Multinationals in Eastern Europe

Multinationals in Eastern Europe

Edited by

Patrick Artisien-Maksimenko
Consultant in International Business

Foreword by Michael Kaser

First published in Great Britain 2000 by
MACMILLAN PRESS LTD
Houndmills, Basingstoke, Hampshire RG21 6XS and London
Companies and representatives throughout the world

A catalogue record for this book is available from the British Library.
ISBN 0–333–71832–1 hardcover
ISBN 0–333–79294–7 paperback

First published in the United States of America 2000 by
ST. MARTIN'S PRESS, INC.,
Scholarly and Reference Division,
175 Fifth Avenue, New York, N.Y. 10010

ISBN 978-0-333-79294-0

Library of Congress Cataloging-in-Publication Data
Multinationals in Eastern Europe / edited by Patrick Artisien-Maksimenko.
p.   cm.
Includes bibliographical references and index.
ISBN 0–312–23131–8 (cloth)
1. Investments, Foreign—Europe, Eastern—Case studies. 2. International business
enterprises—Europe, Eastern—Case studies. 3. Investments, Foreign—Europe,
Central—Case studies. 4. International business enterprises—Europe, Central–
–Case studies. 5. Investments, Foreign—Former Soviet republics—Case studies.
6. International business enterprises—Former Soviet republics—Case studies. 7.
Corporations, Foreign—Europe, Eastern. I. Artisien-Maksimenko, Patrick, 1951–
HG5430.7.A3 M85 2000
338.8'8847—dc21

99–054921

This book is printed on paper suitable for recycling and made from fully managed and sustained
forest sources.

10   9   8   7   6
17   16   15   14   13   12   11   10

Printed and bound by CPI Antony Rowe, Chippenham, Wiltshire

ЭТА КНИГА ПОСВЯЩАЕТСЯ ГАЛИНЕ

Contents

List of Tables

List of Figures

Foreword

Lacking active mechanisms of prices and of interest and exchange rates, the former Soviet Union met its economic end through misinvestment. The deficiencies were less in Central and Eastern Europe, where the full Soviet-type economy was abandoned well before the dissolution of their communist political monopolies in 1989: as contributors to this book point out, Slovenia and Hungary were in the vanguard of adopting market instrumentation.

Ten years of transition into market economies of almost thirty countries has demonstrated the effects of variant inheritances of passivity in prices, interest rates and exchange rates on investment – although the use of such mechanisms is by no means a sole determinant of growth and of welfare. With the exceptions of self-isolated Albania and Romania and Soviet-enwrapped Mongolia, communist governments prior to their fall were allowing the relativities of those three mechanisms to penetrate their own decision-making. Thus Mikhail Gorbachev's leadership (1985–91) dismantled the Soviet foreign trade monopoly, granted state enterprises both substantial financial autonomy and the right to establish joint ventures with foreign firms and made them more sensitive to world market prices by applying coefficients to the officially fixed exchange rate.

Such restructuring (*perestroika*) was far from enough, and it was only in the 1990s that Central and Eastern Europe, the former Soviet Union and Mongolia were infused with foreign direct investment that embodied all three essential mechanisms. Price decontrol, privatization and commercial banking put them also at the disposition of domestic enterprises, but it has been the foreign investor and operator that has brought their application ready-made. Some foreign investment has entered small enterprises, but quantitatively and qualitatively it has been the larger multinationals that have had the most impact. Thus the chapter on the Czech Republic shows that foreign companies account for only 2.7 per cent of enterprises, but employ 8.5 per cent of the workforce and produce 11.2 per cent of total output.

Two of the contributors quote John Dunning's description of multinationals as 'the repository of much of the world's technological capability, managerial capabilities and organizational competences ... ideal vehicles for spearheading industrial restructuring through their ability to transfer technology and management skills'; Terutumo Ozawa is also cited for perception of their 'comparative advantage augmenting investment'. It is a plus for this book that there are chapters by both those authorities among its fourteen authors. With thirteen countries in particular focus and five synoptic chapters the volume emulates its subject in providing real 'value added'.

MICHAEL KASER

Preface

This book is the third in a series of manuscripts on foreign investment in Eastern Europe, published by Macmillan.[1] The editor is grateful to Dr Yuri Adjubei for comments and encouragements.

He would also like to thank Mrs Jenny Firth, who typed the manuscript with promptness and accuracy.

PATRICK ARTISIEN-MAKSIMENKO

---

[1] The first book in the series, *Foreign Investment in Central and Eastern Europe*, edited by Patrick Artisien-Maksimenko, Matija Rojec and Marjan Svetličič, was published in 1993. The second, *Foreign Investment in Russia and Other Soviet Successor States*, was edited by Patrick Artisien-Maksimenko and Yuri Adjubei and released in 1996.

Notes on the Editor and Contributors

The editor

Patrick Artisien-Maksimenko is a consultant in international business, specializing in economic and political risk analysis in Central and Eastern Europe.

Dr Artisien-Maksimenko has worked in the field of East European business for over twenty years. During this period he has acted as consultant to the International Finance Corporation, the Organization for Economic Cooperation and Development, *The Economist*, the Soros Foundation, Oxford Analytica and a number of multinational corporations.

He has authored and edited seven books on foreign investment in Eastern Europe and taught at undergraduate, postgraduate and post-experience levels in Europe, North America, South-East Asia and South Africa.

Dr Artisien-Maksimenko also teaches international business and East European economics at the University of Cardiff, UK.

The contributors

Yuri Adjubei is a member of the Trade Division of the United Nations Economic Commission for Europe in Geneva.

John H. Dunning is Emeritus Professor of International Business at the University of Reading, and State of New Jersey Professor of International Business at Rutgers University.

Philip Hanson is Professor of Economics at the Centre for Russian and East European Studies at the University of Birmingham.

Gabor Hunya is a Research Economist at the Institute for Comparative Economic Studies in Vienna.

Wladyslaw Jermakowicz is Professor of Business at the University of Southern Indiana in Evansville.

xix

Michael Kaser is Visiting Professor at the Institute for German Studies at the University of Birmingham and former Professorial Fellow at St Antony's College, Oxford.

Carl H. McMillan is Distinguished Research Professor in the Department of Economics and the Institute of Central and East European Studies at Carleton University, Ottawa.

Terutomo Ozawa is Professor of Economics at Colorado State University in Fort Collins.

Matija Rojec is Assistant Professor at the University of Ljubljana and Senior Research Fellow at the Slovene Institute of Macroeconomic Analysis.

Faye Sinclair is a former economic adviser to the Centre for Privatization, Investment and Management in Kiev.

Jim Slater is Director of the East Asia-EU Business Research Group at the University of Birmingham Business School.

John Slater is a former member of the secretariat of the United Nations Economic Commission for Europe in Geneva.

Alexandra Swetzer is a member of the secretariat of the United Nations Office in Geneva.

Alena Zemplinerova is Professor of Economics at the Centre for Economic Research and Graduate Education at Charles University, Prague.

Part I

Multinationals in Transition Economies

1
Multinationals in Eastern Europe: An Overview

Patrick Artisien–Maksimenko and Matija Rojec

The process of transforming the previously centrally planned economies of Central and Eastern Europe (CEE) into market economies is now well underway. In most countries, significant progress has been recorded in liberalizing economic activity and setting up the foundations of a market system.

The process of adjustment, however, has been slower than expected, and the early hopes of a painless transition and a recovery in output have in some cases given way to increasingly pessimistic expectations. In some transition countries, the prolonged economic recession, combined with rising unemployment and increasing income differentials, has resulted in mounting political and social tensions.

According to the EBRD:

> While great strides have been made in most countries in the region, the challenges that remain are persistent and difficult ... The generation of institutions for mobilising and allocating savings is an issue at the heart of the transition. (European Bank for Reconstruction and Development 1996)

Since the beginning of the 1990s, foreign direct investment (FDI) and portfolio investment to CEE have been rising and making an important contribution to economic growth; ultimately, however, the host countries' capacity to have prosperous market economies will also require the parallel creation of financial and banking institutions needed to encourage long-term domestic savings through insurance, pension and other funds. Within that context, FDI is seen as a necessary supplement – particularly in the short to medium term – to the limited supply of

3

domestic capital, but not as a panacea for infrastructural shortcomings, themselves the result of distortions following decades of misplaced priorities under central planning.

The EBRD's *Transition Report* also notes that

> Countries at more advanced stages of transition are now grappling with the difficult problems of restructuring, strengthening of financial institutions, building a more commercial infrastructure and overcoming the environmental legacy of the old regime ... Their magnitude underlines the conclusion that the transition is not a process that can be completed in only a few years. (European Bank for Reconstruction and Development 1996)

The perception of FDI in CEE has been coloured by emotional prejudices and political expediency: illusions, on the one hand, that FDI can solve major economic shortcomings at a stroke, and fears, on the other, that national interests – particularly in the public sector utilities – may be 'sold out' to foreign concerns.

Both views appear somewhat extreme: a more realistic approach may be to create an active strategy and policy towards FDI incorporating the upgrading of indigenous competitive advantages, particularly in the areas of underexploited raw materials, human capital and the conversion of technology and R & D to civilian uses.

The scope of this book is very wide, in terms of both countries covered and problems analysed. Selectivity, therefore, was deemed unavoidable: the countries under study differ in terms of size, experience of FDI, economic structure, resource endowment, infrastructure, foreign trade orientation and privatization. The last has been the central focus of institutional reforms, but progress has been hindered by the slow pace of legislative changes, the poor condition of state enterprises and controversies over property restitution. Recent (1996) figures from the OECD, ranking countries according to the percentage of large companies already privatized, show that the Czech Republic, Hungary and Estonia have made the most progress, with Poland, Bulgaria and Romania faring less well. More significantly still, the transfer of ownership *per se* does not necessarily change the behaviour of new but often inexperienced owners: 'genuine' privatization, and with it increased economic efficiency, occurs when 'responsible' owners come into the possession of enterprises. In this context, FDI as a mode of privatization delivers owners with the capacity of implementing quick improvements in the efficiency of domestic companies.

We believe that our representative sample of transition economies provides a sound basis for at least some generalisations. Hungary's early move towards economic reform has made it a favourite destination for foreign investors in Central Europe. Poland's 'big bang' in January 1990 witnessed an upsurge of joint venture investments and placed it second to Hungary in terms of cumulative FDI inflows since 1989. In the Czech Republic, the economy's main industrial sectors – with the exception of financial services – have substantial exposure to FDI, with chemicals, trade and services, electrical engineering and the food sector major recipients of FDI.

Slovenia and Estonia are, with Hungary and the Czech Republic, the main per capita recipients of FDI. All four countries have made considerable headway in terms of macroeconomic stabilization, and investor perceptions of country risk have advanced accordingly.

Within the CIS, the vast markets and natural factor endowment of Russia, Kazakhstan and Ukraine have already been a major influence, and are likely to continue absorbing growing amounts of foreign capital in the years ahead. The smaller markets of the Trans-Caucasus also warrant attention: oil-led growth in Azerbaijan and a nascent economic recovery after years of economic decline in Georgia and Armenia have started to create opportunities for foreign investors.

This first chapter does not purport to present either a complete overview or a systematic analysis of FDI in CEE. The main objective is instead to draw out some of the common characteristics and problems that these countries share, and that are likely to influence economic strategies, both nationally and internationally, to and beyond the turn of the century.

Among the other chapters we have included in this volume is one by John Slater (Chapter 3) on FDI in the transition to a market economy. Slater refers to the daunting restructuring challenges facing many of the successor states of the former Soviet Union: domestically, the obstacles inhibiting investment resources include the small pool of private savings for investment purposes, the lack of confidence in the new market systems being developed and the difficulties of making rational investment decisions based on comparative costs in conditions of high inflation. These are compounded by other constraints, namely the host countries' perceived creditworthiness and political stability, their commitment to sound stabilization and structural adjustment policies as stimulants to growth in the medium term, and their ability to raise funds on international capital markets. According to Slater, investment decisions have been complicated further by the lack of domestic managers with the appropriate techniques for making them, or with experience of exposure to market forces and the rapid and flexible responses which they require. In most of the CIS member states, the weak commercial banking sector, overburdened with uncollectable loans and suffering from a shortage of experienced personnel, has done little to generate confidence, as uncertainty persists as to whether funds can be deposited safely and maintain their values while possible investment opportunities are sought and assessed.

Nevertheless, the CIS, particularly Russia and Central Asia, has the potential to absorb large amounts of foreign capital. For example, the World Bank has identified 60 billion dollars' worth of essential infrastructure investments which will require funding up to the year 2002. However, the conditions for funds to be securely and profitably invested are lacking to various degrees in most CIS states. A scant review of (would-be) investors includes, among the main deterrents, the weak acceptance of the concept of legally binding contracts, endemic corruption, frequent changes to the relevant legislation, weak financial market structures and perceptions that foreigners face threats to their physical security in some parts of the region.

These conditions contrast sharply with those found in Central Europe, where not only have many of the legal and financial obstacles to foreign investment been overcome and privatization pursued more vigorously, but macroeconomic stabilization is well entrenched and there have been several years of growth. Five of the twelve CIS economies shrank in 1996, according to the EBRD, and most of the rest have only recently started to emerge into still problematic growth.

Moreover, although the economies of CEE share a similar systemic background, their ability to attract FDI in the first decade of transition has revolved around a number of variables: first, the path and intensity of the implementation of systemic changes; second, location-specific advantages (resource endowment according to traditional theory); third, infrastructural facilities; fourth, human capital development, particularly managerial, marketing and organizational skills; and political and economic stability.

The level of development of each country *vis-à-vis* the aforementioned prerequisites clearly differs. Central Europe is more advanced in terms of infrastructure and privatization than South-East Europe; yet, its domestic markets still lack the liquidity for large-scale capital raising, as a result of the lack of local institutional investors with an interest in long-term assets. Moreover, domestic banks often lack the expertise or resources to structure the kind of financial packages required for major privately funded projects, such as in infrastructure. Others, like Russia, Kazakhstan and Azerbaijan, are rich in resources. Generally, however, these countries' comparative advantages do not outweigh the infrastructural drawbacks. FDI is more often than not the outcome of a mix of relevant factors, which have been developed to a satisfactory level. Failing that, they represent a barrier to FDI. Vast resources on their own cannot compensate for an underdeveloped infrastructure, which impedes the full exploitation of potential opportunities; this is pertinently highlighted by Adjubei, Swetzer and Sinclair (see Chapters 10, 12 and 13).

Differences do exist in terms of the type of inherited economic structure, the intensity of international economic cooperation and the timing of the implementation of the transformation process. Slovenia, which as part of the former Yugoslav federation departed from central planning as far back as the 1950s, and to a lesser extent Hungary, which was exposed at an early stage to a degree of self-management, are special cases, as Rojec, in Chapter 8, and Hunya, in Chapter 5, show.

We count as systemic changes not only those factors that would help create an adequate infrastructure for FDI, but also those that would usher in a complete transformation of the economic system. Foreign investment laws creating special islands for foreign capital, including free zones, are not sufficient. The whole essence of the system needs to become compatible with that of other market economies to be transparent and understandable to both foreign investors and local entrepreneurs. Only when foreign investors perceive that they are treated on a par with their local counterparts will they be convinced of the longlasting nature of systemic changes.

Instability and unpredictability have not been restricted to the investment climate of the host countries: the attitudes of investing countries have at times added to uncertainty, reflecting their lack of knowledge of market and political conditions in the transition economies. In the Central Asian and Trans-Caucasus republics, in particular, foreign investors must be prepared for long negotiations with the host companies and should not underestimate the time required to secure corporate approval.

From the CEE host's viewpoint, the main contribution of FDI is not restricted to capital injections, which can be done equally efficiently through portfolio investment or loans; it also includes the transfer by foreign strategic investors of a whole package of the ingredients of development, including machinery, equipment, technology, management and marketing. Such transfers are performed predominantly through the vehicle of FDI, the preferred option of foreign strategic investors, who retain control of ownership-specific advantages. The opening up of the East European economies to worldwide competition and the collapse of Comecon markets has brought added urgency for domestic enterprises to enter foreign markets.

In the medium term, most CEE countries are unlikely to face the high, government-induced entry barriers to EU markets; instead, increased natural entry barriers reflecting national competitive advantages are likely to emerge (see Rugman and Verbebe 1990). The CEE countries will, in the foreseeable future, remain subordinated to their Western counterparts because of infrastructural deficiencies, the lack of strong market segments and sophisticated buyers, weak supporting industries and shortcomings in management and labour relations.

In order to increase their level of competitiveness on Western markets, the economies of Eastern Europe need to build up strengths in sectors where their national competitive advantages are optimalized. FDI can help strengthen those advantages in a number of ways: first, MNEs as global players structure their factor cost advantages in response to the host's relative factor endowment. This, in turn, will help promote structural upgrading in the CEE economies and develop their comparative advantages (see Ozawa 1992a).

Second, foreign investors bring with them an integrated package of development 'ingredients' for restructuring and development. In Dunning's words,

> because MNEs are the repository of much of the world's technological capability, managerial capabilities and organisational competences, they are ideal vehicles for spearheading industrial restructuring through their ability to transfer technology and management skills ... and provide much of the competences and initiatives for economic growth. (Dunning 1991)

Third, the future development of the CEE economies also lies in moving from a supply-push to a demand-pull orientation: according to Ozawa,

> given the high level of human capital accumulation and technological sophistication, the region has an excellent capacity to absorb technology from the West and initiate commercial R&D, thereby fostering the development of consumer-oriented assembly-based

industries (differentiated Smithian industries) and the growth of Schumpeterian innovation-based industries. (Ozawa 1992a)

This line of thought suggests that the transition economies' chances of success would be enhanced in industries internationally dominated by FDI. The 1995 UNCTAD *World Investment Report* (1995) found that companies with foreign participation were among the best performers in CEE. The productivity and sales of FIEs in Hungary, the Czech Republic and Estonia have greatly exceeded those of domestic enterprises.

Whether FDI takes on an increasingly important role in the restructuring process will hinge on a number of variables:

1. Growth trends in the major investing countries and the worldwide availability of investment funds: the doubling of FDI inflows to CEE in 1995 ran parallel to a 40 per cent increase in worldwide FDI flows:

2. The path and intensity of market reforms in CEE, combined with the stability and predictability of the political, legal and economic systems:

3. The speed and scope of the institutional integration of the transition countries with the EU. This is significant, as the EU member states are the main investors in CEE. The entry of Greece, Spain and Portugal into the EU was accompanied by a remarkable increase in FDI inflows to those countries from other member states:

4. The future pace of privatization: in parts of CEE the main wave of foreign acquisitions has yet to take its full course. The commitment of foreign strategic investors may depend ultimately on the concept of legally binding and enforceeable contracts in individual countries as ways of minimizing corruption and other forms of criminality.

2
Assessing the Costs and Benefits of Foreign Direct Investment: Some Theoretical Considerations

John H. Dunning

Introduction

Any assessment of the impact of foreign direct investment (FDI), or the activities of transnational corporations (TNCs), on the economic welfare of host countries requires some understanding of the reasons why TNCs undertake FDI in the first place, and also the policies pursued by the host countries which, directly or indirectly, may affect the level and composition of that investment.

This is because the consequences of FDI on a particular host country are a function of the interaction between the competitiveness of its location-bound resources and the competitive advantages of the investing firms. Neither of these sets of advantages is immutable; the advantages are changing constantly over time, *inter alia*, in response to new demands by consumers, technological progress and political and economic developments.

The last decade has witnessed more of these changes than, perhaps, any other comparable decade of the twentieth century. I identify some of these later in this chapter, but one that particularly affects the structure of the interface between the competitive advantages of firms (particularly TNCs) and those of countries is the paradigmatic shift now taking place in the structure of the capitalist system, and in the micro-organization of economic activity (Perez 1983; Best 1990; Gerlach 1992). This change is best described as the movement from *hierarchical* to *cooperative* or *alliance* capitalism, and is occurring as a result of a series of systemic technological and institutional developments that, taken together, are heralding a new paradigm of production – known variously as 'flexible production', 'Toyotism' or 'the new competition'.[1] While, as yet, it is too early to pronounce the demise of the mass, or Fordist, system of production, in several of the industrial sectors, for example autos and consumer electronics, in which scale value-adding activity was once lauded as the 'best practice' system, this new techno-economic paradigm has already been widely adopted – not only by Japanese firms, in which it was first introduced, but by US and European producers as well.

This chapter proceeds as follows. First, in the next three sections, I examine some of the changes that have taken place in the thinking of scholars about the determinants of FDI and TNC activity. I believe such thinking should be of interest to those who administer Central and East European economies as they seek to improve the attractiveness of their own location-bound resources and capabilities to foreign investors, and to evaluate the consequences of such investment for the welfare of their citizens.

After this, the major part of the chapter, consisting of the following three sections, is devoted to examining the main consequences of inbound FDI for the competitiveness of host countries. I have taken the upgrading of national competitiveness (at the minimum possible cost) as the main criterion by which inbound FDI is judged, and I discuss the ways different kinds of TNC activity are likely to impact on different components of competitiveness. I also argue that the economic con-sequences of inbound FDI are likely to depend critically on specific characteristics of host countries, both on the particular legal and institutional infrastructure and on the macro-organizational policies pursued by governments.

Following this discussion, I identify some of the actions that national governments might take to ensure that, in this emerging age of alliance capitalism, FDI can best fulfil its intended purpose. The final section considers some alternatives to inbound TNC activity as a means of securing the resources, capabilities and markets for upgrading compe-titiveness.

From the Perspective of Individual Firms: What Determines FDI?

It is worth emphasizing that all the received theories and paradigms of FDI and TNC activity essentially view the TNC as an independent hier-archy of horizontally or vertically integrated value-adding activities. While the existence of collaborative arrangements is recognized, these are usually perceived as *alternative* forms of economic organization, rather than an *extension of the boundaries* of the firm, and/or as *part and parcel of a system, or network,* of TNC-related *activities.* Moreover, the boundaries of the firm are assumed to be well defined, and to be coincident with its ownership of, or control over, a particular set of resources and capabilities. This means that, while accepting that firms may interact with each other in a variety of ways, the extant literature views the key unit of analysis as the independent firm, rather than the firm as part and parcel of a network of interrelated activities, or, indeed, the network itself.[2]

In such conditions, the theory of the TNC is *a theory of the firm whose boundaries are determined by its ownership*; and the theory of TNC activity is *a theory of the activities of firms of a particular industry, country or region.*

Of the various theories and paradigms of TNC activity[3] that have emerged over the past thirty years, the most comprehensive is the *eclectic paradigm*, which provides a framework within which a number of specific propositions about the determinants of FDI and international production can be accommodated. The paradigm avers that the extent and pattern of TNC activity will be determined by the interaction between the competitive advantages embedded in firms and those embedded in countries, and the way in which firms choose to combine and coordinate these two sets of advantages across national boundaries.[4]

The paradigm essentially considers two main forms of economic organization, viz. *arm's length transactions* and *hierarchies*. It assumes (as does its near neighbour – the internalization paradigm) that these two modalities represent the extremes of a continuum, which range from perfect competition, with zero transaction and coordination costs, to a perfect hierarchy with zero internally administered costs.[5] In between lies a series of intermediate stages, which involve some kind of time-related cooperative agreement between two or more independent firms. As one moves along the continuum, it is assumed the transaction and coordination costs of using markets increase relative to those of, first, quasi and, later, full hierarchical control. However, for the most part, each of these alternative forms is assumed to be a *substitute*, and not a *complement* to the other; and, even in the case of a cooperative arrangement, the unit of analysis is the individual firm, rather than the two or more firms involved in the arrangement.

Turning now to the eclectic paradigm of TNC activity, this paradigm suggests that firms will engage in FDI in a particular country when the following conditions apply:

1. Firms possess a portfolio of resources and capabilities, including organizational and innovatory competencies, that gives them a

unique set of advantages – so-called ownership-specific (O-specific) advantages[6] – over any competitors, or potential competitors, serving, or seeking to serve, the same markets. The necessary conditions for such O-specific advantages to be sustainable over time have recently been set out by Peteraf (1993) in her analysis of the resource-based theory of the firm.[7]

2. Firms find it beneficial to internalize the market for these advantages, rather than to sell the right to use them to other – i.e. separately – owned firms. This they will do whenever they perceive that they can coordinate these advantages with other value-added activities more beneficially than by using markets as an exchange mechanism. These advantages are called internalization (I) advantages and it is these that essentially are the *raison d'être* of hierarchies.[8]

3. Firms' global goals are best met by adding value to these advantages from one or more production sites in a foreign country that offers location-bound resources and capabilities superior to those of the home country of the investing firm.

The eclectic paradigm accepts that the precise configuration of OLI advantages will depend on three main contextual variables. These are:

1. the type and range of products produced by TNCs or potential TNCs;[9]

2. their country of origin, and the country(ies) in which they are contemplating investment and;

3. a variety of firm-specific factors, including the past strategies pursued by the investing companies.

Until the mid-1980s, the literature distinguished between three motives for foreign-owned value-added activity, *viz.* to acquire *natural resources*, to *seek markets* and to *restructure (i.e., rationalize)* an existing portfolio of market-seeking or resource-seeking investments. Most of the operational theories, or models, of TNC activity seek to explain one or other of these three kinds of FDI, or else a particular aspect of all of these.[10]

More recently (see Dunning 1993), the eclectic paradigm has been widened to embrace two other kinds of TNC activity, as follows:

1. The first is where a firm (usually an established TNC) makes an investment to acquire assets that, it perceives, will protect or strengthen its global competitive advantages *vis-à-vis* those of its competitors. Such FDI is called *strategic-asset-seeking investment*. Rather than exploiting existing O-specific advantages, this kind of TNC activity is directed to gaining new advantages. It is particularly

Table 2.1 A reconfiguration of the eclectic paradigm of international production

1. Ownership-specific advantages (of enterprise of one nationality (or affiliates of same) over those of another)

Hierarchy-related advantages	*Alliance or network-related advantages*
a. Property right and/or intangible asset advantages (Oa). Product innovations, production management, organizational and marketing systems, innovatory capacity, non-codifiable knowledge: 'bank' of human capital experience; marketing, finance, know-how, etc. b. Advantages of common governance, i.e. of organizing Oa with complementary assets (Ot). i. Those that branch plants of established enterprises may enjoy over *de novo* firms Those due mainly to size, product diversity and learning experiences of enterprise, e.g. economies of scope and specialization. Exclusive or favoured access to inputs, e.g. labour, natural resources, finance, information. Ability to obtain inputs on favoured terms (due, e.g., to size or monopsonistic influence). Ability of parent company to conclude productive and cooperative inter-firm relationships, e.g., as between Japanese auto assemblers and their suppliers. Exclusive or favoured access to product markets. Access to resources of parent company at marginal cost. Synergistic economies (not only in production, but in purchasing, marketing, finance, etc., arrangements). ii. Those that specifically arise because of multinationality. Multinationality enhances operational flexibility by offering opportunities for arbitraging, production shifting and global sourcing of inputs. More favoured access to and/or better knowledge about international markets, e.g., for information, finance, labour etc. Ability to take advantage of geographical differences in factor endowments, government intervention, markets etc. Ability to diversify or reduce risks, e.g., in different currency areas and creation of options and/or political and cultural scenarios. Ability to learn form societal differences in organizational and managerial processes and systems. Balancing economies of integration with ability to respond to differences in country specific needs and advantages.	a. *Vertical alliances* i. Backward access to R&D, design engineering and training facilities of suppliers; regular advice by them on product innovation and improvement, and implications of projected new production processes for component design and manufacturing. New insights into, and monitoring of, developments in materials and how they might impact on existing products and production processes. ii. Forward access to industrial customers, new markets, marketing techniques and distribution channels particularly in unfamiliar locations or where products need to be adapted to meet local supply capabilities and markets. b. *Horizontal alliances* Access to complementary technologies and innovatory capacity. Access to additional capabilities to captive benefits technology fusion, and to identify new uses for related technologies. Encapsulation of development time. Such inter-firm interaction often generates is own knowledge feedback mechanisms and path dependencies. c. *Networks* i. Similar firms Reduced transaction and coordination costs arising from better dissemination and interpretation of knowledge and information, and from mutual support and cooperation between members of network. Improved knowledge about process and product development and markets. Multiple, yet complementary, inputs into innovatory developments and explanation of new markets. Opportunities to develop 'niche' R&D strategies; shared learning and training experiences, e.g., as in the case of cooperative research associations. Networks may also help promote uniform product standards and other collective advantages. ii. Business districts As per (i), plus spatial agglomerative economies, e.g. labour market pooling. Access to clusters of specialized intermediate inputs, and linkages with knowledge-based institutions, e.g. universities, technological spill-overs.

2. Internalization incentive advantages (i.e. to circumvent or exploit market failure)

Hierarchy-related advantages	*Alliance-or network-related advantages*
Avoidance of search and negotiating costs.	While, in some cases, time-limited inter-firm cooperative relationships may be a substitute for FDI, in others they may add to the I incentive advantages of the participating hierarchies, i.e. R&D alliances and networking (which, for example, when preferred to M&As), may help strengthen the overall hierarchical advantages of the participating firms. Moreover, the growing structural integration of the world economy is requiring firms to go outside their immediate boundaries to capture the complex realities of know-how trading and knowledge exchange in innovation, particularly where such assets are tacit and need to adapt speedily to structural change.
To avoid costs of moral hazard, information asymmetries and adverse selection; also, to protect reputation of internalizing firm.	
To avoid cost of broken contracts and ensuing litigation Buyer uncertainty (about nature and value of inputs (e.g. technology) being sold).	
When market does not permit price discrimination.	
Need of seller to protect quality of intermediate or final products.	
To capture economies of interdependent activities (see (b) above).	Alliance-or network-related advantages are those that prompt a 'voice' rather than an 'exit' response to market failure; they also allow many of the advantages of internalization without the inflexibility of bureaucratic or risk related costs associated with it. Such quasi-internalization is likely to be most successful in cultures in which trust, forbearances, reciprocity and consensus politics are at a premium. It suggests that firms are more appropriately likened to archipelagos linked by causeways rather than self-contained 'islands' or conscious powers.
To compensate for absence of future markets.	
To avoid or exploit government intervention (e.g. quotas, tariffs, price controls, tax differences, etc.)	
To control supplies and conditions of sale of inputs (including technology).	
To control market outlets (including those that might be used by competitors).	
To be able to engage in practices, e.g. cross-subsidization, predatory pricing, leads and lags, transfer pricing, etc. as a competitive (or anti-competitive) strategy.	

Table 2.1 Continued

3. Location-specific variables (these may favour home or host countries)

Hierarchy-related advantages	*Alliance or network-related advantages*
Spatial distribution of natural and created resource endowments and markets.	The L-specific advantages of alliances arise essentially from the presence of local complementary assets, when organized within a framework of alliances and networks. The extent and type of business districts, industrial or science parks and the external economies they offer participating firms are examples of these advantages which, over time, the presence of foreign owned firms might expect cross-border alliance or network relationships may also allow foreign firms to better tap into, and exploit, the comparative technological and organizational advantages of host countries. Networks may also help reduce the information asymmetries and likelihood of opportunism in imperfect markets.
Input prices, quality and productivity, e.g. labour, energy, materials, components, semi-finished goods.	
International transport and communication costs.	
Investment incentives and disincentives (including performance requirements, etc.)	
Artificial barriers (e.g. import controls) to trade in goods and services.	
Societal and infrastructure provisions (commercial, legal, educational, transport and communication).	
Cross-country ideological, language, cultural, business, political etc. differences.	
Economics of centralization of R&D production and marketing.	
Economic system and policies of government: the institutional framework for resource allocation.	

Sources: These variables are culled from a variety of sources, but see especially Dunning (1993a), Kobrin (1993) and Teece (1994).

noticeable in the high-tech sectors serving global markets, and is primarily concentrated within the advanced industrial nations. Much of the cross-border merger and acquisition (M&A) and strategic alliance activity of the last decade falls into this category. Some examples of this kind of FDI are given in chapter 3 of Dunning (1993a).

2. A feature of the modern, large, integrated TNC is that its portfolio of assets consists of a variety of organizational arrangements, each of which it treats as an integral part of a network of activities. While, taken separately, these arrangements are similar to those set out in Table 2.1, collectively they represent an *organizational system* in which each component is not *substitutable* but *complementary* to the others; and each benefits from being associated with the others. One example of such activity is the Japanese *keiretsu*, or network of firms, in which each firm is fused with, or linked to, the others by ownership or by a less formal, but no less committed, mode of bonding. Frequently, and especially in vertical keiretsus,[11] there is a core, or lead, firm – usually a large industrial customer – that determines the structure and composition of the network. In horizontal networks (e.g. clusters of firms engaged in similar activities) there may be no such flagship firm. In the 1990s, there is evidence to suggest that network relationships are becoming increasingly widespread, *and that TNCs and other firms regard the membership of a network as a competitive or O-specific advantage in its own right.*

Because of these two developments in the last decade, which I take up below, it may be appropriate to widen the *de facto* boundaries of the individual firm to include other firms that, as a result of the ongoing relationships it has with them, substantially affect its own O-specific advantages. In practice, this may be an exceedingly difficult thing to do – not only because the precise boundaries of each firm are different, but because each activity of a multi-activity firm might involve a different set of collaborative relationships. At the same time, it makes little sense to argue that, because a firm sheds some of its activities, – for example, disinternalizes part of its value chain, yet immediately enters into a cooperative production or marketing agreement with the firm(s) now undertaking these activities – it surrenders all the advantages that stemmed from its internal governance.

The fact is that, in the 1990s, owing to technological advances and competitive pressures, large TNCs are increasingly disaggregating activities that they perceive do not directly contribute to their core O-specific advantages. Partly, this reflects the growing preference for innovation-led *flexible* production systems, as compared with cost-reducing *mass* production systems; and partly because some of the overhead costs of production, for example R&D, are becoming so astronomical that firms are being forced to limit their product range and innovatory activities. At the same time, the growing interdependence between different technologies,[12] and the need of firms to continue to exert some influence over the disaggregated activities, mean that the form and pattern of their inter-firm relationships are becoming more critical influences on their core competencies. Hence, hierarchy-related transactions are being replaced by alliance-related transactions of one kind or another. And hence, too, when firms go overseas, or increase their foreign value activities, they now pay especial attention to the availability and quality of these complementary activities, which in TNC hierarchies would have been internalized to minimize the costs associated with their coordination and transaction.

The switch of emphasis from *independent* to *relational firms* or *enterprise networks*, and from *hierarchical* to *alliance capitalism*, reflects partly the growing production and coordinating costs of undertaking multiple activities within a single ownership, and partly the increasing perception that inter-firm collaborative arrangements are a viable – and sometimes a preferable – alternative to full vertical or horizontal integration. This change in perception is partly a reflection of technical forces – for example, the increasing costs (and risks associated with such costs) of innovatory activities and the truncated product life cycles. It is also partly a demonstration by Japanese firms that, in the right business culture, informal inter-firm alliances or networks based on trust, mutual support, forbearance and reciprocity *can* adequately protect the proprietary assets of the cooperating parties, while allowing each to exploit the economies of synergy and co-specialization associated with the techno-economic system of innovation-led production.

In the 1990s, the lessening of such market imperfections as opportunism, information incompleteness and asymmetry, uncertainty, and bounded rationality by the establishment of mutually beneficial inter-firm relationships, rather than by the replacement of imperfections by single hierarchies, seems to be an increasingly preferred route of economic organization. It is, indeed, an extension of Albert Hirschman's 'voice' response to the problem of market failure (Hirschman 1970). It is particularly relevant to problems of customer – supplier relationships (for example, high rejection rate, unreliable delivery dates, opportunistic behaviour), where such a response would involve the two parties working together until the problems are corrected; and it contrasts with

Hirschman's concept of an 'exit' strategy, where, for example, the response of a customer to problems with a supplier is to find a new supplier or internalize the market for the product being supplied.[13]

It may be useful to consider how the traditional configurations of the competitive advantages of firms, and their interpretation of the locational activities of countries, are affected by extending the concept of the individual firm to embrace those activities over which it has some influence, and which, it perceives, affect its own competitive position in a significant way. We do this in Table 2.1. Whereas the left-hand side of the table sets out the OLI advantages traditionally identified, as for example in Dunning (1993a, ch. 4, p. 81), the right-hand side suggests how these advantages may be affected, for good or bad, by the cooperative relationships that firms enjoy with other firms – be the relationship that of a dyadic alliance or part of an industrial or spatial network of activities.

Why Should Host Countries Seek to Attract FDI? What Are the Specific Advantages of FDI?

To the extent that host countries want FDI primarily for the O-specific advantages that are unique to the investing firms, and which the former believe they need to promote their long-term economic goals, it might be reasonably supposed that its impact will be most pronounced where these O-advantages are the most distinctive. This is, in fact, the general case, although it is possible that, at the same time, the price the TNC extracts for the provision of these advantages is unacceptable to the host country. To that country, it is the net *benefit* it expects to receive from FDI, – namely, the domestic value added – that is the relevant variable to assess.

The domestic value added by inbound FDI is of various kinds. In particular, we might identify the following:

1. The value added created and retained in the host country by the foreign investment, *less* the value added that could have been generated by obtaining the assets in other ways (including producing them within the country).
2. The 'spill-over' effects on the value added of other firms, for example suppliers, customers and competitors,[14] as a direct result of the investment.
3. The impact of the investment on the allocation and reallocation of indigenous economic activity; and, in particular, the extent to which, by assisting an efficient inter-sectoral or intra-country distribution of resources and capabilities (for example, by promoting increasing

returns to scale and fostering industrial districts), it advances a country's dynamic competitive advantage.

Each of these consequences may be due to the following:

1. The assets (and especially technology and information) transferred by the foreign firm to the host country.
2. The organizational control exercised over the use of these assets and the location-bound assets of the host country used in conjunction with them.

It is, indeed, the way TNCs organize their global resources and capabilities – which often results in a different international division of labour from what would have occurred had the assets been organized by indigenous firms – that is one of the most distinctive features of TNC activity.

For an investing firm, a foreign location is to be viewed in terms of its contribution towards the firm's regional or global economic and strategic objectives. Of course, much depends on the motivation for the investment, whether it is initial or sequential investment, and whether it is a stand-alone investment or one that is part and parcel of a globally integrated strategy (Dunning, 1993a). The response of firms to a set of locational pulls and pushes will also depend on firm-specific characteristics other than the nationality of their ownership. Thus, a small, non-diversified investor may have a view of a particular locational opportunity that is different from that of a large, diversified firm. An oligopolistic firm that takes the initiative of investing abroad may attach values to a given set of locational variables that are different from the values of those who follow it; the response of a leading innovating firm may differ from that of a following imitating firm; a *de novo* foreign direct investor may judge the opportunities offered by a particular host country in a manner quite different from that of a TNC with many foreign subsidiaries.[15] At the same time, the contribution of each of these different types of firms to the objectives of a host country's goals is also likely to be distinctive.

The Need to Understand What Attracts Firms to Locate their Activities in a Particular Country

The second reason for a government of a country to understand the determinants of FDI is to guide it in its own actions in so far as these may affect FDI and its consequences. At the same time, national governments may also wish to know what actions are being pursued by other governments that might affect the locational choice of TNCs. Finally, they may wish to assess the extent to which they can get the benefits expected of FDI by alternative routes, such as licensing or the encouragement of indigenous industries.

I deal with each of these issues as this chapter proceeds. Here, however, I would make the point that governments may affect both the extent to which they attract inbound FDI and the benefits flowing from it in two main ways. The first is by the actions they take to affect the level and structure of FDI. These include the conditions of entry[16] for FDI and the ownership or financial limitations placed on it; the performance or operating requirements expected of foreign affiliates;[17] and any restrictions on the remission of earnings or the repatriation of capital. Clearly, any action that decreases the total revenue, increases the total costs or lowers the net profits of a particular FDI is going to reduce its locational attractiveness to the investing company.

Exactly how much it will affect this attractiveness will depend on the economic rent the TNC is earning and its alternative investment opportunities. These will clearly vary according to firm-, industry- and country-specific considerations. However, the evidence does suggest that TNCs are becoming more sensitive to differences in foreign investment policies pursued by governments – particularly where the FDI is in export-oriented manufacturing and service sectors.

Policies of the second type are more general, but are becoming more important with the growing integration of the world economy. These embrace actions that are not directed specifically to foreign investors, but that nevertheless impinge on their global competitiveness. Moreover, it is important to consider not only the competitiveness of an affiliate, but also that of the TNC of which it is a part.

Of the more important of these, taxation rates, political stability, competition policy and general macroeconomic policies are usually put at the top of the list. However, as capital, technology and other intangible 'created' assets become more mobile across national boundaries, the role of government in affecting the availability and efficiency of location-bound resources that support these assets – for example, transport and communications infrastructure, industrial and/or regional clusters, and some kinds of human capital – has become more important. Also, governments, by some of their non-economic programmes, for instance environmental regulations, affect the competitiveness of their own firms and their ability to offer complementary resources and capabilities to investors.

In the mid-1990s, it would appear that the extent of the complementarity between O-specific resources and capabilities of foreign investors and the L-specific resources and capabilities offered by countries, together with the macro-organizational framework that determines the way these two sets of assets are coordinated, is becoming the critical explanatory factor of the form and composition of TNC-related activity. *Inter alia*, as has already been suggested, this is because of the changes now taking place in the socio-institutional framework of market economies that we have described above as alliance capitalism. The critical feature of alliance capitalism is that firms need to actively cooperate with each other to produce a given product or engage in a set of value-adding activities. This cooperation is tending to replace the internal markets of multi-activity firms, which are a central characteristic of hierarchical capitalism. Such internalization of markets is proving increasingly costly, as firms find they need to devote their attention to building up their core competencies and to combining these with those of other firms.

Alliance capitalism may take various forms. It may be inter-firm or intra-firm. Inter-firm cooperation may be between firms producing at different phases of the value chain, as for example in the case of a keiretsu of assemblers and suppliers in the Japanese automobile industry. Alternatively, it may be between firms producing similar products or using similar processes, as in the case of many strategic alliances in the biotechnology, computer and aircraft industries – particularly in the higher echelons of the value chain – or it may be between firms related in interests grouped in networks or federations, for example cooperative research associations.[18] Another form of cooperation is exemplified by the business or industrial district in which the participating firms reap a variety of agglomerative economies, – that is, economies external to themselves but internal to the district or region in which they operate. In each form of cooperation, the participating firms retain their financial independence. The alliance is formed mainly to exploit the benefits of information-sharing, technological complementarity, the availability of specialized inputs and labour pools, the spreading of risks and costs and the speeding up of the production process. The belief is that, through membership of the alliance (which might be between two firms or very many), the value of each firm's core competencies is protected or increased.

To be successful, alliance capitalism also requires a closer cooperation between the different stakeholders of a firm – and in particular between labour and management – than in the case of Fordism, where workers were servile to the routinizing tasks and the conveyor belt. It is, indeed, a feature of innovation-led production that it relies on shop-floor workers to play a more constructive and critical role in the organization of production. Without their active support for such practices as job rotation, total quality management, continuous product improvement and just-in-time deliveries, the flexible production system, which is now increasingly replacing the Fordist or scale production system,[19] could not operate efficiently. It follows, then, that inward investors who believe that their competitive advantages rest on such a system will prefer a location where the local workers are sympathetic to it – or can be trained to be so.[20]

A final aspect of alliance capitalism concerns the relationship between governments and firms. Again, it is instructive to look at the symbiosis between the objectives and strategies of Japanese firms and the Japanese government, as both have striven to improve the former's competitiveness in world markets.[21] Too often, in the past, the relations between governments in Western countries have been adversarial; and, too often, policy has been limited to advancing the *static* efficiency of domestic resource allocation. Yet, in these days of global and innovation-led competition, governments and firms need to give at least equal weight to upgrading the competitiveness of indigenous resources and promoting *dynamic* comparative advantages. For their part, firms need to be as efficient as possible in the use of their O-specific resources and capabilities. However, to achieve this goal, they need to access the right kind of physical and human inputs, cutting-edge transport and communications facilities, and an efficient legal and commercial infrastructure, each of which is a location-bound resource that governments either provide directly or else influence strongly in its conditions of supply.

The political and economic environment for FDI (and for that matter domestic investment as well) have been discussed at some length because the availability and quality of complementary assets, which are essential to the efficient use of the core assets possessed by foreign investors, are becoming a more important determinant of the locational decisions of firms. While this is most obviously the case with FDI in advanced industrial countries, the concept of alliance capitalism is not confined to these countries.

The division of labour forged by the new production system affects developing and transition economies as well – and affects them increasingly as they move up their development paths. Certainly, any attempt by (for example) Central European governments to attract FDI *purely* on the basis of favourable wage rates, raw material and component prices or fiscal incentives is unlikely to succeed in the long run – for these advantages may only be temporary and do not attract high-value FDI.

For host countries to attract inbound investment of the right kind and on the right terms, they need to assign a high priority to (a) upgrading the availability and quality of their location-bound created assets and (b) encouraging a mentality of, and institutional framework for, alliance capitalism, by which both foreign and domestic firms can draw upon resources and capabilities external to their own assets but internal to those of the alliances.

The Changing World of FDI

The Changing Attitudes of Countries

In the early 1990s, most countries – or more particularly governments of host countries – are welcoming FDI as 'good news', after a period of being highly critical – if not downright hostile – to it in the 1970s and early 1980s.[22] There are several reasons for this change of heart. Some of these are set out in Table 2.2. The first is the renewed faith of most countries in the workings of the market economy, as demonstrated, for example, by the wholesale privatization of state-owned assets, and the deregulation and liberalization of markets over the last eight to ten years. While these events are being most vividly played out in Central and Eastern Europe and in China, the need to remove structural market distortions has also been acknowledged by national or regional governments in many other parts of the world – notably in the European Community, India, Mexico and Vietnam.

The second explanation is the increasing globalization of economic activity and the integration of international production and of international financial markets (UNCTAD 1993). *Inter alia*, and as described below, globalization is bringing structural transformation and a new division of labour in the world economy. It is also going hand in hand with alliance capitalism; and it is compelling both governments and firms to pay more attention to the dynamic competitiveness of the resources and capabilities under their jurisdiction.

The third reason is that the key ingredients – namely currently growing created assets, such as technology, intellectual capital, learning experience and organizational competence – are not only becoming more mobile across national boundaries, but are also becoming increasingly housed in TNC systems.[23]

The fourth reason why governments are modifying their attitudes towards FDI is that a growing number of economies – especially in East Asia – are now approaching the take-off stage in their economic development, so that, as a result, the competition for the world's scarce

Table 2.2 The changing world of foreign direct investment

a. From a country's perspective

- Renaissance of the market system.
- Globalization of economic activity.
- Enhanced mobility of wealth-creating assets.
- Increasing number of countries approaching 'take-off' stage in development.
- Convergence of economic structures among advanced countries, and some industrializing countries.
- Changing criteria by which governments evaluate FDI.
- Better appreciation by governments of the costs and benefits of FDI.

b. From a firm's perspective

- Increasing need to exploit global markets (e.g. to cover escalating R&D costs).
- Competitive pressures to procure inputs (raw materials, components, etc.) from cheapest possible source.
- Regional integration has prompted more efficiency seeking investment.
- Growing ease of trans-border communications and reduced transport costs.
- Heightened oligopolistic competition among leading firms.
- Opening up new territorial opportunities for FDI.
- Need to tap into, and/or monitor, foreign sources of technology and organizational capabilities; and to exploit economies of agglomeration.
- New incentives to conclude alliances with foreign firms.
- Changes in significance of particular locational costs and benefits.
- Need to better balance the advantages of globalization with those of localization.

resources of capital, technology and organizational skills is becoming increasingly intensive.

The fifth reason is that the economic structures of the major industrialized nations are converging, one result of which is that intra-triad competition is becoming both more intra-industry and more created asset-intensive.

The sixth explanation is that the criteria for judging the success of FDI by host governments have changed over the years, and changed in a way that has made for a less confrontational and a more cooperative stance between the host governments and foreign investors. More particularly, the emphasis of evaluating inbound TNCs over the past two decades has switched from the direct contribution of foreign affiliates to its wider impact on the upgrading of the competitiveness of a host country's indigenous capabilities and the promotion of its dynamic comparative advantage.

Finally, the learning experience of host countries about what TNCs can and cannot do for them has enabled their governments to better understand FDI and assess its consequences, and to take action to ensure that it more efficiently promotes their economic and social goals.

The world economy in the late 1990s is, indeed a very different place from that of even a decade ago, and the changes that have occurred have had implications both for the responses of individual nation states to FDI and for the very character of FDI itself.

The Changing Behaviour of Firms

The events just outlined have also affected the attitudes, organizational structures and behaviour of business corporations. Such enterprises, for example, have found it increasingly necessary to capture new markets to finance the escalating costs of their research and development and marketing activities, both of which are considered essential to preserve or advance their competitiveness.[24] Cross-border strategic alliances and networks have been prompted for similar reasons, and to encapsulate the time it takes to innovate and learn about new products, processes and management cultures.

Firms have been no less pressured to reduce the cost and improve the quality of their raw materials and components, while, as a growing number of countries are building their own arsenals of skilled labour and technological capacity, foreign investors are finding it more and more desirable to geographically diversify their information-gathering and learning capabilities. Competition in internationally oriented industries is becoming increasingly oligopolistic, while – as we see in more detail below – both the nature of the competitive advantages of firms and the factors influencing their locational choices are very different in the late 1990s from those only a decade or so earlier.

Finally, in the more complex global environment of the 1990s, TNCs are being forced to pay more attention to achieving the right balance between the forces making for the global integration of their activities and those requiring them to be more oriented towards, and sensitive to localized supply capabilities and consumer tastes and needs – what Akio Morita of Sony has referred to as 'glocalization'. For, alongside the acknowledged benefits of globalization, there is a growing awareness, particularly among the citizens of smaller countries, of the need to preserve – and indeed promote, as a comparative advantage – their distinctive cultures, institutional structures, life styles, working relationships and consumption preferences. TNCs ignore these country-specific differences – which many observers, for example Naisbitt (1994), believe will become important in the future – at their peril.[25]

The Changing Modality of International Commerce

At one time, firms used to engage in international transactions primarily through arm's-length exporting and importing. Today, the main vehicles are FDI and cooperative alliances. We saw above, alliance capitalism is challenging hierarchical capitalism as the dominant characteristic of market-based capitalism. Initially, the foreign-based activities of TNCs were driven by trade; today, they are inextricably fused with trade. Outside the primary sector, upwards of two-thirds of the world's exports of goods and services are accounted for by TNCs, and 30 to 40 per cent of these take place within these same institutions – 60 to 70 per cent in the case of intangible assets such as technology and organizational skills (Dunning 1993a; UNCTAD 1993).

Today, TNCs are the main producers and organizers of knowledge-based assets; and they are the principal cross-border disseminators of the fruits of these assets. It is true that the ambience of innovatory activities, the availability of risk capital and the educational infrastructure are all strongly influenced by the actions of governments. It is also the case that a myriad of small firms and individual entrepreneurs are significant seedbeds of new ideas and inventions.

However, increasingly, economic progress is being shaped by the way new knowledge and organizational techniques are created, systematized and disseminated. Sometimes, the market system is able to satisfactorily perform this task by itself; but, because many emerging innovations are both generic and multi-purpose, and have to be coordinated with other assets to be fully productive, firms frequently find it beneficial to supplement or supplant external markets by their own governance systems. Sometimes – as I have already suggested – and increasingly, the efficient production and use of created assets requires firms to cooperate with each other, and even to be located in close proximity to each other.[26]

To some extent, this has always been the case. One of the earliest definitions of a business enterprise was that it was a 'coordinated unit of decision taking;[27] but, today the firm is better described as 'a coordinator of a network of interrelated value-added activities' (Dunning 1993b) or a 'nexus of treaties'. At one time, the boundaries of the firm were firmly determined by its ownership. Now, *de facto*, they are much fuzzier, as their capability to control the allocation of resources may be exercised through a variety of cooperative arrangements, or networking agreements.[28] The more activities a firm pursues, the more it engages in coalitions with other firms, and the more countries it produces in, or trades with; then, the more its competitiveness is likely to be determined by its ability to systemically integrate these activities.

The systemic view of the TNC[29] implies governance structures very different from those implemented by traditional foreign investors. Rather than acting as an owner of a number of fairly autonomous or stand-alone foreign affiliates, each expected to earn the maximum economic rent on the resources invested in it, the systemic TNC aims to manage its portfolio of spatially diffused human and physical assets – including those owned by other firms in which it has some proprietary interest – as a holistic production, financial and marketing system. Of course, there are costs of coordinating intra- and inter-firm cross-border activities, and these will ultimately determine the extent and pattern of a firm's territorial expansion. However, recent advances in international transport and telecommunication technology have pushed out these limits. In cases where corporations have shed some of their foreign assets, this has been mainly to reduce the scope or diversity of their activities and the form of their networking, rather than that of the geography of their international transactions.

A final feature of the FDI of the 1980s and 1990s, which accords with the systemic view of TNC activity, is that probably as much as 90 per cent of it is currently undertaken by already established TNCs; that is, it is *sequential* rather than *initial* investment. This is not to deny that new TNCs are emerging all the time – probably at the rate of 4000 to 5000 a year,[30] and increasingly from developing countries, notably China; however, as yet, the total foreign capital stake of these companies is thought to be quite small. Now, research has established that *sequential* FDI – which, as far as a particular country is concerned, might be a first-time investment – not only is likely to be more geared to the interests of the rest of the investing company's value activities, but also is likely to generate its own unique costs and benefits – that is, over and above those generated by an initial investment (Kogut 1983; Buckley and Casson 1985). These arise essentially from the consequences of multi-nationality *per se*. They include such gains as those arising from the diversification of exchange risk and economic uncertainty, the spreading of environmental volatility, and the opportunity to better exploit the economies of geographical scope and specialization. They also include the costs of coordinating the activities and markets of foreign affiliates in widely different business cultures and political regimes (Kogut and Kulatihala 1988); and those associated with the setting up and sustaining of a cross-border network of intra- and inter-firm relationships.

The Criteria for Evaluating FDI

Global economic events of the last decade or so, and particularly those driven by technological advances, regional integration and the realignment of economic systems and policies, have, then, fundamentally altered the perception by governments of host countries of how FDI may contribute towards their economic and social goals. These same events have also caused a reappraisal by firms of *why* and *how* – and, indeed, *where* – they need to engage in international transactions. It is for these reasons that the current generation of scholars – not to mention governments and firms – continue to want to know more about the benefits (and costs!) of FDI. To what extent and in what way is the global economy causing these to change? Also, what should national and regional administrations do to ensure that inward TNC activity contributes the most benefits it possibly can to their economic and social needs and aspirations?[31]

While host nations have a multiplicity of economic and social goals they wish to achieve, the priority of which may vary over time, the principal economic criterion by which national administrations appear to be evaluating inbound FDI in the 1990s is *its perceived contribution to the improvement of the competitiveness and productivity of the resources and asset creating capabilities located within their areas of jurisdiction.*[32] This, indeed, is probably the single most important medium-to-long-term economic objective of the great majority of nations, and particularly of those that are most dependent on foreign sources of supply and foreign markets for their prosperity.

How, then, might the competitiveness or productivity of a country be advanced? Table 2.3 identifies five main ways. The first is for a country's firms to produce more efficiently whatever they are currently producing, for example by reducing organizational costs and/or raising labour or capital productivity. The second is by the introduction of new products, production processes and organization structures, or the improvement of the quality of existing ones. The third is by the reallocation of resources and capabilities to produce goods and services that are in better accord with the country's comparative dynamic advantage. The fourth is by capturing new foreign markets – providing this is cost-effective. The fifth is by reducing the costs, or speeding up the process, of structural adjustment to changes in global demand and supply conditions.

Until to fairly recently, most Western economists – especially those of a neo-classical persuasion – have treated competitiveness as a *static* phenomenon, and have been concerned mainly with upgrading the

Table 2.3 The five ways for a nation to upgrade its competitiveness and comparative advantage

---

1. Increase the efficiency of its existing asset deployment; by more effective quality control procedures; e.g. by networking with other firms; by more cost-effective sourcing; by reducing lead times; by raising labour and capital productivity.
2. Improve the allocation of its existing resources and capabilities, e.g. from less productive to more productive activities; and towards those in which its perceived dynamic comparative advantage is increasing.
3. Innovate new products, processes and organizational structures, e.g. by improving national innovatory systems; by better exploiting the economies of the spatial clustering of related activities; by ensuring risk capital is available for start-up firms.
4. Capture new markets, e.g. by improving knowledge about foreign markets and about customer needs; and by better marketing and distribution techniques.
5. Reduce the costs and/or increase the speed of structural adjustment, e.g. by encouraging flexible labour markets; by enhancing the quality of retraining programs; by minimizing bureaucratic inefficiencies; by appropriate fiscal and other incentives for industrial restructuring; by a greater willingness to accept, and adjust to, change.

---

productivity of firms or countries through improving the usage of *existing* resources and capabilities. However, as the focus of raising economic welfare has been increasingly directed to product improvement and innovation, so the concept of *dynamic* competitiveness has gained attention. Such competitiveness refers to the relative capabilities of firms to market new products or production processes and/or to react speedily and appropriately to exogenous changes in demand and/or supply. Global competitive pressures, together with the new techno-economic paradigm of flexible production, are thus impelling policy-makers to increasingly evaluate the merits of different organizational modes by their contribution to upgrading the medium to long-term productivity to their location-bound assets.

The potential contribution of inbound FDI to each of these ways or vectors of upgrading competitiveness is fairly self-evident. It may provide resources or capabilities otherwise unattainable, or attainable only at a higher cost. It may steer economic activity towards the production of goods and services deemed most appropriate by domestic and international markets. It may boost R&D, and introduce new organizational techniques. It may accelerate the learning process of indigenous firms. It may stimulate the efficiency of suppliers and competitors, raise quality standards, introduce new working practices, and open up new and cheaper sources of procurement. It may provide additional markets. It may better enable a host country to tap into, or monitor, the competitive advantages of other nations. It may inject new management talent and entrepreneurial initiatives and work cultures. It may encourage the formation of cross-border cooperative alliances, technological systems and inter-firm networking. It may foster the geographical clustering of related activities that generate their own agglomerative economies. In short, it may interact with the *existing* competitive advantages of host nations and affect their *future* competitive advantages in a variety of ways.

Some of these ways are summarized in the schema set out in Figure 2.1. This figure is an adaptation and extension of Michael Porter's

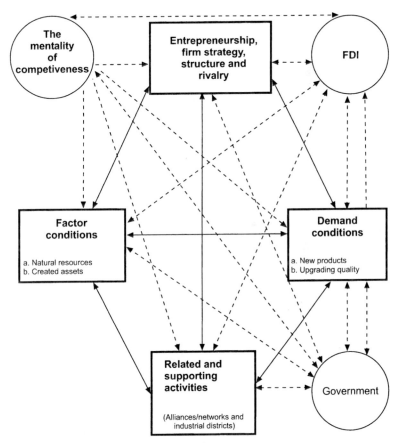

Figure 2.1 The diamond of competitive advantage.

Source: After Porter (1990); modified by the author of this chapter

diamond of competitive advantage (Porter 1990).[33] It suggests that inbound FDI may affect not only the four facets of the diamond but also the actions of host governments, and the mentality of competitiveness of the constituents in the host country. This it may do, for example, by injecting more market-oriented philosophies and practices, by encouraging more harmonious labour relations, and by raising the quality standards expected by consumers.

It is worth noting that the significance of the individual attributes of the diamond of competitive advantage may vary not only between countries, but within a particular country over time. Thus, for example, the relative importance of the production and efficient deployment of created assets, and the means by which these are transmitted over space, has increased as the world economy has become more globalized. Similarly, there are suggestions that the ways complementary activities are organized along the value added chain, and the agglomerative economies to be derived from a spatial clustering of these and other related activities, are becoming more significant. By contrast, the optimum number of domestic firms competing in their home market is probably falling as the geographical focus of competition becomes more regional or global, while the domestic availability of natural resources is generally becoming a less critical competitive advantage than once it was.

It is to be accepted that most of the competitive advantages just described are also available to domestic firms, but, it is my contention that the unique attributes of FDI – and especially those that arise from the multinationality of the investing firms, and their ability to engage in cross-border alliances and networks – offer financial, production, marketing and organizational benefits over and above those that indigenous firms may posses or can acquire.

At the same time, there are costs to a host country of inbound TNC activity. These may be divided into two groups. The first comprise various payments (for example, profits, interest, dividends, royalties, management fees) that have to be made to attract the foreign investor or maintain the FDI. These will vary along a continuum. At one extreme are the payments below which a non-resident firm is unwilling to invest, and at the other the payments above which a country is not prepared to accept the investment. The payments actually made will rest on the relative bargaining skills and negotiating power of the TNCs and the recipient governments. These, in turn, will depend on the price a host country would have to pay to acquire the benefits of FDI in alternative ways and the options open to the investing companies to locate their activities in other countries. In the 1960s and 1970s, the main anxiety of host governments was that the monopoly power of foreign TNCs would enable them – the TNCs – to extract an unacceptably high share of the value added by their affiliates. Today, the greater concern is that, without the inbound investment, host countries may be deprived of the advantages of being part of an internationally integrated production and marketing system (UNCTAD 1993).

The second type of cost of FDI arises whenever the behaviour of the investing firms, which is geared to advance their global objectives, is perceived to produce unwelcome consequences for the host country. These include the restrictions a parent company may impose on the sourcing of raw materials and components by its affiliates, and the markets they may serve. The affiliates may also be limited in the range of products they produce, the production processes they employ, the amount and kind of research and development (R&D) they undertake, and the pattern of their networking with indigenous firms. By transfer pricing manipulation, too, it is possible that income earned in the host country might be syphoned off to the home country (or some tax haven).

Some Determinants of the Net Benefits of FDI

To what extent is it possible to theorize about the net benefits of inbound FDI? Under what conditions will it be of most value to host governments? What can governments do to ensure that such investment best contributes to the upgrading of its indigenous resources and capabilities? The short – but hardly satisfactory – answer is that it all depends on the kind of FDI, the conditions that prompted it, the existing competitive advantages of the host country, and the economic policies pursued by host and other governments. But, fortunately, the economist can go a little further than this by identifying the situations in which a specific host country is likely to gain the most from FDI, and, in sub-optimal situations, what that country might do to increase this gain. In particular, I argue that the benefits to be reaped from FDI critically depend on: first, the types and age of the investment; second, the economic characteristics of the host countries; and, third, the macroeconomic and organizational strategies pursued by host governments.

Types of FDI

Table 2.4 sets out the main types of FDI identified by the literature.[34] The classification is mainly based on the *raison d'être* for the investment.

The first two types of FDI, viz. *resource-seeking* and *market-seeking* investment, represent the two main motives for an initial foreign entry by a firm – be it in the primary, the secondary or the tertiary sector. The latter two embrace the two main modes of expansion by established foreign investors. These *sequential* investments are frequently aimed at increasing the efficiency of the TNC's regional, or global, activities by the integration of its assets, production and markets; these are called *efficiency-seeking* investments. However, sequential investments, and occasionally first-time ones, are increasingly taking the form of *strategic-asset-seeking* investments, the main purpose of which is to acquire resources and capabilities that the investing firm believes will sustain or advance its core competences in regional or global markets. These assets may range from innovatory capability and organizational structures to access to foreign distribution channels and a better appreciation of the needs of consumers in unfamiliar markets.[35] Strategic-asset-seeking investment is frequently the most expeditious way of acquiring these kinds of competitive advantages (Wendt 1993).

In the 1960s and 1970s, most FDI was of the first or second type, although regional integration in Europe and Latin America was beginning to lead to some efficiency-seeking (or rationalized) FDI, particularly by large US TNCs in sectors like automobiles, consumer electronics and office equipment. There was also a small amount of strategic-asset-seeking investment – usually by US firms that had not been among the first of their industry to invest in Europe, but now, encouraged by the prospects of market growth, were seeking a speedy means of catching up with their rivals.

In the 1980s and early 1990s, FDI has been increasingly of types 3 and 4. Exceptions include first-time investments by TNCs from developing countries and a new generation of first-world TNCs. But, upwards of 75 per cent of all intra-Triad TNC activity since the mid-1980s has been by established European or US TNCs, and by Japanese companies, who, from the start of their internationalizing programmes, have sought to coordinate the deployment of their domestic and foreign assets, and have viewed each of their foreign affiliates, and frequently their associated suppliers and industrial customers, not as self-contained entities but rather as part of a regional or global network of activities.

This last point is an important one. I have suggested that, in an age of flexible production systems and alliance capitalism, TNCs are engaging increasingly in a variety of modes of cross-border activity. These should be considered less as substitutes for each other and more as the components of a holistic and integrated network of activities. Sometimes FDI is

Table 2.4 The four main types of foreign direct investment

• *(Natural)-resource-seeking* a. Physical resources. b. Human resources. • *Market-seeking* a. Domestic markets. b. Adjacent (e.g. regional) markets.	Mainly motives for *initial* FDI
• *Efficiency-seeking* Rationalization of production to exploit economies of specialization and scope a. Across value chains (i.e. product specialization). b. Along value chains (i.e. process specialization). • *Strategic-(created)-asset-seeking* a. To advance regional or global strategy by acquiring foreign: i. Information and technology. ii. Organizational capabilities. iii. Markets. b. To tap into the agglomerative and other economies of business networks.	Mainly motives for *sequential* FDI

the appropriate modality, and at others it is some kind of non-equity relationship. However, each is being viewed increasingly as a complementary means of gaining entry into foreign networks of related activities and into foreign markets. Increasingly, too, the competitive advantage of TNCs is being viewed in terms of their ability to coordinate their core competences with those of other firms – and sometimes of the public sector – located outside their home countries. Moreover, host countries, too, are increasingly viewing inbound FDI and cooperative agreements involving foreign firms as a means of advancing the economic interests of their indigenous firms – including those in the same networks as the foreign affiliates.

One very recent phenomenon is the export of vertically integrated networks by Japanese firms to the US and Europe. As yet, this is largely confined to the automobile industry, in which sector, between 1980 and 1988, some 109 Tier 1 Japanese component suppliers – members of the same keiretsu as one or more of the six main Japanese automobile assemblers[36] – established manufacturing facilities in the US (Banerji and Sambharya 1994). However, as Japanese direct investment continues to increase, and as alliance formation becomes a more important part of the strategies of TNCs, one may expect networking FDI to be a feature of the global economy. The extent to which the phenomenon is primarily an intra-triad one remains to be seen. However, a case could be made out that, in transition economies, in order to speed up the full integration of FDI with the rest of the local economy, foreign TNCs might encourage their home-based suppliers either to invest with them or else to conclude non-equity agreements with suppliers in the host country.[37] What is certain, however, is that in making their locational choices, foreign TNCs are now giving more attention to the quality of the supply capability of potential host countries, including that which arises out of being part of a network of related activities.

While FDI in developing countries – which in the period 1988–92 accounted for about a third of all new FDI (UNCTAD 1994) – remains primarily of a market-or resource-seeking kind, this, too, is changing. Increasingly, the liberalization of markets and regional integration in Asia and Latin America is enabling foreign investors to view their production and sourcing portfolios from a regional rather than a national perspective. The sub-region comprising the eastern coastline of China, Hong Kong, Taiwan and Indo-China is a case in point. Increasingly, too, many developing countries are being drawn into the hinterland of the globalizing firms from First World countries, as, in their bid to remain competitive, these firms are continually seeking new markets and cheaper, better quality and more stable sources of supply. Moreover, there is some suggestion that, *within* both developed and developing countries, foreign firms are increasingly locating their activities either in well-established industrial districts (for example Silicon Valley and Route 28 in the US) or in places with the potential to become new business districts (for instance the new automobile complex now developing in North-East England around the Nissan plant.[38]

However, unlike the 1960s and 1970s, most investments now taking place in developing and transition countries by First-World TNCs are not autonomous investments. Rather, they are part of an integrated production system (UNCTAD 1993). This means that the decisions of a TNC on *what* to produce in a particular country, *where* to source its inputs from and *who* to sell its output to are based not only on the locational attractions of that country, *vis-à-vis* other countries, but what is perceived to best advance the global interests of the corporation, rather than the interests of one of its foreign affiliates, or group of affiliates. *Inter alia*, and we shall return to this point later, this requires governments of host countries, in the formulation and implementation of their domestic macroeconomic and industrial strategies – and especially those that affect the decisions of foreign direct investors – to cognize the strategies of governments of other countries whose firms are competing for the same resources and markets (Dunning 1992).

In Table 2.5, we identify some of the attributes of each type of inbound direct investment that are most likely to enhance the competitive advantages of recipient countries. In practice, the precise contribution of each type of investment will be both activity- and firm-specific. It is also likely to vary according to the age of the investment – generally speaking, the local value added of a foreign affiliate is positively correlated with its age – and, perhaps most important of all, it will

Table 2.5 Some likely contributions of different kinds of FDI to the upgrading of competitiveness of host countries

1. Natural-resource-seeking	a.	Provides complementary assets (technology, management and organizational competence).
	b.	Provides access to foreign markets.
	c.	May or may not lead to local spin-off effects on industrial customers, e.g. secondary processing activities.
	d.	Raises standards of product quality.
	e.	May or may not foster clusters of resource-based related activities.
2. Market-seeking	a.	As 1. a above.
	b.	Fosters backward supply linkages and clusters of specialized labour markets and agglomerative economies.
	c.	As 1. d, and also raises domestic consumers expectations of indigenous competitors.
	d.	Stimulates local entrepreneurship and domestic rivalry.
3. Efficiency-seeking	a.	Improves international division of labour and cross-border networking: entices comparative advantage of host country.
	b.	Provides access to foreign markets and/or sources of supply.
	c.	As 2. b above.
	d.	As 1. d and 2. e above.
	e.	Aids structural adjustment.
4. Strategic-asset-seeking	a.	Provides new finance capital and complementary assets.
	b.	As 1. b above.
	c.	As 2. d above.
	d.	As 3. a above.

depend on the organizational strategies and economic policies adopted by host governments. I examine some of these strategies and policies later in this chapter, but in compiling Table 2.5 I have assumed that they are broadly consistent with the dictates of the international marketplace, and, that they are directed primarily towards enhancing the dynamic competitive and comparative advantages of the resources and capabilities within their jurisdiction.

The conclusions from Table 2.5, which summarize a substantial body of research findings,[39] and also the experience of many national authorities, are self-evident. Each type of FDI has its own particular contribution to make to the five ways of upgrading competitiveness, identified in Table 2.3 and the four facets of Porter's diamond illustrated in Figure 2.1. For example, by the resources and capabilities they transfer, the examples they set, their participation in business districts, and their upstream and downstream transactions with related domestic firms, TNCs engaged in both market and resource-seeking FDI have the potential to raise the productivity of indigenous resources and capabilities, improve quality standards and stimulate economic growth. In the right circumstances, efficiency-seeking FDI can assist the host country to restructure its economic activities more in line with its dynamic comparative advantage, it can reduce the costs of structural adjustment, and it can foster more demanding purchasing standards both by industrial and personal consumers. Strategic-asset-seeking investment may help integrate the competitive advantages of the acquired firm with those of the acquiring firm, and make for additional rivalry between domestic firms. However, this type of FDI, unlike the other three, may be undertaken with the specific purpose of transferring the assets acquired from the host to the home country, and this may work to the disadvantage of the competitiveness of the former country.[40]

The contribution of each type of FDI will also vary according to the part, or parts, of the value chain in which it is undertaken. In turn, investment in each part may be differently motivated. For example, some kinds of foreign-owned R&D activities are truncated replicas of those of the parent companies, some are akin to efficiency seeking foreign production, and some are designed to gain an insight into the innovatory activities of the host country, and, where permitted, to participate in foreign research consortia.[41] This latter motive explains the presence of foreign TNCs in regional clusters of R&D activities in the US, the EC and Japan. However, in general, inbound investment, providing it helps advance the dynamic comparative advantage of the host country, is likely to have its most beneficial effects when it is directed to those stages of the value chain where the potential for upgrading productivity is the greatest.

Spatial and Country Influences

So much for the different kinds of FDI, each of which, we saw earlier, is likely to be pushed or pulled abroad by different factors, and thus attracted to different countries. Thus, *market-seeking* FDI will be attracted to countries with large and prosperous markets, or to countries with easy access to such markets (for example, small countries in regionally integrated areas). *Resource-seeking* FDI will be determined almost entirely by the availability and quality of natural resources, together with the level and significance of international transport costs. *Efficiency-seeking* TNC activity will prefer a location consistent with the host country's comparative advantage in that activity on world markets; thus labour-intensive FDI will be directed to countries with low real wages, while TNCs will choose to specialize in high-tech activities in the advanced industrial countries and those that offer the best supporting infrastructure. *Strategic-asset-seeking* investment will be partly firm-specific, but will normally take place in a country similar in economic structure and living standards to that of the investing country, except, perhaps, in the case of natural-resource sectors and where FDI is geared towards buying into unfamiliar markets and distribution channels.

Again, the ownership of foreign facilities is not always necessary to achieve the objectives implicit in these four kinds of FDI. In the hotel industry, for example, the major form of foreign involvement by the leading transnational hotel chains is not FDI, but franchising and management contracts (Dunning and Kundu 1994). As large and medium firms are reducing the scope of their domestic value-added activities, this is also likely to occur abroad as well. However, in place of vertical or horizontal integration, firms are now concluding a variety of non-equity cooperative arrangements, and if this pattern is replicated abroad then we might expect the significance of these arrangements to increase in the years to come. Certainly, in considering the impact of foreign TNC activity on the competitiveness of host countries, it is appropriate that every form of non-equity alliance besides FDI is considered.

Let us now turn to factors determining the location of TNC activity today. How do they differ from twenty years ago? What determines the kind of competitive advantages offered by countries seeking to attract FDI? What should be the attitude and policies of national governments in the 1990s towards FDI, and in the light of globalization? And how do these attitudes and policies differ from those displayed in the 1960s and 1970s?

In answer to the first question, Table 2.6 sets out a selection of some generic spatial characteristics, which scholarly research has shown to most affect the geography of TNC activity. Broadly speaking, the characteristics fall into two main groups:

1. those that chiefly impact on the *production* costs and revenues of the investing firms, and
2. those that chiefly impact on the *transaction* and *coordinating* costs and benefits[42] of the investing firms.

Research[43] has established that each of these characteristics – and their constituent components – will impact differently on each of the kinds of FDI just described. Thus, for example, artificial barriers to trade might encourage defensive market-seeking FDI, but deter efficiency-seeking FDI. Both resource- and efficiency-seeking investors are less interested in the size and character of the local market, which is the main concern of market-seeking investors. Investment incentives and disincentives have been found to be most significant in influencing efficiency-seeking FDI, while sequential investors are less likely to be concerned about cross-country ideological, language and cultural differences than first-time

Table 2.6   Some country-specific attributes affecting FDI

---

1.   Those that impact chiefly on direct production costs and benefits
- Spatial distribution of natural resources, created assets and markets.
- Input prices, quality and productivity (e.g. labour, energy, materials, components, semi-finished goods).
- Investment incentives and disincentives (including performance requirements, etc.).
- Comparative economics of centralization vs. decentralization of different segments of value chain, viz. production and marketing.
2.   Those that impact chiefly on transaction and coordinating costs and benefits
- Cross-border transport and communication costs.
- Artificial barriers (e.g. import controls) to trade in goods and services.
- Societal and infrastructural provisions (commercial, legal, educational, transport and communication).
- Differences in cross-country political ideologies, language, culture, business, customs and the ethos of competitiveness.
- Economic system and policies of host governments. The organizational and institutional framework for resource allocation.
- The opportunities to exploit the agglomerative economies of industrial districts.

Source: Adapted from Dunning (1993a, Table 4.1).

market-seeking investors. Strategic-asset-seeking investors are unlikely to be influenced by input prices or cross-border consumer transport costs to the same extent as are efficiency-seeking investors, while the opportunity to exploit scale economies is likely to be positively correlated with efficiency-seeking FDI, and negatively correlated with market-seeking FDI. Moreover, the significance of the locational variables set out in Table 2.6 will also vary according to the industry[44] of and the asset portfolios and strategies pursued by an investing firm.[45] Finally, such significance will also depend on the attributes of any particular host country – such as its size, stage of economic development, industrial structure, degree of economic interdependence with the rest of the world – and its physical and psychic distance from the main investing country.

Now, most of these spatial characteristics, and the industry-, firm- and country-specific contextual variables that influence them, are well known to both scholars and business enterprises alike. Yet, in the past, the expectations of governments – and particularly governments of lower-income countries – have been frequently frustrated because they have not taken sufficiently into account the unique characteristics of their own resources and organizational capabilities. The benefits of inward FDI for Nigeria or Taiwan are unlikely to be the same as those for India, those now experienced by Chile and Vietnam are quite different from those ten to fifteen years ago, those currently gained in Malaysia and Botswana from efficiency-seeking FDI are scarcely comparable with each other, while those which result from market- and resource-seeking FDI are likely to be highly dependent on the development and macro-organizational policies of host governments, relative to those implemented by other governments competing for the same FDI.

The significance of the spatially related variables set out in Table 2.6 has changed considerably over the last two decades. As their share of total production costs has declined, the drawing power of natural resources and unskilled labour has declined, while that of created assets and the opportunities of networking with local firms has risen.[46] As the unique competitive advantages of TNCs have become both more mobile and systemic, so such firms have chosen increasingly to locate their value-added activities in countries that can offer the most cost-effective complementary assets, and the quality of infrastructure and support services that an integrated international production or marketing strategy requires. In this connection, intending investors usually place their need for state-of-the-art facilities for the cross-border acquisition and transmission of information, technology and finance at the top of their locational priorities. An effective and trustworthy legal framework – particularly in its ability to enforce property rights and resolve contractual disputes – comes a close second. At higher levels of economic development, the quality of a country's educational and technological infrastructure becomes more critical.

More generally, as the organizational and transaction costs of economic activity have become relatively more important – and there is some evidence (Stiglitz 1989; Wallis and North 1986) that these are also positively related to the complexity of a nation's industrial structure – countries that can offer a business environment conducive to minimizing these costs, are, *ceteris paribus*, likely to gain an increasing share of inbound investment. Recently, two surveys have been conducted – one on the determinants of Japanese direct investment in UK manufacturing and the other on the location of international offices (During 1991). In both surveys, transaction- and coordinating-cost-related variables – such as those to do with interpersonal relations, information asymmetries, language and culture, searching for and working with subcontractors, learning about the quality of communications and adapting to local business practices and customer needs, and bureaucratic controls – were ranked considerably higher as investment determinants than were traditional production-cost-related variables.

Host Government Policies

Elsewhere, I have written on the ways in which the actions of national governments might affect – for good or bad – the location and structure of TNC activities. Here, I focus on the main changes in host government organizational strategies that have over the past two decades most affected the level and distribution of FDI.

Foremost among these changes has been a softening in the attitudes of national governments towards FDI. This has resulted in a widespread liberalization of policies that previously constrained TNC-related activity. In the last decade, more than thirty countries have abandoned central planning in favour of market-based policies, and another eighty have liberalized their foreign investment regulations (UNCTAD 1993). In addition, as already mentioned, the criteria by which most countries evaluate inbound TNC activity have shifted from its direct contribution to local value added to its longer-term consequences for the competitiveness of indigenous resources and capabilities.[48] This reassessment has occurred at a time when governments – both of developed and developing countries – have been rethinking their own role and functions in the light of political changes and the globalization of the world economy. The most obvious manifestation of this rethinking has been a widespread deregulation and liberalization of markets and the privatization of many state-owned sectors, together with the removal, or reduction, of a wide range of government-imposed market imperfections, for example, subsidies, tariff and non-tariff barriers, price controls and all manner of rules and regulations.

However, the fact that governments have lessened their direct intervention in markets does not mean that they have abdicated – or, indeed, that they should abdicate – their responsibilities either as *enablers* and *steerers* of wealth-creating activities or as *facilitators* of the private-enterprise system. Indeed, as firm-specific assets become more internationally mobile, while others increasingly take on the form of public goods,[49] the role of government as a coordinator of markets and hierarchies is becoming a more, rather than a less, critical one. Moreover, because of the demands of modern technology and competitive pressures, the organization of economic activity has become more pluralistic. This places additional responsibilities on governments to ensure the continued existence of the resources and capabilities over which they exercise jurisdiction and to capture the synergistic benefits of alliance capitalism.

To a large extent, this remoulded role of national government – it's not so much a question of whether or not governments should intervene in markets, but rather *what kind* of intervention they should make, and *for what purpose* – reflects the changes now taking place in the relative efficiency of different modes of organizing economic activity. The market – as a systemic organizational entity – has been reinstated and upgraded, except in the case of public goods and strategically sensitive products. The current philosophy is that decisions on what is to be produced in a particular country, and how it is produced, are best left to the collective will of thousands of firms and hundreds of thousands, or millions, of consumers. At the same time, this philosophy also presumes that underpinning and sustaining the market as a resource-allocative mechanism lies the strong visible hand of government. For without the complementary assets of an efficient and up-to-date legal, financial and commercial infrastructure, an educated labour force, an adequate transportation and telecommunications network, a strong anti-monopoly policy, a sound macroeconomic policy, and a wealth-creating culture, the market cannot do the job expected of it. We believe that, besides its various social and strategic responsibilities, it is the government's task to cultivate and support – though not necessarily undertake – all of these market-enabling activities.

Possibly, what has been written so far is not contentious. Indeed, the policy implications may seem all too familiar. However, the real challenge facing governments is how best to implement these policies. The particular point I wish to emphasize is that the globalizing economy of the 1990s is forcing national governments – be they large or small, developed or developing – to re-examine their domestic economic strategies in the light of the fact that they are increasingly competing for competition enhancing assets – which are much more footloose than they used to be.[50] Macro-organizational policies that at one time affected only the domestic allocation and use of resources are now as likely to affect trade, FDI and cross-border alliances as much as any tariff, exchange rate change or interest rate hike. If nothing else, the world economy of the 1990s is obliging governments to realign their domestic economic strategies more closely to the needs of the international marketplace.

It is my strong contention that a government that is successful in reducing – or helping hierarchies and collaborative ventures to reduce – the transaction and coordinating costs of economic activity, and that best enables its firms to surmount the obstacles to structural change, is *ceteris paribus*, likely to be the most successful, not only in attracting the right kind of FDI, but in doing so at the least real costs. It is surely no accident that the countries that have performed best economically in the last two decades are also those that have (1) designed and implemented a macro-organizational strategy consistent with upgrading the competitiveness and the dynamic comparative advantage of their location-bound resources, and (2) sought to attract the right kind of inward FDI.[51]

One final difference between the domestic economic policies now being required of governments in a world of quicksilver capital and those practised in the 1960s and 1970s is that, except for cultural or strategic reasons, there is little case for discriminatory action by governments, either in favour of or against inbound TNC activity. Though it is not always admitted (notable exceptions being the cases of particular types of incentives and performance requirements), most governments have downgraded the significance of FDI policies *per se*. Instead, they are preferring to re-examine the appropriateness of their general macroeconomic and macro-organizational strategies *in the light of the globalization of economic activity and the growing mobility of critical wealth-creating assets, as well as on the understanding that FDI and trade-related FDI are the chief modalities by which countries are linked together*. It is, then, the interaction between these policies and the strategies pursued by TNCs that will determine the extent to which inbound FDI is able to upgrade a particular country's competitive advantage.

Alternatives to Foreign Direct Investment

Earlier in this chapter we saw how some large, multi-activity firms are disinternalizing their non-core activities, and in so doing are replacing hierarchical control by a cooperative arrangement. It is also the case that, for many years, some host countries have preferred to purchase the foreign resources and capabilities they need – or the right to their use – on the open market, or by way of a licensing or franchise agreement or management contract, rather than via a foreign direct investment. The desire to maintain control over the use of imported technology and organizational competence has always been a powerful one, although it is by no means the case that ownership of equity capital is necessary to achieve this purpose – a fact that many developing countries found out the hard way following a spate of expropriations in the 1970s.

We have seen that the literature distinguishes between, on the one hand, a particular set of assets and proprietary rights provided to a host country by FDI, and, on the other, control over the use of these assets. Both O-specific advantages are likely to be different when internalized within TNCs from what they would be were they exchanged between independent firms. Host countries clearly have to assess whether the net benefits of asset transfer and usage by way of FDI are greater or less than that by a non-equity route. The answer will clearly depend on the form and extent of the market failure leading to the FDI, and on how far such failure can be reduced by 'voice' rather than 'exit'-type organizational strategies (Hirschman 1970).

The recent experience of Japanese participation in European and US industry has shown that a cooperative venture is sometimes a viable alternative to FDI from an investing firm's viewpoint, although much will depend upon whether, as a result of relational transactions, the proprietary assets of the parties to the exchange can be protected. Earlier, I suggested that technological advances, particularly in inter-firm communications, together with an increasing need for industrial buyers and sellers to tap into each other's assets and work together to ensure that the economies of synergy are fully exploited, are combining to reduce the transaction and coordination costs of alliances or networks. I also averred that various characteristics of flexible production – for instance, the just-in-time inventory system and the greater emphasis on learning from other firms through the exchange and diffusion of superior production technology and organizational routines, etc., together with the increasing inability of 'stand-alone' hierarchies to meet the demands of the global marketplace – are increasingly favouring non-equity cross-border relationships.

Over the past decades, the number of high-tech strategic alliances has considerably outpaced the number of new foreign affiliates and cross-border M&As – at least in the developed world.[52] And, as we have seen, growth through collaboration and the pooling of assets – particularly among small and medium enterprises (SMEs) – is well suited to transitional economies in which there is a lack of suitable information .–processing capability and/or effective governance mechanisms. Certainly, deficiencies in the socio-institutional infrastructure, inadequate and unreliable legal and commercial rules, a rudimentary banking and accounting system, penal taxes, and a paucity of indigenous trained managers have been the most important causes of the lack of hierarchical inbound investment – FDI – in the erstwhile planned economies over the last five years or more.[53]

The extent to which a host country should consider producing its own technology and other assets, rather than importing them via FDI or alliances, will depend strongly on the unique characteristics of that country. However, the key to making the right decision rests on (1) the setting up of a market-facilitating institutional framework that best ensures the promotion of dynamic comparative advantage, and (2) the readiness and ability of the host country's government to pursue the appropriate macroeconomic and macro-organizational policies to foster this advantage.

Japan and South Korea are two examples of countries that, in seeking to promote their long-term comparative advantages, initially limited the role of inbound FDI and created the economic and technological infrastructure to support these advantages from their own resources and from imported knowledge and technology. In doing so, both countries evolved a socio-institutional system that was a mixture of hierarchical and alliance capitalism, into which, as their economic development proceeded, they incorporated FDI. However, the extent to which a newly developing or transition economy can (or should) follow the Japanese or Korean example rests largely on its ability to replicate the organizational and institutional structure of those countries, not to mention the culture of their firms and peoples regarding asset creation networking and business districts, the upgrading of product quality and the macro-organizational policies of their governments.

The current economic situation of most Central and East European countries is very different from that of Japan, or even Korea, twenty to thirty years ago. Nonetheless, lessons can be drawn from the institutional framework and economic strategies adopted by those countries, which directly or indirectly affected the contribution of inbound FDI to their development. Similarly, the experiences of countries as diverse as Chile, India, Indonesia, Nigeria, and Portugal are also worthy of study – sometimes as a guide to what might be done and sometimes as a guide to what ought *not* be done! As has frequently been stressed in this chapter, each country is unique in its economic, social and cultural characteristics, and therefore its assessment of the value of FDI is also likely to be distinctive. Moreover, time may change both the characteristics of a country and its objectives, while, also, technoeconomic developments may affect the appropriate way of organizing the creation and use of resources.

In the 1990s, it would seem that the routes by which countries can gain access to foreign-owned resources and markets are considerably wider than they were even a decade ago. Foreign direct investment is now just one of a plurality of channels a country may use to upgrade its competitive and comparative advantages. Analysts are agreed that, as a general rule, it should be used to *supplement* the creation and deployment of indigenous assets, rather than replace them; and that any macro-organizational policies of governments should be directed to ensuring that foreign and indigenous resources and capabilities are combined such that their static and dynamic competitiveness are optimized. One thing, however, is certain. Whether technical knowledge, managerial expertise, entrepreneurship, marketing skills, financial acumen or organizational capacity are provided by indigenous firms, FDI, cross-border alliances or networks of foreign and domestic firms, in today's global marketplace, where economic progress is decided primarily by the ability of private enterprises to innovate fresh assets and to combine these effectively with other assets (some of which will be government-supplied), a strong and vibrant techno-economic production system and an efficient socio-institutional infrastructure are essential. Moreover, it is only by a conscious and determined effort by government, enterprises and people working together that the critical condition for the success of both foreign and domestic investment can be achieved.

Conclusions and Caveats

This chapter has sought to identify the main contributions that inbound FDI can make to the static and dynamic competitiveness of host countries, and the conditions which must prevail if that contribution is to be optimized. It has also reviewed the changes over the past twenty years in both the determinants affecting TNC activity and the attitudes of governments towards it.

Among the most important of these changes has been the globalization of the world economy, the emergence of a new paradigm of production and the growth of alliance capitalism. These changes and the resulting international division of labour – an integral part of which is the growing mobility of intra-firm intermediate products between countries – is demanding a reappraisal of the economic philosophies and policies of national governments. In particular, the widening locational options of TNCs and the convergence of the industrial structures and trade patterns of advanced countries are forcing national administrations to pay more attention to ensuring that the quality of their location-bound resources and capabilities do not fall behind those of their competitors.

In pursuing these goals, governments have other critical roles to play. These include: the elimination of structural and institutional impediments to efficient resource usage; the active promotion of market-facilitating measures; and the encouragement of an ethos of entrepreneurship together with the promotion of dynamic competitiveness among their constituents. It is the administrations that have gone the furthest in implementing these changes, and in taking a long-term view of their economic strategies, that have been the most successful, not only in attracting inbound FDI but – much more important – in using it so as to best advance their national interests in a globalizing economy.

However, I would end with a couple of caveats. The first concerns a matter already discussed – some of the possible costs of FDI as a competition-enhancing vehicle. There is a saying, much beloved by Western economists, that there is no such thing as a free lunch, in other words all good things have their price. This is certainly true of FDI; the only question is whether the price attached to it is a fair and reasonable one. One difficulty faced by many governments in formulating and implementing policies that affect the costs and benefits of inbound FDI is that they do not know, or at least are uncertain, what these costs and benefits actually are. This is partly because most decisions affecting the behaviour of a foreign-owned affiliate are taken by the parent company on the basis of information and expectations known only to them. This is not to say that these globally oriented decisions necessarily work against the interests of host countries, but it makes life more difficult for a government seeking to optimize the level and pattern of inward FDI and its effects on domestic competitiveness.

In summary, Table 2.7 sets out the main costs and benefits of FDI as they have been experienced by host countries over the past two decades or more. The balance between the costs and benefits of each kind of contribution will vary according to the type of investment, as identified in Figure 2.1, over a range of *firm-* and *industry*-specific features, some of which I have identified in this chapter, and also according to the age and nationality of the FDI. It will further depend on the characteristics of the host country – and especially, as we have seen, the policies of the host government.

The second caveat relates to the nature of a country's competitiveness. As I have emphasized, competitiveness is a relative concept, which analysts use to make comparisons in economic performance between firms, industries or countries, or between the performances of the same firm, industry or country at different times. However, whether or not a country whose firms are uncompetitive in the production of a particular range of goods or services should encourage inbound FDI to improve that competitiveness is a debatable point. Very rarely – if ever – can one country expect to be competitive in the production of all goods and services. Obvious examples include growing bananas in Scandinavia and producing sophisticated electronic equipment in Chad. One of the tasks of the international marketplace – backed by the appropriate government policies – is to allocate resources and capabilities in such a way that each country engages in the kind of economic activities to which it is *comparatively* best suited. FDI can play a useful – sometimes decisive – part in this process. However, what it should not be used for is to prop up activities that can never be internationally competitive. Resources and capabilities must be directed to where they can be most efficiently deployed. After all, one of the functions of trade is to allow a country to import products that it is relatively unsuited to produce for itself and pay for these with products that other countries are relatively unsuited to produce. The success or otherwise of FDI in upgrading the *competitive* advantage of a country's resources and its *comparative* advantage in the international market place should also be judged by this criterion.

Appendix: Measuring the Impact of FDI – Some Methodological Issues

There have been a considerable number of empirical studies assessing the costs and benefits of inbound foreign direct investment, which I will

Table 2.7 Some possible contributions of inbound foreign direct investment to the upgrading of the competitive advantages of host countries

	Positive	Negative	Host country characteristics that favour positive effects
1.	By providing additional resources and capabilities, viz. capital, technology management skills, access to markets.	May provide too few, or the wrong kind of, resources and assets. Can cut off foreign markets, c.f. with those serviced by domestic firms. Can fail to adjust to localized capabilities and needs.	Availability of local resources and capabilities at low real cost, particularly those complementary to those provided by foreign firms. Minimal structural distortions or institutional impediments to upgrading of indigenous assets. Development strategies that help promote dynamic comparative advantage.
2.	By injecting new entrepreneurship, management styles, work cultures and more dynamic competitive practices.	An inability of foreign entrepreneurship, management styles and working practices to accommodate to, or where appropriate change, local business cultures. The introduction of foreign industrial relations procedures may lead to industrial unrest. By the pursuance of anti-competitive practices, it may lead to an unacceptable degree of market concentration.	The policies pursued by host governments to promote local entrepreneurship and a keen and customer-driven work ethic; the character and efficiency of capital markets; the effectiveness of appropriate market facilitating policies. Larger countries may find it easier to introduce some of these conditions than smaller countries.
3.	By a more efficient resource allocation, competitive stimulus and spill-over effects on suppliers and/or customers, it can help upgrade domestic resources and capabilities, and the productivity of indigenous firms; it can also foster clusters of related activities to the benefit of the participating firms.	Can limit the upgrading of indigenous resources and capabilities by restricting local production to low value activities, and importing the major proportion of higher value intermediate products. May also reduce the opportunities for domestic agglomerative economies by confining its linkages to foreign suppliers and industrial customers.	The form and efficiency of macro-organizational policies and administrative regimes. In particular, the benefits likely to be derived from FDI rest on host governments providing an adequate legal, commercial and assigning priority to policies which help upgrade human and technological capabilities; and encouraging regional clusters of related activities, e.g. science and industrial parks.

4.	By adding to the host nation's gross domestic product (GDP), via 1to3 above, and by providing additional tax revenue for government.	By restricting the growth of GDP via 1to3 above, and by transfer pricing (TP) other devices to lower taxes paid by host governments.	See 1to3 above, and by suitable policies by the tax authorities of host governments to minimize TP abuse. Countries with most to offer TNCs are likely to be more successful in implementing these policies.
5.	By improving the balance of payments (B of P), through import substitution, export generating or FDI efficiency-seeking investment.	By worsening the B of P, through limiting exports and promoting imports, and out-competing indigenous firms that export more and import less.	Need to take a long view of importing and exporting behavior of foreign affiliates. The key issue is not the B of P *per se*, but the contribution of FDI to economic efficiency, growth and stability. However, countries with a chronic B of P deficit may find it difficult to completely liberalize their B of P policies.
6.	By better linking the host economy with the global marketplace, and helping to advance economic growth by fostering a more efficient international division of labour (D of L).	By promoting a D of L based on what the investing firm perceives to be in its global interests, which may be inconsistent with dynamic comparative advantage, as perceived by the host country.	As 3 above – and in particular the extent to which host country governments can pursue policies that encourage investing firms to upgrade their value adding activities, and invest in activities that enhance the dynamic comparative advantage of indigenous resources. The gains from 6 are particularly important for smaller countries.
7.	By more directly exposing the host economy to the political and economic systems of other countries; to the values and demand structures of foreign households; to the attitudes to work practices, incentives and industrial relations and foreign workers; and to the many different customs and behavioural norms of foreign societies.	By causing political, social and cultural unrest or divisiveness; by the introduction of unacceptable values (e.g. respect to advertising, business customs, labour practices and environmental standards); and by the direct interference of foreign companies in the political regime or electoral process of the host country.	Extent to which society is strong and stable enough to smoothly adjust to technological and political change. Also, the strength and quality of government determined regulations and norms; the nature of the host country's goals and its perceived trade-off between (e.g.) economic growth, political sovereignty and cultural autonomy. The difficulties in optimizing the benefits of the openness induced by FDI will be greatest in countries that are most culturally distinct from their trading or investing partners.

not review here.[54] I would, however, reiterate some methodological points made in chapter 10 of *Multinational Enterprises and the Global Economy* (Dunning 1993). This is because it is my experience that, in their evaluation of FDI, host governments are frequently inclined to overestimate that part of its contribution which is specifically attributed to its foreignness *per se*.

The problem of attribution is common to all impact studies. Suppose, for example, it is possible to identify the transactions and performance of MNEs or that of their affiliates. For example, suppose it can be shown that German-owned affiliates in Brazil record a good export performance; or that Japanese affiliates in the UK are highly productive; or that Swedish subsidiaries in Malaysia pay their workers above the national average wages; or that French-owned hotels in Jamaica import most of their food; or that UK mining companies in New Guinea limit the markets to which their affiliates can sell; or that US subsidiaries in Canada carry out only a limited amount of R&D; or that as a result of a take-over of a Thai textile company by a Hong Kong foreign investor a large number of redundancies occur; or, that, in order to obtain a permit for building a petrochemical plant that an Italian construction company is found guilty of bribing a Nigerian government official, or that a Dutch and Indian food-processing firm concludes a strategic alliance to drive out a powerful US competitor.

Suppose all these things. To what extent may it then be said that these events are due specifically to the *foreignness* or the *multinationality* of these companies, and to what extent to other attributes they may possess, but which may have little, if anything, to do with their nationality of ownership or degree of multinationality? For it is a fact that, as well as engaging in foreign production, MNEs are often big and diversified; but so are many uninational firms. They may also influence, if not control, sources of supply or marketing outlets: but, so too, might some of their local competitors. By their marketing and advertising practices they may, for good or bad, affect the purchasing habits and values of consumers; but, so too might indigenous firms or foreign firms exporting to the countries in question! In assessing the unique contributions of MNEs, the scholar needs to be constantly careful only to attribute those that are a consequence of their foreignness and/or their degree of multinationality.

There is another, but related, problem. Let us take just one example. How does one measure the impact of the operations of a foreign affiliate of an MNE on the balance of payments of a host country? I will demonstrate that it is not sufficient to calculate the external transactions on capital and current account of MNEs or their foreign affiliates; for these must be set against some estimate of the transactions that would have occurred in the absence of such foreign affiliates – the so-called *alternative* or *counter-factual* position. For example, suppose that a Dutch MNE company finds, that, after two years of operating a foreign affiliate in Pakistan, its exports to that country are only one-half those before the affiliate was set up? How far can this decline in exports be attributed to the foreign investment? The answer depends very much on what would have happened had not the investment taken place. There is also the question of what happens to the resources, for example capital and labour, displaced by exports. Will these be employed elsewhere in the economy where exports might be earned, or will they remain unused? Much in this instance rests on the supply capacity of the home country, and the kinds of macroeconomic, fiscal and employment policies pursued by the home government. But, depending on the answer to these questions, the net balance of payments effects of outward investment may vary from being strongly negative to strongly positive.

Naturally, any alternative or counter-factual position is bound to be hypothetical, as one cannot be sure what would actually have happened in the absence of the foreign investment. Because of this, some researchers have argued that it is more helpful to try and identify the specific characteristics of the *ownership* of foreign affiliates, by making comparisons between the conduct and performance of foreign and indigenous firms or between foreign firms according to the nationality of their ownership or degree of multinationality. Any differences revealed may then be reasonably attributable to the nationality or multinationality of the firm. This is an interesting estimating procedure. At the same time, it does make the implicit assumption that, in the absence of FDI, the output gap would be met by other firms, that is to say, that the resources released by the foreign firm would be utilized.

Such methodological points are critical if the distinctive impact of MNEs is to be properly appreciated and evaluated. Of course it is quite possible that the main contribution of inbound investment to a particular country may have little to do with country of origin. One suspects that this applies particularly in the case of intra-OECD investment in international industries, where the main competitors of foreign MNEs are domestic MNEs. On the other hand, in some cutting-edge technology and information-intensive sectors, e.g. biotechnology, banking and financial services, etc., the nationality of ownership may be a crucial variable affecting technological or organizational competences; and even in other sectors, since foreign-owned firms are often more efficient than domestic firms, their marginal impact on the competitiveness of indigenous resources may be quite substantial.

Notes

1   For a detailed examination of this system, cf. the scale or mass production system, see for example Best (1990), Gerlach (1992), Harrison (1994) and Oman (1994). For a discussion of the interaction between changes in techno-economic production systems and the socio-institutional framework of market economies, see Perez (1983) and Perez and Freeman (1988).

2   What Benjamin Gomes-Casseres (1994) has recently referred to as 'group alliances' and Jorg Sydow (1992) has called 'enterprise networks'.

3   There are several such theories or paradigms, reviewed in Cantwell (1991) and Dunning (1993a).

4   This, of course, may be an advantage in its own right.

5   Not every scholar accepts the idea of a continuum. Powell (1990), for example, argues that it fails to capture the complex realities of inter-firm connectedness in such organizational structures as industrial and regional networks.

6   Because it is unique to their *ownership*. Advantages of firms other than those attributable to the ownership (e.g. size, etc.) we term firm-specific advantages. See Dunning (1993a, ch. 4).

7   These include the heterogeneity and immobility of resources and capabilities and *ex ante* and *ex post* limits to competition (or to the contestability of markets).

8   I cannot accept that the single-activity firm is a market-replacing mechanism. The initial *raison d'être* of a firm is the creation of valued goods and services; markets have never fulfilled this function. However, once a firm engages in multiple activities it replaces transactions, which otherwise might have been undertaken by other single activity firms; and at this point they engage in signalling and allocating resources, which would otherwise have been the function of markets.

9   Such products include both intermediate and final goods and services.

10 For example, product cycle, intangible asset, risk diversification, oligopolistic strategy and sequential theories all seek to explain different types or aspects of TNC activity.

11 Where different stages of the same value chain are linked.

12 For example, to be fully effective, one technology needs to be used jointly with another technology, such as in the telecommunications and biotechnology sectors.

13 For a recent application of the Hirschman concept of 'voice' and 'exit' to customer/supplier relationships in the auto industry, see Helper (1993).

14 Especially when they are part of a spatial network of related firms, for example a business district.

15 The risk diversification thesis identified with Alan Rugman (1979) suggests that the existing geographical structure of a firm's investment may affect its attitude to a subsequent investment. Thus, Japanese firms with existing investments in the UK may prefer an additional investment in France or Italy to diversify their risks in Europe.

16 For example, whether FDI is restricted to certain sectors.

17 For example, local content and/or export requirements; insistence that a certain proportion of scientific managers, or administrative personnel, be nationals of the host country, the adherence to local environmental standards, etc.

18 Localization economies were first identified by Marshall (1920). More recently, their implications have been taken up by several scholars, notably Piore and Sabel (1984), Porter (1990), Best (1990) and Harrison (1994).

19 This system has a long, practical and intellectual heritage. Its genesis goes back to the introduction of interchangeable manufacturing in the mid-nineteenth century, through the rise of large corporations in the 1870s, to the mass production system which added the principle of flow to that of interchangeability, and the application of scientific management control systems as proposed by Frederick Taylor (1967).

20 As, indeed, has happened in the US, which has long had a reputation for adversarial labour–management relations. One excellent example of how a working culture may be changed to fit the needs of alliance capitalism is the joint venture of Toyota and General Motors, viz. New United Motor Manufacturing Inc., or NUMMI, which began operations in 1984. For further details, see Wilms and Zell (1994).

21 Although we accept governments may also need to intervene to counteract the anti-competitive behaviour of firms.

22 There still remains exceptions, and sometimes the rhetoric of governmental officials, is different from the reality. For a critical evaluation of South Korea's policies towards FDI, see *International Herald Tribune* (1994).

23 We use the expression 'TNC systems' deliberately, because although there is a good deal of evidence that uninational – and particularly small to medium uninational – firms continue to play an important role in the generation of created assets, sooner or later, these firms are forced into a network of complementary activities in which the larger TNCs act as the lead or flagship firms. This idea is further explored in Van Tulder and Junne (1988), Gugler and Dunning (1993), D'Cruz and Rugman (1993) and Harrison (1994).

24 This is especially so in the case of dynamic industries where product life cycles are shortening, and the urgency to innovate new products and introduce more cost-effective production techniques is particularly intense.

25 For some illustrations of the failures of TNCs to acknowledge the significance of inter-country cultural differences, and for some ways in which TNCs may, themselves, build upon these differences to their advantage, see an excellent book by the ex-chairman of Smith Kline Beecham (Wendt 1993).

26 The gains of spatial agglomeration or clustering of related industries are one of the four critical variables influencing the competitiveness of firms and countries, as identified by Porter (1990).

27 This definition was popularized in the 1930s, when the nature of the firm as an organizational unit was hotly debated among British economists.

28 These include strategic alliances and long-term contractual relations with suppliers. The widening scope of firms to at least partially control the use of resources and capabilities of other firms in which they have no ownership, and vice-versa, is encouraging scholars to return to the idea of *groups* of related firms as a critical unit of microeconomic analysis.

29   Some writers have contrasted a global system of TNC organized *intra*-firm activities with a global network of inter-firm activities. For the purposes of this chapter, bearing in mind that the main unit of analysis is the TNC, we embrace each and every 'related' transaction of TNCs – be they *intra-* or *inter*-firm – within the context of a TNC system.

30   Estimates of the universe of TNCs, and their affiliates, are constantly being revised upwards. The latest estimates by UNCTAD are that, in the early 1990s, there were at least 37 000 TNCs and 200 000 foreign affiliates (UNCTAD 1994).

31   While this chapter concentrates on the relations to inbound direct investment, an increasing number of governments are also reassessing the benefits of outbound direct investment. Indeed, as we have frequently stressed – notably in Dunning (1993b) -the globalizing economy is forcing governments to take a more integrated view of outward and inward MNE activity, in exactly the way they do of international trade.

32   As, for example, usually measured by its gross national product (GNP) per head or rate of increase in its GNP. The term 'productivity' relates to the efficiency at which a nation is utilizing its scarce resources at a given moment of time. The term 'competitiveness' refers to how well that country is doing *as compared with* other countries; or in some cases, compared with its own performance at a past period of time. The main value of competition-related studies is to help point the way in which a nation, a region within a nation, or a nation's firms can improve its (their) production.

33   For further details, see Dunning (1992). In this version of the diagram, Porter's 'chance' variable has been replaced by a 'mentality of competitiveness' variable, as I believe this to be a more critically important country-specific factor, which not only is exogenous to each of the four attributes of the diamond but also is closely linked to the government and FDI variables.

34   See, for example, Dunning (1993a).

35   For recent examples, see Wendt (1993)

36   Toyota, Nissan, Honda, Mitsubishi, Mazda and Isuzu.

37   In a very interesting paper, Peng (1993) has argued that, because they are often denied routes of growth through generic expansion or through mergers and acquisitions, firms from planned economies, e.g. Central and Eastern Europe and China, are almost compelled to implement a growth strategy through networking, and bilateral alliances. By such a strategy, firms can tap into 'external resources', i.e. assets that are used but not directly owned by them. Although Peng accepts that a network-based growth strategy frequently incurs many of the bureaucratic costs of hierarchies, he argues that such inter-firm collaboration may well lead to lower bureaucratic costs since it does not require substantial transfers of ownership rights. Peng further argues that a network-based strategy also facilitates organizational learning through the exchange and diffusion of superior production technology and organizational routines.

38   For further examples of sub-national regional clusters of economic activity in which foreign firms are often involved see, for example, Teece (1992), Scott (1993) and Enwright (1994).

39   For a summary of these, see Dunning (1993a).

40   But not necessarily, as much would depend on how the owners of the acquired firm spend the proceeds of the transaction, and on how the

location-bound resources released by the acquired firm are subsequently deployed.

41 For a recent examination of the structure of FDI in US R&D facilities, see Dunning and Narula (1994).

42 Defined as costs and benefits that arise as a direct result of internalizing the market for intermediate products, i.e. hierarchical or bureaucratic costs of administration.

43 As summarized in Dunning (1993a, ch. 6).

44 According, for example, to differences in input requirements, costs of transporting intermediate and final products, the extent to which products need to be adapted to local customer requirements, the advantages offered by networking with local firms, the behaviour of competitors, and the need to be sensitive to government mandates and policies.

45 Asset portfolios are the accumulated tangible and intangible assets (that is, resources and capabilities) that a firm owns or has privileged access to. It is these portfolios, their sustainability and the firm's strategic response to them that will determine the kind and range of products it produces, the extent to which it is vertically integrated, the number and character of its associations with other firms, and the geographical distribution of its activities. In turn, the strategy of a firm will be affected by its age, size, organizational competences and long-term objectives.

46 Exceptions include some resource-seeking and manufacturing assembling investments in the poorer developing countries.

47 See especially Dunning (1991, 1992, 1993b and 1994).

48 What might be thought of as a shift from a 'micro-income' to a 'macro-asset' perspective.

49 Examples include many capital-and technology-intensive products and those that, in their exchange, yield external costs and benefits, that is to non-market participants.

50 The idea of 'competing' governments has a very respectable intellectual heritage. It has so far been used by public-choice economists to explain how individuals, by exiting from the country, or 'voting with their feet', can act as a constraint on governments in their tax policies and in the services they offer their taxpayers. See, for example, Brennan and Buchanan (1985). But the idea could easily be extended to explain how a whole range of actions by governments that affect the profitability of firms may also influence their locational preferences.

51 There are examples of countries that have attracted FDI, but have not grown, and vice-versa. However, sensible macroeconomic and macro-organizational policies have led to FDI being attracted to most competitive sectors of the economy, or to those that are potentially the most competitive.

52 For an analysis of strategic alliances concluded in the 1980s, see Hagedoorn (1993).

53 For a recent and vivid account of the difficulties facing foreign firms contemplating investment in Russia see Goldman (1994).

54 The reader interested in the results of mainstream research on the consequences of FDI on the economic welfare of host countries should see Dunning (1993a, ch. 11 and 13–18).

3
Multinationals in the Transition to a Market Economy

John Slater

Foreign capital inflows have been an important though not always an indispensable element in the development of the societies great and small that have industrialized successfully. This chapter attempts to provide a framework for the country-specific ones which follow, and draws on some of their commentary on the background to and possible role of external investment in the Soviet successor states.

The constraints on investment in general due to the output collapse in these new countries, as well as the additional constraints of political uncertainty on foreign direct investment (FDI) – which the foreign partner can always direct elsewhere – are only too clear. Yet the Soviet successor states also offer important advantages for foreign investors. It is clear that a population of 280 million constitutes both a huge potential market and an important source of supply to, especially, European and Japanese producers. At the same time, the pressing need for foreign investment to supplement the as yet limited supply of domestic capital, as well as the potential domestic demand for up-to-date technology and know-how, should be a strong incentive for the successor-state governments to create favourable conditions for FDI. Foreign companies have the marketing know-how and are indeed integral players in the economies which hold the external debt incurred by the former Soviet Union. They are thus in a unique position to assist the successor states to begin reducing this debt and to lessen its present dead weight on their economies. Foreign-run companies could moreover not only contribute directly to improved economic performance and restructuring through their own economic success, but could additionally offer an indirect but extremely important demonstration effect, by their very presence on the successor states' soil, in disseminating basic knowledge of how to manage a business under modern market conditions.

This chapter begins with a brief survey of some areas of Soviet economic policy that seem to have played a major role in the progressive decline and ultimate collapse of the socio-economic system initiated after the First World War. This is extended to cover the main changes in Soviet policies towards the outside world up to the end of the Gorbachev era. The consequences of Soviet central planning, as practised in the Soviet Union, for its successor states' investment requirements are discussed next. The attempted transition to a market economy now under way points to the possibility that certain analogies may exist with the process of take-off achieved in the past by Tsarist Russia and the present-day industrialised countries, and some of these are then presented briefly. The present size, country distribution and prospects for FDI in the Soviet successor states which draw upon the country chapters which follow, are discussed finally.

The Current State of the Former Soviet Economies

For more than seventy years, the laws of economics were suspended in the Soviet Union in favour of 'socialist economics'. During this period, the implicit assumption of central planners was that this was distinct from capitalist economics, was governed by different rules and that its success must be adjudged by different criteria. After the Second World War, attempts to move from the Stalinist *status quo* to reform, to radical reform, and ultimately to perestroika blurred these basic differences, but the essential unity of economic science, whether communist or capitalist, as distinct from differences in policy objectives and policy instruments, was never admitted as long as communism lasted.

The central objective of economic policy was the expansion of output of selected product lines, and of output overall, by almost any means. The allocation of investment was based upon political priorities which at various times ranged from the building of socialism more or less independently of the world production system, the maximisation of output of what were seen as prestigious products at particular times – steel and electricity in the 1920s and 1930s, petroleum, natural gas and chemicals in the 1960s and 1970s, investment goods throughout the Soviet era – and an inflated defence hardware budget. What was not taken into account was the cost of these selections or any notion of maximising welfare on the basis of least-cost choices. Indeed, the calculation of real production costs was impossible, given a system of administered input and output prices that functioned as accounting units only. Because output prices were not dictated by demand, shortages exerted no upward pressure on prices and profits, and in the resulting shortage economy few gluts occurred to exert any downward impetus. Irrational pricing thus contributed to irrational attitudes to macroeconomic decision-making by hiding, even from the planners themselves, the real costs of those decisions.

With hindsight, it seems likely that the expansion of imports of Western technology in the 1970s was one of the last throws by central planners to reverse the incipient economic collapse with which they, if not Western or even Soviet students, were clearly being confronted by the unpublished data controlled by the Central Statistical Administration and the KGB. Even the published data provided increasing evidence of faltering economic performance. The final years of Soviet power constituted an effort to advance on a still wider front: to reconstruct economic agents' behaviour by inducing them to react to economic imperatives in a manner similar to their Western counterparts. In the event, and despite numerous experiments with new systems of economic management within the planning system, it proved impossible to induce economic agents to react to such stimuli in the absence of a fully fledged market.

The central weakness was the continuous decline in factor productivity. The slowdown in output growth rates, continuous falls in the Soviet share of Western markets of manufacturing, and the increasing cost of growth increments were all recorded at length during the 1980s in many Western commentaries, while the contrast between the material quality of life in the Soviet Union and the West became embarrassingly obvious even to casual observers. This had been implicitly acknowledged by the Soviet planners from the beginning of the 1970s, when policies to 'intensify' the pattern of economic growth by reducing the level of labour, capital and other inputs per unit of output became the central strategy of successive five-year plans up to the last one, which covered the period 1986–90. The accelerating weaknesses in Soviet economic performance, and the total failure of the 'intensification' campaign, became increasingly clear in the 1980s. But the real extent of what we can now, with hindsight, perceive as a comprehensive breakdown of the system was obscured, partly by failure to publish socio-economic data, but also by countervailing successes in prestige space programmes and by the unremitting priorities given in resource allocation to Soviet military and political power.[1]

By the end of the 1980s, several communist countries of Eastern Europe, in addition to Poland where it had happened much earlier, had begun to register substantial falls in output. The Soviet Union followed suit in 1990 after an unprecedented period of decelerating output growth, which had accompanied President Gorbachev's attempts to combine radical reform with the maintenance of most of the old institutions of central planning. In that year labour unrest, the start of the disintegration of the old centralised supply system and increasing uncertainty which decreased investment demand all contributed to an officially announced national material product (NMP) decline of 4 per cent, sharply reversing, if the earlier official figures are to be believed, a post-war record of uninterrupted output growth. Since then, the output decline accelerated in the CIS member states taken together to 10 per cent for GDP in 1991 and to over 18 per cent in 1992.

The output collapse, which had accelerated during the year and into the early months of 1993, was reflected in all domestic demand categories.[2] Investment expenditure, the vital component for the future restructuring of production, fell in 1993 by a massive 45 per cent in the CIS countries as a whole and in Russia, by 40–45 per cent in Kazakhstan, 40 per cent in Ukraine, and by an apparently more modest 17 per cent in Belarus. No other CIS country had reported investment data for 1992 at the time of writing (December 1993), but a further 10 per cent decline at least can be expected for the CIS countries as a whole in 1993.[3] In the Baltic states the investment collapse has been much bigger still.

The Foreign Economic Relations of the Soviet State

Inward capital flows in general and foreign private investment in particular were hindered by heavy ideological baggage and probably – to judge by the post-Soviet rhetoric of communists-turned-nationalists – by xenophobia too, even if the latter was, like pervasive anti-Semitism, rarely openly acknowledged. Attempts were nonetheless made from time to time to enlist foreign money in the development process. In the 1920s a very small number of foreign-owned and run firms ('concessions') were set up to encourage investment in Soviet industry. But these are estimated to have accounted for less than half of 1 per cent of census-reporting industrial output by 1926–7. In the late 1920s and 1930s the role of foreign entrepreneurship was confined to the purchase of technology and know-how from big Western companies to accelerate the development of specific key sectors. These technical assistance contracts numbered about 40 by the end of 1928, mainly with US and German companies.[4] They included the purchase of turnkey tractor factories from Ford US, electricity-generating plant from Vickers UK and even defence-related as well as other technologies from Germany and also France. During that period, capital goods imports are estimated to have risen considerably before the arrest and trial of the Vickers engineers for alleged espionage. From the eve of the Nazi–Soviet pact in 1939 to the death of Stalin, capital and technology flows from the West remained modest.

Not until the 1970s did the Soviet government look westwards on a large scale to supplement its supply of development means. The big difference was the new Soviet willingness to enlist foreign capital flows for the first time by borrowing from private as well as government sources to finance the purchase of investment goods – as well as 'disembodied' technology and know-how.[5]

The techniques involved varied. The Soviet state trading organs, banks, and even ministries, arranged loans from private and public Western sources of finance. The capital goods exporters were often given export credit guarantees by their own governments. In other cases, several types of so-called industrial cooperation agreements were concluded. Here, a variety of technical imports, ranging from turnkey plants and whole production complexes – sometimes on a very large scale – to specific investment goods lines were financed, wholly or partly, by credits reimbursable from the proceeds either of resultant products supplied to the Western partner by the Soviet producer, or by 'compensation' deals involving other unrelated types of goods. But this fell well short of direct investment. There was no continuous involvement by lenders in the management of the projects which were set up. There was sometimes a role for lenders in the choice of project. But there was no visible risk element – or so it appeared at this time of effective Soviet state guarantees – since it accepted that no participating Soviet enterprise would be permitted to go bankrupt should it not make a profit on its borrowings for imported technology. Lenders' participation in the management of such investments was limited at best to technical back-up and the marketing of the product on Western markets in the case of compensation and other kinds of buy-back agreements.

These imports of capital goods and technology, and the consequent build-up of large debts to Western governments and financial institutions, continued unabated from the early 1970s until the break-up of the Soviet state at the end of 1991. In that year, investment goods amounted to about 44 per cent of total OECD exports to the Soviet Union (see Table 3.1). The fall in their share in the early years of the 1980s seems to have been a short-term response motivated by the need to restrain the growth of foreign debt at minimum short-term cost. The

Table 3.1 OECD exports of investment goods to the Soviet Union 1971–92
Investment goods are defined as the total of SITC/BEC 41, 42, 53 and 521 plus
large diameter pipelines.

	1971–5	*1976–80*	*1985*	*1990*	*1991*	*1992*
Total exports ($bn)	6.5	16.9	21.0	26.9	28.2	26.7
Whereof: investment goods ($bn)	2.9	7.4	7.1	11.4	12.3	9.8
Share of total (%)	44	44	35	42	44	37

Source: United Nations Comtrade Data Base.

relative stability of this share bears witness to the importance attached
by central planners to the potential contribution of Western technology
to Soviet growth – even though it was rarely openly acknowledged by
Soviet policy-makers. Even in 1992, when investment fell by nearly half,
investment goods still accounted for 37 per cent of the total imports of
the Soviet successor states.

Investment Requirements in the Successor States

(a) Structure of Investment

Before turning to FDI as such, a brief examination of the size of the task
for investment in general seems appropriate. It must be acknowledged
that no precise quantification of this basic task can be undertaken, since
the starting point – the situation in the last years of Soviet power – can
still not be quantified properly because of the nature of the Soviet
statistical series involved, and notably their expression in arbitrary,
centrally fixed prices. The resulting price relatives diverged substantially
from world market prices. This seriously reduces the accuracy of even
basic statistical aggregates such as the structure of investment by sector
and branch. Even so, the data for the 1970s and the 1980s do suggest the
build-up of important structural imbalances in investment and hence in
the structure of the capital stock. They also illustrate the latter's growing
obsolescence, and hence go some way to document the underlying
reasons for Soviet technical backwardness.

For what they are worth, data on the last decades of Soviet power
indicate a steady deterioration in output growth and labour productivity. The share of investment in total resource allocations fell sharply
during the 1970s, but an apparent reversal of this trend during the 1980s
did not achieve any stimulation of output growth, and capital productivity continued to fall (see Table 3.2)

Table 3.2 Soviet Union: growth and productivity indicators, 1970–89 (average annual % changes)

	1975/1970	*1980/1975*	*1985/1980*	*1989/1985*
NMP	5.6	4.3	3.2	2.8
Gross industrial output	7.4	4.5	3.5	4.0
Gross fixed investment	7.0	3.4	3.6	6.7
Labour productivity	4.3	3.3	2.7	2.5
Capital productivity	−2.8	−2.9	−3.0	−2.0

Source: United Nations Economic Commission for Europe Common Data bases.

With regard to the sector and branch structures of investment, industry increased its share of the total from 48 to 53 per cent between the mid-1970s and 1989 – mainly at the expense of agriculture. The non-material (services) sector, transport and communications also lost ground. Within industry, investment in fuels rose from 18 to no less than 30 per cent of the total over the same period; the big loser branches were chemicals, which fell from about 10 to 5 per cent of the total, but the share of all other branches fell.

Since this took place against a long-term background of decelerating annual investment growth rates (by nearly a third between 1971–5 and 1985–9), the heavy industries previously favoured under central planning, except for fuel, began to record falls in investment levels in the final years of Soviet power. This, and a marked tendency to reduce scrapping rates, led to a deteriorating age structure of the capital stock. The share of assets under five years old in the total capital stock of material production sectors (that is, excluding consumer services) fell from 41 per cent in 1980 to 35 per cent in 1989. The lowest shares of this vintage (under a quarter of the total) in the latter year were in transport and communications, trade and also in the public and consumer services sectors (education, health care and medicine). The corresponding share in industry fell from 41 to 37 per cent and was lowest in the energy, ferrous metals, chemicals and paper branches. In contrast, it rose to over 70 per cent in the fuel extraction branches.

There is thus enough Soviet information available to indicate the parlous state of the capital stock at the outset of restructuring and the extent of the modernisation effort which will be necessary. But on top of this, the restructuring effort will require scrapping of much capacity which is unlikely to be competitive however recent the capital stock is, either because the output mix does not correspond with an underlying pattern of demand which is now freed from the distortions of central planning, or because the technology, styling and quality of products and/or their resource costs are unlikely to be competitive either on external markets or, on domestic markets, with imported goods. An undervalued rouble or other CIS currency could, in principle, partially redress the balance for a time at least, but it is not a long-term option to ensure an adequate return on exports to repay external debt and to finance domestic producers' imports of up-to-date foreign technology.[6]

(b) Restructuring Challenges

The restructuring tasks confronting the newly independent states are indeed daunting. They include conversion of the inflated defence sector to the production of civilian goods, the upgrading of the consumer branches, and improvements in the technological quality of engineering output, especially in the production of new investment goods. Quality needs to be allied to quantity. The precondition for this will be investment, not simply at a much higher level than in the recent past but directed at those areas likely to yield the highest returns. Removal of the obstacles now inhibiting this is the key to the emergence of the former Soviet states from their present predicament. The main constraints on domestic investment resources are:

1. the small pool of private savings available for investment purposes;
2. the solution of the all-important questions relating to confidence in the new market systems now being developed; and
3. the near impossibility in most cases of making rational investment decisions based on comparative costs under conditions of near hyper-inflation.

With regard to savings, the inflation of the past two years has largely wiped out the large savings which had built up due to shortages of consumer goods in the last decades of the Soviet regime. Whereas at the end of 1990 the total value of bank deposits in the old Soviet banking system had reached R216 billion, equivalent to some 34 per cent of nominal GDP in that year, by the end of 1992 they were valued at R658 billion, or only 3 per cent of GDP. This reflects above all the shortfall in income growth relative to inflation, but also the primitive application of banking logic. Negative interest rates in every month between January 1992 and June 1993 represented a strong disincentive to save, and the banking system as a whole has in any case seen its role as bailing out enterprises by providing short-term credits to finance production expenditure and operational losses rather than mobilizing and channelling funds towards investment.[7] Regulations on the obligatory surrender of foreign exchange imposed on exporters have led to capital flight, further reducing the availability of domestic funds for investment.

Investment decisions are complicated by the lack of managers with the appropriate techniques for making them, or who have any experience of exposure to market forces and the rapid flexible responses which they require. Moreover, most of the institutions of resource mobilisation for the investment process are lacking – a gap extending from banking and the assessment of risk criteria to checks on performance which can only take effect through responsive markets for stocks and shares. These factors are intimately linked with confidence – uncertainty whether funds can be deposited safely and maintain their value while possible investment opportunities are sought and evaluated. The inflation of 1992–3 has effectively removed such options; despite the freeing of most prices from government regulation, it is now rapid changes in absolute and relative prices which prevent the calculation of the potential costs and profitability of investment prospects and still more their projection into the future.

To the constraints stemming from macroeconomic uncertainty can be added the lack of confidence engendered by some aspects of the new laws regulating business activity in general, and foreign business activity in particular. In most developed and fast-developing countries, business legislation applies without distinction between domestically owned firms and those which are wholly or partly foreign-owned, apart from some restrictions to safeguard state security notably with regard to defence-related industries. As noted in the country chapters which follow, this is not always the case in the Soviet successor states. The basic laws on foreign capital participation go far in the direction of equality of treatment for foreigners and, in some respects, foreign-owned firms even benefit from more favourable conditions than domestic firms (tax holidays, exemption from surrender of export earnings). In practice, however, they may effectively be discriminated against, as witness the measures limiting foreign participation in Russian banking, insurance and other financial sector activities. But the main problem seems to be the volatility with which provisions may be modified at short notice by subsequent regulations in different areas of the country, or by different administrations in the same area. Some uncertainties also remain as to how far privatisation legislation applies to foreign individuals and firms: a recent Russian presidential decree on land privatisation, for instance, does not apply to foreign individuals or firms.

Finally, confidence is also sapped by institutional shortcomings. The Soviet industrialisation process took place in a totally different environment from that in any other area of the world, and this in itself has given rise to an unprecedented set of problems for the transition process. The fundamental institutions of the market economy are still lacking – at the level of both the formal organs of banking, financial markets and commercial law codes, courts and arbitration procedures, as well as the actual mechanisms for carrying out and regulating such basics as financial settlements between economic agents, accounting standards, insurance, and so on.

Although many banking and legal institutions and codes existed in the Soviet era, their functions diverged at an early stage so widely from their nominal counterparts in capitalist countries that the similarity of nomenclature was in effect without significance.

Are There Any Lessons to Be Learned from Elsewhere?

FDI and Economic Development in Other Countries

The successful negotiation of a major economic turning point has always entailed the development of new institutions. Some were based on primitive but historically deeply rooted indigenous precursors, of which some were adapted to new uses, whereas others simply disappeared. In the Soviet case, the October revolution was followed by the dismantling of the complex banking and financial system and its replacement by a simplified system of transmission belts for the imposition of party and government decisions.

At the outset of the industrial revolutions in Britain and other European countries, where capital to finance expansion into new types of activity was available largely from indigenous sources (in Britain's case largely from the proceeds of textile exports), new home-grown financial and other institutions developed gradually and pragmatically in response to the new opportunities offered by the increasing stock of individually held wealth. This contrasts with both Tsarist Russia and nineteenth-century North America, where the presence of foreign capital in search of profits was the great liberating factor. But though foreign (and immigrant) entrepreneurs played a significant role both in institutional adaptation and in the build-up of productive infrastructure in the two latter regions, they were by no means alone. The development process resulted from a partnership between foreign and indigenous capital and entrepreneurship.

In other cases, such as Meiji-era Japan, a totally new type of economic system replaced the existing one in a short space of time – usually following a severe internal or external shock. The process was accompanied by the rapid implantation of new institutions, based partly on foreign models but adapted in new ways to the country's own traditions. Foreign capital participation was low. More recent cases of economic take-off include the newly-industrialised countries of South-East Asia and the South European countries of the European Union – and particularly Spain. These in fact had little in common at the outset of the economic acceleration. Not only did the countries in both of these regions successfully achieve take off, but they did so largely by attracting considerable sums of foreign capital, technology and know-how. It thus seems that a foreign capital contribution is a common ingredient of economic take-off in most but not all countries which have achieved or are in the process of achieving developed-economy status.

As noted, the main and very important exceptions were the developments in Europe during the successive national industrial revolutions in the nineteenth century, and also in Meiji-era and indeed post-Second-World-War Japan. It may be that the necessary condition in achieving economic take-off is, simply, the awakening of social awareness of the need for change. Foreign capital may then, additionally, provide a means of accelerating the process and, perhaps, of avoiding some of the worst disruptions which took such a toll on British and perhaps, though in different ways, on Japanese social life. This awareness may develop from below in society at large, be part of the baggage brought in by immigrants or be spearheaded by conscious government policies. It is clear that the last has played an important role in some countries, though it took very different forms in different economies. In North America, the 'manifest destiny' doctrine, common to a strong majority of nineteenth-century US legislators and to the populace alike, ensured that what needed to be done in the form of permissive legislation to encourage land ownership, the development of a transport and communications network and the provision of physical protection, policing and the law was, in contrast with the present situation in the Soviet successor states, actively promoted. Moreover, in the 1930s and up to the Second World War, the US government budget, via the New Deal programme, was a big contributor to major infrastructural projects, including the inter-state highway system, rural road networks and large-scale water control – despite arch-capitalist ideological objections. Japan traditionally, and other Asian countries currently, have managed the process of economic change through enforced compliance with industrial development strategies elaborated by governments in the course of close consultation with big and small business representatives.

FDI and the Tsarist State

Tsarist Russia is arguably more psychologically akin to post-Soviet Russia than any other country in which foreign capital has played a key role in achieving economic take-off – and psychology is ultimately perhaps the most important element, *ceteris paribus*, in achieving economic success. Moreover, many of the geographical opportunities and constraints have not changed that much since Russia's pre-industrial era – despite, or more likely because of, seventy years of ostensibly planned but in fact usually chaotic and irrational activity under central so-called planning.

By the 1860s some new features had appeared in Russian society: a distinct class of industrial bourgeoisie, merchants, industrialists and bankers with important capital resources. The emancipation of the serfs gave labour mobility and hence flexibility for the first time. Although the economy remained unbalanced due to the small scale of heavy industry, textile and other food and light industrial branches were beginning to grow rapidly, and the Ural mining industry was well established. By 1880, the first attempts at financial and monetary reform had begun. Good harvests increased trade surpluses, and it was no doubt as a result of the confidence arising from these social, institutional and economic factors that the inflow of foreign investment picked up to unprecedented levels from the 1880s onwards. By the turn of the century it had risen to nearly 3 per cent of national income and had probably averaged around 10 per cent of total investment in the economy during the 1890s. This is considerably larger than the overall resource flows to the CIS countries, estimated at about 1 per cent of GDP annually (see below). In Tsarist Russia, foreign investment was facilitated by the development of private banking after the 1860s, and foreign banks entered the picture by the purchase of shares in private banks or by the creation of banking syndicates with them. At all events, it was the banks which channelled both domestic and foreign resources into productive investment, often by banks with a specialized involvement with particular industries. Other large sums from abroad were raised by the government for budget-financed transport and infrastructural investment. It appears that about a quarter of foreign capital was directed toward mining, with metal processing (30 per cent) being the other main recipient, and with credit and other commercial enterprises accounting for about 15 per cent and textiles and other light industries for a tenth of the total.

The large share of mining anticipates the actual pattern of post-1990 FDI (see below) and also that of Soviet era industrial cooperation agreements. Russian mineral resources are likely to remain an important attraction for foreign investors. However, the sector and/or branch spread of pre-revolutionary FDI was rather better balanced overall than the post-1990 CIS structure, the vast bulk of which was confined to fuel and other mineral resource branches.

FDI in the Soviet Successor States

No previous economic turning point provides a clear analogy to the tasks now confronting the Soviet successor states. Following decades of priority ostensibly given by government to the tasks of 'modernisation', 'catching up' with the technically advanced capitalist countries, raising living standards and other progressive-sounding objectives through a unique science of 'socialist economics', it became increasingly clear to the Soviet leadership – as much as it already had to dissident intellectuals – that economics is, simply, economics and a vast theoretical apparatus has now been consigned to the rubbish heap of history. But the lack of credible existing institutions and the distorted production structures and waste to which economic pseudo-science gave rise remains. A huge physical and psychological detritus of communism underlies the attempted transition to the market now under way in the former Soviet Union. Possible lessons and issues concerning the role and structure of FDI in the Russian imperial past and from other countries could be assessed on the basis of a wide-ranging study of actual patterns of FDI in these other instances, but this is beyond the scope of the present study. Nevertheless, some general issues suggested by experience in Tsarist Russia and other countries are noted in the following paragraphs. The first of these concerns the size of FDI in the CIS countries. Of the total of 17000 joint ventures and wholly-owned foreign subsidiaries registered in the Soviet successor states up to April 1993, less than half (8000) were accounted for by the CIS states. The rest represent ventures in the three Baltic states, half of them in Estonia. Within the CIS states, Russia accounted for 3500, Ukraine 1400 and Belarus for about 850.[8] The total value of accumulated investment commitments in the Soviet successor states taken together amounted to some $5.9 billion up to July 1993, whereof $188.5 million in the Baltic states, $5.5 billion in the CIS as a whole. Russia had received $2.9 billion, Ukraine some $515 million and Belarus $282 million.[9]

It is clear, first, that in terms of ventures per unit of GDP, the Baltic states have been relatively far more attractive than the rest of the former Soviet Union, and that within the CIS countries Russia has been less attractive than either Ukraine or Belarus. At the same time, the overall size of FDI in relation to GDP is considerably less, as noted earlier, than was achieved in Tsarist Russia – less than 1 per cent on an annual basis for the Soviet successor states taken together compared with nearly 3 per cent at the end of the last century for imperial Russia. The amounts concerned are also very low compared with the East European transition countries; many of them appear to be 'foot-in-the-door' arrangements, and the average value of the total number of FDI projects is no more than a few million dollars. Nevertheless, this pattern is reminiscent of Spain, when the number of exploratory foreign investment agreements initially rose fast but where the actual commitment of investment funds was rather low; when it became clear that real change was imminent, there was a very rapid expansion based on these initially small beginnings.

A second general issue concerns the basic sectoral and industrial branch allocations of FDI. There is a potential conflict between the need to engage in widespread physical improvements in transport, communications and other basic services which will be necessary if productive investment is to reach its full potential, and those projects which contribute immediately and directly to increasing the amount of goods. But though the former is an enabling factor, its effects on productive potential will take time to realise. So far, the main sectors involved have been industry – about 75 per cent of the total number of ventures in Russia. Less detailed information is available for other CIS countries, but the bulk of these activities in Ukraine also appear to have been in industry.[10] Within industry, data for the CIS countries as a whole indicate a relatively large commitment in mineral resource branches. Between 1990 and the beginning of 1993, projections based on the first four years of operation in fourteen projects for which data are available (out of a total of thirty-nine projects) alone indicate a total investment value estimated at an ultimate total of over $9 bn,[11] or nearly twice as high as the total cumulative value of FDI in the CIS countries up to July 1993 noted above.

Russia is of course, perhaps together with Kazakhstan, exceptional among the CIS countries with regard to its natural fuel and mineral riches. The available information suggests that the attractions of its natural resources, and especially its fuel reserves, are well recognised by Western investors, and especially by the multinational oil corporations. As noted in several of the country chapters below, it seems that the main brake on further FDI in this area in Russia is uncertainty, owing to the long and complex negotiations involved and, on occasion, to the calls for the revision of ostensibly final agreements before signature when they are referred back to ministries or legislatures for ratification. Some of these hesitations can be traced to still unresolved conflicts between republican and other local bodies, on the one hand, and the central authorities on the other. Similar problems have been experienced in Kazakhstan, and they are likely to persist there and in Russia until the adoption of new constitutions which set out clearly reciprocal rights and obligations between the two levels of government.

In other cases, uncertainties persist with regard to unexpected changes in the implementation of regulations on taxation, profit repatriation, surrender of foreign currency export revenues, liability to duties on imported equipment and export licences and taxes.

Nevertheless, the current attractiveness of the fuel – minerals sector is an economic reality, and it has gone some way to redress the disincentive effects of economic instability up to mid-1993. Investment in manufacturing and in infrastructure has clearly yet to begin on more than a minor scale. At the same time, there are ways in which some of these real concerns could be addressed. This type of agreement could, for instance, proceed in parallel with the development of domestic manufacture of the machinery and equipment to be used with the assistance, on commercial terms, of the Western principals or partners. There is no reason why the Western firms concerned should not, in future, show greater interest in such extended partnerships, but carefully thought-out project detail needs to be placed on the negotiating table in advance by the recipient countries.

Government Policy

With regard to manufacturing in general, the fact that the implantation of new Western-financed firms on a partlyowned or whollyowned basis will and should take place exclusively for commercial reasons does not detract from the need for CIS governments to put in place appropriate industrial policies. This will be especially important in the Baltic states, Ukraine, Belarus and other countries lacking relatively easily exploitable natural resources. Coherent industrial policies are as yet virtually nonexistent in the Soviet successor states at the present time, but the need for them will become acute as the privatization programmes get under way.

It is important that governments develop a strategic view of the role of FDI and how it might be accommodated within the existing production and factor input structures. Clearly, there is no single criterion for gauging the directions of structural change other than profitability and efficiency. But governments can take a position on the kind of industrial and enterprise structures which are likely to be viable and productive in the longer term. How can indigenous technology be best combined with imported capital and expertise? What might be an optimal mix between labour-intensive industry based on imported R&D and management, and capital-intensive operations based on domestic resources? How would the desire for technology-intensive FDI fit in with policies to absorb growing employment? What kind of incentives should be given to encourage competition and the setting up of new industries – whether domestically financed or foreign? Other important areas will be the development of performance, safety and quality standards for finished goods and packaging, environmental and safety standards at plant level and the coordination of education and training programmes. Foreign firms could provide important feedback to regulatory bodies for dissemination to industry as a whole.

Choice between directly productive and infrastructural projects points up a third general issue – the role which will be played by public sector involvement and decision-making. The size of both the overall and infrastructural investment effort required, particularly relative to current low levels of private domestic savings, suggests that this is likely to be considerable – in relation both to the total investment effort and to FDI, and indeed to other aspects of the transition process. Here a distinction needs to be made between different methods of state intervention in the development process. Direct involvement in day-to-day business decisions of the kind invoked under central planning is not in question, but its evident failure should not be used as a reason to discredit all other types of state involvement. In Japan, the role of government in strategic planning and selection of projects via formal and informal consultations and the granting or withholding of machinery and equipment import licences persisted well into the second half of this century. The evidence of imperial Russia, furthermore, suggests that a partnership between foreign capital and expertise and state strategic planning in, for example, developing the transport sector, yielded good results in the past. Given the state's unique role in the transition economies as currently one of the few sources of domestic wealth concentration, the Tsarist experience thus suggests a potentially useful role for the state under the new circumstances of transition. For the immediate future, however, a serious constraint is the current impossibility of the successor states servicing the massive build-up of public sector foreign debt in the last two decades of Soviet power, a problem which must be dealt with before any large-scale expansion of government debt can be contemplated in the immediate future.

There are, of course, other government actions which could facilitate the growth of development potential. The expansion of transport and communications infrastructure in nineteenth-century North America and Britain was financed almost entirely from private sources, but occurred against a background of business-conscious legislatures. They reacted on the whole very quickly and positively to the requirements of domestic and foreign capital in terms of legislation facilitating new forms for the acquisition of land access and rights of way. North America's size and the consequent importance of transport and communications offer analogies for Russia and Kazakhstan. An important psychological factor was the existence of many historical precedents, ranging from the legislature's role in Britain in permitting the transfer of common land to private ownership (the enclosure movement) to the granting of vast areas of land in crown ownership to private entrepreneurs in the colonies. Some of the precedents on which these acts were based had been fixed for several hundred years before the industrial revolution. This was also the case with regard to mineral rights, where guidelines to settle disputes between central and regional administrations and between them and private entrepreneurs had been in existence for many centuries. In contrast, there was no such build-up of precedents in the former Soviet Union which would assist the successor states in delineating the respective rights of the state *vis-à-vis* domestic and foreign private capital.

A distinction should be made between FDI requirements to swell the total volume of investment and the qualitative aspects, notably the need for technology and know-how to modernize the obsolescent technology which is the norm in the Soviet successor states outside the space, defence and a few other sectors. This raises the question of how to cope with the human and natural resource factor endowments.

Labour costs in the successor states are now considerably lower than in other countries with similar per capita consumption levels. The labour force is comparatively well educated and the level of basic skills, ranging from literacy to vocational skills, is also high in comparison with other large-scale capital importers. Yet the quality of the skills and education are qualitatively deficient compared with what is needed for absorption into the world economy. Over 10 per cent of the working population have completed secondary education. This compares favourably with the Western share. Yet, to take managerial qualifications alone, the appropriateness of a thorough grounding in Marxian economics is, to say the least, questionable in relation to modern managerial, marketing and personnel requirements, while the expertise needed to compete on foreign markets is virtually non-existent. Low production engineering standards give rise to high production costs and the low technological level of final products of the manufacturing branches also militate against the development of high quality output in the short term.

In contrast, some activities such as fuels and other natural resources branches have the advantage that output does not depend on a technology input; the technology content of such goods is related to extraction techniques and their carriage to the market. Thus, unlike some other powerful economies, the vast natural resources of the biggest of the successor states are such that they must inevitably become major players in the world commodity markets and are as well or even better placed geographically than the United States, and indeed some other primary producers, to supply both Europe and the Far East.

Full participation in world markets for manufactures will doubtless take much longer to achieve. The oil, natural gas and mineral ore extraction branches could benefit even in the short term from production engineering and improvements in enterprise management. These branches, which are generally expected to be competitive on domestic and world markets, appear to offer the best short-term prospects for FDI. Stable demand and profitability prospects not only offer potentially high profits for foreign participants, but could also supply Russia and some other republics with quickly realisable foreign exchange earnings which could substantially improve debt servicing prospects and provide resources for the purchase of technology needs for other branches.

With regard to these other branches, the key factor will be first and foremost the provision of a stable macroeconomic environment on which rational investment choices can be made. The size of output losses since the market transformation started is such that the potential for considerable, if as yet unrealisable, growth in demand exists. Once the output decline is reversed, the sheer size of the successor states' market should begin to attract both domestic and foreign investment.

The collapse of communism and the exposure of Soviet backwardness in most areas of economic development has also perhaps provided a salutary psychological shock. Revelations of economic weakness can provide a strong stimulus to catch up. The process will be helped by some elements at least of the previous system – literacy levels similar to those in other advanced economies and the physical equipment of the education sector. At another level, however, the legacy of Soviet power is likely to be negative. Past teaching syllabuses in areas ranging from economics to administration have not only failed to equip generations of administrative and managerial workers to function under a market economy, but have also left behind attitudes which are actively hostile to it. This can be detected in the attitudes of some political groupings to Western firms' participation in the privatisation process, and in warnings that Western strategies are designed to transform the successor states into raw material supply appendages. These sensitivities will need to be taken into account by Western companies wishing to operate in these areas, which are, moreover, where FDI is likely to be most attracted in the short to medium term.

In sum, the situation of the Soviet successor states is unique in the annals of economic development. Not only are they obliged to develop new institutions, mechanisms and attitudes appropriate for all levels of the economy, but they are obliged at the same time to attempt to reverse the collapse of output and investment of the highly industrialised but inefficient and fundamentally unbalanced economy inherited from decades of central planning.

In other industrialised countries, foreign capital inflows and the technical know-how at many levels which accompanied them have not always been indispensable. But the need for a rapid transformation of these economies, to avoid the social unrest which is likely to follow a prolonged drop in living standards, seems to indicate an unusually acute need for a substantial foreign contribution of resources and expertise as early as possible. Political stabilisation is a prerequisite for this and, as successful experience in several foreign countries suggests, for the development of a partnership between the state, domestic industry and foreign entrepreneurship to coordinate legislation, strategic planning and any direct state participation seen to be necessary.

Most official aid so far granted has been in the form of debt-creating balance-of-payments assistance. The uncertain investment climate, due to the often inconsistent and usually volatile nature of existing transformation programmes and back-up legislation, has so far limited spontaneous foreign capital inflows. But only this can ultimately provide a dynamic and adequate foreign contribution for rapid economic restructuring on the scale needed. There are many potentially profitable areas for foreign profit-seekers. Initially, the exploitation of natural resources, which do not require much transformation of the final product, may offer the speediest returns. But manufacturing activity, to supply the potentially very large Soviet market in the first instance, also offers the advantages of a low-cost but well-educated labour force. The recent past shows, however, that these advantages will not attract business on the scale required until the implementation of government transformation programmes is perceived to be proceeding in a wholehearted and coherent manner.

Notes

1 Western economists who tried to stick to an honest interpretation of the biased and often deliberately misleading statistical and other facts available could not unambiguously demonstrate what most of them nonetheless suspected.

2 Except stockbuilding. Monopoly enterprises, protected by inflationary credit expansion and subsidies, apparently continued to produce quantities of unsaleable goods.

3 January-June 1993 data from the CIS Statistical authority show a further 7 per cent decline compared with the same period of 1992, and by August this was estimated at 54 per cent of 1990 levels on an annual basis and about the same volume as in 1974 (see Statistical Committee of the Commonwealth of Independent States, *Statisticheskii byulleten*, Moscow 1993, no. 14, p. 18, and no. 16, p. 7). In Russia, the decline between the first halves of 1992 and 1993 was 6 per cent, rising to 12 per cent between the first three quarters of those two years (see Russian Federation State Committee for Statistics, *O razvitii ekonomicheskikh reform*, Moscow, Jan.-Jun. 1993, p. 56, and Jan. Sept. 1993, p. 65).

4 See Davies (1989 pp. 33–4).

5 See Wienert and Slater (1986, pp. 18–30).

6 As in the 1960s in the Netherlands when the Slochteren gas field came on stream, it could prove difficult for the fuel-producing successor states to avoid an unwelcome currency revaluation at some stage, given the high share of fuel in their total exports; in Russia, fuel accounted for about 52 per cent in the first half of 1993, despite a fall in prices compared with year-earlier levels. It should also be noted that so far the fall in the external value of the rouble in 1992–3 had no obvious incentive effect on non-fuel Russian exports which, apart from aluminium and a very few other items, fell substantially between 1992 and 1993.

7 Real monthly interest rates changed from −20 per cent in the first quarter of 1992 to about −2 per cent in July–September of the same year. In the final quarter they were still negative (−4 per cent) in June 1993. See *Russian Economic Trends* (1993) p. 21 (Table 13).

8 United Nations Economic Commission for Europe (UN/ECE) 1993b, p. 15.

9 UN/ECE Secretariat. Not all commitments are actually disbursed and follow-up disbursements are not always included.

10 UN/ECE (1992) pp. 23 and 26.

11 UN/ECE 1993a, pp. 21–28.

4

The Legacies for Russia of Soviet Foreign Investment Policy

Carl H. McMillan

It is clear that there are great potential benefits from increased participation of foreign investors in the development of the USSR and its integration into the world economy. Indeed, success in attracting substantial flows of foreign investment could be crucial in the transition to a market economy.

(IMF, World Bank, OECD and EBRD, *A Study of the Soviet Economy*, vol. 2, p. 75 1991)

Having returned to the world economic system, we believe that Russia will become a fast-growing market. We hope to accommodate foreign investment to the tune of hundreds of billions of dollars. We have scientific potential, natural resources. We have skilled scientists. We have low wages, measured by world standards.

[The new agreements] will open the door for a powerful influx of private capital, and these will not be credits ... [but] will be direct investments from private companies.

(Statements by Boris Yeltsin, on the occasion of his triumphal visit to Washington in June 1992, as president of the newly independent Russian Federation, *New York Times,* 18 June 1992, pp. A18 and A19).

In the final years of its existence, the Soviet Union attempted to break out of its traditional economic isolation and to assume a new role on the world economic stage. Foreign investment was to be an important element in this new external economic strategy.[1] In a dramatic departure from the course set by Stalin in the early 1930s, and pursued without deviation for more than half a century, the Soviet government announced in 1986 that it would open the economy to limited forms of direct investment from abroad, including investment by private, capitalist firms. The new policy took effect in January of the following year.

The Soviet past continues to weigh heavily on the Russian present and future. Any attempt to assess foreign investment in Russia requires that we place it fully in the context of the Soviet experience that preceded it. This chapter therefore reviews the development of Soviet foreign investment policy in what proved to be the last five years of the Soviet state, 1987–91. It also assesses the results of the new Soviet policy, in terms of foreign investment response to the opportunities that it opened up. My purpose is to identify the legacies of the Soviet foreign investment experience for the policies in this domain of the Russian successor state. I first examine the historical context and the rationale for the Soviet policy initiative.

The Historical Context

When, in the 1920s, the young Soviet state began to emerge from the international economic isolation imposed by world war, revolution, civil war and allied intervention, it experimented with limited forms of foreign investment, outward and inward. It undertook investments in companies located abroad and engaged through them in banking, insurance, shipping and trade (Baykov 1946). It also allowed limited forms of foreign capital participation in Soviet enterprises. The most economically important of these were the 'concessions' that allowed foreign firms to engage in projects for resource extraction and development, and even in manufacturing ventures, through long-term leasing arrangements with the Soviet state.[2]

In the unfavourable international political climate of the times, these attempts to attract foreign capital and technology enjoyed little success. The concessions played only a marginal part in the recovery of the Soviet economy in the period of the New Economic Policy (NEP), 1921–6. They were more important in the longer term in establishing policy precedents, precedents that were associated personally with Lenin, the founder of the Soviet state.

It was less their obvious lack of economic success, however, than the course of Soviet domestic politics that put a virtual end to this early Soviet flirtation with foreign investment.[3] Lenin's death and the rise of Stalin brought the relatively liberal policies of the NEP to a close. Soon the economy was converted to the Stalinist system of pervasive state ownership and strong central planning and control. These developments ushered in a period of an increasingly closed economy and growing international isolation in the years leading up to the Second World War.

Pre-war Soviet isolation, broken temporarily by the wartime alliance, resumed after the war and was soon reinforced by the political tensions of the cold war. The Soviet Union did, however, develop economic relations with 'fraternal, socialist countries', especially in Eastern Europe, and with certain newly independent countries in the Third World with which it had established close political ties. With neither of these groups of countries, however, did growing economic relations extend to their capital participation in joint enterprises on the territory of the USSR.[4]

Beginning in the late 1960s, however, the Brezhnev leadership began to express an interest in developing, at the enterprise level, non-equity forms of long-term 'industrial cooperation' with foreign partners, especially with private, capitalist firms from the Western countries.[5] The hope was that such cooperation would prove an effective vehicle for the acquisition and assimilation of industrial technologies that the USSR had failed to develop and apply on its own. Improved access to Western technology was one of the principal objectives of the Soviet government's policy at this time of pursuing a *détente* in its political–military relations with the West, especially with the USA. Industrial cooperation agreements were perceived as providing many of the benefits of FDI, while avoiding the ideological and legal problems entailed in granting formal ownership rights to foreign firms.[6]

Most substantive Soviet industrial cooperation arrangements were limited to so-called 'compensation' deals, by which equipment, technology and know-how for a capital project were supplied on credit by the Western partner or partners and repaid in kind through exports of the resulting output, once the project had become operational.[7] In a 1976 speech to the 25th Communist Party Congress, Brezhnev himself criticized the Soviet failure to advance beyond such simple agreements, which, he noted, were concentrated in the extractive sector.[8] The failure in 1977 of negotiations with the Bendix Corporation of the United States for the joint construction and operation of a spark plug plant in the USSR showed the difficulties of pushing the industrial cooperation format more deeply into Soviet industry.[9] Thus, even such arrangements proved, in practice, too radical for the rigid Soviet system.[10] The USSR engaged for the most part only in limited forms of industrial cooperation with the West. The cooperation strategy failed to provide the desired stimulus to the flagging Soviet economy, and *détente* soon foundered in a rising sea of East–West confrontations and disputes.

Ten years later, a more vigorous Soviet leader, Mikhail Gorbachev, brought a fresh perspective to the old but increasingly urgent problem of how to get the stagnant Soviet economy moving again. His response was a programme, soon known to the world as 'perestroika', that was intended to inject a new dynamism into the economy and society.[11] The Soviet Union's limited participation in the mainstream of international economic intercourse was now more openly accepted as a factor contributing to the economic decline. The official decision, announced in 1986, to permit foreign capital participation in joint enterprises (ventures) on Soviet territory was part of a broad policy initiative designed to end the international isolation of the Soviet economy.[12]

Gorbachev used the precedents established by Lenin at the time of the New Economic Policy to legitimize his own new policy course (perestroika), politically and ideologically. There were NEP precedents to draw on in support of various of its aspects, including the new joint venture policy. In concept, however, Gorbachev's joint ventures considerably exceeded Lenin's concessions. In particular, direct foreign participation was now seen not as a temporary expedient to help put the economy back on its feet, as it had been in the early 1920s, but as a central feature of a new phase in Soviet economic development which would involve greatly expanded, 'organic' links to the world economy.[13]

The Policy Rationale

The Communist Party resolution that announced the new foreign investment policy also covered a number of other measures to open up the Soviet economy. These included steps to liberalise central control over foreign trade and payments, and to allow greater autonomy in these areas to Soviet state enterprises. They were the beginnings of a process that would eventually lead to a substantial dismantling of the old system of Soviet state trading, which had served effectively to keep the economy closed. The 1986 party resolution declared general allegiance to a new, more open strategy of development for the economy.

There is little doubt that one of the principal architects of the new policy of openness was an academic economist, Ivan D. Ivanov. One of his country's foremost experts on FDI and multinational enterprises in the world economy, Ivanov was appointed early in 1986 to a senior post in government as deputy head of the newly created State Commission for Foreign Economic Ties. The commission was designated to be the senior government agency in the sphere of external economic policy and was charged with spearheading the reforms in this area. In a number of speeches and articles, Ivanov set forth the official rationale for the new policy.[14]

Foreign investment would support the more open strategy of development in a number of ways. The positive effects on productivity of the technology acquired through foreign investment would be reinforced by the more direct links to world markets that it would also bring. Partnerships with foreign firms would expose Soviet management and labour to international performance standards, and would help to raise their awareness of competitive requirements on world markets. Direct exposure to international technical norms and developments would have beneficial feedback effects on Soviet industrial technology. With the support of foreign investors, Soviet exports would have a better chance to break into world markets, to which access was limited by trade barriers and imperfect competition. Greater reliance on exports would stimulate Soviet enterprises to raise their technical levels and pay more attention to production efficiency and product quality. In sum, direct foreign partnerships would help to break down the isolation from world market conditions that had contributed to the relative backwardness of many Soviet enterprises.

In the historical circumstances described in the preceding section, the 1986 announcement that the Soviet Union would now permit foreign investment was a clear signal to the Soviet public, and to the world at large, of the seriousness of the intent to open up the economy. Coming little more than a year after Gorbachev's accession to power, it demonstrated in a dramatic, highly visible fashion that his approach to long-standing problems was new in substance as well as in style. No other economic measure taken at the time could have had such powerful, international announcement effects.

Certainly, the traditional aim of forming links at the enterprise level as a means of boosting Soviet productivity through Western equipment, technology and know-how remained central to the new policy. This aim was even more urgent now than in the period of *détente*, because the economy had continued to slow down to the point where some observers believed that it had reached close to zero growth.[15] Gorbachev had announced an ambitious new 12th Five-Year Plan in March 1986 which relied on higher rates of domestic investment to jump-start the economy. Foreign investment would complement this strategy.

Brezhnev's attempts to inject Western equipment and technology into Soviet industry on a massive scale were recognized as having failed to reverse the long-term downward trend in performance. The Brezhnev strategy had relied on techniques that were conservative even by East European standards. There was an increasing awareness that much of the imported equipment, and the technology embodied in it, had in fact been wasted. It now seemed evident that more radical approaches were required. Foreign direct investment served as a vehicle for intensive flows of new technology and know-how among capitalist countries. As one of the keys to their continued economic strength and prosperity, it needed to be emulated.

At the end of 1985, the world market for oil had weakened. The subsequent fall in the world price of oil, whose export was the Soviet Union's principal source of foreign exchange, quickly began to undermine its hitherto relatively strong external financial position. These developments increased Soviet policy-makers' interest in measures which could potentially lead to significant inflows of foreign financial capital. Later, oil production and export declined because deposits became increasingly inaccessible to existing Soviet technology. The application of foreign technology and know-how to oil exploration and development, through the direct involvement of foreign firms, was seen as a means to reverse the downward trend in this vital branch of Soviet industry.

In these various ways, foreign investment would promote the restructuring and revitalization of the state sector of the economy. (It may be recalled that massive privatization was not foreseen at this time.) These were the basic aims to which all aspects of the perestroika programme were directed; but internal reforms were more likely to encounter strong domestic opposition, and would therefore probably take longer to become effective. In this sense, the reform of external relations seemed an easier and faster means to pursue desired ends. At the same time, it was understood that external reforms would be insufficient in themselves to turn the giant Soviet economy round.

Gorbachev had made clear that he regarded a settling of outstanding issues with the West as a precondition for successful domestic reform. Opening the economy to foreign investment could serve as a powerful method to enlist foreign support for the aims and processes of perestroika. It would demonstrate to Western governments the Soviet government's goodwill in an area of relations that had never been reciprocal. Foreign investment would give Western firms a direct stake in the success of the reform process. They could thus become influential advocates of perestroika within Western societies.

Policy Evolution and Implementation in the Gorbachev Period

The new policy was made effective by several government decrees issued in early January 1987.[16] This was just the beginning of a process of policy development in the following years, which was in turn reflected in a rapidly growing body of foreign investment regulations. The process was frequently haphazard and the regulatory environment for foreign investment confusing to all concerned. Nevertheless, certain basic lines of policy evolution are discernible. To this end, it is useful to divide the five-year period under consideration into three sub-periods.

The policy context can of course be defined broadly to include measures in a wide range of areas that indirectly affect foreign investment. In tracing the evolution of policy here, I necessarily have to be more selective. Nevertheless, I do not limit myself to measures directly governing foreign investment, but also examine the course of policy change in the vitally related area of currency convertibility.

1987–8

The provisions of the January 1987 decree that set the new foreign investment policy were drafted in general terms that left many questions open.[17] The Soviet drafters apparently were themselves uncertain how to resolve these questions and opted for a pragmatic approach, designed to 'learn by doing' through negotiations with more experienced foreign firms. The first few years were devoted to filling in some of the blanks, and a series of follow-up regulations on accounting, financial and tax aspects served this purpose. At this time, as well, a registration process was established under the Soviet Ministry of Finance, which was also responsible for making the registrations public.

Several basic principles set forth in the initial decrees governed foreign investments at this stage. Foreign investment had to take the organizational *form* of a jointly owned enterprise (a limited partnership or a joint-stock company) in which both foreign and Soviet entities participated. The foreign partners could be physical or juridical persons, while, on the Soviet side, not only enterprises and other state economic organisations in all sectors of the economy (as well as organs of government at various levels) could participate, but also enterprises formed as 'cooperatives', which were outside the state sector.[18] With respect to *ownership*, foreign capital participation was limited to a minority share of the equity in an enterprise in which the Soviet partner (or partners) held a majority. The maximum allowable foreign equity share in the joint venture was 49 per cent. Finally, *profit repatriation* was restricted by a provision linked to the inconvertibility of the rouble. All convertible currency expenditures of the joint enterprise, including any repatriated foreign profits, would have to be covered by its convertible currency revenues. This stipulation served to dictate export-orientated investments, although officials held out the possibility that import-substituting activities, which resulted in demonstrable convertible currency savings, could also justify the state bank's support of profit repatriation requests.

A series of privileges and preferences granted at this time were intended to encourage foreign investment. Joint enterprises were not to be subject to the national economic plan, but this was both an advantage and a disadvantage in a planned economy.[19] They enjoyed greater freedom in the area of foreign exchange, and could choose to use foreign currencies for settlement purposes. They were granted special tax terms, including a two-year tax holiday on profits. Special economic zones were to be created in which joint ventures could operate virtually free of regulation. Many of these special privileges proved illusory, however, as the Soviet economic system underwent rapid change in the following years. In particular, the creation of special economic zones was much delayed and the concept never fully realized.

1989–90

A second period of policy evolution was initiated by a sweeping decree of the Council of Ministers issued at the end of 1988.[20] Like the 1986 party resolution, this new decree set a further reform agenda for the entire external sector, one in which foreign investment was to play an important role. Meanwhile, progress had been made in speeding up the joint venture registration process.

The decree significantly liberalised some of the conditions originally imposed on foreign control of jointly owned enterprises in the USSR. The 49 per cent maximum foreign share in a joint enterprise was relaxed to allow a foreign majority holding. Although not explicit, the decree clearly implied that foreign equity in a joint enterprise could, in principle, rise to upwards of 99 per cent. The liberalising effects of the decree went beyond the ownership question, however. It removed an earlier stipulation that the board chairman and managing director of a joint enterprise must be Soviet citizens. It also granted joint enterprises greater freedom to hire and fire and to negotiate their own wage terms with employees.

The December 1988 decree granted direct access to foreign markets not only to joint enterprises but also to all other enterprises, associations and cooperatives producing exportable goods or services. A follow-up decree, issued in March 1989, laid down the registration procedures for enterprises applying for foreign trade rights.[21] Thus, joint enterprises that were duly registered no longer needed to export and import through the intermediation of state foreign trade organizations.

The liberalizing trend at this time extended to outflows as well as inflows of FDI. As noted earlier, limited foreign investments by Soviet state enterprises had continued to be made throughout the Soviet period, and this activity had gained momentum in the 1970s and 1980s. Like foreign trade, however, foreign investment was essentially the prerogative of a few dozen state foreign trade organizations subordinate to the Ministry of Foreign Trade. Now all enterprises with the right to engage directly in foreign trade, including cooperatives and joint enterprises, could also invest abroad, and were in fact encouraged to do so. A decree issued in May 1989 served this purpose and clarified the procedures governing the process of outward investment.[22]

Policy change in this period was not all in the direction of liberalisation, however. Growing concern about 'profiteering' by enterprises that exercised their new, direct foreign trade rights to profit from the differential between state-controlled, domestic prices and market-determined, world prices led in the spring of 1989 to the imposition of export and import licence requirements for designated goods. In an effort to prevent any windfall profits based on price differentials from accruing to enterprises outside the state sector, the March 1989 decree made it illegal for joint enterprises and cooperatives to play an intermediary role in foreign trade. Thus joint enterprises could export only their own production and import only for their own use, and could not act as trading intermediaries.

The December 1988 decree also affected foreign investment, indirectly but significantly, in another way. As noted earlier, the inconvertibility of the rouble imposed effective limitations on the repatriation of rouble profits from foreign investment. The decree initiated the first real steps towards rouble convertibility, a goal that had been increasingly endorsed by Soviet leaders as well as reform economists.

Of course, all market-orientated reforms of the Soviet economic system could be viewed as preconditions for convertibility, as inconvertibility was a symptom of the command economy.[23] Nevertheless, it is possible to identify, as important, early steps towards convertibility, the export-incentive schemes that had been introduced in 1986. These allowed exporting enterprises to calculate the profitability of foreign trade transactions by means of currency conversion 'coefficients' more advantageous to them than the overvalued official exchange rate, and to retain a certain share of the resulting foreign exchange earnings for their own use.[24]

The December 1988 decree carried this liberalization further. It reinforced the right of enterprises to share in foreign exchange earnings, it anticipated the establishment of foreign exchange auctions, through which enterprises could obtain or dispose of funds in foreign exchange, and it adopted the principle of a new exchange rate system that would effectively lead to a devaluation of the rouble. Measures to follow up these new policy directions led to substantial progress towards establishing a more decentralized system of foreign exchange allocation in the next few years.

1990–1

The progressive relaxation of restrictions on foreign ownership was brought to a logical conclusion in October 1990, when a special presidential decree allowed wholly foreign-owned companies to be established, in the form of branches or subsidiaries.[25] The decree, moreover, created the legal basis for foreign investors to buy into – and even buy out – existing Soviet enterprises, as these were privatized. It thus reflected the considerable evolution of Soviet thinking on the question of private ownership and the new intent to move towards a system of varied and competing forms of ownership.

Meanwhile, a new foreign investment law made slow progress in the Supreme Soviet. Its intended function was to consolidate and clarify the mass of existing regulations governing foreign investment that had been issued in piecemeal fashion since 1987. After considerable delay, the legislation was signed into law on 5 July 1991, less than six months before the dissolution of the Soviet Union. Almost concurrently, on 4 July, the Chairman of the Supreme Soviet of the Russian Republic, Boris Yeltsin, signed a law on foreign investment in the Russian Republic. It was the 4 July Act that was to serve as the governing law in Russia, following the dissolution of the USSR a few months later.

The competing foreign investment laws did not diverge significantly in their underlying principles. Both allowed enterprises to be wholly foreign-owned and granted foreign investors the right of access to land and other natural resources.[26] Both guaranteed national treatment to enterprises with foreign capital participation (article 5 in the Soviet law; article 6 in the Russian law).

These were years when Soviet power was in rapid decline, however, with inescapable effects on the investment policy climate. To the continuously changing regulatory framework for foreign investment at the federal (all-union) level, there was added an additional element of instability in the final years of the Soviet Union, as the struggle for power between Moscow and the republics escalated. This was the so-called 'war of laws'. It reflected the attempt by various central government agencies and different levels of government to assert their own jurisdictions by issuing regulations, which were often conflicting. This added further uncertainty to an already confusing situation for foreign investors, who did not know what authority to look to for guidance or approval, nor how long a jurisdiction under which they had carried out their negotiations would last. At the same time, continual reorganisations often led to major changes in the functions and responsibilities of Soviet joint venture partners, and even to their disappearance as independent entities.

The reactionary government of Valentin Pavlov, which came to power in January 1991, gave signs of a less favourable attitude towards foreign investment than that of his predecessor, Nikolai Ryzhkov. In February, Pavlov publicly accused foreign banks operating in the USSR of engaging in a plot to destabilize the rouble (*Wall Street Journal*, 13 February 1991, p. 3). At about the same time, he authorized the KGB to make unannounced searches of the premises of joint ventures suspected of illegal activities (*Financial Times*, 28 January 1991, p. 14). These actions, which attracted enormous international publicity, were scarcely designed to raise foreign investor confidence in an increasingly chaotic political and economic environment.

On the more positive side, progress continued towards enlarged rouble convertibility, following up two interdependent principles established in the influential decree of December 1988. A decentralised system of foreign exchange allocation was to replace the system of administrative allocation that had kept external transactions under tight control. Market stimuli, operating through an operational exchange rate mechanism, would then replace administrative directives as guides to export and import decisions.

Through the device of auctions, organised by the State Bank for Foreign Economic Relations (Vneshekonombank), foreign exchange began to be allocated increasingly by a price mechanism rather than by administrative bargaining. Access to foreign exchange auctions was steadily expanded. Towards the end of 1990, a few joint (Soviet–foreign) enterprises were quietly granted access to them. In 1991 the auctions were opened up to all enterprises and organizations that were juridical persons under Soviet law (*Business Eastern Europe*, 18 March 1991, p. 84). The auctions were also held with increasing regularity and in different locations. Ultimately, the system of direct enterprise participation in the auctions was superseded by the grant of authority to deal in foreign exchange to a network of officially designated commercial banks.

The auction rate of exchange was determined by bids and offers on what was a limited market. In a parallel approach, the administratively set values of the rouble were revised, in staged, official devaluations. The first step had been taken towards the end of 1989, when a new 'special' rate for the rouble was introduced to govern individual (including tourist) transactions. Until this time there had been a single, official rate, fixed at a level of about 0.6 roubles to the dollar.[27] The new, non-commercial exchange rate, initially set at 6 roubles per dollar, represented a dramatic 90 per cent devaluation of the rouble. It was nevertheless well below the black market rate and below the value subsequently established in the currency auctions.

The second step occurred just one year later, in November 1990, when a new 'commercial' rate for the rouble was introduced to govern all transactions involving enterprises, associations and banks. Its initial level, set at 1.8 roubles to the dollar, represented a two-thirds devaluation. The commercial rate replaced the cumbersome, multiple-rate system of some 6000 differentiated conversion coefficients that had been employed by enterprises to calculate the rouble profitability of their import and export transactions, that had been introduced in 1986.

As the Soviet Union entered what was to be its final, eventful year, there were four exchange rates legally in effect: the old official rate, now used purely for accounting purposes; the special rate, used for individual, notably tourist, transactions; the commercial rate for commercial transactions; and the rate set in the official foreign exchange auctions. The first three were administratively set; the last was determined by forces on the limited auction market.

The special and commercial exchange rates were thus introduced ahead of the timetable originally set in the December 1988 decree. This was a departure from the more typical Soviet practice of delaying announced reforms. They also represented a greater devaluation than originally foreseen, reflecting official recognition of price inflation in the Soviet economy.

These changes in exchange rate policy created more flexible and realistic conditions for the conversion between roubles and foreign currencies. In this respect, they represented a significant improvement in the regulatory environment for foreign investment and for the operation of foreign-owned businesses in the Soviet Union. They served to relax the original convertibility constraints on profit repatriation by foreign investors.

On the other hand, the foreign exchange regime in 1990 and 1991 was based on a 60 to 90 per cent foreign exchange surrender requirement placed on enterprises and a still very thin foreign exchange auction market.[28] Moreover, the devaluation of the rouble represented a depreciation in the international value of rouble assets already acquired by foreigners. The move towards a more flexible exchange rate system, combined with the increasingly uncertain economic and political conditions in the country, raised the exchange rate risk associated with foreign investment in the Soviet economy.

On the tax front, developments were less favourable to foreign investment. Soviet legislation, adopted in 1990, instituted a new system of income taxes (on corporations and on individuals) potentially affecting the profitability of joint enterprises.[29] New export taxes introduced in 1991, especially on oil exports, also applied to joint ventures and directly affected the net convertible currency earnings, and hence the profitability, of the more export-orientated. Though many joint enterprises seem to have been able to avoid their full effects, these measures served (whether by design or by inadvertence) to undermine the financial incentives established originally to attract foreign investment. Moreover, as republics and regions began to enter the taxation field, the issue was caught up in their 'war of laws' with Moscow.

The Investor Response

As noted earlier, the announcement effects of the decision to open up to foreign investment one of the world's largest, but hitherto most closed, economies, were powerful and received both immediate and maximal publicity. Moreover, intense international press coverage of the 'Gorbachev revolution' in the Soviet Union ensured that this new possibility would not quickly fade from the attentions of potential investors abroad.

The opening of the Soviet economy also stimulated a great deal of interest and excitement within the Soviet Union. This was reinforced by the traditional Soviet-style 'campaign' through which the government sought to promote the new joint venture possibility. Western firms already doing business in the Soviet Union came under strong pressure from Soviet business partners to convert their relations to the new, politically preferred format. Foreigners in general, visiting the Soviet Union in the late 1980s, found themselves besieged by Soviet counterparts with proposals to enter into joint ventures.

Despite the intense surrounding publicity, the general mood of euphoria generated by the rapid pace of change in the USSR and Eastern Europe, and the improved 'post-cold-war' international political climate, the investor response was cautious and the results ultimately far below expectations. We shall present and analyse the evidence for this conclusion below, but first some words of caution about the data.

If it was often difficult to bring the policy picture into sharp focus, it is even more difficult to penetrate the veil of frequently misleading data available on foreign investment in the Soviet economy in the period 1987–91. This was a new area for Soviet statistical agencies, and in the best of circumstances it would have required time to establish appropriate recording and processing procedures and to disseminate the resulting information. The circumstances were far from the best, and the responsible agencies were burdened with many new reporting tasks, in a climate of great political and bureaucratic uncertainty.

The most immediately available data were based on information obtained in the process of official registration of 'joint ventures with foreign capital participation', as they were established. Most data on foreign investment in the Soviet Union were derived from these registrations: their number, location, activity and statutory capitalization, and the nationality and share of foreign partners. At best, information based on these registrations represented intentions; formal commitments frequently did not translate into actual investment activity.

There is reason to believe that, even as expressions of intent, registrations must be treated with considerable caution. As noted earlier, Western firms were under considerable pressure from Soviet partners to convert existing arrangements to the joint venture format. In these cases (which were apparently an important share of the first registrations), so-called new investments were simply old deals dressed in new clothing. Tax and other preferences granted to joint enterprises led to the creation of ventures that constituted more legal 'shells', designed principally to take advantage of these advantages. Even if intentions were serious at the time of registration, they often changed thereafter, so that registration data poorly reflected subsequent reality with regard to activity and capitalization. Moreover, the responsible government agencies were under considerable political pressure to produce evidence of positive policy results.

As the number of joint venture registrations grew, the Ministry of Finance began to find its attendant public information responsibilities too much to cope with, and publication of registration data became more irregular. Meanwhile, the State Committee for Statistics had begun to publish data on the activities of joint enterprises that had become operative. These data, although more substantial and more economically significant than those based on registrations alone, necessarily became available with a lag and represented a considerably reduced phenomenon (in 1990, for example, less than half of registered joint ventures were operational).

Moreover, as the Soviet Union began to disintegrate in 1990–1, so did the central agencies that had been the source of comprehensive foreign investment data. The Soviet Ministry of Finance ceased registering new investments in the last quarter of 1990 and the responsibility was shifted to republican ministries. At the same time, republican statistical offices increasingly took over the functions of the Soviet state committee. These major organizational changes affected the continuity of foreign investment statistics well before the final break-up of the Soviet Union.

With these considerations in mind, let us turn to the data presented in the accompanying tables. These tables, all based on registration data, show trends over time and present additional information on activities and location as of the end of 1990. It should be emphasized that these data are based on original commitments and not on capital transfers or actual investment operations.

As reflected in new registrations, foreign investor interest began to grow rapidly after 1987 (Tables 4.1 and 4.2). The initial slow start in 1987 was perhaps unavoidable, given the unprecedented nature of the registration task and the slowness of the Soviet bureaucracy to respond to departures from the routine. The data show rapid growth to a peak in the second quarter of 1989 and then a fall-off in the first three quarters of 1990. These trends would correspond to the rise in international confidence in the Soviet reform process in the late 1980s, followed by a decline in confidence as the process seemed to reach an impasse in the 1990s, and led ultimately to the disintegration of the Union. At the same time, the 'war of laws', preceding the formal break-up of the USSR, created an increasingly chaotic and uncertain regulatory climate.

In these terms, the officially reported rebound in numbers of registrations, beginning in the last quarter of 1990, is difficult to explain.[30] It would in fact seem paradoxical in view of the events then transpiring: the centre – republican power struggle, the conservative crackdown on joint venture 'abuse', increasing uncertainty leading up to the

Table 4.1 Number of new joint venture registrations in the USSR, by year and quarter, 1987–91

Quarter	1987	1988	1989	1990	1991	Total
1		13	181	209	494	
2	5	27	328	271	300	
3	3	42	253	297	1655	
4	15	86	321	855	900	
Total	23	168	1083	1632	3349	6255

Sources: United Nations (1992 p. 115, table 2); East–West Project, Carleton University.

Table 4.2 Foreign capital investment in the USSR,[a] January 1987 to October 1991.

Period	Flows ($m)	Stocks ($m)
1987	89.3	89.3
1988	416.6	505.6
1989	1692.2	2198.1
1990	953.6	3151.7
1991 (first three quarters)	2498.3	5650.0
Q1	725.0	3876.7
Q2	415.0	4291.7
Q3	1358.3	5650.0

[a] Rouble values converted to $US at current official exchange rates.
Sources: United Nations (1992, p. 115, table 2); East–West Project, Carleton University.

August 1991 *coup*, and then chaos following the collapse of central institutions in the final months of the year. We must recall, however, that beginning precisely in the last quarter of 1990, responsibility for registration was shifted to the republican level, and the data are, in this respect, not strictly comparable with those for the preceding quarters. The data for the five final quarters of the Soviet statistical record on foreign investment thus remain an anomaly that may be the result of changes in recording practices.

The Soviet investment option attracted investors from a wide range of countries (Table 4.3). The major sources of foreign investment were private Western firms, primarily in West European countries (56 per cent of foreign capital committed as of the end of 1990), which had traditionally been the most important Western trading partners of the USSR. North America was also an important source, but Japan was

Table 4.3   Sources of foreign direct investment stocks in the USSR, end 1990 (current million US dollars)

Source	Number	No. as % of total	Foreign share of capital[a]	Foreign share as % of total foreign share
Western Europe	1168	57	1759.7	56
of which:				
Finland	183	9	356.9	11
Germany	281	14	346.1	11
USA	247	12	360.2	11
Canada	53	3	86.7	3
Japan	33	2	46.4	1
Other developed countries	40	2	50.4	2
Developing countries	153	7	162.0	5
Economies in transition[b]	186	9	364.3	12
Non-European CPEs[c]	46	2	58.6	2
Other countries	124	6	263.1	8
Total[d]	2050	100	3154.6	100

[a] Only foreign share of foreign affiliate capital.
[b] Bulgaria, Czech Republic, Slovakia, Hungary, Poland, former Yugoslavia.
[c] Democratic Republic of Korea, People's Republic of China, Vietnam.
[d] Figures may not add to totals, due to rounding.

Source: United Nations (1992, pp. 119–20, table 9).

notable by its relatively limited role. The overwhelming share (three-fourths) of investments was directed to the Russian Federation, as Table 4.4 indicates, and was highly concentrated in the major industrial centres of Moscow and St Petersburg.

The data also record few surprises in terms of sectoral distribution (Table 4.5). Nearly half (48 per cent) of the ventures were in the service sector, with the largest share in consumer-related services. Services were not only an underdeveloped sector of the Soviet economy, long neglected under official investment priorities, but also required less capital investment and this entailed less investor risk. The official data do not clearly reveal activity in the important energy sector. The Soviet oil industry, long effectively closed to any significant direct foreign involvement, possessed some of the world's largest oil reserves. The investment opportunities and their potentially high returns attracted the interest of most of the major Western oil companies, but the scale of follow-up investments was below expectations.

In sum, the Soviet Union, despite its enormous market size and wealth of natural resources, attracted relatively modest levels of capital in the

Table 4.4   Distribution of foreign direct investment stocks by republic, end 1990 (current million US dollars)

Region	No. of joint ventures	Foreign share of capital[a]
Armenia	14	34.3
Azerbaijan	12	24.3
Belarus	43	57.2
Estonia	105	63.2
Georgia	61	81.7
Kazakhstan	14	11.5
Kyrgyzstan	1	0.5
Latvia	46	29.8
Lithuania	18	39.0
Moldova	21	35.3
Russian Republic	1535	2485.5
of which in:		
Moscow	982	1410.1
Moscow Region	48	72.3
St Petersburg	178	199.0
St Petersburg Region	16	19.6
Other	311	784.6
Tajikistan	3	1.6
Turkmenistan	1	2.0
Ukraine	148	206.5
Uzbekistan	24	61.2
Unknown	4	18.1
Total[b]	2050	3151.6

[a] Only foreign share of foreign affiliate capital.
[b] Figures may not add to totals, owing to rounding.

Source: United Nations (1992, p. 121, table 9A).

five-year period 1987–91. Even in terms of funds committed (registration data), the stock of foreign investment by the end of the period was not great by international standards, especially if the relative size of the Soviet economy is taken into account. By the end of 1991, official registration data reported a stock of foreign capital committed in the neighbourhood of $6 billion. Although data on actual (realized) investments are not available, they probably constituted less than half of commitments (under $3 billion). By way of comparison with other economies in transition, China reported total commitments of over $60 billion and realised investments of nearly $30 billion in 1991 (with inflows in that year alone of well over $3 billion). The stock of realized foreign direct investment in Hungary by end 1991 exceeded $3 billion (inflows alone to Hungary in 1991 were nearly $2 billion).[31]

Table 4.5 Distribution of foreign direct investment stocks by activity, end 1990 (million US dollars)

Sector	Number	Foreign investment[a]
Agriculture, hunting, forestry	26	41.4
Fishing	10	39.6
Mining and quarrying	7	15.1
Manufacturing	1032	1936.6
Construction	94	110.2
Wholesale, retail trade	68	164.4
Real-estate development (including hotels and restaurants)	144	253.1
Transport, storage, communications	64	48.9
Financial intermediation	5	117.7
Renting of machinery and equipment	25	15.1
Computer, related activities	117	70.2
R+D	11	14.2
Other business activities	268	116.1
Education	22	8.5
Health and social work	46	79.4
Sewage and refuse disposal	11	12.4
Cultural and sporting activities	85	64.4
Other services	5	1.7
Multi-sectoral and other[b]	10	42.6
Total	2050	3151.6

[a] Only foreign share of foreign affiliate capital.
[b] Including purification of water.

Source: United Nations (1992, pp. 117–18, table 7).

The Soviet Legacy

The Soviet foreign investment experience of 1987–91, now rapidly receding into the past, forms part of the closing chapter of Soviet economic history, an important element in the final, failed attempt to revitalize the Soviet economy and to save the Soviet state. As such, it helps us to understand that failure. It is also the backdrop against which Russia and other newly independent successor states to the Soviet Union must now develop their own foreign investment policies and build their own foreign investment record.

The Soviet experience we have reviewed here cannot be regarded as constituting a rich legacy. It was late and brief; foreign investment was, in many respects, just getting under way in the final Soviet year. That year, 1991, saw the passage of the first, comprehensive foreign investment law, the culmination of five years of policy experimentation.

This would appear to be the most important legacy of the Soviet experience. It provided Russia with the basics of a legal framework for foreign investment activity, a necessary first step in the development of any foreign investment process. Moreover, it constituted a significant break with the past, in terms of ideology, policy and institutions. At the same time, there was progress in the related areas of foreign trade and foreign exchange reform, where there was a fundamental shift from centrally planned and conducted state trading to indirect regulation of foreign trade transactions, and from a system of centrally administered foreign exchange allocations to a limited foreign exchange market.

The piecemeal approach to fashioning a foreign trade regime led, however, to inconsistencies and confusion that tended to defeat the purpose. It was to an extent dictated by circumstances, reflecting lack of experience, bureaucratic apathy and political opposition. It also no doubt reflected the over-confidence of Soviet policy-makers. They apparently felt that capitalist investors were beating at the long-closed door. When foreign investment failed to come flooding in on the original Soviet terms, the government was forced to engage in successive liberalizations.

A legacy of the Soviet period has been the divergence between regulatory principle and practice. To an extent this has reflected the gap between economic theory and Soviet/Russian reality. For example, in the evolution of the Soviet foreign investment regime, there was a trend from a system of special exemptions and preferences granted to foreign investors to an investment regime based on national treatment. The latter principle was embodied in the foreign investment law, on the basis that Soviet national enterprises now operated under a liberal regulatory regime. In fact, national treatment placed foreign firms at a disadvantage, given the chaotic mix of the old and the new that had emerged with partial reform and the lack of transparency surrounding actual practice. The removal of preferences was arguably premature in these circumstances and its deterrent effect was one of the reasons for poor investor response.[32]

The jurisdictional battles between levels of government – the 'war of laws' – further contributed to the problematic regulatory environment for foreign investment. Foreign investors found themselves enmeshed in conflicting lines of authority. Although initially a symptom of the disintegration of central Soviet authority, the problem has persisted in the post-Soviet period. Conflicting lines of authority and regulatory instability are thus negative legacies of the Soviet experience.

A negative psychological legacy should be noted. For decades, Soviet ideology preached the superiority of national economic practices and industrial technology, as well as the evils of capitalist foreign investment. The population at large has not been taught to appreciate the need or the value of foreign investment in Russia. This has provided fertile soil for political and economic interest groups in Russia hostile to foreign investment.

The Soviet legacy was weaker in terms of substantive foreign investments than the data based on registrations presented in Tables 4.1 to 4.5 suggest. Although the data are poor, it is clear that Russia inherited only a small body of foreign investment projects by the end of 1991, probably not more than two thousand.[33] Most of these were located in Russia, but were concentrated in Moscow and St Petersburg. Only a handful of major Western companies were represented; a significant Western multinational presence had not been achieved. Average investments were small and most were directed not to manufacturing but to services.

To be sure, aggregate, quantitative measures can lead to an underestimate of the real investment impact, especially on economies in transition, where the qualitative dimensions of foreign investment are unusually important. A few, successfully operating foreign companies can have a major demonstration effect on an industry, even if they constitute a small part of it.[34] The Soviet experience left a legacy of a few, well-established foreign firms, in a wide range of activities and in a position to introduce international standards, inject new elements of competition and generally to serve as examples of what could be done. Service investments (such as hotels and communications) helped to improve the infrastructure required to attract more foreign business.

Foreign investments cannot have the desired impact, however, if economic and political conditions are not favourable. One of the legacies of the Soviet experience was the clear lesson that political and economic instability can serve as major impediments, however attractive the investment opportunities and the nominal regulatory treatment. Investor surveys indicate that it was investor perceptions of the risks posed by the policy vacillation of the final years of the Soviet Union that kept the Soviet legacy of actual foreign investments from being more substantial.[35] These same conditions undermined the impact of those foreign investments made.

In sum, as Russia embarked on its own foreign investment path, it had rather modest foundations to build upon in terms of inherited policies and investments. The lessons (often negative) of the Soviet experience were potentially the more valuable legacy for Russian policy-makers. The record of foreign investment in Russia is examined below, in Chapter 10.

Notes

1 Hough (1988) and Hewett (1992) analyse the evolution of Soviet external economic policy in this period. Boguslavsky and Smirnov (1989) discuss the legal aspects.

2 Sutton (1968) is one of the most comprehensive sources in English on this subject. In Russian, there is a more recent treatment by Dongarov (1990).

3 Although they put an end to inward investment, outward investment on a modest scale continued in subsequent decades, before and after the Second World War, then began to grow in significance from the mid-1960s. See McMillan (1987).

4 It was not until 1983 that a Soviet decree permitted joint equity ventures on Soviet territory between Soviet enterprises and state enterprises from its closest foreign economic partners, the fellow member states of the Council for Mutual Economic Assistance (Comecon). See Matejka (1988).

5 The Soviet strategy in this regard is discussed by Maximova (1977) and Shmelev (1978).

6 Gutman and Arkwright (1974) set industrial cooperation in the context of the internationalisation of production.

7 In this period, senior Soviet agencies (most notably, the State Committee for Science and Technology) signed 'scientific and technical cooperation' agreements with prominent Western firms, but these were little more than protocols of intent. One of the largest, and most politically controversial, compensation deals was the export gas pipeline project concluded in the early 1980s with several West European gas companies and pipeline equipment suppliers. See Jentleson (1986).

8 Brezhnev stated that 'it is perhaps time to extend the operating sphere [of agreements] so as to include the manufacturing sector, and to look for new approaches to cooperation in production' (Brezhnev, 1976, p. 69; author's translation).

9 See the discussion in Barclay (1979), pp. 478–9.

10 The USSR did not push the co-operation strategy as far as did some of its East European allies. In the more reformist of these – notably Hungary and Poland – enterprises concluded more elaborate arrangements with Western partners, including joint equity ventures. McMillan (1977) reviews the experience of the East European countries in this perspective.

11 There is now a sizeable body of literature on perestroika and the reasons for its failure. See, for example, Hewett (1988), Hanson (1992a) and Ellman and Kontorovich (1992).

12 Although preceded by official hints that it was coming, the decision was formally embodied in resolutions of the Central Committee of the CPSU and the USSR Council of Ministers of 19 August 1986, published in the official Communist Party newspaper *Pravda* on 24 September 1986. The resolutions established the guidelines for a programme of reform in the external sector of

the Soviet economy. The Russian term *sovmestnoe predpriyatiye* is often translated as 'joint venture'. I use the terms 'joint enterprise' and 'joint venture' interchangeably in this chapter.

13　See Gutman (1992) for a more extensive contrasting of the two approaches.

14　The most comprehensive in English is Ivanov (1987).

15　See the 'Overview' chapter of Ellman and Kontorovich (1992) and Khanin (1992).

16　The key implementing legislation took the form of three decrees issued on 13 January 1987. The English language texts of these and other relevant Soviet regulations can be found in the annexes to United Nations (1988). Their provisions are discussed by Russian legal specialists in Institute of the State and Law (1989). The participation of Soviet enterprises in joint ventures was confirmed by the Law on the State Enterprise of 30 June 1987.

17　For an initial reaction and appraisal in the specialized Western business press, see *Business Eastern Europe*, vol. xvi (1987), nos. 6, 19 and 20.

18　The Law on Co-operation (26 May 1988) confirmed the right of cooperatives to form joint ventures.

19　Because wholesale trade was not yet well established, they had to compete with state enterprises in obtaining scarce materials through the state supply system. To market their products domestically, they had to work through the state system of internal trade and to export them, through state foreign trade organizations.

20　USSR Council of Ministers Decree of 2 December 1988 ('On the Further Development of the External Economic Activity of State, Co-operative and other Public Enterprises, Associations and Organisations').

21　Starting from 1 April 1989, any enterprise – state, cooperative or joint (Soviet–foreign) – could register for the right to engage directly in external economic activity on its own behalf. By the autumn of 1990, over 20000 enterprises had been registered.

22　Council of Ministers Decree no. 412 of 18 May 1989.

23　Holzman (1991) traces the systemic roots of Soviet foreign exchange controls.

24　Cf. International Monetary Fund *et al.* (1991, ch. iv. 3).

25　The decree, dated 26 October 1990, introduced a number of general principles designed to encourage foreign investment. It established the right of foreign firms to buy shares in Soviet enterprises, to own and lease property in the USSR and to establish joint ventures, not only with Soviet legal entities, but also with natural persons. It also guaranteed foreign-owned enterprises legal treatment at least equal to that granted to Soviet enterprises. See *Business Eastern Europe*, vol. xix, 5 November 1990, p. 363.

26　The text of the Soviet law was published in *Izvestiya* on 25 July 1991, the Russian law in *Sovetskaya Rossiya* on the same date.

27　The Soviet Union had differed in this respect from the East European countries, most of which had long had two official exchange rates, commercial and non-commercial.

28　See the discussion in United Nations (1992, pp. 60ff).

29　The 1990 Soviet law on personal income tax set a tax of 60 per cent on the high income bracket into which most expatriate Western businessmen would fall. The full effect on foreign firms of the new tax regulations would depend upon the existence and nature of any bilateral tax treaties between the USSR and their home countries. See *Business Eastern Europe*, vol. xix (1990) nos 21, 35 and 36.

30 The related financial data (Table 4.2) show a substantial fall in investment inflows in 1990, but a rebound in 1991 of scarcely credible magnitude, especially in the third quarter, the last for which quarterly financial data are available.

31 See Young (1993).

32 On these points, see Evgeniya Yakovleva in Astapovich and Grigor'ev (1993).

33 The State Committee for Statistics reported (*Vestnik Statistiki* 6/1991) that 1027 joint enterprises were operative as at the end of 1990. This represented 35 per cent of registered joint enterprises at the time. Official data for operating joint enterprises in the USSR at the end of 1991 are not available, but if the same ratio of operating to registered held, the number would have been 2190.

34 See United Nations (1992, pp. 125ff., table 17) for listing.

35 See, for example, Sherr *et al.* (1991), McMillan (1991) and *Business International* (1992). For a general discussion of the perceived obstacles, see International Monetary Fund *et al.* (1991), especially vol. 2, pp. 75ff.

Part II

Central and Baltic Europe

5
Hungary

Gabor Hunya

Introduction

Hungary has been the most successful East European country in attracting foreign direct investment (FDI), with 13 billion dollars or about 40 per cent of the total cumulative capital invested in the area at the end of 1995. In 1992–5 it was among the first five net-capital-importing countries in the world per capita. This uniquely high degree of foreign penetration, when compared to the other transition economies of Central and Eastern Europe, is the result of specific economic policy features.

The overall economic performance of Hungary seems to contradict the expectations connected with the penetration of foreign capital: it is characterized by slow economic growth and serious imbalances in the current account and government budget. This chapter examines some of the reasons behind this contradiction. Some lie with the general features of the transformation policy; others are connected with the behaviour of foreign-owned firms. The benefits of foreign investment are more obvious at the microeconomic level, where the fast restructuring of enterprises is taking place. As a result, the increase of labour productivity in Hungarian manufacturing and the shift in export structures towards higher-value-added commodities have been more rapid than in other transition economies. At the same time, a duality can be identified in the performance of the Hungarian economy along the lines of foreign and domestic ownership.

The Economic Policy Environment for FDI

Several features of the Hungarian economy during the transition years benefited the inflow of FDI; these included the following:

- The early start and positive track record of the market reforms, when Hungary established itself as a stable and reliable partner.
- The cutting of subsidies and strict implementation of a bankruptcy law, under which the assets of state-owned enterprises (SOEs) in financial difficulties were sold off.
- The pursuit of privatization mainly through direct sales, permitting foreign investors to outbid domestic ones.
- High foreign debt service obligations that necessitated a permanent inflow of foreign capital.
- Despite privatization and FDI suffering a temporary setback in 1994, severe foreign trade and budget deficits that made the sale of more state-owned assets to foreign investors unavoidable in 1995.

During 1990–2, transformation 'shock measures' in the form of import competition, price liberalization and the loss of East European export markets adversely affected Hungarian companies. Hungary's economic policy did not provide relief through hidden subsidies, currency undervaluation or import surcharges, as in the Czech Republic and Poland. The removal of subsidies and the introduction of tough bankruptcy laws and modern accounting regulations were aimed at enforcing hard budget constraints. The rapid restructuring of production, the redirection of sales and the adoption of new technologies were expected to take place on a large scale.

The aforementioned policy measures fell broadly within the parameters of the traditional economic reform thinking prevalent in the 1980s. The socialist economic system described by Janos Kornai as a 'shortage economy', where enterprises operated under 'soft budget constraints', was to be replaced by a market economy governed by free competition. The economic reforms of the 1980s ushered in the gradual opening of the economy, competitive prices, realistic exchange rates and the tolerance of small-scale private initiative. The reform of the taxation system (1988), the introduction of a two-tier banking system (1987), the authorization of majority foreign-owned companies (1988) and the setting up of a stock exchange (1990) were all instigated by the last communist government. The autonomy of state-owned enterprises was guaranteed, allowing for the development of marketing and management skills; spontaneous privatization and asset-stripping also took place before real privatization started in 1990. Thanks to the advance of economic reforms in the early transformation period, privatization could be carried out as an economic process, a 'bargain between buyers and sellers', and the application of voucher schemes practised in less-mature transition economies could be avoided.

The changes of the early transformation period came abruptly: 90 per cent of all imports were liberalized in just two years (1990–1), when most subsidies were cut. In addition, the tight monetary policy introduced to curtail inflation with high interest rates was detrimental to companies with large debts. State-owned enterprises, which had borrowed heavily for investment purposes during the 1980s, and their commercial banks ran into financial difficulties. The first transition measures taken by companies were defensive: they curtailed production and employment, cut back capacity and closed down or sold production sites. The bankruptcy law of 1992 speeded up the exit of enterprises in financial distress.

At the same time, extensive foreign takeovers, small investments with high productivity gains and the emergence of new production units added dynamism to the economy. Tens of thousands of new private companies were founded, which partly replaced the production of state-owned enterprises and also provided services to them. New enterprises channelled profits from the public to the private sector. The advance of institutional reform and privatization aroused the interest of foreign investors ahead of other transition countries. State-owned enterprises survived mostly by selling assets or inviting foreign investors. The privatization policy, which favoured cash sales to the highest bidder, was advantageous to foreign takeovers as domestic investors lacked the capital to compete.

The chosen policy of privatization stimulated the foreign penetration of Hungarian productive assets and markets. Not only was the sale of companies relatively widespread in Hungary, but the decline of state-owned enterprises, their bankruptcy or closing down also occurred on a fairly large scale. When domestic producers started to curtail production, their market shares were taken over by imported goods and the products of local subsidiaries of foreign firms. The real estate of bankrupt or down-sized firms was offered cheaply, and a trained workforce was also available to the incoming owner.

The business sector is relatively free of state intervention; management skills and linguistic abilities are adequate; ownership rights are transparent. Foreign investors have been relatively successful in lobbying for government support, if required. The benefits and tax holidays provided by the government to foreign investment enterprises (FIEs) were often ineffective and subject to frequent changes. However, the liberal legal framework for offshore activities has been a special point of attraction. Most large, export-oriented investment projects have received 'free-zone' status, exempting them from Hungarian customs, currency and book-keeping regulations. These foreign-owned companies, mostly greenfield investments, were established without much contact with the local economy. The lack of spill-over effects from such offshore companies is even more noticeable than in the case of other FIEs.

The unexpectedly severe recession that affected some industrial policy measures in 1993–4 did not change the main rules of the economy. The budget constraints of some major state-owned enterprises and banks were softened in an expensive debt and debtor consolidation programme. The sharp edge of the bankruptcy law was blunted and the automatic trigger for bankruptcy abolished. Privatization policy changed in favour of domestic investors, who received subsidized credit schemes and compensation vouchers. Nevertheless, the mainstream of economic development was still determined by the expansion of foreign and domestic private firms as well as by the further contraction of the larger state-owned companies. A turning point in economic development was reached in mid-1993, when GDP took off and more pronounced investments and growing industrial production put an end to the depression of the early transition years. By 1994 most 'surviving firms' were able to consolidate their position and gather some optimism for the future, while macroeconomic imbalances deteriorated. New policies aimed at correcting these imbalances have of late tempered growth expectations.

The high level of inherited foreign debt was one of the unfavourable starting conditions for the Hungarian transformation. Instead of costly rescheduling, subsequent governments carried out debt management by replacing old debts with bonds and new loans with longer maturity. Debt-service obligations remained high with net interest payments reaching 15 per cent of exports, while the repayment of principal reached 40 per cent of exports in 1994. The inflow of new credits and FDI facilitated the discharge of payment obligations and the accumulation of reserves, but the situation remained fragile. Revenues from FDI counterbalanced interest payments on the foreign debt but did not result in direct financial gains in net terms. Foreign investment revenues became essential when the current account plummeted to large deficits in 1993 and 1994. The exit of major producers and import-intensive investment projects, in addition to radically changing demand structures, led to a deterioration of the foreign trade balance in 1993 and 1994. The basically successful shift of exports from the former CMEA to Western markets during 1989–92 was partly based on loss-making production, which could not be indefinitely sustained under hard budget constraints. No transitory protection was afforded to loss-making exporting firms. On the other hand, the closedown of capacities as well as foreign takeovers generated excessive imports of semifinished goods, machinery and consumer goods. In 1993 exports shrank while imports expanded, and in the following year the pace of import growth exceeded that of exports. The 1994 foreign trade deficit, which reached 36 per cent of exports (customs statistics), was too high for the country's strained foreign financial situation, even if deficits were interpreted as a normal effect of recovering economic growth. As FDI did not add to available resources, it could not give much growth incentive to the economy as a whole. This is the reason for the coexistence of high FDI inflows and slow economic growth.

The central government's budget deficit, which increased to 7.5 per cent of GDP in 1994, was another problem. As the available budgetary means were limited, programmes promoting investment and FDI were weak and short-lived. The government was forced to sell fixed assets in order to reduce outstanding debts and in consequence spend less on debt-servicing.

To avoid any further aggravation of macroeconomic imbalances, an austerity package was announced on 12 March 1995. Measures to curtail the current-account deficit included a one-time 9 per cent devaluation and the introduction of a crawling-peg regime for the next two years. An 8 per cent temporary surcharge on imports was introduced: it excluded energy and allowed refunding for investment-related imports and bought-in components incorporated in export products. The import surcharge is valid for two years and represented an emergency measure under WTO rules. Measures to halve the budget deficit included, first of all, severe cuts in outlays. Under the new system of social spending, universal eligibility was to be replaced by eligibility below a certain per capita income. In addition, wage increases were to be curtailed and fringe benefits cut in the public sector.

Attracting FDI was confirmed as a key element in the government's financial strategy for 1995. The Hungarian National Bank and the government realized that any increase in net debt was hazardous; hence, the current account deficit had to be lowered and FDI revenues increased. The need to reduce the budget deficit gave another stimulus to foreign investors in late 1995. No direct incentive for foreign investors was introduced, but an increase in offers for privatization sales was planned. Significant stakes in electricity works, gas distributors and the Hungarian oil company were prepared for sale. In addition, one of the main commercial banks and a pharmaceutical company were offered for privatization and sold to foreign investors. Privatization-related foreign inflows in 1995 surpassed their accumulated value for 1990–4. In privatization contracts, foreign investors in the energy sector committed themselves to further investments in the next few years to the tune of some 3 billion dollars.

FDI inflows outside the privatization process continued at a stable rate in 1995 and the first half of 1996. Hungary has thus become dependent on foreign investment capital and the decisions of transnational enterprises. Its future economic development will to a large extent be affected by the behaviour of foreign investors.

The Foreign Sector at National Level

It is not easy to measure the size of the foreign sector, but at national level the data from majority foreign-owned companies can be separated from other sectors in the economy. Companies outside the financial sector that produced 48 per cent of Hungary's GDP in 1993 fell into three categories of ownership: companies with majority public ownership that produced 43 per cent of value added; companies with majority foreign ownership producing 15 per cent of value added; and the remaining domestic private companies (42 per cent) (see Table 5.1). The foreign sector's share was estimated at 9 per cent of total GDP in 1993; this rose to 12 per cent in 1994, about three times as much as in the Czech Republic and Poland, on a par with Austria, but below Spain and Portugal.

Increasing efficiency and profitability can be expected as a result of foreign investment. Calculations of the foreign sector's profitability are based on the national accounts for 1993 (Central Statistical Office 1995). The operating surplus (value added *less* employees' compensation *plus*

Table 5.1 Hungary: gross value added of companies with double-entry bookkeeping, 1992–4

	1992		*1993*		*1994*	
	F bn.	*%*	*F bn.*	*%*	*F bn.*	*%*
Public	730.7	57.5	618.2	41.9	—	—
Majority foreign	130.2	10.3	241.9	16.4	—	—
Domestic private	409.0	32.2	615.0	41.7	—	—
Total	1269.9	100.0	1475.1	100.0	1868.8	100.0
FIEs	259.4	20.4	447.5	30.3	732.2	39.2

Sources: Central Statistical Office (KSH), Budapest, 1994, 1995, 1996.

net taxes and subsidies) of all non-financial corporations made up 23 per cent of value added in 1993, but 35 per cent in the case of foreign companies, thus signalling the latters' higher profitability. Foreign companies, producing less than 15 per cent of valued added, generated 22 per cent of the operating surplus in the Hungarian economy.

By deducting payments on capital – that is, property-related income – from operating surpluses, we arrive at the primary income balance, which can be associated with retained earnings. This amounted to 13 per cent of value added in the case of all companies, and to 19 per cent for foreign firms. Retained earnings are an important source of capital investments. As foreign companies had a relatively high share (21 per cent) of total retained earnings in 1993, the assumption is that they had a higher growth potential than their counterparts in the domestic sector. Foreign companies paid 24 billion forints in gross dividends to their owners. Assuming that foreign-owned companies repatriated half of their dividends, the income generated for the domestic economy was 58 billion forints. This corresponds to 23.7 per cent of foreign companies' value added, a higher share that than of the domestic sector (17.5 per cent), which had no registered transfer of dividends abroad. In sum, The Hungarian economy did benefit from the high profitability of the foreign sector in 1993.

FDI in Foreign Investment Enterprises (FIEs)

In contrast to the group of foreign companies, which includes only firms with majority foreign ownership, FIEs include all firms with a share of foreign ownership. In FIEs minority foreign owners frequently obtain a controlling position in management: this can lead to improvements in efficiency, particularly if the majority owner is a public company. The state retains only the right to dispose of its share in the company's capital and does not normally participate in managerial decisions.

The economic and financial data of FIEs and their share in the overall economy are analysed below to shed light on the size and behaviour of the foreign sector. A comparison between the performance of foreign and domestic-owned companies is carried out at both macro and sectoral levels. The analysis differs from other FDI-related investigations, which rely either on case-studies or company surveys, which suffer from difficulties in finding the right sample. The set of data analysed below is based on aggregate company balance sheets, which are deemed most representative.

At the end of 1993 the total stock of FDI was reported to be 7400 million dollars, while the foreign capital in FIEs covered by our analysis amounted to 6542 million dollars. A year later the total foreign investment stock was 8700 million dollars, of which FIEs amounted to 7480 million. The discrepancy is the result of three main factors:

1. Not all companies have double-entry book-keeping, which forms the basis of the statistical reports.
2. Not all companies registered during the year provided a balance sheet for that year.
3. FDI not registered as capital increase in a company is not included in the FIE data.

Foreign capital penetration in the Hungarian economy rose significantly following the opening of the economy in 1989 (see Table 5.2). In 1994 foreign capital was present in some 23 500 companies (out of a total of 170 000), while FIEs accounted for a third of the nominal capital. Foreign investment made up a fifth of total nominal capital. Other Central European countries do not come close to Hungary's degree of openness to foreign capital (see Table 5.3). In all four countries foreign capital displays common characteristics: FIEs tend to have higher labour productivity, are more export-oriented and have more intensive investment activities than domestic firms.

In the early years of the transformation process, foreign investment was concentrated in joint ventures with state-owned enterprises where foreigners held a minority position. Investors sought maximum security in a predominantly state-owned economy and shared the investment risks with the state. Later on, as the state withdrew from the economy, the foreign share started to increase: first, fresh foreign capital was injected in joint ventures that could not be financed by the Hungarian partner; second, unilateral capital increases resulted in foreign dominance in share distribution (in new acquisitions, foreign investors targeted majority shares to gain control); third, new ventures were increasingly set up as 100-per-cent foreign companies and greenfield investments.

In 1990, 62 per cent of FDI capital and 81 per cent of nominal capital in FIEs was located in joint ventures, while only 6 per cent of FDI was invested in totally foreign-owned companies. These proportions changed considerably with new projects and capital increases. In 1991 only 34 per cent of FDI was in minority companies, and 18 per cent in wholly foreign-owned firms. In 1994 minority companies had only 16 per cent of the FDI capital, while wholly foreign-owned firms made up 41 per cent.

Table 5.2 Foreign investment enterprises in Hungary, 1989–94 (share in nominal capital and employment)

Year	Nominal capital		FDI in nominal capital		Employment	
	(F bn.)	(%)	(F bn.)	(%)	(000 persons)	(%)
1989	30	2	12	1	—	—
1992	713	20	402	11	360	14
1993	1113	27	663	16	400	20
1994	1398	32	833	19	476	24

Source: Central Statistical Office (KSH), Budapest, 1995, 1996.

Table 5.3 Share of foreign investment enterprises in the Hungarian, Czech, Polish and Slovak economies[a]

	Czech Republic 1994	Hungary 1994	Poland 1993	Slovak Republic 1994
Nominal capital	7.4	31.9	7.0[b]	5.0
Employed persons	6.0	22.6	5.6	3.8
Output	9.4	38.6	10.8[c]	7.7[d]
Export sales	n.a.	50.6	16.4	n.a.
Investment	16.5	38.0	11.2	11.8

n.a. = not available
[a] Czech Republic, Slovak Republic: non-financial corporations with at least 25 employees; Hungary, Poland: companies supplying tax declarations.
[b] Estimated.
[c] Income from sales and financial operations.
[d] Value added.

Source: Based on national statistical data collected in the framework of the research project on FDI carried out by the Wiener Institut für Internationale Wirtschaftsvergleiche.

The two economic activities where minority foreign participation dominated in 1994 were the telecom and oil-refining sectors. In the first, foreign partners controlled 27 per cent of shares in the national company MATAV. A management agreement ensured the leading role of the German shareholder in managerial matters. In 1994 the foreign share acquired in the national oil company was marginal.

Foreign Penetration by Sector

In 1994 foreign investment was negligible in agriculture, as foreigners were not allowed to buy agricultural land. In the energy and public utilities sectors privatization had yet to start. In other activities FIEs had more than a third of the companies' nominal capital.

Mining is mostly in domestic hands, with the exception of stone, sand and gravel mining, where FIEs dominate. The mining of construction materials is dominated by foreign interests. In other construction-related industries, the share of FIEs is about 76 per cent.

The expansion of foreign capital in manufacturing in 1994 was as high as 60 per cent. Above-average shares of foreign capital are found in the food industry, and foreign control is almost complete in the beverage and tobacco sectors. In textiles, apparel and leather, the share of FIEs in the total nominal capital was about 45 per cent. The growth of foreign control in 1994 was slow, as foreign investors had already selected the most successful companies.

The production of chemical products and rubber are activities with increasingly high foreign penetration, while the crisis-hit steel industry is still mainly in domestic state ownership, with the exception of processed metal goods, where the share of FIEs is above 50 per cent. In some machine-building activities FIEs control more than three-quarters of the nominal capital, namely, office machines, electrical machinery and motor vehicles.

Trade and tourism were among the first targets of foreign investors after the opening up of the economy. In trade, car distribution and wholesale are more foreign owned than the retail sector. Transport and telecommunications are the primary targets of FDI. Hungary was the first of the Central European countries to privatize the national telecoms company to foreign strategic investors and open up the mobile telephone business for competition. In financial intermediation, foreign companies control the whole insurance business and have strong interests in banking. High foreign shares in education and health are misleading, because the bulk of these activities are performed by public budgetary institutions not providing tax declarations.

In sum, foreign penetration is strongest in branches with a relatively stable or promising domestic market. Some sub-branches of the food industry, including edible-oil production, breweries and tobacco factories, are almost exclusively foreign-owned. Household equipment and cars also have good prospects on both the Hungarian and foreign markets. In general, industries with a high level of internationalization abroad have been the target of foreign capital, particularly in the machine-building and car industries.

Employment in FIEs

FIEs employed 24 per cent of the total workforce in 1994. The share of FIEs in employment is smaller than that in respect of the amount of invested capital. FIEs are less labour-intensive than domestic firms in all branches of production – with the exception of financial services – and in all sub-branches of manufacturing. The lower labour intensity and higher capital intensity of FIEs, when compared with domestic companies, seems to be the result of different company strategies. One may tentatively conclude that foreign firms are faster in restructuring and laying off redundant workers; they also employ more labour-saving technology than domestic firms. Data on investment activity support the view that FIEs have a more recent capital stock than domestic companies.

The employment level of foreign companies increased in all branches of the economy in 1993 and 1994. If we consider that the employment increase took place partly because privatization transferred workers from the public to the private sector, genuine job creation in the foreign sector must have been negligible. Indeed, the years of transformation witnessed a severe depression in the Hungarian economy, with rapidly rising unemployment. Structural change enforced by the transformational depression was mainly defensive and labour-shedding. Foreign companies and, to some extent, domestic private companies took over several state-owned enterprises where they speeded up restructuring and layoffs. Also, in the immediate future, foreign investments will hardly mitigate the problem of unemployment.

Employees in FIEs are better paid on average than those in domestic companies. Per capita annual salaries in the companies surveyed amounted to 374 000 forints, and to 488 000 forints in FIEs, or 30 per cent more than in 1993. In 1994 the difference narrowed and salaries in FIEs reached 552 000 forints, a quarter more than in the total economy. Salaries were particularly high in fully foreign-owned companies: some 43 per cent higher than the average. It is not known to what extent this result is related to the presence of high-income expatriates in FIEs. Press reports suggest that foreign companies are not generous to local blue-collar workers, and try to economize on wages and demand intensive work.

High capital intensity and efficient use of labour have resulted in higher productivity in the foreign sector. FIEs reported per capita net sales 64 per cent higher than the average of all companies both in 1993 and 1994, while wholly foreign-owned firms had two and a half times higher than average labour productivity. These turned out to be a special type of firm, mainly greenfield, equipped and operating with modern technology.

The Sales and Exports of FIEs

The importance of FIEs has been more pronounced in output than in nominal capital or employment. FIEs contributed 33 per cent to the total *sales* of enterprises in 1993 and more than 38 per cent in 1994. Higher-than-average sales per unit of invested capital were registered in three branches: financial services, real estate and consulting services, and transport and telecom. FIEs provided 40 per cent in 1993 and 55 per cent in 1994 of sales in manufacturing, with the highest foreign shares in beverages and tobacco.

The export sales of FIEs made up half of the total exports of Hungarian companies in 1993, and 60 per cent in 1994. The share was higher still in the case of the most important export branch, manufacturing, with 65.5 per cent in 1994 (see Tables 5.4 and 5.5). Two-thirds of machinery exports and almost 60 per cent of exports in the food industry originated from FIEs.

Average companies exported 13 per cent of their sales in 1994, somewhat more than in 1993, but less than in 1992. FIEs exported 20 per cent of their sales in 1993, 21 per cent in 1994 and 22 per cent in 1992. The decline in export shares in 1993 reflects the overall decline in Hungary's exports. The upturn in exports in 1994 was to large extent due to the increasing activities of FIEs.

The highest export shares in 1994 were recorded in manufacturing: 25.4 per cent for all companies and 30.1 per cent for FIEs. Within manufacturing, machine-building had an average export share of 35 per cent – 47 per cent for FIEs. The difference was even larger in textiles: 39 per cent on average against 58 per cent for the FIEs. In these sub-branches, processing for exports must have been an important motivation for investing in Hungary. The food industry, on the other hand, was highly domestic-oriented. The relatively low export share – 16 per cent in the case of FIEs – reveals that investments in the food industry were motivated by access to the domestic market. Nevertheless, FIEs provided almost 60 per cent of food industry export sales.

Actual trade flows are documented in foreign trade statistics based on customs declarations. An important discrepancy exists between the export sales quoted by companies and *exports leaving the country*. The method of data collection and the range of companies involved make such a difference unavoidable. Indirect exports and exports by companies in duty-free zones are covered in a different way by the two sources. The difference is most significant in the case of FIEs, which reported export sales to exceed actual exports. One reason is that duty-free-zone

Table 5.4 Hungary: share of FIEs in the total economy,[a] by selected industries, 1994 (percentages)

ISIC Code	Industries	Employment	Nominal capital	Sales	Export sales	Investment[b]	FDI[c]
A, B	Agriculture, hunting, forestry, fishing	2.9	6.2	6.2	21.7	10.0	1.2
C	Mining and quarrying	13.4	30.3	24.9	21.5	29.6	1.1
D	Manufacturing	35.3	60.8	54.0	65.5	79.0	48.6
F	Construction	14.4	40.5	28.2	35.7	36.8	4.7
G	Wholesale and retail trade	23.6	40.1	33.5	55.7	53.7	14.1
H	Hotels and restaurants	46.1	50.1	31.6	42.6	40.0	3.6
I	Transport, storage, communications	10.8	36.3	35.1	56.6	47.0	7.9
J	Finance	46.0	47.9	78.5	84.0	37.6	8.9
K	Real estate, renting	13.0	25.9	23.8	58.0	31.2	8.5
	Total	22.6	31.9	36.7	60.0	40.2	100.8

[a] All companies providing tax declarations.
[b] Gross fixed investment.
[c] Distribution of FDI among branches (%).

Source: Central Statistical Office (KSH), Budapest, 1995.

Table 5.5 Hungary: share of FIEs in manufacturing, 1994 (percentages)

ISIC Code	Branches	Employment	Nominal capital	Sales	Export sales	FDI %
15–16	Food	38.3	63.4	49.3	70.4	32.7
17–19	Textiles	29.6	43.4	41.0	56.8	4.1
20–22	Paper	24.1	42.7	44.2	54.7	6.4
23–25	Chemicals	53.2	72.5	73.0	67.8	13.4
26	Non-metallic mineral products	40.0	76.2	58.1	70.4	8.2
27–28	Metallurgy	21.7	43.3	35.2	50.5	6.3
29–35	Machinery	38.8	61.0	57.5	77.9	27.6
36–37	Other	23.7	32.2	29.2	55.1	1.3
	Total	35.3	60.8	54.0	65.5	100.0

Source: Central Statistical Office (KSH), Budapest, 1995.

companies are all foreign-owned: they report their sales outside Hungary as exports in their balances, but do not fill in customs declarations. In fact, Hungarian national foreign trade data do not cover the activity of these important firms (Opel, Suzuki, Philips, and so on).

The export and import shares of FIEs were significantly larger than their contribution to value added, nominal capital or employment. FIEs also tended to import more than they exported, thus exacerbating the foreign trade deficit. In 1993 and 1994, when the country accumulated dangerously high foreign-trade deficits, FIEs generated 46 per cent and 65 per cent respectively of the deficit (see Table 5.6).

Several specific *conclusions* can be drawn as to the role of FIEs in foreign trade:

1. The high foreign trade intensity of FIEs suggests that many are engaged as subcontractors in outward processing activities with low domestic value added.

Table 5.6 Hungary: Foreign trade of FIEs 1992–4 (billion forints current prices)

	1992			1993			1994		
	Total	FIEs	FIE (%)	Total	FIEs	FIE(%)	Total	FIEs	FIE (%)
Export sales	812.5	325.9	40.1	878.2	438.9	50.0	1130.7	684.5	60.5
Exports	843.6	272.9	32.3	819.9	357.1	43.6	—	614.1	54.4
Imports	878.5	323.6	36.8	1162.5	514.7	44.3	—	880.1	57.3
Deficit	34.9	50.7	145.3	342.6	157.6	46.0	—	266.0	65.1

Source: Central Statistical Office, Budapest, 1995.

2. Disproportionately high imports can be interpreted as a sign of low levels of integration in the domestic economy. The 'enclave' mentality of some foreign companies, which receive their inputs from abroad but sell their products domestically, begs the question of the extent of spill-over effects and the potential for local sourcing.
3. The high import intensity of foreign companies is also due to their immature stage of development. During the buildup period, companies import a greater percentage of machinery and components than at a later stage.
4. The smaller decline in FIE exports in the recession year of 1993 may mean that foreign companies rely more extensively on secure foreign markets than do domestic companies.
5. FIEs in the trade sector show a higher import intensity than domestic companies. Some FIEs, especially in wholesale trade and car distribution, were established with the aim of penetrating the Hungarian market with foreign-made products. Foreign-owned retail networks, when operating in the higher price echelons, also show high import ratios.

Gross Fixed Capital Investment and R&D in FIEs

The investment setback in Hungary started bottoming out in 1992 at 84.5 per cent of the 1988 level. In 1993 a real growth rate of 2.7 per cent was recorded, followed by 10.4 per cent in 1994. Thanks to the recovery, 95.8 per cent of pre-recession levels was reached in 1994. (The new setback of investments since the middle of 1995 is not covered here.) Recovery was faster in the business sector than in the rest of the economy: economic entities with legal status (all companies plus government, social security and non-profit organizations) invested the same amount in real terms in 1994 as in 1988. The investments of 'organizations without legal status' (households and auxiliary activities and artisans) invested only 82.4 per cent of pre-recession levels. A shift of activities between sectors certainly played a role in the divergence of investments. Also, the composition of investments was uneven: construction investments were more hit severely by the recession and their recovery was slower than in machinery, where 43 per cent of the invested machinery was imported in 1988, rising to 57 per cent in 1994.

Some three-quarters of total investment in 1994 were carried out by companies with double-entry book-keeping, of which 262.5 billion forints, or 40 per cent, was done by FIEs. If business investments (excluding budgetary institutions) are taken into account, the share of FIEs is above 50 per cent and increasing. The most rapid increase in investments is among wholly foreign-owned enterprises and minority foreign ventures. The shift of Hungarian companies to the foreign investment sector (for example MATAV) seems to have been more important than the increase of investments in older joint ventures. Investments per 100 forints of nominal capital in 1993 amounted to 12 forints for the whole economy, and 16 forints for FIEs; the respective figures for 1994 were 14 and 19. This shows a higher investment propensity for the foreign sector, although the improvements in 1994 took place in both domestic- and foreign-related firms.

FIEs invested below average in buildings and above average in machinery, mostly imported. The FIEs' share of machinery investments was between 45 and 50 per cent in 1992–4, and 50 per cent in imported machinery. This suggests that the contribution of FIEs to economic modernization through machinery investments and imports of modern technology is outstanding. On the other hand, the increase of Hungarian imports and the deterioration of the current-account situation must be attributed partly to the investment activity of FIEs.

An important item on the cost side, namely R&D expenditure, shows the growing role of FIEs as well. Total outlays on R&D in 1992 amounted to 1284 million forints, of which 37 per cent was spent by FIEs. The sum more than doubled in 1993 to 3507 million forints, of which 41 per cent was spent by FIEs. Most of the yearly increases were due to FIEs, which played a greater than proportional role in the otherwise low-key R&D activities of Hungarian companies. It should be added that foreign investors were interested in investing substantial amounts in acquiring Hungarian companies with significant R&D activity (Ganz, Tungsram and Richter). Access to the domestic R&D potential was clearly an attraction to foreign investors.

The Profitability of FIEs

The findings in this chapter have been aggregated from FIEs' tax declarations, but have not been converted into the national accounts methodology, and thus show somewhat different trends from those outlined previously. Post-tax profits in the Hungarian economy were negative in 1993. FIEs recorded a-quarter of total losses (30 billion forints), only slightly less than their share in invested capital. Losses in 1993 were half the losses in 1992 for both domestic companies and FIEs. In 1994 the financial results of companies improved as losses were halved compared with the previous year at current prices. FIEs recorded losses of only 5 billion forints, or 11 per cent of the total. Manufacturing turned into the black for both foreign and domestic companies, while trade remained the major loss-maker. Losses incurred during these two years were caused by two sets of factors, besides profit-hiding. First, the Hungarian economy was in a state of general depression until 1994. Fixed costs and employment did not decrease as rapidly as sales. Unit costs increased more than sales revenues. Some foreign investors overestimated the expansion of the domestic market and suffered from underutilized capacity. The downsizing and selling off of assets reduced fixed costs and generated revenues for domestic companies, but not fast enough to compensate for operational losses. Second, new investments had a launching period during which no profit was made. Foreign investors usually provided their Hungarian subsidiaries with a grace period of 2 to 5 years before expecting profits. Subsidiaries even increased their capacity during periods of negative profitability to achieve an optimum size of operations and the best product range.

Losses in manufacturing amounted to 40 billion forints in 1993, of which 7 billion forints were recorded by FIEs; both sets of figures were higher in nominal terms than in the previous year. Some sub-branches, however, were exceptions: in the chemical industry both domestic and foreign companies made profits. This was the result of a very selective privatization process affecting healthy sub-sectors. The food, beverages and tobacco sector was profitable among FIEs, but recorded losses among domestic firms, as the best enterprises were allowed into the privatization process. The greatest losses occurred in metallurgy and machine-building. In the latter the foreign sector's losses were higher than those of the domestic sector. Old industries were being streamlined while new ones such as the car industry were being built up, resulting in temporary losses in anticipation of future profitable operations.

In 1994 manufacturing FIEs had net profits of 27 billion forints, primarily because machine-building, textiles and clothing stopped generating losses. The chemical industry continued to be the most profitable sector.

In 1993 FIEs showed a slightly higher return on total capital (1.4 per cent) than all companies (1.1 per cent). The gap widened in 1994, but both groups of companies showed improvement (2.71 per cent for FIEs and 1.62 per cent for all companies). Foreign companies operated with higher capital costs and lower wage costs per unit of output than their domestic counterparts. All companies, including FIEs, reported low profits, suggesting that repatriated dividends must have been low.

However, the suspicion of transfer pricing and other ways of unrecorded transfers subsisted.

Lessons From International Comparisons and Case-Studies

The features characterizing FIEs in Hungary are in line with worldwide trends (Rojec 1995): FDI is more pronounced in capital- and technology-intensive branches than in labour-intensive sectors. The higher the technological level in an FIE, the higher the foreign partner's share. Telecommunications and utilities are common exceptions.

The development of manufacturing enterprises under foreign ownership has become dependent on decisions in multinational corporations. The fast tempo of restructuring in Hungarian manufacturing is the result of large-scale foreign penetration, which has also made the development of whole industries foreign-dependent. By comparison, in the Czech Republic and Poland, most companies have tried to preserve their independence even at the cost of slower restructuring, but in the hope of being able to pursue advantageous strategies.

In respect of microeconomic restructuring, the Hungarian transformation process for 1990–4 has differed from the Czech approach. Hungary's industrial labour productivity in 1995 was 34 per cent above 1989 levels, contrasting favourably with the Czech Republic, where it was 4 per cent lower. The Czech economy is characterized by 'capital hoarding, postponed bankruptcies and missing financial capital for restructuring' (see Zemplinerova and Benacek 1995) and Zemplinerova *et al.* 1995). Under such conditions the chances of preserving old structures are higher, while restructuring is slower but less painful. Czech privatization was effected mainly through vouchers and not capital investment, hence capital costs remained low in firms with amortized assets. Export revenues were increased through the sales of products with a low unit-value. As the pressure to invest was not very strong, most firms survived in domestic hands.

The current research supports the global developments of the past few decades: intra-industry and intra-multinational company trade leads to more successful and dynamic specialization, as in the Hungarian case. If the changes are too abrupt, however, this may increase the need for imports and external financial resources. This was instrumental in retarding dynamic economic growth in Hungary.

Successful initial restructuring by foreign investment is no safeguard for future success. It is still premature to judge whether Hungarian subsidies will be carefully integrated into the global networks of multinationals and succeed in raising their technological knowhow.

Foreign ownership, though beneficial at the initial stage of restructuring, limits the choice of future company strategies. Incorporation into global sourcing implies a narrower assortment and competition for higher-standard products inside the multinational network; it also sets limits on R&D activity. Import dependence on other members of the multinational group may increase without a test of alternative supplies. This increases imports and may remove traditional domestic suppliers. Market access is also restricted by the multinational owner. A recent study of the car industry in Hungary by Somai reveals the difficulties experienced by local companies in becoming subcontractors to multinational car producers. While Suzuki aims to increase local sourcing, European investors (such as GM, Audi and Ford) operate as islands with marginal local sourcing.

Some Conclusions

On the basis of aggregate company data, a high level of foreign penetration can be identified in the Hungarian economy. The foreign sector shows higher productivity and is more export-oriented than the domestic sector. It also plays a primary role in capital investment as well as in R&D. Differences between FIEs can be identified according to branches of economic activity and investing country. Expanding and export-oriented enterprises exist alongside stagnating and rent-seeking ones.

FIEs have been the most dynamic part of the Hungarian economy. In 1993 they accounted for about half of all investments and exports, while their share in industrial production reached one-third. According to some estimates, the FIEs' share in exports reached 70 per cent in 1995.

Hungary has now embarked on a more mature stage of FDI-penetration. Among newly established firms, greenfield investment has become increasingly important. Capital investment into existing ventures and reinvestment of profits have taken on an increasing share of FDI. In December 1995 a new stage of privatization began with the partial sale of the gas and electricity distribution companies.

Relatively high and increasing foreign penetration has become a specific feature of the Hungarian economy. FIEs have had a high impact on microeconomic development (subordinated to the global strategy of multinational enterprises) and are likely to influence future economic development (rapidly increasing openness).

Given the success to date in attracting foreign capital, the Hungarian authorities have been under little pressure to grant special incentives to foreign investors. There is scope, however, for improving the investment climate. First, in order to reduce investment risks, legal and institutional transparency and stability must improve. Second, taxation, social security contributions and other cost-related items should be fixed for longer periods of time and not depend on annual state budget requirements. Third, incentives must also be more lasting and easily calculable: the time horizons of government action (one year) and company-level investment decisions (ten to fifteen years) should move closer to each other.

A problem related to FDI in Hungary is the large part of the current-account deficit associated with the activities of FIEs. This was larger than the inflow of new and reinvested FDI in 1992–4.

Strong foreign penetration of the Hungarian economy brought about a serious dichotomy between the foreign and domestic sectors. Foreign engagement concentrates on specific industries, is located in a few privileged regions and attracts mainly the younger and more educated part of the workforce. Areas with a long industrial tradition located in the west of the country have benefited more than the eastern regions. Education policy has been pushed into training elites with foreign-language skills, while general public education has suffered from organizational and financial shortcomings. The low proportion of the workforce benefiting from relatively high salaries in FIEs has limited their popularity.

Closer integration by the foreign sector in the domestic economy should receive priority in policy-making, as it would lead to a wider choice of favourable investment locations and help preserve and develop human capital. The dichotomy might be partly overcome by spill-over effects in the wake of economic growth. In addition, regional and labour policy measures seem to be necessary. Infrastructure investment and regional policy instruments must be implemented. Action stimulating labour mobility towards the more affluent regions should also be considered. The budgetary means for such expenditures seem to be neither abundant nor well-placed; improvements in this respect would benefit economic growth and simultaneously promote FDI.

6
The Czech Republic

Alena Zemplinerova

This study examines the behaviour of foreign investment enterprises (FIEs) in the economy of the Czech Republic. It covers the extent, the structure and the dynamics of these companies, their performance compared with domestic firms, and their links to the privatization process. According to my estimates, foreign companies employed 8.5 per cent of the total workforce of the Czech economy in 1995 and produced about 11.2 per cent of the economy's total output. However, as these 20 000 foreign companies account for only 2.7 per cent of the total number of registered firms, they are substantially outperforming their domestic counterparts.

While the Czech Republic still has a long way to go before it is thoroughly integrated into the world economy, the rate of foreign direct investment (FDI) has clearly accelerated during the last few years: the older firms continue to perform well, suggesting that growth will continue in the future. In manufacturing, the FIEs not only are more productive and export more on average than other firms, but also invest more in new technology. Foreign manufacturing enterprises apparently restructure faster, getting rid of redundant employees but also paying higher average salaries than domestic firms by about 20 per cent. Foreign penetration varies significantly according to sector. The allocation of foreign investment also follows a different pattern from its domestic counterpart. Measured by share of output or size of the labour force, foreign participation in manufacturing is highest in motor vehicles, printing and publishing, rubber and plastics, non-metallic minerals, tobacco and foodstuffs. A high share of foreign investment is also recorded in electronics and medical instruments. Privatization turns out to have been a mixed blessing. On the one hand it has created investment opportunities, but on the other it has also thrown up barriers that have slowed or in some cases deterred altogether the involvement of foreign investors. According to my estimates, about three-quarters of FDI assets come from the privatization of former state enterprises.

Introduction

Before 1989 the number of FIEs operating in the Czech economy was negligible. Since 1990 FDI has grown markedly, thanks to several large privatization deals, principally joint ventures like Volkswagen-Skoda, Nestlé-Cokoladovny or TelSource-Telecom. At the same time, a large number of small FIEs appeared, often not recorded in official statistics, but with an important and dynamic role in the economy.

According to balance of payments statistics, investments by foreign firms in the Czech Republic reached 7.2 billion dollars by end 1996. Between 1991 and 1995, FDI investments had been determined on the whole by privatization policy. As elsewhere, investors' decisions to expand or relocate production abroad have been influenced by both macro-and microeconomic policies. The key macroeconomic reforms in the Czech Republic were put in place in January 1991, when prices were decontrolled, the currency was declared to be 'internally convertible', and foreign trade was liberalized. Since then, conservative fiscal and monetary policies have produced a relatively stable and reliable investment climate.

Microeconomic reforms – such as the creation of a new legal framework, privatization, and enterprise restructuring – have also progressed steadily since reforms began, but naturally at a slower pace than the macroeconomic measures. Privatization, for example, has been a mixed blessing. On the one hand it has created investment opportunities, but on the other it has also thrown up barriers that have slowed or in some cases deterred altogether the involvement of foreign investors. Other than splitting up unwieldly conglomerates and monopolies, the problem of restructuring has been left with few exceptions to the post-privatization owners. Relatively high expectations for the restructuring of former centrally planned economies were related to foreign investment. It is the main purpose of this study to contribute to the knowledge of the extent, structure, dynamics and performance of FIEs in the Czech economy in general and privatization in particular.

The analysis is based on both traditional and non-traditional sources. The 'standard' source of data on foreign direct investment capital flows is the balance of payments series. This refers to cash payments made through banks from outside the country, recorded by percentage ownership of the firms' assets. In the next section, FDI is analysed according to sector, geography and size, beginning with foreign capital flows and then developments between 1990 and June 1996.

Balance of payments statistics do not, however, give an account of more detailed foreign penetration by economic sector, nor do they allow for the evaluation of the efficiency of foreign investments.

Therefore, in the following section, entitled 'Foreign and Domestic Enterprises by Sector and Size', we look at additional sources related to foreign direct investment. These include data on individual enterprises obtained from the Czech Statistical Office (CSO), which allow identification by owner. Firms are divided into two groups, FIEs and domestic enterprises. We focus on distribution patterns among foreign investors, as well as on the size and structure of firms. We then compare the performance of domestic and foreign enterprises, first for the economy as a whole and its sectors, then for the manufacturing sector and its component industries. Such an approach is particularly useful in revealing several important aspects of foreign involvement in the Czech economy, especially with respect to its restructuring.

There then follows a section discussing government policies affecting FDI. The final section examines the privatization process as it has affected foreign investment, and puts forward empirical evidence of the experience and behaviour of foreign investors during privatization and of the linkages with domestic industry.

General Features of Foreign Capital Inflows

The world-wide asset value of FDI can be estimated at about 2500 billion dollars, of which the volume in 1995 amounted to 235 billion dollars, according to the United Nations Conference on Trade and Development. The Czech Republic's share in the flow of FDI world wide was just over 1 per cent in 1995. FDI stock ownership, however, was lower, at only 0.2 per cent, indicating how far the Czech Republic has still to go before it is successfully integrated into the world economy (see Table 6.1).

It needs to be stressed, however, that Czech balance of payments statistics may not describe all performing FDIs. For example, some share transactions may escape public monitoring, and thus remain unidentified within group portfolio investments. Other deals, especially in the case of small businesses, may not be reported as foreign buyouts, as FDIs valued at less than 100 000 korunas often escape statistical monitoring altogether. Also, the reinvested profits of foreign companies are not always included in FDI figures.

Table 6.1   FDI, portfolio investment, foreign credits and deposits in the Czech
Republic, 1990–5 (million dollars)

	1990	1991	1992	1993	1994	1995
FDI	49	595	1003	568	862	2559
FDI/GDP in current prices (in %)	0.09	2.45	3.53	1.80	2.39	5.45
FDI/total gross investment	0.7	10.7	14.1	6.5	7.4	16.3
Portfolio investment	n.a.	n.a.	−26	1059	819	1651
Long-term capital	n.a.	n.a.	320	528	860	3173
Short-term capital	n.a.	n.a.	−1275	535	−75	233
Total foreign capital/ GDP (in %)	n.a.	n.a.	n.a.	9.6	9.2	18.4

n.a. = not available.

Source: *Bulletin of the Czech National Bank* (1993–4–5).

Before 1993, FDI was the prevalent form in foreign capital influx to
the Czech Republic. Later, portfolio investment[1] as well as the extension
of credit by foreign banks also became important. There was significantly less foreign investment during 1993 and 1994, as compared with
either 1992 or 1995. Accordingly, the figures for FDI as a percentage of
gross investment or GDP fell in those years as well. A number of factors
contributed to the investment decline:

• Political uncertainties related to the separation of the Czech and
  Slovak Republics in January 1993.
• Voucher privatization which excluded foreign investors from more
  than a third of privatised assets.
• Warning signals picked up by the international investing community. One widely cited example was the repurchasing of shares in CSA
  airlines, originally sold to Air France, because of a failure to meet
  restructuring commitments. Another was the decision by the City of
  Prague not to approve the construction of a major new Canadian
  hotel in the old city centre.
• The success of domestic investors over foreigners in several important
  tender offers, coupled with the failure of several key foreign privatization bids, such as that by Mercedes for the state truck manufacturers.

The low volume of FDI in 1993 and 1994 was partially compensated
for by an increase in investments by foreign mutual funds and other
institutional investors, which are, in reality, hard to separate from FDI.
These reached 819 million dollars in 1994.[2] Despite some speculative

investing, the majority of foreign institutional holdings are long- or medium-term.[3]

There have also been large amounts of foreign capital flowing into the country in the form of foreign loans. Since the first half of 1994, credit extended to Czech enterprises by foreign banks accelerated, reaching a level of 3.6 billion dollars by the end of 1995. Large loans represented only 15 to 20 per cent of the total. The majority were small and med-ium-sized loans, or were related to the establishment of new joint ventures. Some 30 per cent of loans went toward investments in tech-nology, 40 per cent for the purchase of real estate, 26 per cent for trade activity, both domestic and international, and the remaining 4 per cent for other miscellaneous investments. Most of the credit was extended by German banks.

Foreign capital inflows increased radically in 1995, especially in the form of FDI, for the following reasons:

- The acceleration of economic growth.
- Progress in the privatization of large enterprises, particularly in tele-communications, and the final instalment in the transfer of Skoda to Volkswagen;
- Continuing macroeconomic and political stability, reflected in a gen-eral perception of low risk by the investment community.
- Membership of the OECD in September 1997.
- Full convertibility of the koruna in current account transactions, as established by article VIII of the IMF agreement, and partial deregula-tion of capital account transactions.
- Relatively low share prices of Czech securities for portfolio and insti-tutional investors, coupled with anticipated high returns.
- High interest rates on the domestic money markets coupled with a fixed exchange rate, which attracted foreign loans and portfolio investments.

Regarding the balance of payments, high foreign capital inflows were partially counterbalanced by a trade deficit, which reached 8 per cent of GDP in 1995. Thanks to the surplus in services, the current account deficit was in the end only half the trade deficit, just under 2 billion dollars. Thus, 1995 closed with a balance of payments surplus as in previous years and a doubling of foreign exchange reserves at the Czech national bank. Hence, the Czech government had no need to attract additional foreign direct investment to correct a balance of payments deficit, as was the case in Hungary. On the contrary, thanks to the real appreciation of the currency resulting from a policy of fixed exchange rates and relatively high inflation, the national bank needed to sterilize the money supply of any net foreign exchange inflows. More FDI would have added inflationary pressure and complicated the efforts of the national bank to curb the growth in money supply.

FDI by Sector, Size and Country of Origin

While no details are available of industrial sectors in balance of payments source statistics, a clear pattern of foreign direct investment emerges, as seen in Table 6.2, which varies significantly with the sector and time period involved.[4] During the period from 1990 to June 1996, the highest level of FDI was directed at the telecommunications industry (22.6 per cent of the total), followed by the automotive industry (17 per cent) and the tobacco industry. In all, over 50 per cent of the FDI investment total was in manufacturing, including those manufacturing investments listed under 'other industries'.[5] Nevertheless the percentage of investment in manufacturing appears to be declining over time as other sectors – such as telecommunications, oil refineries and banking – open up to foreign investors.

Table 6.2   FDI inflows to the Czech Republic by sectors, 1990–June 1996 (million dollars)

	1993	1994	1995	1996 Jan.– June	1990– 6 June
Transport, telecommunication	n.a.[a]	n.a.[a]	1349.8	n.a.[a]	1364.5
Automotive	10.0	266.1	307.8	n.a.[a]	1025.2
Consumer goods and tobacco	244.0	59.2	179.3	40.0	851.9
Construction	65.0	107.9	n.a.[a]	27.6	490.6
Banks and insurance	55.0	132.4	n.a.[a]	n.a.[a]	443.0
Foodstuffs	35.0	71.2	121.5	n.a.[a]	478.1
Engineering	57.0	n.a.[a]	158.2	n.a.[a]	n.a.[a]
Chemicals	19.3	43.6	89.7	214.9	n.a.[a]
Trade	40.0	n.a.[a]	147.3	71.7	n.a.[a]
Electronics	22.4	86.2	n.a.[a]	20.0	n.a.[a]
Fuel and energy	n.a.[a]	n.a.[a]	n.a.[a]	56.5	n.a.[a]
All others	20.3	95.9	204.9	27.4	1402.2
Total	568.0	862.4	2558.5	458.0	6039.4
of which manufacturing (in %)[b]	70.0	38.8	37.5	63.0	57.7

n.a. = not available.
[a] Individual statistics not available; included under 'others'.
[b] Data include only the Czech Republic; Slovak enterprises are excluded for the period 1990–2.

Source: Czech National Bank, 1995.

Data about the size distribution of FDI based on the balance of payments statistics are not very detailed. Alongside major foreign investments, there are numerous cases of small and medium-sized foreign investments, as illustrated in Table 6.3. Very small foreign investments (up to 18500 dollars, or 0.5 million korunas) are not recorded in the national bank survey of business activity and are therefore excluded from these statistics. We can assume on the basis of personal observation and informal reports that this figure is made up of a great number of separate small investments. Therefore the average size of these investments must be rather small, often with only the minimum capital requirement of 100 000 korunas.

The volume of FDI grew dramatically, thanks to five large privatization deals. Almost half of the total foreign direct investment comes from these large projects – Skoda-Volkswagen, Tabak-Philip Morris, Cokoladovny-Nestlé, Technoplyn-Linde and SPT Telecom-Telsource, four of which are in manufacturing.

The first large deal was signed in April 1991 between Skoda Mlada Boleslav and Volkswagen. The Volkswagen investment was divided into three stages. The first stage took place in 1991, the second in 1994 and the last in 1995, after which Volkswagen altogether acquired 70 per cent of the equity in Skoda Auto for 0.9 billion dollars. Philip Morris acquired 77 per cent of Tabak Kutna Hora for about 0.5 billion dollars, and Nestlé-BSN 69 per cent of Cokoladovny for 0.2 billion dollars. The largest foreign investment in 1995 was by the Dutch–Swiss consortium Telsource for 27 per cent of SPT Telecom at a price of 1.3 billion dollars.[6]

Altogether, the German-speaking countries (Germany, Switzerland and Austria) represent 50 per cent of the total FDI in the Czech Republic. The EU countries as a whole make up 68 per cent and the OECD countries 97 per cent (see Table 6.4). In 1994 the Czech Republic was

Table 6.3 Size of FDI in the Czech Republic
1 US dollar = 26.55 koruna

Foreign investment ($)	Number of enterprises (% of total)
18500–37000	25.2
37000–370000	22.3
370000–3700000	29.4
3700000–37000000	21.1
> 37 million	2.0

Source: Czech National Bank, 1995; Ministry of Privatization.

Table 6.4   FDI in the Czech Republic by country of origin (per cent)

Country	1990–June 1996
Germany	29.6
USA	14.5
Switzerland	13.7
Netherlands	13.5
France	8.8
Austria	5.8
Other	14.0
Total	100.0

Source: Czech National Bank, 1996.

the sixth most important recipient of all German FDI. With transfers of 1132 million Deutsch marks, by 1994 the Czech Republic became the second largest recipient of German capital of all the Central and Eastern European countries after Hungary. Germany's position as the largest foreign investor remained unchallenged through 1996. The FDI ranking of the Czech Republic's Western neighbours may be even stronger than it appears, because of numerous small foreign investments that are often excluded from statistics. Small foreign business owners often come to the Czech Republic from Austria or Bavaria, with which traditional trade and investment links were recently revived.

In 1994 and 1995 'other' in Table 6.4 included investments from the Bahamas (Stratton Investments), Italy, the European Bank for Reconstruction and Development, the UK, South Korea, Norway and Sweden. After a two-year setback the position of the USA picked up in 1996. A solid presence of French and Austrian investors is in marked contrast with the rather slack performance of Japan. Japanese multinationals have only recently started to show an interest in Central Europe, particularly in the case of greenfield investments involving new infrastructure and facilities.

Foreign and Domestic Enterprises by Sector and Size

In this section, we examine in greater detail the patterns of foreign investment by sector and size, and the investment performance of both foreign and domestic enterprises.

We begin with data from the companies register, which includes the total population of firms from all size categories, with location (address), form of ownership, activity and size (number of employees). It was not feasible from these data to establish how many firms (especially small businesses) were operational.[7]

In order to obtain more information, we used a reduced set of data based on financial statements of output, investment and profit. According to the methodology used by the Czech Statistical Office (no. 8, April 1993), eight types of ownership are distinguished.[8] For our purpose, we divided the enterprises into two groups according to ownership: FIEs, that is enterprises with any foreign participation, and domestic enterprises (all others, both private and state-owned).

First, the analysis was carried out for the whole economy and included all registered enterprises (all sizes and sectors as well as individual entrepreneurs): 1.31 million firms were registered in 1995, of which 32 946 were partly or fully owned by foreigners. The second stage involved non-financial enterprises, of which 365 were under foreign control. This group included enterprises fully owned by foreigners and those in which foreigners had a majority or controlling interest. Our findings confirmed that this group was almost identical to the group of FIEs. We also found that, in most cases, foreign investors preferred to acquire a majority position, and calculated that FIEs were primarily under foreign control (Zemplinerova 1995b). This is supported by the evidence in the section below dealing with foreign investment and privatization.

Our inquiry concluded with an analysis of manufacturing enterprises. At end 1995 there were 2 288 manufacturing businesses (with 100 or more employees), of which 216 were wholly or partly foreign-owned. For the period 1992–4, we have complete balance sheet and export data for all businesses with 25 or more employees. As of 1995, however, the Czech statistical office altered its methodology and started to record balance sheets for enterprises with 100 or more employees, limiting comparability. Since 1995 export data have not been recorded. Hence we have conducted our own analysis of the manufacturing sector for 1994 and of the economy as a whole for 1995. Companies register data also became available in mid-1996.

Our first observation is of startling growth – an increase of 85 per cent in the number of FIEs in just over two years, as compared with an 11 per cent increase for all firms. For firms that are totally foreign-owned, the rate of increase is a dramatic 264 per cent, revealing growing investor confidence in the Czech economy. By mid-1996, 23 721 of the 1 390 459 registered firms were wholly foreign-owned, and another 13 772 partly foreign owned, amounting to 2.7 per cent of all registered firms, up from 1.1 per cent in 1993.

The percentage of foreign enterprises varies considerably according to sector, showing a markedly different pattern of investment from that in domestic businesses. Foreign investment is concentrated in real estate, mining, wholesale trade and services. By June 1996, the percentage of foreign businesses in real estate had reached 11.4 per cent and that in wholesale trade 8.7 per cent (see Table 6.5).

In absolute terms, there are now more than 22 700 FIEs in wholesale and retail trade and in excess of 6500 in manufacturing and construction. There are some 3700 FIEs providing business services and 1400 in real estate. Between 1993 and mid-1996 the number of FIEs increased dramatically in all sectors: it grew six-fold in construction, four-fold in retail, three-fold in real estate, and doubled in manufacturing and transport.

Table 6.5　FIEs in the Czech Republic by industry, 1993 and 1995

	% of total number		Number of foreign enterprises	
	1993	*1995*	*1993*	*1995*
Mining and quarrying	1.54	6.11	16	37
Manufacturing	0.65	1.55	1488	2863
Electrictiy, gas and water supply	0.74	1.07	10	16
Construction	0.33	1.86	574	2647
Sale and repairs of motor vehicles	0.82	0.99	169	235
Wholesale trade	7.40	8.56	4600	11263
Retail trade	1.18	3.37	2491	8578
Hotels and restaurants	0.50	0.93	332	502
Transport, storage, communication	0.78	1.21	374	563
Financial intermediation	2.66	1.93	101	161
Real estate activities	8.04	10.86	438	1201
Renting of machinery	0.34	2.26	68	116
Computer and related activities	1.25	1.71	204	333
Research and development	3.21	4.50	35	30
Other business activities	1.46	1.96	2593	3453
Public administration and defence	0.29	0.01	47	85
Education	0.12	0.56	24	56
Health and social work	3.04	0.21	27	69
Sewage, sanitation, similar activities	1.09	4.80	257	304
Recreation, cultural, sporting activities	0.07	0.12	21	54
Other service activities[a]	0.46	0.38	140	147
Total	1.12	2.51	14052	32946

[a] Includes public administration, extra-territorial organisations and home-based businesses.

Source: Register of Firms, Czech Statistical Office, 1993–5.

Most foreign businesses are small, following a pattern similar to that of domestic enterprises documented in Table 6.6. Only nine companies employed more than 2000 employees and only three foreign companies had more than 5000 employees.

For businesses with 100 or more employees, foreign penetration is highest in the hotel and restaurant sector, where almost a quarter of all employees work for foreign companies (see Tables 6.7 and 6.8). In real estate, trade and other services, foreign employment is also well above average. A similar pattern holds for the share of foreign companies in total output. Even in healthcare and education, where only a small part of the sector is made up of enterprises operating as separate legal units available for investment, foreign businesses accounted for a remarkable 14 per cent of total output. This situation should continue, as FIEs account for a high percentage of total investment, especially in manufacturing, but also in trade, hotels and restaurants and services generally.

Foreign enterprises are more productive and invest more than domestic firms, and also achieve higher value added per employee and pay higher salaries. The profitability of FIEs varies significantly according to sectors and is highest in mining, construction, trade, hotels and restaurants, education and healthcare. These findings are illustrated in Table 6.8.

FIEs in Manufacturing

Foreign manufacturers in the Czech Republic employ 70 per cent of all FIE workers and staff and produce 80 per cent of total FIE output. In 1995, FIEs employed 9.6 per cent of the total workforce in manufacturing companies of more than 100 employees, compared with only 2.6

Table 6.6 Czech Republic: size distribution of enterprises between 1993 and 1996

Number of employees	domestic		foreign	
	1993	1996	1993	1996
1–5	76.37	74.25	76.80	66.61
6–24	10.25	18.67	16.03	23.90
25–99	7.68	5.18	4.94	6.80
100–499	4.41	1.59	1.72	2.22
500–999	0.71	0.19	0.34	0.27
1000 and more	0.57	0.12	0.17	0.20
	100.0	100.0	100.0	100.0

Source: Register of Firms, Czech Statistical Office, 1996.

Table 6.7 Share of FIEs in total workforce, output and other indices by industrial sectors in the Czech Republic, 1995 (per cent)

	Work-force	Output	Wage fund	Own capital	Book VA	Fixed capital	Invest-ment
Mining and quarrying	0.58	0.82	0.53	0.43	0.91	0.45	0.57
Manufacturing	7.88	13.19	9.49	10.90	11.59	10.07	22.04
Construction	1.41	1.92	1.60	2.07	1.84	1.59	1.69
Wholesale, retail trade	8.72	14.16	12.41	5.24	11.52	10.71	24.60
Hotels, restaurants	24.35	24.73	23.39	10.75	21.72	11.70	18.83
Transportation, communication	0.36	3.20	0.69	0.15	2.68	0.16	0.56
Real-estate activities	9.21	12.73	11.46	1.32	9.90	2.27	10.01
Education, healthcare	3.81	13.97	7.18	4.19	14.89	3.72	10.24
Total of above	5.15	8.66	6.23	4.48	7.38	5.00	8.88
Total economy	8.50	11.20	n.a.	n.a.	8.5	n.a.	n.a.

n.a. = not available.

Sources: Czech Statistical Office, 1995, and author's own computation.

per cent in 1992. Their share of output increased from 5.6 per cent to 16.5 per cent. They earned 27 per cent of total manufacturing profits and 27.5 per cent of total manufacturing investment in 1995.

Foreign manufacturing enterprises also restructure faster than enterprises owned solely by domestic investors, getting rid of redundant employees and investing in new technology. FIEs also pay higher average salaries than domestic firms by about 20 per cent, reflecting higher labour productivity and an apparent ability to attract more managers and skilled workers.

On average, capital endowments per employee are also higher in FIEs than in non-foreign enterprises, belying the general opinion that foreign companies invest primarily in low-wage, labour-intensive industries (see Table 6.8). The average rate of depreciation reveals that foreign plant and equipment are usually more modern than that in domestic companies, reflecting a concentration of foreign investment in state-owned enterprises with the most recent equipment.

Labour productivity is markedly higher in firms with foreign capital involvement than in domestic firms, because of both higher capital investment and greater capital efficiency. Foreign enterprises invest four times more per employee than domestic firms and are also major exporters (see Table 6.9).

The role of FIEs differs significantly by industry. The period 1992–4 saw large privatizations that included acquisitions in the automobile

Table 6.8 Comparison of enterprises by ownership and sector in the Czech Republic, 1995 (thousands)

	Output per employee	VA per employee	Average salary	Profit output	Fixed capital per employee	Investment per employee
mining and quarrying						
domestic enterprises	642	321	10306	4.47	1550	92
foreign enterprises	905	503	9349	23.93	1182	91
manufacturing						
domestic enterprises	844	245	7870	3.53	982	58
foreign enterprises	1500	376	9649	3.08	1285	192
construction						
domestic enterprises	819	216	9017	3.63	439	29
foreign enterprises	1123	285	10302	9.46	497	35
wholesale, retail trade						
domestic enterprises	452	209	7442	4.74	950	58
foreign enterprises	781	285	11040	6.96	1194	198
hotels, restaurants						
domestic enterprises	552	231	8313	−0.82	1475	115
foreign enterprises	564	199	7885	0.66	607	83
transportation, communication						
domestic enterprises	434	181	8350	11.90	1295	140
foreign enterprises	3920	1364	15865	3.76	570	216
real estate and like						
domestic enterprises	653	286	9823	9.60	1266	50
foreign enterprises	939	310	12530	5.85	290	54
education, healthcare						
domestic enterprises	531	273	8287	9.25	817	59
foreign enterprises	2179	1208	16206	29.28	797	169
Total						
domestic enterprises	776	253	8254	6.14	1163	95
foreign enterprises	1358	372	10114	3.48	1128	171

Source: Czech Statistical Office, 1995, and author's own computation.

industry (Volkswagen, Steyer Daewoo), food processing and tobacco (Nestlé, Philip Morris, Pepsi-Cola, Bass Breweries), rubber and plastics (Intercontinental), printing and publishing (the majority of newspapers and magazines are owned by foreigners, many of whom have invested heavily in private production facilities), non-metal minerals (Glaverbel-Asahi Glass, Italcementi), chemicals (Linde, Dow chemicals, Procter & Gamble), and electronics (Siemens AG, Asea Brown Boveri).

In 1994 foreign investment expanded into textiles (Marzotto, Shoeller), paper (Assi Doman) and furniture (Lyra). In other industries, the development of foreign involvement was more gradual, occurring

Table 6.9   FIE Share of total employment, output, value added, investment and export of manufacturing in the Czech Republic, 1992–5 (per cent)

	1992	1993	1994	1995
Labour force	2.6	6.2	7.2	9.6
Output	5.6	9.8	11.6	16.5
Fixed assets	3.4	n.a.	10.2	14.9
Value added	4.0	8.2	9.2	19.1
Own capital	n.a.	n.a.	12.6	16.7
Wage fund	3.1	7.4	8.9	11.6
Investment	n.a.	22.4	26.9	27.5
Export	9.9	15.1	16.0	n.a.

n.a. = not available.

Source: Czech Statistical Office, 1995.

through reinvested profits and cash flow retrenchment. This was the case in processed metals, communications, equipment, machinery and wood products. Measured by the share of output and labour force, foreign participation in manufacturing is concentrated in the automobile sector, printing and publishing, rubber and plastics and non-ferrous minerals. A high foreign presence is also reported in electrical equipment and medical instruments.

Thus, FIEs in the Czech Republic are very active in the export market, often considered one of the positive effects of foreign direct investment. And in most manufacturing industries – cars and trucks, rubber and plastics, processed foods and tobacco, as well as electrical equipment and medical instruments – the export market penetration of FIEs is significant. In addition, foreign firms export substantially more than domestic firms: this is most evident in the cases of rubber and plastics, metals, electrical equipment, medical instruments, transportation equipment and furniture and wood products. Three-quarters of all FIEs' sales in apparel, wood products and furniture, and more than half of sales in leather goods and shoes, chemicals, metals, medical equipment, automobiles and furniture are destined for the export market.

FIEs are more productive than domestic businesses, especially in manufacturing, where economies of scale play a large role and foreign investments have been substantial – as in automobiles, chemicals, paper, printing and publishing, and food products and tobacco. The same set of industries also records both high productivity and high levels of investment per employee.

Capital endowments are generally higher in FIEs, particularly in large-scale industries such as paper, printing, publishing, chemicals, non-ferrous metals, automobiles, food products and tobacco. In the more traditional industries, such as textiles, leather products, shoes and machinery, domestic firms have a higher level of capital investment, as well as in newer industries such as business machines and recycling.

Government Policy Towards FDI

Over the last few years, the Czech government has taken the position that the best way to encourage economic development is to provide a stable economic and political environment, and to liberalize key regulations that have slowed the formation or expansion of business activity.[9] In the long run, it is assumed that this approach will create and maintain a climate conducive to sustained economic growth and mitigate risks.

After the first free elections of 1990, the Czech government experimented with a variety of investment subsidies – as in the Skoda–VW venture – with mixed success. The programmes were expensive, and the company results rarely as promised. They also created a climate of favouritism, which discouraged competitors. After the June 1992 elections, the new government adopted a significant policy shift, aiming instead for a 'level playing field' of stability and equal opportunity for all entrepreneurs, domestic and foreign. We can expect this approach towards foreign business to remain unchanged in the foreseeable future.

This is good news for investors, as the Czech Republic has attained a solid foundation of stability, both politically and economically. The country continues its reintegration with the developed world market through macroeconomic stabilization and the orientation of its trade towards the European Union market. At the time of writing (1997), the Czech Republic was the only post-communist country with an investment grade rating for government bonds from Moody's Investors' Service, a Baa 1 grade (as of November 1995), a BBB+ from Standard and Poor's and an A rating from the Japanese Bond Research Institute. According to the *Institutional Investor* magazine, the Czech Republic is ranked 13 out of 135 countries in terms of creditworthiness.

With a low level of foreign debt and high foreign reserves, the Czech Republic is enjoying somewhat easier access to international capital markets than other Central European countries. It also has a relatively highly skilled labour force, a strong work ethic and a long tradition of industrialization, which preceded the communist era. Because of this the Czechs do not feel the same pressing need for foreign investment as some of their Central European neighbours, and have had fewer problems sourcing managerial skills and technology from the domestic market.

But even though foreign direct investment may not be deemed crucial to the successful transformation and privatization *per se*, it is expected that foreign investors will play a significant role in restructuring enterprises. In the medium term – once equity markets are operating efficiently – the Czech Republic should become readily integrated into international capital markets.

At present, foreign investors can become owners of a company by:
- purchasing shares on the stock exchange;
- participating in tenders for shares;
- purchasing shares directly from the property's owners;
- participating directly in a new stock issue; and
- setting up a greenfield subsidiary.

Under the current law, foreign persons and legal entities can conduct business in the Czech Republic on equal terms with Czech investors with a few minor exceptions, where special provisions apply.

The Czech Republic has set no upper limit to the level of foreign investment or ownership; other than in banking and insurance, no state approval is required for the establishment of a corporate body with foreign participation. The repatriation of profits and capital abroad is guaranteed through various foreign currency and investment protection agreements. Foreigners can also freely repatriate any foreign assets in the form of commercial paper, bonds or other securities in foreign currency that relate to their business activities in the country.

There are very few special incentives[10] for foreign investors; in fact, some protective measures were enacted in recent legislation in an attempt to strengthen the position of domestic firms. One new regulation introduced in 1995 requires that foreign firms underbid domestic firms by 10 per cent in order to win a public contract bid. An amendment to the Trades Licensing Act in November 1995 set a deadline of 31 December 1996 for all representatives of foreign companies (joint-stock, limited-liability or subsidiary-office) to receive work and residence permits, prove unimpeachable character, and demonstrate proficiency in the Czech language.

The equal treatment standard has been set aside in the case of certain large and prestigious FDI projects – but at the regional, rather than the national, level. Recently, Matsushita decided to invest 66 million dollars in a plant at Pilsen for the assembly of Panasonic TV sets. Although the

Czech government refused to provide special incentives for the Japanese investor, the local Pilsen government not only sold the land (17 hectares) at below market price (11.5 dollars per square metre), but also agreed to install the necessary infrastructure valued at some 4 million dollars, as part of a planned industrial zone in the area. It also agreed to provide assistance with training employees, public transportation links, and housing for Japanese staff. The Czech producers of television sets (Tesla TV), which control 20 per cent of the domestic market, feel threatened by the Matsushita project, because of what they perceive as 'the unfair legislative relief conceded to the Japanese'.

Although Matsushita promises to cooperate with Czech suppliers, some experts have expressed doubts, as Czech parts producers lack the skills and experience of foreign competitors. The expectation is that the new plant will be an assembly line for imported parts, preferentially imported under a tariff shield; a six-year tariff deferment has also been discussed.

The Czech legal environment is still in its infancy: it is over-regulated and often bureaucratic. Laws are often difficult to interpret and burdened with inconsistencies and loopholes. Many informal codes of ethical or corporate behaviour are missing altogether or are going through a slow process of evolution. In addition, the state judiciary infrastructure is overburdened to the point of paralysis, lacking both the human and financial capital necessary to enforce either statutes or contracts.

FDI and Privatization

From the outset in 1991, privatization has been considered the key to the transformation of the economy. It began with the restitution and privatization of small-scale assets, now complete except for a few restitution claims being settled through the Ministry of Finance. For large privatization projects, the Czech Republic has combined standard methods[11] with voucher privatization.

The large-scale privatization programme involved property valued in excess of 930 billion korunas (35 billion dollars) over 5 to 6 years, of which about a third was done through voucher privatization (see below). Out of this property list, 93 per cent was privatized by the end of 1995. Today (1997), the Czech economy has the largest share of private ownership in Eastern Europe – between 60 and 80 per cent depending on the source and methodology of data-gathering.

Institutionally privatization has been handled primarily through the National Property Fund, the Ministry of Privatization, and other economic branch ministries. Recently the Ministry of Privatization was closed and the National Property Fund became the government's repository for state shares and only institution responsible for the final stages of the privatization process. In some cases, the administration of state shares has been delegated to the Ministry of Economy and Trade.

The programme's goal was to privatize about 80 per cent of the country's assets by mid-1996, with the goal of achieving a ratio of private to state-owned entities similar to that of developed market economies. Postal and telecommunications services have been separated, with the former remaining under government control, and other telecommunications activities and services being partially privatized. Of these, 27 per cent are held by foreign investors. Public utilities have also attracted foreign interest. Recently, it was decided that banks and financial intermediaries would also be privatised. So far, 30 to 45 per cent of shares in these financial institutions have been sold under the voucher privatization programme, while the remainder are held by the National Property Fund.

Natural resources and most traditional public utilities will remain in the public sector. Nevertheless, general disillusion with central planning, state ownership and the role of the state bureaucracy has led to a refusal to accept any coordinating role for the state in guiding economic activity. This has lent support to an important faction of politicians and economists advocating the extension of privatization to almost every type of economic activity, including public utilities such as electric power, transportation, education and healthcare. If implemented, these would result in more far-reaching privatization programmes than in some established market economies.

Privatization and Foreign Investors

Although foreign participation represents only 1.2 per cent of all projects submitted, foreign investors have been the source of more than half of all proceeds from large-scale privatization (in all a total of $4.6 billion). Because of investment commitments over the next few years, foreign investment is expected to become an increasingly important factor in company restructuring. Given the penalties for non-fulfilment of contracts, foreign investor privatizations have been closely monitored by the National Property Fund and other official bodies, and most commitments so far have been fulfilled. Table 6.10 illustrates the size of foreign investment commitments at end-1995.

Table 6.10 Size of foreign investments in Czech privatization

Value of privatization transaction (US $m.)	% of total number of transactions
< 1	6.9
1–5	30.6
5–10	19.4
10–20	21.5
20–50	13.9
50–100	4.2
> than 100	3.5
Total	100

Source: Ministry of Privatization, 1996.

A total of 315 privatization projects involving in excess of 200 enterprises with proposed foreign participation were submitted. Of these, 144 with a total transaction value of $4.2 billion were approved. The remaining privatization projects either were turned down by the Czech authorities or collapsed as the foreign partners withdrew, often losing interest in the lengthy negotiation process. The average purchase price has been close to book value, but the market to book value ratio ranges widely, between 0.5 and 4.5.

Projects with foreign participation have been subject to particular scrutiny and, as they affect the best enterprises, have tended to be controversial. In evaluating projects with foreign investment, specific attention has been paid to both the deal structure (debts versus equity, plans to increase equity) and social issues such as employment and environmental protection. Newly privatized companies have normally taken over the obligations of the former enterprise, including environmental liabilities.

A standard purchase contract form and two separate standard contracts for the sale of assets (enterprise purchase agreement) and equity (share purchase agreement) are in circulation. These have been helpful in unifying contractual conditions and improving and accelerating the negotiation process. As a rule, foreign investors are given the standard contracts at the initial meeting to highlight the relevant business and legal issues of privatization in the Czech Republic. Negotiations would follow before the project is submitted for review to the Approval Commission. These standard agreements have been continually updated to reflect new governmental resolutions and policies.

The process of privatizing a company through the National Property Fund varies in duration from several months to more than a year. The bid may be initiated by submitting a takeover intention to the relevant ministry, which may tender out for competing projects. The procedure requires the approval of the Ministry of Privatization. Other government authorities may also be consulted, including the Council of Economic Ministers, the Ministry of Finance and the Ministry of Economic Competition. To accomplish this, a thorough review of business plans, financial statements, environmental audits and other relevant information must be conducted. Successful bids often involve commitments by the foreign firm to invest, train management and employees, improve the environment and provide new technology and access to export markets. Pricing policy, remuneration strategy and guarantees to preserve domestic competition are other important considerations.[12] Table 6.11 shows that foreign investors prefer majority ownership of the shareholding: over 88 per cent of all investors acquired majority ownership.

The National Property Fund and Privatization

By the end of 1995, the National Property Fund held equity positions in some 1500 Czech companies. In 410 – nearly a third – it held an interest above 20 per cent, including 38 companies where it was the sole owner. In another 94 companies it held more than two-thirds of the stock; in 80 companies it had a majority interest, and, in another 100 companies, a qualified minority of more than 34 per cent. In yet another 1000-plus firms, it held up to 20 per cent of the equity.

The Czech state ultimately intends to privatize much of the aforementioned portfolio, but will probably continue to hold permanent or provisional stakes in about 228 of the 410 companies referred to above. Of the 228 companies, 58 companies have been selected as 'strategic': these are mainly in finance, energy, mining, metallurgy, chemicals and transportation, as well as telecommunications and healthcare.

Table 6.11   Stakes acquired by foreign investors in Czech privatization

% acquired	% of transactions
1–30	4.9
31–50	6.9
51–70	32.6
71–99	21.5
100	34.1
Total	100.0

Source: Ministry of Privatization, 1996.

Privatization and Restructuring

In most cases, the government has avoided restructuring enterprises prior to privatization, leaving it to the new owners to reorganize as they have judged best. In cases where companies were sold outright to foreign investors, as with Skoda or Cokoladovny, control was transferred immediately to the new owners and/or managers, who rapidly began improving company performance. By contrast, if the ownership remains ill-defined, with neither direct state control nor effective private owners, the restructuring can be delayed and necessary changes slow in coming.

The acquisition of the chocolate producer Cokoladovny by Nestlé/BSN is a good example of restructuring by a foreign owner. Following privatization, the Cokoladovny-Nestlé/BSN company headquarters were completely reorganized with a new emphasis on marketing and sales. First, a marketing department was established to provide market research, new product ideas and improvements in packaging. For instance, the company decreased its number of candy varieties from 500 to 150 to market them more effectively.

Second, there was a new focus on human resources and training. The company restructured the personnel department and provided better training. It also prepared a social programme to improve the working environment and help prepare workers for lay-offs arising from job duplication. The new management also initiated a major campaign to improve communication within the company: by giving workers more insight into company planning and development, it sought to increase their motivation. With this programme in mind, Czech middle managers are sent abroad for training.

Third, the company centralized all materials purchasing from domestic suppliers and importers.

Fourth, the company separated the sales operation from both distribution and logistics and set up a local sales network and four regional distribution warehouses to improve the efficiency of product delivery. Previously, customers were resupplied monthly by each production unit with an often incomplete range of goods. Now, the company is able to deliver virtually the entire assortment (90 selected products, representing 80 per cent of sales) every two weeks. The sales department was increased from 10 to 200 employees, reflecting an increase in the number of clients and a new emphasis on improving customer service.

Fifth, the company created two production-management divisions at headquarters for chocolates and non-chocolate sweets, for which there are eight production locations; and for biscuits, with seven.

Sixth, the company installed a new computer network with Nestlé management software; new cost control modules now generate complete financial profiles on individual plants.

Once the management changes were in place, the objective was to replace the former top-down management with a more horizontal, collaborative approach preferred by Western managers. Plants receive targets for quantity, quality, efficiency and production deadlines. Financially, the plants are accountable only for operating within a budget; they are not responsible for pricing their endproduct, nor do they deal with marketing or market research. Investments are focused on concentrating production, increasing specialization and adjusting capacities to market size.

Nestlé estimates that productivity has been improved by some 25 per cent through the more efficient use of existing resources, better management and higher capacity utilization. Having learned the specifics of their new business as a result of these changes, Nestlé committed themselves to additional large capital injections.

Privatization and Monopoly

Before 1990, the supply of most commodities was controlled by a handful of Czech state enterprises, and monopoly was a general phenomenon in the economy (Zemplinerova 1995b). The centrally planned system set up numerous administrative and legal barriers isolating industries from external competition and regulating the entry and exit of firms. Since 1990, the legal restrictions that institutionalized the monopoly control of various industries have been relaxed, and the market pressure for rational economic behaviour is expected to increase. In general, firms are getting smaller, both through the break-up of large state enterprises prior to and during privatization, and through the spontaneous, explosive growth of small independent businesses.

In January 1991 parliament passed the Competition Protection Act. The law is similar to EU legislation and the German Anti-Cartel Law; it has been amended twice since 1991. The Ministry of Economic Competition, which had jurisdiction for this law, will now be turned into an independent agency.

During privatization, the Ministry was empowered to approve each privatization project with a view to reducing industry concentration. The heavy volume of privatization projects led to administrative overload and serious delays. In market economies, antimonopoly (anti-trust) offices usually deal with tens of cases per year. In the Czech Republic, as in other transitional economies, there were hundreds of enterprises with market shares exceeding 30 per cent. Therefore, the Ministry chose to rely more extensively on direct methods of demonopolization, by removing entry barriers and creating a favourable climate for fair competition.

In such a small country, the legal system and regulatory ministries are necessarily relatively weak vehicles for maintaining a competitive environment. To date, the application process for merger approval has not been frequently used.

During privatization, the government was usually faced with a choice of selling the monopoly control of an entire market to one foreign investor, or breaking up the enterprise for the benefit of a particular investor. There are no clear guidelines as to the most appropriate way to handle this, although the development of competitive markets is certainly an important consideration. In evaluating the Czech FDI record to date, it seems that in several cases it might have been preferable to have set a lower initial purchase price for the company, and to have strengthened the free market by refusing the high levels of protection that so dampen competition. However, this can still be done. By opening up the Czech economy to foreign trade and improving conditions for the growth of new firms, some of the more important market sectors should gradually adjust of their own accord.

Conclusions

Although foreign penetration in the Czech Republic (as measured by the level of foreign direct investment) is still limited in comparison with that in open-market economies of a similar size, it is increasing steadily. In manufacturing, the share of FIEs in the total work force increased to almost 10 per cent in 1995 from 2.6 per cent in 1992. Although foreign companies account for over 20 per cent of manufacturing employment, foreign involvement in the Czech Republic is about half of that in developed market economies. Real GNP growth was about 5 per cent in 1995 and the economy is expected to continue growing in the future. Although inflation has been curbed to single figures, salaries are growing at about 17 per cent a year. The recent increases in the foreign trade and current account deficits call for compensating growth in foreign direct investment to finance these deficits in a more stable way than more mobile capital would provide.

The Economist Intelligence Unit expects this 'catch-up' to continue, and estimates that the amount of FDI to the Czech Republic during 1996-2000 will reach 15.5 billion dollars. Nevertheless, the real FDI inflows, and by implication the expansion of FIEs in the Czech Republic, can significantly differ from this forecast depending on economic growth rates, the balance of payments situation, exchange rate and trade policies, labour cost developments, taxation, the existence of bureaucratic obstacles to investment, and the progress of integration to the European Union. New foreign investment will also be influenced by outstanding government privatization decisions.

Prior to 1995, the main source of FDI was privatization. FDI amounted to 1.4 billion dollars in 1996, down from 2.6 billion the previous year. This was primarily because of the absence of large deals such as the Telecom privatization of 1995. Large-scale privatization is essentially over, although there are some existing investment commitments which should come to fruition over the next few years.

Privatization has generally slowed down. Future inflows of foreign investment arising from privatization will depend on developments in the banking sector, the utilities and strategic sector enterprises. There are also large outstanding blocks of shares in state hands that could be privatized. The Ministry of Industry and Trade, for example, administers holdings that will probably be privatized, at least partly, in the future. These include raw materials industries, such as coal mines and steel works, and a variety of manufacturing enterprises. Holdings in the oil giant Unipetrol and other energy distributing enterprises are also likely to be partly privatised.

The bulk of future FDI is likely to be channelled into modernizing and restructuring companies that have already been privatized, or into greenfield investments. The analysis above has shown a sizeable level of investment activity by FIEs in the Czech economy. The foreign managers of these projects are planning for the long term and are developing strategies for beyond the turn of the century. Domestic investors have so far not paid much attention to strategy or long-term planning; instead, they have directed their efforts towards acquiring operational control. They also face the additional problem of how to finance such a strategy and carry the responsibility of repaying or servicing a heavy debt burden. Foreign companies usually have both the expertise and the financial means for their strategic and restructuring objectives. Foreign investors have also helped establish the small-business sector, which did not exist at the beginning of the transformation process.

Notes

1 The stock exchange opened in spring 1993, and the shares of more than 600 companies were originally traded, primarily companies privatized in the

voucher privatization. Voucher shares that do not qualify for the stock exchange are traded in the 'over-the-counter-market', which was based on the technology originally developed to implement bidding in voucher privatization.

2 The origin of portfolio investment at the end of 1995 was as follows: UK 50 per cent, USA 22 per cent, Germany 6 per cent, Slovakia 5 per cent (voucher privatization holdings excluded), Austria 5 per cent, Cyprus 3 per cent and other countries 9 per cent. The industrial structure of portfolio investment in 1995 was as follows: banking (including government bonds mediated through the Czech national bank) 54 per cent, energy 17 per cent, transport 17 per cent, construction 3 per cent and other industries 9 per cent.

3 In 1994 250 million dollars' worth of Prague town hall bonds were sold abroad, as well as 126 million dollars of Eurobonds held by the Czech national bank.

4 The sectoral structure is too aggregated, and detailed information was not available from the Czech national bank.

5 'All others' in Table 6.2 includes not only services and transport but also machinery, electronics and other manufacturing industries.

6 There was a disinvestment in the case of Air France, when the state repurchased Air France's share in CSA.

7 Recent results from the Panel Peco Project, published by the Czech statistical office (1996), assessed the quality of the companies register in the Czech Republic. According to this analysis, 36 per cent of units in the Register are non-active. The most frequent reason for non-operation was closure (57 per cent).

8 • *Foreign ownership:* unit established by a foreign physical or legal unit, non-resident of the Czech Republic, owning 100 per cent of assets (total equity).
   • *International ownership:* joint ventures established jointly by domestic and foreign units, that is units with domestic and foreign capital (enterprises with any foreign contribution, with the exception of total equity).
   • *Private ownership* of private domestic physical or legal units.
   • *Cooperatives.*
   • *State ownership*: units of public administration, enterprises founded by the ministries or other central administrative bodies, or other institutions set up from state sources, joint stock companies where the state is the only shareholder.
   • *Municipal ownership.*
   • *Non-governmental organizations*: ownership of parties, associations and church.
   • *Mixed ownership* of more than one domestic founder with a mixed ownership. Mixed ownership is a combination of private and state ownership. In 1994 some large firms were still under this indeterminate arrangement.

9 Among the comparative advantages that have attracted foreign investors to the Czech Republic are more than 150 years of established industrial tradition, the high technical skills of the workforce, a steep learning curve, a stabilized political climate and long-lasting experience with parliamentary democracy, acquired in the 1920s and 1930s, a European cultural heritage, social peace and a favourable geographical position.

10 As of 21 July 1993 joint venture companies in the Czech Republic, with at least 30 per cent foreign ownership (equalling no less than 1.7 million dollars), were allowed one year's exemption from customs duties on raw materials or semi-processed goods imported through the foreign partner for manufacturing. The law, intended to encourage new companies, was valid for established enterprises until July 1994 or, in the case of new enterprises, for one year after their foundation.

11 Restitution to original owners or their heirs; sale of property to domestic or foreign investors through public auctions and tenders; direct sale to a designated owner; transformation into a joint-stock company with the subsequent sale of shares; and free transfer of property to the municipalities.

12 The assessment is usually carried out by an independent international real estate company or a team of foreign advisors paid by the Czech government. Though relatively free of corruption, this process has been criticized for being bureaucratic, subjective and slow.

7
Poland

Wladyslaw Jermakowicz

Although Poland has been a recipient of foreign direct investment (FDI) since 1976, the real acceleration in FDI began after the first free elections of June 1989 and the 'Big Bang – Balcerowicz Programme' of January 1990. These political and economic factors influenced the new FDI legislation and dramatically improved the business climate.

Over the past nine years, the number of new firms with foreign participation has grown considerably. The evolution of FDI went through various phases. We examine in turn the influx, origin, and strategy of FDI, and use a well-established investment-development-path model to determine whether Poland's FDI development fits within a more global pattern.

The Investment-Development-Path Model

John Dunning (1993c) has developed an investment-development-path model that corresponds to three types of adjustment mechanisms. Taking into account Narula's contribution, this model comprises four stages: factor-driven, domestic-investment driven, export-investment driven, and innovation-driven (see Table 7.1; Dunning and Narula 1993).

The Factor-Driven Stage

At this stage nations draw their advantages mostly by mobilizing an abundance of basic and inexpensive factors. Little technology is created locally, and domestic firms use imported technology mostly through licensing and joint ventures. Factor-driven development is supported by a relatively low level of inward investment and, more importantly, by subcontracting and outward processing. Usually a large number of small firms arise: joint ventures and minority foreign investment are dominant. Traditional industries based on local resources are prevalent.

The Domestic-Investment-Driven Stage

This stage is dominated by investment in manufacturing standardized products for the domestic market. Domestic market conditions, buttressed by import-substitution policies, are dominant with regards to balance of payments constraints. Inward FDI through direct acquisitions develops as a major source of technology transfer.

The Export-Investment-Driven Stage

At this stage, advanced factor conditions attract investments to the export-driven mass production of medium-technology products. Inward FDI increasingly concentrates on economies of scale, because low labour costs are no longer sufficient grounds for establishing local production. Growth measured by the number of FDI slows down as the ownership advantages of MNEs *vis-à-vis* domestic firms weaken. The average size of firms is high. Firms enter the market with global investment strategies. Greenfield inward investments predominate.

The Innovation-Driven Stage

During this stage the national innovation system reaches a level of maturity that enables the economy not only to appropriate and improve from foreign locations but also to create its own innovations. The bulk of inward investment now seeks strategic assets through applied and basic research. Outward investment grows rapidly, and inward and outward investment become increasingly complimentary. Thus, the national innovation system becomes the main source of a country's competitive advantage, systematically acquired through generating new knowledge and technological capabilities.

Historical Development of FDI in Poland

Calculating inward FDI in Poland is fraught with difficulty. The Polish State Foreign Investment Agency publishes data only for large firms with investments exceeding $1 million, while the Polish Statistical Office's data sources are not always reliable or comparable. In this chapter, data from the Ministry of Privatization and the State Foreign Investment Agency will be used.

Table 7.1 includes data for all firms as well as large firms with investments exceeding a million dollars. The data for all firms come from the Ministry of Privatization for 1987–96; for larger firms, the source is the

Table 7.1 Investment-development-path model

Investment strategy stage	Characteristics of firms	Strategy seeking	Entry modes
Factor-driven	Large number of small firms	Resources Cost efficiency	Licensing Joint ventures Subcontracting
Domestic-Investment driven	Limited number of average size firms	Domestic market	Inward direct investment Direct acquisition
Export-investment driven	Limited number of large firms	Foreign market	Inward direct investment Greenfields
Innovation-driven	Investment in R&D institutes	Human capital R&D assets	Inward direct investment equals outward direct investment; non-equity

Sources: Dunning (1993a), Dunning and Narula (1993).

Polish State Foreign Investment Agency for 1989–96. While at the beginning of the period large investments were practically non-existent, by 1996 they constituted 93 per cent of all investments.

Poland has experienced increasing FDI inflows since 1987: in 1988 it played host to a mere 30 investments with a total capital value of 6880 dollars; in 1989, 518 foreign firms invested 96410 dollars (Table 7.2). The ten-fold increase in capital and joint ventures in 1988 was exceeded the following year, when the number of joint ventures increased by a factor of 16.7 and capital by 13.7. Such growth levels clearly could not be sustained in the medium term.

The second wave of FDI growth occurred in 1992, when new laws and economic reforms gave foreign investors the security needed to enter the Polish market. In 1992 the amount of invested capital tripled over the previous year. The average size of firms with foreign participation more than doubled, and the share of large firms exceeding 1 million dollars was over 50 per cent of all investment.

The third wave of inward FDI took off in 1995, when the value of annual investment nearly doubled in comparison with 1994, accumulated capital grew 1.5 times, and the ratio of large investments to all investments exceeded 80 per cent. The stock of small firms with capital below a million dollars became marginal. By 1996 the total value of inward FDI exceeded 12.5 billion dollars.

The statistical data on FDI to Poland confirm the usefulness of Dunning's investment-development-path model. The first wave resembled a

Table 7.2 FDI stock and flows to Poland, 1987–96

	Growth of FDI by number		Growth of FDI by capital ($)			Average size of firm (%)			
	Number	Accumulate	Capital	Accumulate	Dynamic %	Large	$ in all %	Yearly	Accumulate
1987	3	3	696	696			0	232.0	232.0
1988	30	33	6 880	7 576	1 089		0	229.3	229.6
1989	518	551	96 413	103 989	1 373	8 000	8	186.1	188.7
1990	1 493	2 044	204 458	308 447	297	97 000	47	136.9	150.9
1991	3 125	5 169	425 096	733 543	238	219 000	52	136.0	141.9
1992	3 456	8 625	1 500 645	2 234 188	305	1 084 000	72	434.2	259.0
1993	4 179	12 804	2 014 657	4 248 845	190	1 633 000	81	482.1	331.8
1994	4 023	16 827	1 675 437	5 924 282	139	1 280 000	76	416.5	352.1
1995	3 421	20 248	3 045 874	8 970 156	151	2 511 000	82	890.3	443.0
1996	3 654	23 902	3 578 942	12 549 098	140	3 323 000	93	979.5	525.0

Source: Author's own calculations based on data from the Ministry of Privatization.

typical factor-driven stage: during this period the Polish advantage lay in the abundance of cheap raw materials and an inexpensive labour force. Local firms provided infrastructure, buildings, labour and materials, while foreign partners supplied the capital and technology. At this stage a relatively low level of inward investment was observable. The second wave resembled the domestic-investment-driven stage, with large firms exceeding 50 per cent of all FDI. Average-sized firms grew and the import of technology became more visible. The third wave witnessed export-investment-driven activities: large firms with a clearly global approach prevailed. As yet, there is no sign of the beginning of the fourth stage in FDI development.

Greenfield vs. Acquisitions

A foreign company's decision to invest abroad involves selecting the most appropriate investment mode. This decision depends largely on the investor's motives and the nature of the industry. There are three basic investment modes: greenfield investment, indirect acquisition (via joint ventures) and direct acquisition (through the purchasing of shares in local companies). The last mode is used most frequently in the privatization process.

Table 7.3 illustrates the changes in the structure of investment modes between 1988 and 1996. Although the value of all modes of investment significantly increased, the proportions of greenfields and privatizations changed most over these years.

Table 7.3   Greenfield investment, indirect and direct acquisitions in Poland, 1987–96

Year	Greenfield		Indirect acquisition		Direct acquisition		Total	
	000's $	%	000's $	%	000's $	%	000's $	%
1987	82	11.8	614	88.2	0	0.0	696	100
1988	1 686	24.5	5 194	75.5	0	0.0	6 880	100
1989	26 514	27.5	54 399	56.4	15 500	16.1	96 413	100
1990	58 066	28.4	91 266	44.6	55 126	27.0	204 458	100
1991	126 254	29.7	126 796	29.8	172 046	40.5	425 096	100
1992	454 695	30.3	398 673	26.6	647 277	43.1	1 500 645	100
1993	689 013	34.2	276 853	13.7	1 048 791	52.1	2 014 657	100
1994	646 719	38.6	187 541	11.2	841 177	50.2	1 675 437	100
1995	1 495 524	49.1	165 436	5.4	1 384 914	45.5	3 045 874	100
1996	1 800 208	50.3	152 365	4.3	1 626 369	45.4	3 578 942	100
Total	5 298 759	42.2	1 459 137	11.6	57 912 014	46.1	12 549 098	100

Source: Author's own calculations based on data from the Ministry of Privatization.

First, an impressive increase in greenfield investment flows is observable: from only 82 000 dollars in 1987 to 1.8 billion at end 1996. This suggests an increase in confidence in the Polish market and a growing willingness to start new ventures.

A second observable trend is the increase in receipts from direct acquisitions: from 15.5 million dollars in 1989 (16.1 per cent of all inward investment) to 1.6 billion (or 45.4 per cent of the FDI total) in 1996.

Third, there has been a decline in the number of joint ventures (4.3 per cent in 1996): this suggests that greenfield investments and privatizations have become more attractive modes of entry.

Fourth, greenfield investments have grown relatively faster than direct-acquisition (privatization) investments. Although privatization made up over half of all FDI in 1994, I believe that greenfield investments are now set to increase at a faster rate than privatizations. Poland has already privatized its most attractive enterprises, and privatization is meeting increased resistance among the population. Adding to the interest in greenfield investments is the growing investor confidence in political stability and the potential for high returns.

The role of greenfield investment is even more impressive in terms of the number of enterprises. In 1995, 10 422 greenfield investments constituted 88.3 per cent of all FDI, compared with 1115 indirect acquisitions (9.4 per cent of foreign investors) and 266 direct acquisitions (a mere 2.3 per cent of all cases). In terms of capital invested, however, direct acquisitions have contributed 30 per cent more capital than have greenfields.

Investors acquiring Polish firms in the framework of privatization between 1989 and 1993 contributed 1 938 741 million dollars, or 45.6 per cent of total FDI. But the average foreign share in capitalization per firm differed significantly: greenfield investments amounted to only 130 100 dollars per firm, joint ventures 855 400 dollars (nearly six times more) and direct acquisitions 7 288 500 dollars (56 times more). Greenfield investments involved mostly small investments in retail premises; by contrast, direct acquisitions comprised mostly large firms.

Table 7.4 compares the modes of market penetration in selected East European countries. Foreign investors entering the Polish market have chosen greenfield investments more often than their counterparts in other post-communist countries (32.9 per cent vs. 17 per cent). This is partly the result of Poland's more liberal investment climate. Table 7.4 also shows that indirect acquisitions through joint ventures have been more prevalent elsewhere in Eastern Europe (50 per cent against 22.4 per

Table 7.4 FDI distribution by types of investment in Eastern Europe, December 1993

	Number	%	Capital $	%	Average size of firm ($)
Mode of investment in Poland					
Greenfield	10 422	88.3	1 356 309	32.9	130.1
Indirect acquisition	1 115	9.4	953 795	22.4	855.4
Direct acquisition	266	2.3	1 938 741	45.6	7 288.5
Total	11 803	100.0	4 248 845	100.0	164.3
Mode of investment in the Russian Federation					
Greenfield	2 077	26.0	31 525	1.0	15.2
Indirect acquisition	5 672	71.0	2 774 816	88.0	489.2
Direct acquisition	240	3.0	346 852	11.0	1 447.2
Total	7 989	100.0	3 153 200	100.0	394.7
Mode of investment in the Czech Republic					
Greenfield	1 650	33.0	102 650	5.0	62.2
Indirect acquisition	1 650	33.0	656 960	32.0	398.2
Direct acquisition	1 700	34.0	1 293 390	63	760.8
Total	5 000	100.0	2 053 000	100.0	410.6
Mode of investment in Hungary					
Greenfield	6 011	28.0	1 741 653	29.0	289.7
Indirect acquisition	7 728	36.0	2 162 052	36.0	279.8
Direct acquisition	7 728	36.0	2 101 995	35.0	272.0
Total	21 468	100.0	6 005 700	100.0	279.8
Mode of investment in CEE					
Greenfield	9 738	28.0	1 875 835	17.0	192.6
Indirect acquisition	15 051	44.0	5 593 828	50.0	371.7
Direct acquisition	9 668	28.0	3 742 237	33.0	387.1
Total	34 457	100.0	11 211 900	100.0	325.4

Source: Author's own calculations based on data from the Ministry of Privatization.

cent in Poland). This would suggest that the Polish economy has entered a more mature stage in terms of attracting FDI, as joint ventures are normally associated with infant economies.

In the Russian Federation joint ventures predominate, and greenfield investments are negligible: this supports the argument that high risk levels have prompted foreign firms to take the shared-risk approach offered by joint ventures. In the Czech Republic, the extensive voucher privatization schemes have encouraged direct acquisitions. Hungary's position bears similarities to that of Poland, with one exception: a higher share of joint ventures. The investment-path model thus suggests that in 1993 Russia was still at stage i, while the Czech Republic,

Hungary and Poland were entering stage ii. Since 1996 Poland has entered stage III, with neighbouring countries being expected to follow suit (with the exception of Russia).

Majority and Minority Stakes

Table 7.5 shows the relationship between acquisitions and greenfield investments in terms of equity ownership. The general trend suggests an investor preference for majority holdings, although some discrepancies occur between greenfield and acquisition-type investments.

The past nine years have witnessed a radical increase in majority interests (from 9.6 per cent in 1988 to 79.6 per cent in 1996. The first stage (1988–92) was characterized by minority foreign involvement, with the exception of larger firms entering the market as greenfield investments (such as Intercell, Sigma and Hyatt Regency). Foreign acquisitions dominated the second period (1993–5), when both acquisitions and greenfield investments helped secure foreign majority control. In the third period (1996 onwards), greenfield investments have shown steady growth; at the same time, a surprising decline in foreign acquisitions has also been observed.

Sectoral Patterns of FDI

The FDI stock shifted between sectors in the first two years of the transition (1990–1), when foreign investors faced high levels of uncertainty and essential changes took place in target industries for FDI. During 1992–4, a gradual level of stabilization was introduced; since 1994, sectoral stabilization has occurred.

Table 7.5   FDI distribution in Poland by Foreign capital shares, 1988, 1993 and 1996

Foreign share in capital (%)	Total		Foreign acquisitions		Greenfield investments	
	50% and less	*51% and more*	*50% and less*	*51% and more*	*50% and less*	*51% and more*
1988	90.4	9.6	100	0	39.1	60.9
1993	28.9	71.1	43.3	56.7	26.9	73.1
1996	20.4	79.6	57.6	42.4	17.3	82.7
Total	60.4	39.6	64.4	35.6	26.3	73.7

Source: Author's own calculations based on data from the Ministry of Privatization.

Table 7.6 shows that the two highest-ranked sectors (in technological terms) (1 and 2) received the smallest portions of FDI (about 10 per cent) in the first period. Sector 3, characterized by low human and physical capital, was dominant, and included such industries as footwear, clothing, metals, and furniture. FDI in this period was attracted by location advantages. During this factor-driven stage – dominated by subcontracting – access to resources and low production costs motivated foreign investors.

The second period was export-driven: sector 4 including such industries as motor vehicles and textiles, became dominant, with low human capital but high physical capital. The principal reason for the strong performance of sector 4 was the drive to capture the strongest share of the domestic market. Investment into scale-based industries attracted less investment, not because of cost–efficiency considerations, but rather because of lagging demand for standardized, mass-consumption products (Kubielas 1996).

In the third period, a clear increase in human-capital-related sectors (sectors 1 and 5) seems to indicate that export-driven factors are gradually beginning to dominate.

Origin of Investors

A comparison of FDI over time shows important changes not only in the size of invested capital but also in the ranking of different countries. In the first period, the most striking trend is the dominance of countries

Table 7.6 Sectoral distribution of FDI in Poland, 1990–5

	Sector	1990	1991	1992	1993	1994	1995	1990–5 % point change
Stock structure in %	1	1.9	15.3	12.8	12.6	21.5	18.4	+16.5
	2	8.5	19.2	14.9	11.8	14.1	17.4	+8.9
	3	64.4	22.2	17.0	11.8	11.5	12.5	−51.9
	4	6.3	30.2	21.5	37.1	35.3	30.5	+24.2
	5	19.0	13.1	33.7	26.7	17.6	21.2	+2.3
Flow structure in %	1	1.1	19.3	11.6	12.5	48.9	12.9	
	2	3.4	22.4	12.7	9.6	21.3	23.3	
	3	71.2	9.8	14.4	8.3	10.3	14.3	
	4	5.8	37.2	17.1	47.7	29.7	22.0	
	5	18.4	11.4	44.1	21.9	−10.2	27.5	

Source: Author's own calculations based on companies' balance sheets from the Central Statistical Board.

bordering Poland. Germany, including West Berlin, contributed 29.8 per cent, followed by Sweden and Norway (Table 7.7).

In the second period (up to December 1993) geographical proximity played a lesser role. Italy and the United States topped the table, followed by Germany. Low costs, abundance of resources and proximity to markets took on greater importance. During the third period (1994–6) the United States was ranked first, followed by Germany. Little deconcentrating of inward foreign investment has taken place so far. In 1988 the top ten investor countries provided 92 per cent of all capital; in 1993, of the 93 countries whose capital was present in Poland, 10 accounted for 87 per cent of all FDI. Italy occupied first position with 30.2 per cent of all foreign capital. The average size of Italy's firms amounted to 887.9 million dollars, the result of large capital investments by Fiat, the Luccini Group, and Frotrade Financing. Germany, by contrast, has invested in a large number of firms with an average capital of 67900 dollars per firm. The situation changed in 1996: the 10 major investing countries engaged just under 70 per cent of all inward investment.

The impact of historical relationships on the size and structure of investment warrants some attention. In the first period they were important as investors relied on familiarity with the region. Firms from Germany, Sweden and Austria were less wary of Poland and tended to invest greater amounts. In the second period, more non-European

Table 7.7 Origin of FDI in Poland, 1988–97 (value of FDI)

LP	31 December 1988			31 December 1993			31 December 1996		
	Country	$m.	%	Country	$m.	%	Country	$m.	%
1	Germany	42.6	22.8	Italy	546.1	30.2	USA	2399.4	24
2	Sweden	19.7	10.6	USA	347.7	19.2	Multinational	1467.3	14
3	Norway	18.3	9.8	Germany	214.8	11.9	Germany	1335.6	13
4	Netherlands	16.8	9.0	Netherlands	143.7	7.9	Italy	953.1	9
5	Multinational	15.4	8.2	France	83.7	4.6	Netherlands	839.1	8
6	West Berlin	13.0	7.0	Sweden	70.1	3.9	France	657.4	6
7	USA	10.3	5.7	Austria	65.9	3.6	UK	393.8	4
8	Italy	10.5	5.6	UK	59.9	3.3	Austria	316.4	3
9	Austria	8.9	4.8	Norway	40.3	2.2	Australia	298.0	3
10	UK	5.7	3.0	Switzerland	40.2	2.2	S. Korea	290.5	3
	% of EU countries		87.3	% of EU countries		78.8	% of EU countries		56.0
	Total top ten	171.5	91.9	Total top ten	1,572.2	86.9	Total top ten	8,950.6	71.3
		186.6			1,809.9			12,549.1	

Source: Author's own calculations based on data from the Polish State Investment Agency.

firms entered the Polish capital market. Australian, South Korean, Canadian and Japanese firms significantly increased their investing profile. Yet another trend was the growth of multinational capital in the form of international investment funds and institutions, particularly in the post-1993 period.

In terms of FDI structure, two-thirds of EU investments consisted of acquisitions and one-third of greenfield ventures. The ratios were reversed for the rest of the world. Geographical distance seems to be an important factor: the closer the investor is to Poland, the more investment takes place via acquisitions, and vice versa. Little investment originates from other East European countries: Russian investment is concentrated in the building of a gas pipeline from Siberia to Western Europe.

Investment Projects

According to the Foreign Investment Agency the total financial involvement of the 373 largest foreign investors in Poland (equity and credit) in mid-1996 amounted to 10.1 billion dollars. The investment commitments of these 373 firms totalled 8.4 billion dollars. Table 7.8 lists the 10 largest foreign investors during the period 1988–96. At end 1988 the Kvaerner Gdynia Shipyard joint venture was the largest investor with a mere 17.5 million dollars (the joint venture was registered but never came to fruition). In 1993 and 1996, a joint venture between Fiat and the Car Factory FSM in Bielsko-Biala topped the league table in terms of actual and committed investments.

In 1988 the top 10 foreign investments amounted to 64.7 million dollars or 34.7 per cent of total FDI. This went up to 1 billion in 1993 and 3.3 billion in 1996.

In the period up to 1988, of the top 10 firms, 3 came from the United States, 2 from Germany, and the others from Norway, Sweden, West Berlin, the Netherlands and Italy. The United States presence increased to 6 of the 10 ten firms in both 1993 and 1996.

Legislative Changes

The first joint venture law allowing full foreign participation was passed by the Sejm (lower house of the parliament) on 23 April 1986. At that time foreign capital participation was restricted to small-scale production and joint ventures with foreign minority interests. These companies were subject to complex authorization procedures that excluded entry into sectors deemed important for social or state interests. Severe restrictions also existed on the repatriation of profits and capital

Table 7.8 The ten largest foreign investors in Poland, 1988, 1993 and 1996

	31 December 1988		31 December 1993			31 December 1996		
	Foreign investor	$m.	Investor	$m.	$m. future	Investor	$mn	$m. future
1	Kvaerner Gdynia	17.5	Fiat	180.0	830.0	Fiat	702.1	1581
2	Intercell	10.0	Coca-Cola	170.0	50.0	EBRD	608.3	0
3	Hyatt Regency	7.6	International Paper	120.0	175.0	ING Group	343.7	0
4	Inter-sport Club	6.6	Warimpex	100.0	80.0	Intern. Paper	340.1	30
5	Schooner	6.0	ABB	100.0	20.0	Polish-American Enterprise Fund	316.3	33.6
6	Polish Cable TV	5.0	Curtis International	100.0	0.0	IFC	277.2	0
7	Poloval	4.7	Unilever	96.7	0.0	Coca-Cola	275.3	0
8	Sigma	3.8	Polish American Enterprise Fund	82.3	29.0	Philip Morris	227.2	70
9	Polepan	3.5	EBRD	72.1	0	Nestlé	210.0	49
10	International	3.2	Procter & Gamble	60.2	130.0	Thompson C.E.	184.5	0
	Total 10	64.7		1 021.0	1 314.0		3 299.6	1 714.6
	Total all	186.6		4 248.8	3 467.0		12 549.1	8 467.0
	%	34.7%		24.0%	37.9%		26.3%	20.3%

Source: Author's own calculations based on data provided by the State Investment Agency.

invested, which depended ultimately on the availability of hard currency. In the absence of compensation guarantees against expropriation, with licences usually issued for only ten years, and the restricted transfer of ownership interest even within Poland, it is not surprising that these partnerships usually adopted fast-profit strategies. The average capital investment per firm was low (usually the minimum capital requirement of 50 000 dollars).

The foreign investment legislation was liberalized in April 1986: more sectors of the economy were opened up to foreign investors; the full transfer of profits abroad was permitted, and investors acquired greater control over the ventures.

A new law introduced on 14 June 1991 abolished the 50 000 dollars minimum investment requirement. In its place, a minimum start-up capital of 1000 dollars was introduced for limited-liability companies, and 26 000 dollars for joint-stock companies. Moreover, the 20 per cent minimum stock ownership requirement was abandoned, and foreign companies became subject to the same levels of taxation as Polish firms. Special permits were no longer required, with the exception of investments in seaports and airports, real estate, defence, the wholesale trade of imported goods, and consulting and legal services.

These new regulations providing for full national treatment constituted the most important factor in the second wave of FDI inflows in 1992. Foreign investors increased significantly their stake in established joint ventures in terms of both percentage participation and average capital invested.

The period 1994–6 saw a concerted attempt by the government to improve Poland's image as a favourable investment location. Various incentive schemes were introduced to encourage the entry of large investors: these included the creation of special economic areas with preferential treatment (including tax exemptions) to trade and manufacturing industries; the setting up of barriers for imported products, especially in the car industry; the reduction of corporate income tax; and accelerated depreciation and exemption from import duties. These incentives, however, were of the hidden-type and tended not to be publicized.

Conclusions

The impact of FDI on Poland's economy has been limited. The first objective of attracting substantial amounts of foreign capital has not been met. Poland's 12.8 billion dollars of investment stock constitutes approximately 14 per cent of total FDI in Eastern Europe and only 0.2 per cent of worldwide investment.

The second objective of accelerating privatization has not been achieved either. Approximately 4.0 billion dollars of FDI in privatized Polish companies as of December 1996 amounted to only 42 per cent of all invested capital and a mere 5.3 per cent of state-owned equity, as valued in 1989. The internationalization of Polish enterprises has been a weak contributor to Poland's economic structure and activity.

A third objective – the introduction of modern technologies and management practices – has been partly achieved and only in the case of large firms. Large firms' investments in key industries seem to have contributed to Poland's economic recovery. This recovery was fostered by an increase in domestic automobile production fuelled by foreign investment in the industry (by Fiat and GMC *inter alia*). Likewise, in brewing – the best-performing subsector of the Polish economy – most major breweries are owned by foreign companies (United Nations Conference on Trade and Development 1994). Another important contribution by large transnational firms has been the transfer of modern technology and management practices to Polish affiliates and supplier firms. In the case of International Paper, a series of technology-transfer contracts was signed between headquarters and the Polish subsidiary in Kwidzyn. Furthermore, human-resource developments and local labour-force training aimed at raising Western quality standards in both manufacturing and services have been a successful outcome of FDI in Poland. For example, Fiat undertakes the training of all its employees in specially designed schools (Automotive Survey 1994), while Citibank spends 400 000 dollars on training each year (Bobinski 1994). Moreover, the transfer of many soft technologies has been complemented by the provision of unique services formerly unavailable (or unknown) in Poland (Lipsey and Zimmy 1994).

The fourth objective – integrating local markets with European markets – was only partially achieved. Large firms have fared better than small ones. Multinationals from Western Europe in particular have helped establish new trade linkages between Eastern Europe and the European Union, sometimes in the framework of regional core network strategies. For example, Asea Brown Boveri's affiliate in Poland now provides electrical engines on a globally integrated basis (Robinson 1994). As a result, the share of foreign affiliates in foreign trade has risen: they account for 10 per cent of total exports and 12 per cent of imports. To the extent that trade plays an important role in promoting growth and facilitating adjustment, the role of large corporations has been more significant than other indicators regarding the importance of FDI in Poland would suggest. Smaller firms, on the other hand, have not fulfilled the expectations of strengthening ties with EU markets. Their share in the total sale of goods and services is approximately 10 per cent. Over 40 per cent of small firms with foreign participation are in the trade sector, while most others are in simple food-processing, textile production and commodities.

On the whole, FDI in Poland has been fairly small and uneven, but part of this unevenness does suggest that FDI has been relatively important in a number of industries and in key areas to growth and the transition process.

8
Slovenia

Matija Rojec

Introduction

For over four decades Slovenia practised an inward-looking, import-substituting development concept backed by a highly protected domestic (Yugoslav) market. In principle, the structure of the manufacturing sector that developed under those circumstances did not reflect the actual pattern of Slovenia's relative factor endowments, and hence was not based on its comparative advantages. Slovene firms remained competitive abroad by setting export prices at below factor costs and compensating for the shortfall by selling at much higher prices to the protected domestic market. The main objective of exporting firms was to earn (deficitary) foreign exchange, while domestic market sales were intended to maximize profit.

When Slovenia seceded from the Yugoslav federation in 1991, a relatively large protected domestic market disappeared. Slovenia took steps to reduce the level of economic protection and turned to an outward-looking, export-oriented development concept as the only reasonable development policy for a small country of 2 million. Effective rates of protection were reduced from 53.0 per cent in 1986 to 7.03 per cent in 1993, and are set to be further reduced to 5.85 per cent by 2001. The share of exports (goods and non-factor services) in GDP increased to 55.7 per cent in 1995.[1] A parallel process of restructuring took place in non-domestic sales. In the 1990–5 period, sales to the other republics of the former Yugoslavia decreased from 6.6 billion dollars to 1.1 billion, while exports to other countries increased from 4.1 billion dollars to 6.9 billion.[2] The Slovene economy, notably its manufacturing sector, was obliged, under pressure, to reorientate its non-domestic sales and enter into an export-oriented development strategy. As a consequence, a number of Slovene enterprises lost not only the Yugoslav market but also the grounds for exports at below-cost prices. By contrast, another segment of Slovene enterprises, whose development and export competitiveness had been hindered by the import-substituting development concept and administrative restrictions (such as administrative prices favouring some and disfavouring other industries, and compulsory sales of foreign exchange earnings of administratively set foreign exchange rates), began to prosper under a more export-oriented development policy.

What, then, is the potential role of foreign direct investment (FDI) in the restructuring process? As far as macroeconomic restructuring is concerned, Ozawa's comparative-advantage-augmenting FDI seems to be the most suitable conceptual background. When a host country follows an outward-looking, export-oriented development policy, factor-cost-advantage-seeking FDI will go into those manufacturing industries in which a host country has superior factor endowments. In this way, FDI will foster the upgrading of a host country's comparative advantage. The theoretical background for the microeconomic restructuring impact of FDI in a host country – that is, the impact of FDI on the increasing efficiency of a company, in the first instance a foreign investment enterprise, followed by the spill-over effects on domestic enterprises – is fairly clear. It relates to the ownership-specific advantages of foreign investors, as a precondition for investing abroad, and to the internalization advantages originating from being a part of a multinational enterprise (MNE) network (Dunning 1993a; Buckley and Casson 1985). This is even more pertinent for factor-cost-advantage-motivated (export-oriented) FDI, where the efficiency of one subsidiary affects that of others and of the parent company itself. In Dunning's words,

> because they (foreign firms) are the repository of much of the world's technological capability, managerial capabilities and organizational competencies, MNEs are ideal vehicles for spearheading industrial restructuring through their ability to transfer technology and management skills, through their introduction of up-to-date industrial practices and quality control techniques, through their example and spillover effects on local entrepreneurship, suppliers and competitors, and through their network of international linkages – with both large and small firms, they can provide much of the competencies and initiatives for economic growth. (Dunning 1993c)

This chapter seeks to assess the role of foreign investment enterprises (FIEs) in the Slovene economy: their performance, operating characteristics and relevance to various sectors, in particular manufacturing. It also compares the performances of the foreign and domestic sectors in Slovenia and examines the extent to which FDI has contributed to macro- and microeconomic restructuring. The major methodological tool will be the income statements and balance sheets of both FIEs and domestic enterprises. For the purpose of this analysis, and in accordance with the OECD definitions of FDI, FIEs are defined as companies with at least a 10 per cent foreign equity share. All others are treated as domestic enterprises.

The Legal Framework for FDI

FDI legislation in Slovenia (then as part of the former Yugoslavia) was first enacted in 1967, and the first joint ventures with foreign partners date back to the early 1970s. However, only a specific form of contractual joint venture was allowed until 1988. In that year, new FDI legislation introduced the national treatment principle and permitted equity FDI in the form of joint ventures and wholly foreign-owned companies. Today, the legal framework for FDI exhibits the following features:

1. *National treatment:* All forms of foreign investments enjoy the so-called 'full national treatment'; that is, companies with foreign capital participation and wholly-foreign owned companies registered in Slovenia have the status of Slovene legal persons and are subject to Slovene regulations. Equal treatment of foreign and domestic companies is provided.
2. *Sectors open to foreign investors:* All sectors of the economy are open to foreign investors. The foreign share has not been capped, but wholly foreign owned companies are not permitted in military equipment, rail and air transport, communications and telecommunications and insurance. Majority foreign-owned insurance companies cannot engage in reinsurance. In auditing companies a maximum 49 per cent foreign share is permitted; in publishing and broadcasting 33 per cent; in stockbroking companies 24 per cent; and in investment companies (for the management of investment funds) 20 per cent.
3. *Capital structure:* The minimum founding capital for establishing a new company (applicable to all companies, whether or not there is foreign participation) is 1.5 million tolars for a limited liability company and 3 million tolars for a joint stock company.[3]
4. *Real estate ownership:* Legal persons established and duly registered in Slovenia, regardless of foreign share, are entitled to own real estate.

Foreign natural and legal persons are persons of foreign law and cannot own real estate.

5. *Business registration procedure:* Companies established with foreign capital or share acquisitions in existing companies acquire legal status upon registration with the local registry.

6. *Transfer of profit/repatriation of capital:* Foreign shareholders are entitled to the unrestricted transfer of profits abroad in foreign currency.

At the time of writing (1997), Slovenia still had a Foreign Investment Act. With the intention of fully applying the national treatment principle, this Act is to be abolished when a Foreign Exchange Operations Act is adopted. These enactments will, together with the existing Company Act, make up the backbone of the legal framework for FDI in Slovenia.

Basic Trends and Characteristics of FDI Inflows

The foreign investment legislation of December 1988 was a decisive turning point in Slovenia's legal framework for FDI. The number and amount of FDI increased accordingly: at the end of 1988, there were only 28 joint ventures, with 114.3 million dollars of invested foreign capital; by the end of 1995, the number of enterprises with foreign equity participation had increased to 1348, with a foreign share estimated at 1642.8 million dollars (see Table 8.1). At present (1997), FDI is

Table 8.1 Foreign investment in Slovenia at end 1993, 1994 and 1995 (millions dollars)

	1993	*1994*	*1995*
FDI[a]			
Number of companies	1 100	1 345	1 348
Total value[b]	954.3	1 275.4	1 642.8
of which:			
1. Equity	709.7	919.1	1 133.1
2. Long-term liabilities to foreign investor	346.6	472.8	646.3
3. Long-term claims to foreign investor	102.2	116.5	136.6
Portfolio[c]	35.3	47.7	50.5
Total	989.6	1 323.1	1 693.3

[a] Foreign direct investment = 10 per cent or higher foreign equity share (OECD benchmark definition of FDI).

[b] Total value = equity long-term liabilities to foreign investor – long-term claims to foreign investor.

[c] Foreign portfolio investment = less than 10 per cent foreign equity share.

Source: Bank of Slovenia.

assessed at approximately 2 billion dollars. In the second half of 1996, the interest of foreign portfolio investors for shares in newly privatized Slovene companies was around 150 million dollars. Most successful FDI projects in Slovenia developed from previous cooperation between foreign and Slovene companies.

The largest FDI projects were structured as foreign acquisitions or joint ventures. Greenfield investments are usually predominant in small projects. According to existing foreign investors, the major reasons for choosing Slovenia among alternative investment locations (particularly the other East European countries in transition) are company-specific: they include the quality of the Slovene partner/target company (reliability, management and technical staff, expertise, tradition, export orientation and adequate production programmes) and satisfactory experiences in previous cooperation. More general location-specific advantages have been only of secondary importance (Rojec 1994).

Major Investing Countries

Most FDI in Slovenia originated from Austria (24.5 per cent of the total foreign equity stock at end 1995), Croatia (22.2 per cent), Germany (19.3 per cent), France (9.4 per cent), Spain (5.2 per cent) and Italy (5.2 per cent) (see Table 8.2). Croatia's and France's high shares do not, however, accurately reflect the overall picture. In the case of Croatia, it

Table 8.2   Major investing countries in Slovenia (FDI equity stock at end 1995)

Investing country	Value ($m.)	Share (%)
Austria	277.4	24.5
Croatia	251.0	22.2
Germany	219.1	19.3
France	106.5	9.4
Spain	58.9	5.2
Italy	58.5	5.2
Switzerland	56.6	5.0
United Kingdom	40.8	3.6
USA	21.3	1.9
Denmark	12.7	1.1
Netherlands	12.7	1.1
Other countries	17.7	1.6
Total	1 133.1	100.0

Source: Bank of Slovenia.

is distorted by the co-ownership of the nuclear power plant at Krško (built in the 1970s), while Renault's investment in car manufacturing makes up much of French investment. The six countries mentioned above accounted for as much as 85.6 per cent of FDI equity stock at the end of 1995. Slovenia's proximity to the EU and traditionally strong economic ties with Germany, Austria, Italy and France explain the pre-dominance of investors from those countries. A typical foreign investor in Slovenia is a small to medium company from one of the EU countries, which are also major foreign trade partners.

In value terms, however, FDI is heavily concentrated in a dozen large projects with European MNEs,[4] including the investments of Renault in car manufacturing, Saffa (Italy) and Brigl & Bergmeister (Austria) in paper manufacturing, EGO (Switzerland), Siemens and Kirkwood Industries (USA) in electrical machinery and apparatus, Reemtsma (Germany) and Seita (France) in cigarette manufacturing, Pfleiderer (Germany) in non-metallic mineral products and Henkel (Austria) in the manufacturing of chemical products.

FDI by Sector

Manufacturing industry is by far the most important recipient of FDI in Slovenia, followed by electricity production (the nuclear power plant at Krško), financial, technical and business services (notably R&D activity, financial institutions and trade-related services) and retail trade (see Table 8.3). FDI in manufacturing is concentrated in the production of transport equipment, electrical machinery and appliances, paper and paper products. Such a distribution is determined by the handful of large FDI projects listed above.

Although an intensive restructuring process is underway, the structure of the Slovene manufacturing sector today was formed mostly in the framework of the import-substituting policy of the former Yugoslavia.[5] On the other hand, the industrial structure of FIEs was set up, with a few exceptions, mostly in the post-independence period when the outward-looking, export-oriented development concept was emerging. This accounts for the different role of FIEs and domestic enterprises in Slovene manufacturing. Transport equipment, electrical machinery, paper and paper products and cigarette manufacturing absorb as much as 68.6 per cent of all manufacturing assets of FIEs, but only 19.8 per cent of those of domestic enterprises. FIEs are overrepresented in transport equipment manufacturing, paper and paper products, tobacco and electrical machinery, but underrepresented in fabricated metal products

Table 8.3   Industrial distribution of FDI in Slovenia: FDI equity stock at end 1995

EKD No.[a]	Industry	Value ($m.)	Share (%)
0112	Non-metallic mineral products	30.6	2.7
0113	Fabricated metal products, except machinery	8.7	0.8
0114	Non-electrical machinery, professional, scientific etc. equipment	14.9	1.3
0115	Transport equipment	98.4	8.7
0117	Electrical machinery apparatus, appliances and supplies	122.7	10.8
0118	Industrial chemicals	38.4	3.4
0119	Other chemical products	39.9	3.5
0121	Other non-metallic mineral products	7.9	0.7
0123	Wood products, including furniture	1.9	0.2
0124	Paper and paper products	127.8	11.3
0126	Wearing apparel	4.5	0.4
0130	Food manufacturing	8.0	0.7
0131	Beverage industries	9.2	0.8
0134	Printing and publishing	2.8	0.2
0101	Electricity production[b]	n.a.	n.a.
0105	Petroleum refineries[b]	n.a.	n.a.
0129	Rubber products[b]	n.a.	n.a.
0133	Tobacco manufacturers[b]	n.a.	n.a.
Total	0101–0133[b]	208.3	18.4
0501	Construction of buildings	1.5	0.1
0605	Land transport	10.2	0.9
0701	Retail trade	37.5	3.3
0702	Wholesale trade	41.8	3.7
0703	Foreign trade	16.4	1.4
0801	Restaurants and hotels	0.5	0.0
0901	Repair services	1.5	0.1
0902	Personal and household services	3.2	0.3
1003	Sanitary and similar services	4.0	0.4
1101	Financial institutions	88.1	7.8
1102	Insurance	3.4	0.3
1103	Trade related services, including storage	64.9	5.7
1104	Technical services	9.3	0.8
1106	R&D activity	116.6	10.3
Total above 32 industries		1 122.9	99.1
Other		10.2	0.9
Total		1 133	100.0
of which			
Industry and minery (incl. electricity production)		725.8	64.1
Manufacturing industry		567.3	50.1
Financial, technical and business services		282.6	24.9
Trade		95.7	8.4

n.a. = not available.

[a] Unified Classification of Activities.

[b] Industries for which data are not disclosed, as each of them contains less than three FDIs.

Source: Bank of Slovenia

(except machinery), iron and steel basic industries, apparel, wood products (including furniture) and food and beverages.

Significant differences in the industrial distribution of foreign and domestic enterprises suggest that the restructuring of the Slovene manufacturing sector is going on through FDI. Nevertheless, the fact that major FDI projects in Slovenia have been structured as foreign privatizations makes the macroeconomic restructuring impact of FDI dependent on the destination of the proceeds from foreign privatizations. An informed guess is that the Slovene Development Fund – the major recipient of privatization proceedings – has frequently been used as a 'fire brigade' to settle the most urgent financial problems (such as debt and wage arrears in enterprises listed in the fund's portfolio),[6] rather than as a development agency.[7]

FIEs in the Non-Financial Corporate Sector

Table 8.4 highlights two trends: one is the relatively unimportant role of FDI in Slovenia; the other, based on income statements and balance sheets (especially exports, imports and profit), shows that FIEs hold surprisingly high shares. FIEs account for only 3.4 per cent of the total population of enterprises in the Slovene non-financial corporate sector; they hold 7.4 per cent of all equity, 8.2 per cent of all assets and 6.0 per cent of all employees in that sector.

FIEs realize 11.5 per cent of total net sales, 15.3 per cent of total net operating profits and 6.1 per cent of net operating losses; they also pay out 15.5 per cent of all profit taxes, import 19 per cent, export 20.1 per cent and account for no less than 23.9 per cent of the total imports of the Slovene non-financial corporate sector. The importance of FIEs in the Slovene manufacturing industry is also considerably higher than that in the non-financial corporate sector in general. The general impression is that FIEs have become important actors in the Slovene economy, particularly with regard to foreign trade, net operating profits and profit taxes.

Financial and Operational Characteristics of FIEs

Table 8.5 shows that FIEs are outperforming their domestic counterparts. Our findings suggest that in six major areas FIEs show different operating indicators that might explain their superior performance. These are company size, capital intensity, the structure of assets, the level of export orientation, the structure of financial sources and solvency. Compared with domestic enterprises, FIEs possess the following features:

Table 8.4   Selected income statements and balance sheets items of domestic and foreign enterprises in Slovenia, 1995 (million dollars)

Item	All enterprises	Domestic enterprises	FIEs	Share of FIEs in all enterprises (%)
TOTAL	33 609	32 463	1 164	3.4
No. of enterprises	25 079	23 218	1 862	7.4
Equity	46 743	42 897	3 846	8.2
Assets	484 602	455 465	29 137	6.0
No. of employees	38 676	34 213	4 463	11.5
Net sales	9 460	7 561	1 899	20.1
Exports	7 509	6 077	1 432	19.1
Imports	1 951	1 484	467	23.9
Exports – imports	8 249	7 575	674	8.2
Value added	999	846	153	15.3
Operating profit	1 131	1 061	70	6.1
Operation loss	−132	−216	84	n.a.
MANUFACTURING				
No. of enterprises	5 594	5 365	229	4.1
Equity	7 543	6 556	987	13.1
Assets	14 306	12 525	1 781	12.5
No. of employees	239 788	219 301	20 487	8.5
Net sales	14 282	11 774	2 508	17.6
Exports	6 906	5 305	1 601	23.2
Imports	4 278	3 477	801	18.7
Exports – imports	2 628	1 828	800	30.4
Value added	3 654	3 253	401	11.0
Operating profit	318	251	67	21.0
Operation loss	498	465	33	6.7
Net profit/loss	−181	−214	33	n.a.

n.a. = not available.
Source: Institute for Macroeconomic Analysis and Development, Ljubljana.

1. *Much greater size*: In terms of average equity, assets, employment, sales and exports, FIEs are distinctly larger than domestic companies. With the exception of exports, these differences are even more marked in the case of manufacturing firms. Although, in numerical terms, most FIEs are small and medium-sized companies, FDI (by value) is concentrated in a few large projects, as noted above.
2. *Greater capital-intensiveness*: Assets per employee are 40 per cent higher for FIEs than for Slovene firms (52 per cent in manufacturing); productive assets (especially machinery and equipment) are over three times as high. These differences are also reflected in the higher

labour costs and salaries per employee in FIEs, suggesting greater use of skilled labour.

3. *Better asset structure*: The capital productivity of FIEs is increased by tying up a smaller proportion of assets in land and buildings, and through a higher proportion of machinery and equipment: in the manufacturing sector, where FIEs hold 45.8 per cent of fixed assets in machinery and equipment, the figure for domestic firms is only 30.1 per cent. The share of intangible fixed assets, although a small part of total assets, is also much higher in FIEs (particularly in manufacturing). This may reflect the transfer of technology and skills between foreign parent companies and their Slovene subsidiaries.

4. *Greater export orientation*: Not surprisingly, the indicators of export intensity are also higher in the case of FIEs. For instance, FIEs in the manufacturing sector export 63.8 per cent of their net sales; the corresponding share for domestic enterprises is 45.1 per cent. The reasons given by foreign investors for their involvement in Slovene companies include a past record of successful cooperation with these enterprises, export performance and established trade links.

Table 8.5 Major financial indicators of FIEs and domestic enterprises in Slovenia, 1995

Indicators	*All enterprises*	*FIEs*	*Domestic enterprises*	*Index FIEs/ domestic enterprises* (%)
1. Net sales per assets (%)				
Total	77.8	109.2	75.0	146
Manufacturing	93.9	132.5	88.4	150
2. Net sales per employee (000 $)				
Total	79.8	153.2	75.1	204
Manufacturing	59.6	122.4	53.7	228
3. Operating profit per equity (%)				
Total	3.7	7.7	3.4	226
Manufacturing	4.0	6.4	3.6	178
4. Operating profit per employee (000 $)				
Total	2.1	5.3	1.9	279
Manufacturing	1.3	3.3	1.1	300
5. Value added per employee (000 $)				
Total	17.0	23.1	16.6	139
Manufacturing	15.2	19.6	14.8	132

Source: Institute for Macroeconomic Analysis and Development, Ljubljana.

Table 8.6   Major operational indicators of FIEs and domestic enterprises in Slovenia, 1995 (index for FIEs, domestic enterprises = 100)

Indicator	Index (%)	
	Total	Manufacturing
A. INDICATORS OF SIZE		
1. Equity per company	227	353
2. Assets per company	254	333
3. No. of employees per company	181	219
4. Net sales per company	369	499
5. Exports per company	711	707
B. INDICATORS OF CAPITAL INTENSITY		
6. Assets per employee	140	152
7. Machinery/equipment and other fixed assets (except land/buildings) per employee	292	223
C. INDICATORS OF ASSETS' STRUCTURE		
8. Fixed assets as a share of assets	88	96
9. Tangible fixed assets as a share of assets	97	104
10. Intangible fixed assets as a share of assets	230	314
11. Machinery/equipment and other fixed assets (except land/buildings) as a share of fixed assets	237	152
12. Current assets as a share of assets	123	105
D. INDICATORS RELATED TO VALUE ADDED		
13. Value added as a share of gross revenue	69	58
14. Costs of commercial goods, materials & services as a share of gross revenue	107	114
15. Labour costs as a share of net sales.	59	52
E. INDICATORS OF EXPORT ORIENTATION		
16. Exports as a share of net sales	192	142
17. Exports per assets	280	212
18. Exports per employee	392	323
F. INDICATORS OF LABOUR COSTS AND SALARIES		
19. Labour costs per employee	119	118
20. Salaries per employee	118	118
G. INDICATORS OF FINANCIAL STRUCTURE		
21. Subscribed capital as a share of equity	85	83
22. Ratio between long-term and current liabilities and equity	129	90
23. Equity as a share of total equity and liabilities	89	106
24. Equity and long-term provisions and long-term liabilities as a share of total equity and liabilities	100	106
25. Current liabilities as a share of total equity & liabilities	96	85
26. Ratio between financial revenues and financial expenses	96	136
H. INDICATORS OF SOLVENCY		
27. Ratio between current receivables and cash and current liabilities	113	133
28. Ratio between net sales and long-term and current operating receivables	120	136

Source: Institute for Macroeconomic Analysis and Development, Ljubljana.

5. *Distinctive features of financial structure*: A comparison of the financial structure of FIEs and domestic firms shows different results. FIEs in the manufacturing sector use more equity (but relatively less subscribed capital) and less debt financing. Further, FIEs have relatively fewer current liabilities and correspondingly more long-term financial sources than domestic enterprises; they also show a better ratio between financial revenues and expenses. The FIEs' consolidated financial situation and easier access to foreign loans, as integral parts of MNEs, probably contribute to this pattern.

6. *Better solvency*: Compared with domestic enterprises, FIEs have higher ratios of current receivables and cash to current liabilities, and of net sales to receivables. These solvency indicators are stronger in manufacturing enterprises, and may in part reflect the stronger links established with reliable customers through foreign parent networks.

Motivation of Foreign Investors

In general, gaining access to or enlarging a domestic market share has traditionally been the most important motive of foreign investors in Slovenia. In 1995 FIEs in the Slovene manufacturing sector exported as much as 63.8 per cent of total sales (the corresponding share for domestic enterprises was 45.1 per cent); this indicates that FDI in Slovenia is fast becoming a factor-cost-advantage-seeking investment. Therefore, foreign investors generally have multiple objectives (growth, profitability, expansion of exports) in their Slovene ventures. They also rank as important the reduction of production costs and establishing an export base to third countries. The author's findings (Rojec 1994) on the motivation of foreign investors are summarised below.

1. Successful previous cooperation with Slovene joint venture partners/ target companies.
2. Relatively high purchasing power (GDP per capita is higher in Slovenia than in alternative investment locations in Central Europe) and growth potential of a small local market.
3. Established trade links with other parts of the former Yugoslavia and with Central and Eastern Europe.
4. High export orientation and established market shares of Slovene companies on West European markets.
5. Relatively high management and technical and/or technological expertise.
6. A traditional industrial environment with technological capacities allowing the rapid absorption of foreign technology.

7. Low transport costs and proximity to major investing countries.

Future FDI Flows to Slovenia

The determinants of future FDI flows to Slovenia are likely to include: (1) the small size of the domestic market and access to foreign markets, including those of the former Yugoslavia; (2) the process of ownership consolidation after privatization; (3) political, legal and economic stability; and (4) Slovenia's integration into the EU.

1. A Small Local Market

The small size of the domestic market is a major constraint on future FDI inflows. Slovenia's integration into CEFTA has extended its market, but in terms of foreign investors' considerations of where to locate capacities for 'feeding' the CEFTA market, Slovenia has no obvious advantages.

The potential affirmation of Slovenia as a springboard to the other markets of the former Yugoslavia could be a reason for more FDI inflows. This will depend on whether Slovenia can establish preferential access (such as a free trade agreement) to some of these markets. Although Western companies may decide to establish a direct presence in the other states of the former Yugoslavia, it is unlikely that they would invest sizeable amounts in such a high-risk area.

Foreign investors could be persuaded to set up regional headquarters in Slovenia to service other markets of the former Yugoslavia if it can maximize its comparative advantages as a low-risk destination offering an in-depth knowledge of the regional market.

2. Privatization and FDI

Once the first, formal phase of privatization (distribution through the use of ownership certificates and internal buyout at considerable discounts) is over, it is probable that the willingness of domestic enterprises to attract foreign investors will increase, as new owners (individuals as well as privatization funds, which collected a high proportion of certificates) cash discounts from internal buyouts. Foreign investors may also use the opportunity to make cheap company acquisitions.

It is likely, however, that foreign investors will be selective in their choice of companies. First, foreign firms operating in Central Europe have shown above-average interest in the following industries: (a) the manufacturing of consumer goods, principally cars, food, soft drinks, cigarettes, detergents, cosmetics and electric and electronic consumer goods; (b) the paper industry, the construction materials industry and the chemical industry; (c) banking, insurance, telecommunications, trade and public services (such as gas distribution); (d) industries show-ing signs of fast growth and intensive restructuring; and (e) overall, any where the production of inputs for the foreign partner requires high quality and accuracy.

Second, the attractiveness of any individual Slovene enterprise to strategic foreign investors is likely to be determined by the following factors: (a) its market share on the domestic market; (b) its monopolistic or oligopolistic domestic market position; (c) its showing signs of speedy restructuring and absorbing new technology; (d) its previous or existing cooperation with the target companies; (e) its possession of well-known trade marks on the domestic market; (f) its having a market share on foreign markets; (g) its lower labour and other input costs; and (h) the purchasing price of the target company, together with the costs of restructuring versus greenfield investments.

For the time being, foreign investors in Slovenia have responded more to individual companies (as target companies or joint venture partners) than to individual manufacturing sectors. With the exception of the service sector, wholly foreign-owned greenfield investments are almost non-existent. Given the existing pattern of FDI in Slovenia, relatively high labour costs (compared with other countries in transition) and ongoing contractual negotiations, in the medium term foreign investors are most likely to turn their attention to capital-intensive industries such as construction materials, rubber products, car parts, electrical machinery and pharmaceuticals. Given the government's passive approach to greenfield ventures, foreign acquisitions will probably remain the major mode of investment in the foreseeable future.

3. Political, Legal and Economic Stability

Political, legal and economic stability are arguably the most important elements in a country's attractiveness to foreign investors. Slovenia, as a new state in transition bordering the unstable southern flank of Europe, is unlikely to attract foreign investors from far afield; instead, the con-centration of foreign firms from neighbouring Germany, Austria and Italy is likely to continue; so is the attraction to foreign firms with an existing presence in or previous association with Slovenia.

4. Slovenia's Future Membership of the EU

Slovenia's accession negotiations with the EU represent a strong incen-tive for FDI among both member and non-member states. There is little doubt that Slovenia's future membership of the EU will increase FDI inflows. At present, however, Slovenia's associate membership is based on the Europe Agreement, which eliminates some constraints on FDI, but is unlikely to bring immediate increases in FDI inflows. Its more likely impact in the medium term is on the harmonization of Slovene laws with EU standards, as a step towards membership.

Slovenia's Strategy and Policy Towards Inward FDI

The major liberalization of the legal framework for FDI since the late 1980s has not been accompanied by an active policy of seeking foreign investors. Slovenia's only relevant investment incentive – duty-free imports of foreign investment in kind, mostly machinery and equipment – was abolished in 1984.[8] The Trade and Investment Promotion Office lacks resources and instruments to attract FDI. In sum, Slovenia's existing policy towards inward FDI is of the passive type.

This chapter has demonstrated that FIEs display better performance indicators, are more export-oriented and generate higher value added per employee than domestic enterprises, which suggests that Slovenia should adopt a more proactive, open and export-oriented approach to FDI. In the long term, the development of Slovene national comparative advantages could be based on factors that are mostly in the possession of MNEs, another reason for initiating an open attitude to FDI. FDI is not only a source of additional capital to Slovenia, but principally an input of development factors, including technology, access to foreign markets, better management and organization, integration in the international economy and knowledge and skills. In evaluating FDI, Slovenia should consider not solely the direct performance of foreign subsidiaries but also, more importantly, the impact on the development of indigenous capabilities, particularly in terms of restructuring and upgrading comparative advantages.

By signing the Europe Agreement, Slovenia committed itself to ensuring that companies from the EU were treated on a par with Slovene firms. This applies to the setting up of new companies, subsidiaries and branches. Moreover, in the transition period to membership, Slovenia should refrain from adopting new regulations or measures that discriminate against EU-based companies. The submitted draft proposals of the Takeover and Foreign Exchange Operations Acts (which are due to replace the present outdated investment code) adhere fully to the national treatment principle, and thus bring the Slovene legal framework in line with the provisions of the Europe Agreement.

In accordance with the principle of national treatment, foreign acquisitions are regulated by the Takeover Act. In the interest of national treatment of foreign acquisitions, the government should encourage enterprises and shareholders to regulate takeovers above a certain percentage of all enterprise's shares. In the transitional period leading up to accession, the foreign acquisitions of large privatized companies will be dealt with in accordance with the Europe Agreement provisions and article 83 of the draft Takeover Act, which states that:

> When the value of the share capital of a company/issuer of shares which has undergone the process of ownership transformation exceeds 800 million tolars at the time of taking down the legal effects of ownership transformation in the court register, a special permission issued by the government of the Republic of Slovenia on the proposal of the Ministry of Economic Relations and Development is required to acquire more than 25 per cent of the shares of the individual issuer, issued pursuant to the Ownership Transformation of the Enterprises Act.

This provision is valid for five years after the legal effects of ownership transformation of an enterprise have been taken down in the court register.

Slovenia should be searching for foreign investors among (1) neighbouring countries, which are also its major foreign trading partners; (2) smaller and medium sized foreign firms; (3) foreign firms with prior knowledge of the Slovene market; (4) and foreign firms with an above-average inclination to do business in Central Europe. In the framework of its industrial policy, the government should actively attract key FDI projects for the restructuring and development of the economy. It should seek to diversify the geographical structure of foreign investors and attract major projects from the USA, the UK and Japan.

Openness and equality of treatment should dominate Slovenia's attitude to foreign investments, as they promote the efficient allocation of investment resources. Temporary legal or practical constraints limiting the inflow of foreign investment should be used as a last resort, and removed as soon as the political agenda permits.

Notes

1 Data provided by the Statistical Office of the Republic of Slovenia.
2 Data of the Institute of Macroeconomic Analysis and Development of the Republic of Slovenia.

3   The average exchange rate in 1996 was 1 US dollar = 135.3654 tolars.
4   The largest 29 FIEs account for 72.9 per cent of the total assets of FIEs and the largest 17 FIEs account for 76.7 per cent of total FIE equity.
5   The current restructuring process has been slowed down by a number of factors, but principally by the slow pace of privatization.
6   The Development Fund was established to help restructure Slovene enterprises in severe financial difficulties but deemed viable. Under this scheme, a number of companies transferred their ownership to the Fund.
7   Stankovsky found no correlation between economic growth and FDI inflows in the transition economies. This might be due to the fact that most FDI to the transition economies up till now has taken the form of foreign privatizations, whose proceeds have usually not been used for investment purposes.
8   This incentive was widely misused by Slovene companies.

9
The Baltic States

Philip Hanson

Introduction

The three Baltic states – Estonia, Latvia and Lithuania – have followed a post-communist economic trajectory that is a mixture of that followed by Russia, on the one hand, and that followed by the more successful Central European states, on the other.

Like Russia, the Baltic states shed entrenched communist rule slightly later than Central Europe – in late 1991 – and then experienced a steep fall in output and very high initial inflation. The output collapse of 1990–3 and the near-hyperinflation of 1991–2 were probably unavoidable. These three small states, with a total population of only 8 million, housed a population of production units that were deeply enmeshed in the input–output relationships of the old Soviet economy. The customary demand and supply linkages could not be changed quickly. The three new economies also shared the rouble currency with Russia until Estonia established the kroon in June 1992. Initially, the Baltic economies could not escape the turmoil that Russia was passing through.

Like Poland, the Czech Republic, Slovakia, Slovenia and, less clearly, Hungary, however, the Baltic states went on to exhibit effective macro economic stabilization and, subsequently, a sustained recovery of output. From about 1993 – in Estonia, the foundations for stabilization and recovery were laid in mid-1992, with the successful launch of the Estonian kroon (EEK), pegged to the deutschmark (DM) under a currency-board arrangement at EEK 8 = DM 1 – the Baltic economies moved on to an output recovery curve similar to that seen in Central Europe, but still (in 1999) awaited in Russia.

The three Baltic states have differed among themselves in their economic policies and economic outcomes. But they have had in common

– despite changes in government, some unstable political coalitions and three national banking crises – a reasonably consistent pursuit, by their policy-makers, of liberalization, stabilization and privatization. These often painful policies have been made sustainable by broad popular support for the aim of getting away from the communist order imposed on them by Moscow. By the same taken, their governments have on the whole kept impediments to foreign investment low.

The unpleasant business of sticking to these policies has also been made slightly more palatable to the population by hopes of joining Europe. Not only financial discipline, price decontrol and the creation of a strong private sector have been on the policy-makers' agenda, but so also has conformity of legislation and commercial practice to European Union (EU) models. This, too, has supported the efforts to create an environment favourable to foreign investment.

The European Commission recommended in summer 1997 that Estonia, judged capable of being eligible for EU membership by 2002, be included in the short list of five potential first-wave Eastern entrants to the EU.[1] That recommendation, which reflects the conventional wisdom in the wider world that Estonia is ahead of the other two Baltic states in economic transformation, understandably provoked criticism from Latvian and Lithuanian politicians. It is true that any discrimination by the EU among the Baltic states offers Russia a change to stir up trouble between them. For the time being, however, all three have association agreements with the EU, while Estonian entry is unlikely before 2005 and might be impeded in a great many ways. For the present, at least, the status of the three Baltic states as host countries for foreign investment is much the same.

This chapter contains an assessment of the present position and prospects of Estonia, Latvia and Lithuania as recipients of foreign investment. The next section gives a summary of the general economic background of the three states when they regained their independence in September 1991. Then the subsequent development and the early 1997 state of the Baltic economies are reviewed. This section is followed by an account of the foreign investment flows that have so far been tracked, and the main influences on them. In the final section, some thoughts on future prospects are set out.

The Economic Background at Independence

The three Baltic states regained international recognition as independent nations in September 1991, after the failure of the August *coup* attempt in Moscow. Their incorporation into the Soviet Union in 1940 had been forced. It followed directly from the Molotov–Ribbentrop agreement, in which Stalin's Russia and Hitler's Germany divided the lands between them. Thus the Baltic states, though they had been part of the Russian Empire before 1917, had an independent inter-war existence. That, in combination with their long previous history as a trading region, meant that they started post-communist life with an inheritance of economic culture that was closer to that of East–Central Europe than was the case with other parts of the former Soviet Union.

Before 1940 these three countries had traded extensively with Western Europe. Estonia and Latvia had reached development levels comparable to that of Finland at the time. Lithuania was, and still is, appreciably less developed than the other two (Hanson 1990, especially the historic sources).

On the eve of the break up of the Soviet Union, the three Baltic republics accounted together for 2.8 per cent of Soviet population, and something like 3.5 per cent of Soviet GDP. Wages were higher than the Soviet average. Table 9.1 gives some of the key aggregates and shares.

Development levels in the former Soviet Union are even harder to assess than they are for Eastern Europe. There is a starting range of estimates for Soviet per capita GNP in dollar terms in the last years of the Soviet period. Something in the order of 4000 dollars in 1990 (marginally above the PlanEcon purchasing power parity assessment for Poland, though average consumption levels must have been lower in the Soviet Union than in Poland) may be reasonable. In any event, the order of magnitude of the Baltic states' levels of real final domestic expenditure per head would be slightly higher than that for the USSR as a whole.

The relative strengths of these economies within the former Soviet Union were in agriculture (mainly livestock production), services (especially transport and port services), light industry and food-processing. All these assessments are problematic because of the weakness of Soviet statistical reporting and the distorted nature of Soviet prices. The available numbers show the three states accounting for 4.5 per cent of Soviet farm output in 1990 (against 2.8 per cent of population), and having a relatively large net export of farm products to other republics in inter-republic goods flows. Unpublished Soviet official data for 1985 industrial-sector employment indicate that the military production sector was very much less important in the Baltic republics than in the Soviet Union on average (for details see United Nations Economic Commission for Europe 1992; and Hanson 1992b).

As the Gorbachev leadership struggled to hold the Soviet Union together in 1988–91, a great many official figures were put out in Moscow showing that the Baltic republics – and indeed every other non-Russian republic – were heavily dependent on Russia. This is not the place to delve into these numbers and the extensive literature about them. It is sufficient here to make the following points.

There was some substance in Moscow's claims. Estonia, Latvia and Lithuania were apparently delivering goods equivalent to around half their GDP to the rest of the USSR (of which very little was to one another). Their imports of oil and gas from the rest of the USSR were recorded at internal Soviet rouble prices; a shift of all Baltic – other – USSR trade to world prices would entail a dramatic increase in these energy import prices, relative to the prices of other items being traded. Taken together, these two points would indicate that newly independent Baltic states suddenly obliged to trade at world prices with all their trade partners would suffer a substantial terms-of-trade shock to their national income. If in addition they were obliged to settle trade imbalances in convertible currency then they would be in extreme difficulties, since they had almost no reserves and extremely small exports to the West. This scenario, however, was always worse than any plausible worst-case economic scenario for independence could be, for a number of reasons.

The rouble figures for cross-border flows were distorted to the apparent detriment of the Baltics by the incidence of turnover tax and the omission of extensive cross-border shopping in the Baltic republics by residents of other republics. Also, imports into the Baltic states were in some – not negligible – measure for Soviet troops stationed there.

Services transactions would also need to be taken into account, and both tourism and above all transport and port services would, for independent Baltic states, be sources of relatively large net earnings. Much of the grain imported into the Soviet Union came in through Muuga, near Tallinn. All the oil products shipped to the Rotterdam market went out through Ventspils in Latvia. With the break up of the USSR, Moscow lost direct control of about half the thirty-seven ports that had served the European USSR. Russian port-handling capacity became 149 million tons a year, where European USSR port handling capacity had been 382 million tons a year. (*Financial Times*, 9 September 1992); United Nations Economic Commission for Europe 1992; Van Arkadie and Karlsson 1992). Part of that port capacity was lost to Ukraine, but a large part was Baltic.

Above all, the flows of goods across Baltic–former – USSR borders, and in time the location and composition of output generally, could be expected to be very substantially different in a post-Soviet economic world. Energy-intensity of given lines of production, for instance, could be expected to decline, and so – to take an example of special relevance to Baltic agriculture – would the heavy reliance on grain as animal fodder (creating a systemically determined dependence of Baltic live-stock production on non-Baltic grain). Prices, of course, would also change sharply.

This adjustment would take time, but in the meanwhile the disinte-gration of central control over the Soviet economy and the *de facto* shift of priorities towards food and consumer goods could be expected to strengthen the hands of Baltic enterprises negotiating directly with enterprises in Russia, Belarus, Ukraine and other republics.

Finally, the leaders of the Baltic states' drive for independence in 1988–91 knew that if the three states gained international recognition then they ought to be able to reclaim gold to the value (in 1991) of around 300 million dollars that was held in Western Europe for the pre-war Baltic governments. They would resist the notion of taking on a share of the USSR's external debt. So there was a hope that the three states could, soon after achieving independence, have at least some international reserves (Hanson 1992);

Despite all these offsetting considerations, however, it was hard in 1991 to see how the Baltic states could easily avoid, in the year following independence, a substantial drop in GNP and a need to finance a cur-rent-account deficit of perhaps 3 to 5 billion pounds (United Nations Economic Commission for Europe 1992). Provided, that is, that they settled imbalances with the rest of the former USSR in hard currency. It was also hard to see where sufficient financial assistance to cover such a deficit would come from.

Farm exports to the West would be blocked by the European Community's Common Agricultural Policy. The EC's protectionism over sensitive manufactures could also be relied upon to block at least part of their potential export of consumer goods. Most observers, accordingly, forecast an extremely difficult time for the three states, with the usual problems of economic transformation compounded by high costs of disentangling themselves from an extremely close involve-ment in the Soviet economy.

For Latvia and Estonia, the presence on their territories of a large Russian-speaking population, mostly settled there after the Second World War, added a source of political instability. Not all the non-Estonians in Estonia or the non-Latvians in Latvia are Russians in the sense that their old Soviet internal passports contained the nationality identification 'Russian'. There are also Ukrainians, Belorussians and others. But, for these two states, it is the broader category of 'Russian-speaking' people that is the problem. Most of these residents do not speak the language of the basic nationality. They formed in 1990 slightly more than half the industrial labour force in these two states. There are some regions where they are heavily concentrated, forming a Russian enclave – notably in north-eastern Estonia. The hostility of many Latvians and Estonians to people they regard as occupiers, together with the lack of linguistic integration, has proved to be a threat to political stability.

In Lithuania this particular problem is not so serious (see Table 9.1), though there is a significant Polish minority for whom Lithuanian independence has been a source of social tension.

Economic Developments since Independence

It has already been noted, in the Introduction, that output in all three Baltic states collapsed in 1990–3, and inflation was extremely high in 1991–2. In effect, the three small countries could not at first get out from under the price explosion and output implosion that hit the whole former Soviet Union. Official statistics show the gross domestic output of all three, in 1993, at less than 50 per cent of the 1989 level.

It has become clear, however, that the data available for this period overstate the fall in economic activity. There are many distorting effects at work, but in particular the motivation of producers reporting output to the statistical authorities changed with the collapse of communism from (typically) incentives to overstate output to (typically) incentives

Table 9.1   The Baltic economies around 1990 (population, wages, and ethnic mix)

	Population at 1 Jan. 1991 (000)	Share of titular nationality, 1989(%)	Average state wage, 1990 (roubles/month)
Estonia	1 582	61.5	340.7
Latvia	2 681	52.0	290.9
Lithuania	3 728	80.0	283.3
USSR	290 077		274.8

Sources: Narodnoye khozyaistvo SSSR v 1989 g., pp. 16, 52; *Narodnoe khozyaistvo SSSR v 1990 g.*, pp. 38, 66.

to understate it; and the statistical coverage of a new, emerging *de novo* private sector (which is relatively dynamic) was significantly less thorough than that of the old state and, later, privatized enterprises. One skilful attempt at recalculation puts Russian 1995 industrial output at about 75 per cent of the 1990 level, against a Russian official figure of 50 per cent (Kuboniwa 1996). Industrial output probably declined slightly more, initially, in the Baltic states than in Russia, but probably by less than the official numbers indicate, and GDP perhaps by about the same proportion.

The inflation data (for consumer prices, at least) are probably somewhat better than the industrial output and GDP measures for this early period. They do suffer however from being based at first on rather sketchy sampling procedures and from a more general difficulty that would be faced in any country in measuring very high rates of inflation in a reliable way.

Suffice it so say that there was a steep output decline and very high inflation at first, and that the three countries began to emerge from this chaotic period in 1992–4. Table 9.2 summarizes the output recovery from 1994.

Macroeconomic policy was tough from an early stage in both Estonia and Latvia. Lithuania, initially under the nationalist leadership of Vytautas Landsbergis, had less consistent policy-making at first. Under the reformist ex-communist, Algirdas Brazauskas, however, Lithuanian policies became more compatible with those advocated by the International Monetary Fund (IMF). Lithuania's stabilization and recovery therefore started a little behind those of its Baltic neighbours.

The methods adopted to bring inflation under control have differed among the three. Estonia led the way out of the rouble area when it established the kroon in June 1992. The kroon money supply must by

Table 9.2   Overall output growth in the Baltic states, 1994–8 (year-on-year percentage change in real GDP, recorded (R) and projected (P))

	1994	1995	1996	1997[c]	1998[c]
Estonia	−2.7	4.3[a]	4.0[b]	11.4	4.2
Latvia	1.9	−1.6	2.8[a]	6.6	3.9
Lithuania	1.0	3.0[a]	3.6[b]	6.1	4.5

Sources: European Commission, *Forecast Summary* (10 December 1996), except

[a] Bank of Finland, *Russian and Baltic Economies, The Week in Review* 15 (11 April 1997).
[b] Eesti Pank, *Statistical Data Sheets*, information as at 1 August 1997.
[c] United Nations Economic Commission for Europe, *Economic Survey of Europe*, No. 1, 1999, Table B.1.

law be at least 100 per cent backed by foreign currency, at a rate of 8 kroons to the Deutschmark. The rate, and indeed the whole currency board arrangement, could be altered by legislation, but not easily. The national bank of Estonia (Eesti Pank) is not allowed by law to lend to the government or to commercial banks, though it can influence the latter by altering their obligatory reserve requirements.

A currency board has much of the rigidity, and also much of the anti-inflationary effectiveness, of the gold standard. The central bank has little room for discretionary behaviour. If the economy builds up its reserves of foreign currency through a positive basic balance of payments (current plus capital), the domestic money supply expands (in the Estonian, modified version this upwards linkage is not automatic; some discretion is allowed). If the foreign exchange reserves fall from an initial 100 per cent backing of the domestic money supply, the latter must be reduced. So long as the reserves reflect mainly trade performance (in both goods and services), there is a crude but powerful anti-inflationary device in place: if the country suffers from inflation at a higher rate than its trade partners, so that its producers become less competitive and its current account goes negative, the reserves fall, the domestic money supply therefore also falls, and aggregate monetary demand is reduced, imposing downwards pressure on prices. As and when that process reduces the domestic inflation rate, restoring competitiveness, the reserves increase and the money supply can rise again.

A currency board should work more effectively in a small, open economy, in which exports and imports of goods and services are large, relative to GDP, and where capital flows do not complicate this basic adjustment process too much. Like any monetary system, it requires, confidence: it helps if firms and households initially expect it to work (and not to be tampered with by politicians). It has the considerable additional benefit, if it is widely accepted by the markets, that currency risk for a little-known currency is greatly reduced: in this case, the kroon becomes a near-perfect substitute for the Deutschmark (how imperfect it is can be measured by differences between EEK and DM interest rates).

In the Estonian case, the currency board is generally considered to have worked well. Consumer prices rose 940 per cent during 1992, but by 10.8 per cent in the 12 months through June 1997 (Bank of Finland 1997). At end April 1997 interest rates on five year bank loans in kroons were about 11 per cent, close to German rates (Eesti Pank Bulletin 1997). Production was continuing to recover strongly (see Table 9.2), unemployment in April 1997 was 5.7 per cent, and consumption was 25 per cent up on 1994.[2]

Lithuania adopted a currency board for its currency, the lit, later than Estonia, in 1994. Inflation was brought down to an annual average rate of just under 25 per cent in 1996, and falling during the year and into 1997. The present centre-right coalition government, led by the Homeland Union's Gediminas Vagnorius, was committed to scrapping the currency board in 1998 but did not do so. Unemployment at end 1998 was 6.9 per cent (UNECE 1999).

In Latvia, monetary discipline has been achieved by more or less classic restrictive monetary policies without resort to the device of a currency board. Informally, the Lat has been tied to the IMF Special Drawing Right (SDR) – a basket of currencies. Inflation in the 12 months to end 1998 was 4.7 per cent (UNECE 1999).

All three countries, in short, have managed to get inflation under control, albeit with some differences in method and timing. The output recovery normally associated in East and Central Europe with clear macro stabilization has followed, and has been sustained.

In each of the three countries the recovery was jolted for a time by a banking crisis, first in Estonia, then Latvia and then in Lithuania. Those crises seem to have been overcome, with the weaker banks having been weeded out in the process. The culls of commercial banks have been helped by bank supervision and regulation based on meeting EU and Bank for International Settlements prescriptions on capital adequacy and liquidity ratios and the risk-weighting of assets. The regulation of banks has probably been most effective in Estonia (where the capital adequacy ratio has been set at a minimum of 10 per cent from 1 October 1997). The three largest Baltic-state commercial banks, Hansapank, Eesti Hoiupank and Eesti Uhispank, are all Estonian.[3]

In liberalization of price, output and foreign exchange controls, and in the development of market-friendly legal and institutional environments, all three countries have made substantial progress. Most prices were de-controlled early, with rents and public transport the main exceptions. The kroon, the lat and the lit have full internal convertibility, and the kroon is traded abroad.

Tariff and non-tariff barriers to trade are low in all three countries. For small economies outside a major trading bloc, there is in the long run no alternative to being open to the outside world. It was nonetheless extremely difficult for these countries to open up economies distorted by decades of Soviet planning and with producers whose initial orientation was overwhelmingly to the Soviet market. The strategy adopted (first and most clearly in Estonia) was to provide a sort of blanket protection to producers of tradable goods in the form of an undervalued exchange rate. The idea was that this would provide producers with some time to adapt to a more competitive existence, providing a stimulus to exports and a disincentive to imports, and that it would not require the government even to attempt to assess, product by product, where long-run comparative advantage might lie, and then to provide product-specific protection – which would be hard later to withdraw – to supposedly promising lines of production.

On the whole that strategy has had some success. Of course, the pegging of currencies while inflation remained higher than in Western Europe has led to real appreciation of the Baltic currencies over time and to claims that exporters are losing out. Lobbies making that claim in Lithuania were behind the Vagnorius government's pledge to get rid of the currency board for the Lit (Economist Intelligence Unit 1997).[4]

In general, despite their broadly effective domestic policies and a remarkable success in reorienting trade towards Western partners, the Baltic states have run into some difficulties in *foreign trade*. In 1998 all three ran current-account deficits equivalent to about 10 per cent of GDP (United Nations Economic Commission for Europe 1999, p. 105 – based on January–September data). This sort of development was common to almost all the ex-communist countries of Central and Eastern Europe. At least part of the explanation is that the recovery in the region (sucking in imports) has coincided with a slowdown in Western Europe (dampening export demand). In the case of the Baltic countries, some blunting of their producers' competitive edge has probably also occurred, as their currencies have become – if not overvalued – less undervalued than before. The real effective exchange rate of the Estonian kroon, for example, appreciated by 110 per cent against the currencies of developed industrial economies between 1993 and 1996 (this figure has been derived from Eesti Pank 1997, p. 24).

For countries whose cross-border transactions through 1991 were overwhelmingly with the rest of the USSR (and very little with each other), Estonia, Latvia and Lithuania have all managed to alter the partner-composition of their trade remarkably quickly. To some extent the collapse of Russian and other Commonwealth of Independent States (CIS) output made reorientation scarcely avoidable. But the growth of exports to, as well as imports from, the West has been dramatic. Even Latvia, for which Russia was still the largest single trade partner in 1996 (22.8 per cent of Latvian exports and 20.2 per cent of Latvian imports) was doing close to half its trade with the EU (44.7 per cent of exports and 49.3 per cent of imports. (Economist Intelligence Unit 1997). In the case of Estonia, Finland has been the largest single trade partner from 1995 onwards (*Eesti Pank Bulletin* 1997, p. 26), and more than half of Estonia's merchandise trade is now with the EU.

The reorientation to new markets and new sources of supply may have been successful, but the development of the merchandise trade and current account balances since 1994 has raised questions about the sustainability of the recent growth of the Baltic economies. In the case of Estonia, whose combined exports of merchandise and services in 1996 were equivalent to nearly 83 per cent of GDP, there were two worrying structural problems. First, the growth of merchandise exports has been stronger for processed re-exports than for goods of mainly Estonian manufacture, and this outward processing trade, generating merchandise exports equivalent in 1996 to 16.6 per cent of GDP, is dependent on something that will be a declining advantage if Estonia continues to make progress: cheap labour. Second, the merchandise exports in which value was added predominantly in Estonia (food products, timber, clothing and chemical products) are a mixed bag, some of which may have rather limited growth prospects.[5]

The strong growth of services exports, especially of tourism and transit (including port) services, is a favourable factor common to all three Baltic states. Transport probably brings in over 1 billion dollars a year to the three Baltic states, and has been developing strongly; it is, however, vulnerable to changes in political relations with Moscow.[6]

The current account deficits experienced by all three Baltic states in 1996, though large, were exceeded by the net capital inflows (see Table 9.3). That demonstrates the confidence of both Baltic peoples and foreigners in these economies (Russia continued to have a large net capital outflow, of the order of 3 per cent of GDP). It also meant that growth did not have to be checked in order to deal with a balance of payments crisis. By the same token, however, the large inflows left the Baltic monetary authorities with the problem of containing inflationary pressures at a time when export performance needed to be improved. It is clearly of particular importance for all the Baltic states that a large part of the capital that comes in helps to boost long-run export growth.

Meanwhile the Baltic states look, on most financial indicators, rather healthy. Table 9.3 provides some numbers that characterize the size of these economies and give some key external financial indicators.

Table 9.3   The Baltic economies in 1996: some indicators of size and external financial status

	Estonia	Latvia	Lithuania
Population (m.)	1.48	2.49	3.71
GDP ($bn., ppp conversion)	6.4	8.5	15.8
GDP per cap. ($, ppp)	4444	3421	4255
Cumulative FDI to end 1996 ($ mn.)	752	775	261
Sovereign credit rating	BBB−	BBB	BBB+
Net capital inflow/GDP (%)	8.5	10.1	7.7
Gross foreign debt/exports (%)	9	15	29

Notes: The GDP and GDP per capita figures come from separate sources and do not always correspond precisely. The sovereign credit ratings are all investment grade and all as of April–June 1997, but they do not necessarily all relate to exactly the same category of government paper, and are not all from the same rating agencies, so they are not precisely comparable.

Sources: Derived from United Nations Economic Commission for Europe (1997); Eesti Pank Bulletin (1997); Jamestown Foundation Monitor, 17 June 1997; Economist Intelligence Unit (1997); Bank of Finland, Russian and Baltic Economies: The Week in Review, 11 April 1997.

The credit ratings place Estonia and Latvia in the company of the more successful Central European countries, and above Romania, Bulgaria, Russia and Kazakhtan, which all had, in mid-1990, ratings below investment grade as did Lithuania. Estonia was late in seeking a sovereign credit rating, since its legislation was originally intended to require a balanced budget, so that the government would not be issuing debt. However, Estonian municipalities have run deficits and issued bonds.

All three countries might be described as underborrowed, and financially in good shape. The 1996 Estonian consolidated budget deficit was equivalent to only 1.6 per cent of GDP, and total government gross debt was only 8 per cent of GDP (Eesti Pank 1997, pp. 34 and 36). Estonia and Latvia are external net creditors (to the rest of the world) and Lithuania is a net external debtor on only a very small scale (United Nations Economic Commission for Europe 1997).

Privatization, and the growth of new private firms, have now gone a long way in all three Baltic states. All have looked to foreign investors from the outset of their large-scale privatization programmes in 1991–2.

Estonian privatization of large enterprises was influenced strongly by the approach of the German Treuhand, the body responsible for managing privatization in former East Germany. Groups of large enterprises were prepared for privatization and then offered for sale. The Estonian Privatization Agency (EERE) started with a list of 38 enterprises offered for sale in November 1992. In principle, these were available for purchase by either foreign or domestic investors. This approach was continued through a succession of such tenders.

In Lithuania the arrangements were at first less open. The Central Privatization Committee had the power to decide which of a batch of enterprises to be privatized might be available to foreign buyers, and which not. In addition, Lithuania was operating for some time without a convertible currency, so that it was not always clear how a foreign investor might be able to repatriate profits. The declaration, in a very early (December 1990) Lithuanian law on foreign investment, that foreign investors were guaranteed non-discriminatory treatment left many practical questions unanswered.

Latvian legislation in the early 1990s excluded foreign ownership in certain sectors (arms production, the media, port management and some others) but was otherwise quite liberal for the time. Profits-tax breaks were offered for the first two years of profitable operations, on the lines of the Soviet and Russian arrangements.

Laws on property rights in general and foreign investment in particular have become more sophisticated and more comprehensive over time. The tax systems have been elaborated. The shift to a private enterprise economy has continued, with new, small firms growing strongly. Certain problems that loomed large in 1991–2 have receded: fears of Russian buying up of the Baltic economies have waned (allowing what is presumably mutually advantageous Russian investment to occur);[7] at least some of the complications arising from political commitments to restore property to former owners have been resolved; the establishment of convertible currencies and moderate rates of inflation have removed such uncertainty; and the development of securities trading has allowed portfolio investment to begin. At the same time, the clarification of property rights in land–real estate in general, not just farm land–has been slow even in Estonia. It remains a potential problem for some foreign investors in the region.

For all the problems along the way, these are now basically private-enterprise economies with substantial foreign-controlled activity. In Estonia, by end September 1996, the percentage division of net sales (close to, but not identical with, value added) was as follows: state and municipal sector 13.8, Estonian private sector 67.4, foreign-owned sector 18.8 (Eesti Pank 1997, p. 14). Precisely comparable figures are not, to the author's knowledge, available for the other two Baltic states, but the private–state division of output is broadly similar in Latvia and Lithuania.

Foreign Investment Trends

Cumulative foreign direct investment estimates for all three Baltic states at end 1996 have already been given in Table 9.3. It goes without saying (or rather, it should) that the numbers are problematic and not reliable as precisely comparable measures. They are however derived by the UN/ECE in ways that are as far as possible comparable between the ex-communist economies: they are cumulative flows from 1988, on a balance-of-payments cash basis. A compilation of foreign shares in authorized capital in reported joint ventures and wholly foreign-owned companies, for example, would give different figures. On a per capita basis, by 1998 these cumulative totals put Estonia behind only Hungary, and Latvia only two places lower in the pecking order (after Slovenia), among ex-communist nations. But then it helps, in such calculations, to be small. An investment of 1800 dollars in Robinson Crusoe would have put him ahead of Hungary.[8] The fact remains that, as other chapters in this volume make clear, FDI in the European ex-communist countries has been very modest so far. However, annual FDI inflows into Estonia and Latvia have in 1996–98 been over 5 per cent of GDP – which is a better way of putting them into perspective.

In fact, FDI fell in 1996 and again in 1998 in most ex-communist countries. The shifting patterns among these countries in the past few years suggest that the bunching of rapid privatization of large enterprises tends to be associated with surges in FDI inflows into a country. With most of the initial large-scale privatization already accomplished, FDI in 1996–7 was driven mostly by investment in new businesses and additions to capital of existing companies, supplemented by late growth in countries where mass privatization had been delayed (notably Poland) and/or where foreign investors' perceptions of a country had brightened (Poland again, but also Lithuania).

The three Baltic states, given the small size and relative poverty of their populations, were disposed towards privatization with a heavy emphasis on searching for foreign strategic investors, a strategy closer to the Hungarian than to the Russian or Czech approach to large-scale privatization. (It should be stressed that the privatization of small state businesses – shops, cafés, small building firms, road haulage concerns and the like – has been predominantly a matter of sales to local buyers in all the ex-communist countries. Similarly, the growth of new small firms has also been a largely indigenous phenomenon. Both these processes have important aggregate consequences, and have been relatively straightforward – and are generally rather neglected in most analyses of 'privatization' and of foreign investment.)

The recent decline in rates of FDI into the Baltic states and into the ex-communist region as a whole should therefore not be seen as an alarming symptom. This is so, not only because of the connection with initial large-scale privatization, but also because the channels through which foreign finance for investment can flow into these countries have become more numerous.

The development of stock markets – something that was possible only after large-scale privatization had been under way for some time – makes foreign portfolio investment in equities a possibility. Growing acquaintance with international financial markets on the part of Central and East European officials and executives, combined with greater confidence in the West in the prospects of the European emerging markets, allows companies in the ex-communist countries to raise loans on Western money markets, issue corporate bonds or make international issues in the form of American depository receipts (ADRs) or global depository receipts (GDRs).[9]

The scale on which these additional financing flows have developed so far as the Baltic states are concerned is depicted in Table 9.4. As far as possible, the numbers shown here should correspond to private financing to the private sector; flows of assistance are certainly excluded, but some public sector borrowing on commercial terms may be included.

It is evident that total international commercial financing of investment in these countries no longer corresponds closely to net FDI

Table 9.4 Baltic states: international inflows of finance for investment, 1994–6 inclusive ($m.)

	Estonia	Latvia	Lithuania
Bond issues + syndicated loans	64	41	185
International equity issues	10	n.a.	21
Net FDI	525	739	217
Net portfolio investment	139	−261	144
Total	738	519	567

n.a. = not available

Note: The net FDI figures for Latvia and Lithuania include 1996 totals extrapolated from the figures for the first three quarters. The net portfolio investment figure for Estonia specifically includes only equity investment; the figures for Latvia and Lithuania may include some purchase of bonds.

Sources: Derived from United Nations Economic Commission for Europe (1997) and Eesti Pank (1997).

inflows. A number of different market channels for such flows have developed, and the three Baltic states do not receive funds from the different channels in closely similar proportions.

FDI, however, is still of particular importance. Loans have to be repaid, so they represent a future burden on the balance of payments, quite apart from the interest paid on them. Portfolio investment brings no transfer of technology or management skills with it, and is liable to be withdrawn abruptly. So far as the long-run development of the Baltic economies is concerned, FDI inflows are to be preferred.

On the other hand, investment finance is investment finance. Around 30 per cent of all investment in Estonia in 1997 was estimated by Eesti Pank economists to have been externally financed – an amount very roughly equivalent to about 10 per cent of GDP (Eesti Pank 1997, p. 25).[10] This assessment takes the whole current account deficit as a source of domestic financing – which in a national-income-accounting sense it is – rather than the identified commercial financing shown in Table 9.4. However, the difference is not large: the net inflows for 1996 incorporated in the Table 9.4 data for Estonia (381 million dollars) are, at the annual average exchange rate, equivalent to 8.7 per cent of GDP.

The outside world, in other words, is enabling Estonia to invest about 10 per cent more of its GDP than it saves. Household saving in Estonia had risen (in 1996) to about 10 per cent of disposable income – a very respectable saving rate. But the consolidated (national plus local) budget had gone from net saving to net borrowing, albeit very modest net borrowing. Were investment in the Estonian economy to be restricted to what could be financed from Estonian household and business saving, net of the budget balance and of any outward investment, then growth prospects would be substantially poorer than they are.

In the light of international experience of economic growth, this is a somewhat unusual situation. In most countries at most times, the proportion of national income invested is close to the proportion saved. In other words, even in today's supposedly globalized economy, foreign investment finance seldom seems likely to make a large difference to a country's rate of growth in the long run. This is not at present the case in Estonia, and the indications are that Latvia and Lithuania are not in this respect far behind. These countries may yet do well out of being small but well-thought-of.

What investments is the foreign finance supporting, and where is that finance coming from? These questions are more difficult to answer about the other components of the inflows than they are about FDI. In Estonia in 1996 the percentage breakdown of FDI by broad sector was distribution 36, financial services 27, industry 24 and other (including transport and communications) 13. By country of origin the breakdown was Finland 35, USA 28, Denmark 10, Sweden 9 and other 18 (*Eesti Pank Bulletin* 1997, p. 32). For Lithuanian cumulative FDI at end 1996 (using figures derived quite differently from those so far used here, and which are substantially higher) the leading country of origin was the US, followed by Germany and Sweden, in that order (Economist Intelligence Unit 1997, p. 41).

The specific investment projects involved are extremely diverse. A short selection follows. Latvia: airlines (Baltic International Airlines with SAS), fast food (McDonalds), cereals production (Kellogg), hotels (Radisson and others), telecommunications (Cable and Wireless and Telecom Finland); Estonia: cement production (Atlas Nordic Cement at Kunda), telecommunications (Telecom Finland and Telea Sweden), production of ski equipment (HTM Sport), electric cooker manufacture (Electrolux), textiles (Boras Wafveri, at Narva), telephone manufacture (Elcoteq and Ericsson), electricity generation (NRGE, at Narva); Lithuania: electronics (Motorola), cigarette production (Philip Morris), oil terminal reconstruction (Lancaster-Distral).

There is a mixture of three main elements in the kinds of projects to be found in the Baltic states. One component is the development of a network by a leading consumer goods company, are which one or more production or distribution units in the Baltic states are part of the establishing of a presence across the whole Central and East European region (McDonald's, PepsiCo, hotel chains). The second is the development of transport and communication networks that, again, transcend the small Baltic economies, though they may form part of a Scandinavian–Baltic niche in a still wider world market (Telecom Finland, SAS). The third is sourcing for a wider market (Electrolux, Philip Morris, Boras Wafveri and much of the textile and clothing investments, which shade into arm's-length arrangements for outsourcing part of a production process, using available cheap labour). It must be rare for any substantial investment to be made in any of the Baltic countries that is expected ever to contribute more than a small part of the foreign investor's overall business.

That characterization of FDI into the Baltic states, however, is entirely compatible with inflows of investment continuing into those countries that, in aggregate and in their cumulative effects, make a substantial difference to growth and prosperity there.

Portfolio investment from abroad has been significant relative to the size of the (so far small) Baltic stock markets. It is estimated that about

40 per cent of the shares on both the Riga and Tallinn stock markets are owned by non-residents, with Estonian investors owning a substantial part of the Latvian shares and Nordic investors a large slice of the Estonian shares (*East Europe Daily Brief*, 2 September 1997, I). Some integration of the three Baltic stock exchanges is beginning to occur, partly through Estonian acquisition of Latvian and Lithuanian broker-age firms. This process makes portfolio investment in the region easier for outsiders. It is likely to help the performance of these new stock markets, which all grew strongly (from next to nothing) in 1997.

Conclusions and Prospects

The three Baltic economies have adapted, on the whole, rather success-fully to the collapse of communist rule from Moscow. They have all developed an alternative economic lifestyle fairly quickly. There are differences between them; the common perception, that Estonia, the smallest, has so far exhibited the most coherent and successful adapta-tion, is probably correct. They are small, open economies, at present outside a major economic bloc, for which foreign investment can make a difference, and needs to be cultivated. In fact, they have all benefited substantially from external finance of investment – at first entirely through foreign direct investment, but increasingly in the past four years from portfolio investment and other channels as well. This should have enhanced their growth prospects, even though these are not coun-tries whose internal markets are likely to loom large in any multina-tional company's plans.

The European Commission's provisional identification of Estonia as a potential first-wave EU entrant, perhaps in around 2005–7, does not change anything fundamental for the time being. It should however tend to make Estonia more attractive than before as a destination for foreign investment. The risk is that it may sour the other two Baltic states' relations with the EU and perhaps make them seem in some way less attractive as FDI destinations than they were before (though it would be hard to provide any sound argument for such an interpreta-tion of events). It might also increase the (probably slender) chances of Moscow driving wedges between the three.

In general, the three Baltic states need both continued Scandinavian and EU support and improved relations with Moscow. Russia's prox-imity entails a tinge of political risk, associated with any instability in Russia itself. Russian political instability apart, their large neighbour also matters in a more immediate business sense: smoother arrangements for the transit of freight from Kaliningrad through Lithuania (and to a lesser extent on through the other two Baltic states, if the freight is going to North-West Russia) would be beneficial to all involved. Purely practical, depoliticized arrangements over Russian transit cargoes through Baltic-state ports are also worth preserving and strengthening. The Russian lobby for building additional Baltic ports on Russian territory may be incapable of leading to anything more than an expensive boondoggle; but it could (at an investment cost to Russia that would be hard to justify) cut into Baltic-state transit earnings.

External finance for investment is more important for these countries than it is to most other ex-communist countries. Foreign direct investment is only part of this, but it is likely to be the most constructive part by far. As elsewhere, it is the basic domestic economic environment that matters most in attracting FDI: low inflation, convertible currency, political stability, clear property rights, a stable and moderate tax regime, well-enforced laws, a skilled and reasonably cheap workforce. The three Baltic states have on the whole done well in providing these basics, and should be able to maintain them. If they can also raise domestic savings rates, thereby enhancing their long-run growth prospects, they will, paradoxically, both reduce their need for external finance and at the same time increase their long-run chances of attracting more of it.

Notes

1 Commission *avis* of 16 July 1997.
2 The unemployment rate quoted here is for unemployed job-seekers as a percentage of the employed plus job-seekers – higher than the figure for registered benefit claimants but probably somewhat less than would emerge from a labour force survey, using the International Labor Organization's preferred methodology.
3 For more background on the banking sector see Korhonen, (1996).
4 This claim fits rather oddly with calculations that put the 1996 Lithuanian GDP at 15.8 billion dollars on a purchasing power parity (ppp) basis and 7.7 billion dollars at the pegged exchange rate of 4 lit to the dollar, which suggest that the exchange rate undervalues the Lithuanian currency by more than 50 per cent. It is likely that the claims really are exaggerated; however, the appropriate p.p.p. for converting GDP (including non-tradable goods and services) is likely to be at least somewhat different from that appropriate to tradable goods only. Also, with a dollar currency peg, Lithuanian exporters, whose main markets are in Western Europe, are affected by changes in the fortunes of the US dollar relative to European currencies.
5 Calculations derived from the 'Balance of Payments...' chapter and the note by Raimund Hagelberg, 'On Some Features of Today's Economic Environment', ibid. pp. 22–37 and pp. 37–40, respectively.

6   A Russian source (Interfax, 26 August 1997) says Russian companies paid $600 million for freight transport to foreign companies (in Baltic countries, from the context) in 1996. *Eesti Pank Bulletin* (1997, p. 29) gives about 200 million dollars for earnings from freight transport only that year, and 442 million dollars for all transport (including passenger and 'other'), so 1 billion dollars for all three Baltic countries for all transport is probably a conservative estimate.

7   For example, when the Russian Baltic exclave of Kaliningrad briefly lost its official status as a Free Economic Zone in 1995–96 (it is now officially a Special Economic Zone), a number of Kaliningrad firms relocated to Lithuania (author's interviews with officials in Kaliningrad, July 1997).

8   A note for pedants: or 3000 dollars after the arrival of Man Friday.

9   ADRs and GDRs are certificates of ownership of shares in a non-US company, issued by US banks and traded in US securities markets (ADRs) or in several international markets (GDRs). They are comparatively recent devices, but by late 1994 ADRs and GDRs from 1100 issuers in 54 countries were traded on US securities markets.

10   These are preliminary estimates.

Part III

Russia and the Commonwealth of Independent States

10
Russia

*Yuri Adjubei**

Introduction

The Russian Federation is the largest former constituent republic of the Soviet Union. It occupies 76 per cent of former Soviet territory, and accounts for 51 per cent of its population (170.8 million inhabitants in 1991). National income produced in this country makes up about 61 per cent of the ex-Soviet total, and national income produced in industry almost 64 per cent (1988).

The share of the Russian Federation is even higher in the output of major commodities. In 1990, it accounted for over 90 per cent of oil output and 79 per cent of natural gas production. The weight of the republic was also predominant in the output of timber (92 per cent), coal (56 per cent) and iron ore (45 per cent).[1]

Russia represents a large potential market for foreign companies, particularly in the consumer goods sector. First, the latter is underdeveloped in terms of per capita consumption of major consumer goods and services, as compared with that of the developed market economies. It is also inhibited structurally, that is as compared with investment and state collective consumption. In 1989, the share of final household expenditure in the GNP of the former Soviet Union amounted to 48 per cent, as compared with 54 per cent in Germany, 58 per cent in Poland, 60 per cent in France, 64 per cent in the UK, and 66 per cent in the USA.[2] In the mid-1980s, in the former USSR, the share of retail trade in food in GDP amounted to 5 per cent, as compared with 12 to 13 per cent in France and the UK, and close to 16 per cent in the USA.[3] These comparatively low proportions give an idea of structural

* The author works for the secretariat for the United Nations Economic Commission for Europe. The views expressed are his own, and do not necessarily reflect those of the secretariat.

imbalances in the former Soviet economies, inherited from years of rapid industrialization and arms race in the cold war period.

The level of education of the Russian population, illustrating the quality of human resources, is relatively high. In 1989, over 80 per cent of adults had higher or secondary education. Of those, over 11 per cent had higher education.[4] This well-educated labour force earns wages and salaries comparable to those of less developed countries. In the mid-1990s, the average monthly salary was equivalent to about 120 dollars. The relatively low labour remuneration illustrates a potentially significant cost effectiveness of labour-intensive production.

Finally, the Russian subsoil contains enormous deposits of oil, gas, coal, iron and non-metallic ores, precious metals and stones, and other minerals. As an example, the seismological tests carried out during 1990–1 revealed some 250000 million barrels (39683 million tonnes) of oil. This estimate brings the oil resources of the successor states of the USSR (90 per cent of which are on Russian territory) close to those of Saudi Arabia.[5] Siberian forests constitute 52 per cent of the world supply of timber.[6]

In spite of the enormous potential for natural resource development, a large and undersupplied consumer market and a relatively well-educated and inexpensive labour force, the inflow of foreign entrepreneurial capital has been small. On 1 January 1996, 14500 enterprises with foreign participation (foreign investment enterprises, or FIEs) were registered in Russia. On the same date, the cumulative value of foreign investment did not exceed 5.9 billion dollars. For the sake of comparison, at the beginning of 1996 Hungary had attracted an estimated 13.7 billion dollars' worth of investment, and Poland about 7.8 billion dollars' worth.

This chapter outlines the legal framework for foreign investment, including the participation of companies from abroad in privatization, highlights the scale of foreign capital penetration in various sectors of the Russian economy, and assesses the present stage and prospects of the Russian Federation as a host to foreign investment.

Regulatory Basis

Since the disintegration of the Soviet Union, foreign investment inflows in Russia, together with the activities of FIEs, have been governed by the foreign investment law enacted on 1 September 1991, and the relevant legislation on taxation, foreign trade, prices and finance. It was also in 1991 that the legislation on privatization was enacted.

With regards to the rights of FIEs, and the promotion of foreign investment, the foreign investment law went further than the all-Union legislation.

Rights and Guarantees to Foreign Investors

As compared with all-Union legislation, the Russian law strengthens the legal guarantees for foreign investment: foreign investors' property in Russia can only be nationalized, requisitioned or confiscated in exceptional circumstances relating to the public interest. In this event, 'prompt, adequate and effective' compensation (including the lost profits plus accrued interest) is guaranteed. Equally important is the provision that foreign investors must be spared losses stemming from government regulations and the deeds of government officials contradicting the acting legislation. The law explicitly stipulates the 'national treatment' of foreign investors, that is, the enjoyment of a legal regime identical to that of local counterparts.[7]

Revisions of the law on foreign investment discussed in Parliament in the mid-1990s aimed at protecting foreign investors against the deterioration of legal conditions of investment. For five years after its establishment the FIE would be able to invoke the legislative stipulations that existed at the time of registration.[8]

Further guarantees to foreign investors are given by the bilateral investment protection agreements. At the beginning of 1993 Russia concluded such agreements with twelve countries. In addition, in December 1992 parliament ratified a convention on the Multilateral Investment Guarantee Agency (MIGA), which provides guarantees to FIEs against damages caused by civil strife, expropriation, inconvertibility of the local currency and governmental non-compliance with obligations *vis-à-vis* foreign investors.[9]

Access to the Economy and Restrictions

The law on foreign investment requires registration with the Ministry of Finance, which must be delivered within 21 days. Foreign investment projects in the oil, gas and coal industries, and those with capitalization in excess of 100 million roubles, must be approved by the Council of Ministers.[10] The approval of large-scale projects may require expertise bearing upon the environmental and public-health consequences of the investment.

The law does not restrict the areas of activities of foreign investors: however, enterprises engaged in banking, insurance and financial intermediation must obtain licences from the central bank and the Ministry of Finance, respectively. In addition, the law empowers the Council of Ministers to determine other types of activity which may require permission for FIEs.

The law does not set any equity limitations on foreign investors. Joint ventures, wholly foreign-owned subsidiaries, unincorporated branches of foreign companies, as well as foreign participation in the stock of existing national firms, are allowed in the form of joint-stock companies and all other partnerships 'permitted by law'. However, according to the law on insurance adopted at the end of 1992, insurance companies may not have a foreign stake exceeding 49 per cent of the equity.[11]

Mineral Deposits

The law on subsoil adopted on 21 February 1992 sets further legal conditions for the participation of foreign investors in the development of mineral resources. According to this law, foreigners are entitled to national treatment in exploiting natural resources (excluding radioactive minerals). In order to develop mineral resources, FIEs must buy licences through tenders and auctions. The rental payments are fixed as a percentage of the value of minerals extracted by the licence-holders (5 years for exploration plus 20 years for exploitation).[12]

Taxation

The foreign investment law promulgates the general principle of 'national' treatment for FIEs with regard to taxation. At the same time there are exceptions to that principle: enterprises operating in priority sectors of the economy and particular regions can apply for preferential tax treatment. More recently, the taxation of enterprises in Russia has been constantly revised: this makes it particularly difficult to determine the basic tax rates applicable to FIEs at any particular time.

This being said, the law on profit tax, enacted in January 1992, set the basic rate on enterprise profit at 32 per cent; at the same time, profits derived from mediatory operations, including commodity and stock exchanges and brokerage operations, are taxed at 45 per cent.[13] Income from securities issued by private enterprises (non-state securities) is liable to 15 per cent tax (this rate also applies to the repatriated income of foreign parent companies).

The affiliates of foreign banks are subject to a 30 per cent tax on income derived from financial activities on Russian territory. Their 'portfolio' incomes, unrelated to banking operations (dividends, interest, rents and licence fees), are taxable at 18 per cent. The incomes of the foreign partners of banks are subject to 15 per cent tax when repatriated, unless international treaties stipulate otherwise.[14]

When compared with the rates of other transition economies, Russia's basic income tax ranks in the middle of the range. It is lower than in Hungary or Poland (40 per cent in each case), but higher than in the Czech Republic (20 to 25 per cent), Ukraine (21 per cent) or Kazakhstan (25 per cent).[15]

Taxable income is reduced by the value of productive investment aimed at modernizing production and increasing output by enterprises extracting oil and coal and those manufacturing medical and food industry equipment. In the same way, 30 per cent of investment in environmental protection is deductible from taxable income.

The reinvested profits of small enterprises (with an average number of employees of 200 in industry and construction) are tax-free. However, total tax deductions must not exceed the amount of tax payable by more than 50 per cent. In agriculture, consumer goods, food and construction material industries, small companies are eligible for a two-year tax holiday from the date of registration.[16] These rules are intended to encourage small Western enterprises to pass on beneficial 'demonstration effects' to local producers in the areas of managerial practices and general business culture.

FIEs are also subject to other taxes, the most important of which is a value added tax. Initially, the basic rate was set at 28 per cent, 21.88 per cent in the case of goods and services delivered at 'regulated' (state-controlled) prices, which already included the value added tax.[17] As of 1993 the basic rate was reduced to 20 per cent, or 10 per cent for food products.[18]

Operating Conditions and Non-tax Incentives

Although under conditions of price liberalization this incentive is rather obsolete in most economic sectors, the foreign investment law authorizes FIEs to set up freely prices and conditions of delivery when buying from, and selling to, local producers. Equally, FIEs wholly owned by foreign investors, and those in which the foreign share exceeds 30 per cent of equity, are allowed to export without licences the goods and services they produce. The law also relieves FIEs of the obligation to sell part of the resulting foreign currency revenues to the state.

The property of foreign investors brought in as a contribution to the statutory capital of FIEs, as well as inputs imported for production purposes, is exempt from duties. This also applies to the personal belongings of the expatriate workers of FIEs.

Foreign capital is also granted a preferential regime in free economic zones. This involves a simplified registration procedure (enterprises with a statutory capital not exceeding 75 million roubles can be registered by the zones' administrations); tax reduction of up to 50 per cent of prevailing tax rates; reduced rental payments for land and natural deposits; long-term leases (up to 70 years) and sub-leases; and lower customs duties and simplified customs and border formalities. At the time of writing, few free economic zones in Russia have gone through this organizational period.[19]

Profit Repatriation

The foreign investment law guarantees the unrestricted repatriation of after-tax investment incomes. To this end, foreign investors can buy foreign currency on the domestic foreign exchange market. FIEs producing important import-substituting goods can buy foreign currency for profit repatriation purposes from the 'state funds' at agreed exchange rates.

Inconsistencies in Regulations

By and large foreign investment regulations in the Russian Federation seem as liberal as those of the other East European economies in transition. Legislative changes in Russia have gradually eliminated the specific advantages granted to FIEs and introduced a similar legal environment for companies with and without foreign participation. On the negative side, the lack of consistency, precision and stability in regulations remains a major stumbling block to foreign investors, who are confronted by the danger of arbitrary decisions by the authorities.[20] Equally detrimental to the foreign investment climate are the unpredictable and sudden changes in regulations that interfere with the business plans and feasibility studies of investment projects. For example, a new tax law introduced in early 1992 eliminated the two-year tax holiday for joint ventures stipulated in the former all-Union law. This measure could be interpreted as a step towards the national treatment of foreign investors. However, this clearly contradicted the purpose of attracting foreign investors for whom, in Russia at least, tax holidays used to be a considerable incentive. Moreover, in some cases, these new tax regulations were applied retroactively -that is, to FIEs that had been registered before the regulations were enacted.[21] Later that year, the two-year tax holidays were restored for FIEs engaged in 'material production' (that is, not in services).[22] Press reports have since suggested that some foreign investors have been considering plans to redirect investments to countries with a more stable tax environment, such as Kazakhstan.[23]

Another instance refers to the obligatory sale of convertible currency by exporters. In December 1991, a presidential decree obliged all exporters, including joint ventures with a foreign share exceeding 30 per cent, to sell 10 per cent of export revenues to the state at market rates. In February 1992, the state bank exempted FIEs from that obligation.[24] In June 1992, however, a presidential decree required this category of foreign investors to sell 50 per cent of their foreign exchange export revenues to the domestic market.[25] Finally, in March 1993, a presidential decree exempted petroleum-refining enterprises and those extracting oil and gas from the 50 per cent obligatory sale of convertible currency receipts from exports for 1993, if those exports were 'carried out according to the needs of the state'.[26]

In principle, the obligatory sale of convertible currency earnings on the domestic market may be considered as a step towards internal convertibility of the local currency. However, it goes counter to the foreign investors' right spelled out in the foreign investment law (article 25). More important still is that, under conditions of rapid inflation and freefall of the rouble's external value, this requirement may entail considerable losses to the FIEs. Moreover, when implemented in such a contradictory fashion, the convertible currency surrender requirement can interfere with the marketing strategies and profitability targets of foreign investors.

Some operational regulations are less beneficial to FIEs than to other business ventures. In March 1992 export tariffs were reduced by an average of 20 per cent; however, this reduction was not extended to legal entities exempted from convertible currency surrender requirements, namely those enterprises with more than 30 per cent foreign participation and wholly foreign-owned subsidiaries. As a result, the duties on basic commodities (crude oil, coal, wood, nitrogen fertilizers) exported by FIEs increased by 44 per cent (including a surcharge of 15 per cent).[27]

The tax on oil exports (26 ecus a tonne, or more than 5 dollars a barrel in May 1992), in particular, is considered a strong deterrent to foreign investment in this sector. For example, the White Nights joint venture involving the two US companies Anglo-Suisse and Phibro found that the profit, export and value added taxes levied by different government bodies totalled nearly 100 per cent of the Western partners' revenues.[28] For this reason, the venture was compelled to curtail its convertible currency expenditure: the use of imported equipment was cut down and the number of expatriate personnel reduced by half.

Abrupt changes in regulations pertaining to taxation, export procedures and duties, and mineral deposits development, together with contradictory signals from the authorities at various levels, add to confusion
among foreign investors, who already have to operate under conditions
of deepening recession coupled with spiralling quasi-hyperinflation.

Foreign Investment and Privatization

Foreign participation in privatization is a recent phenomenon and is not
well documented. As regards foreign investment in existing enterprises,
the foreign investment law establishes the right of foreign investors to
participate in privatization and use legally earned roubles to buy shares
in state enterprises undergoing privatization. The rights of foreign investors in this respect are spelled out by the privatization legislation.

The privatization law of the Russian Federation enacted on 3 July 1991
gave Russian citizens and domestic investors preferential rights to own
state assets and considerably restricted the participation of foreigners in
the privatization of both small and large state companies.[29]

Foreign investment was officially encouraged in:

- loss-making enterprises;
- suspended or unfinished construction projects;
- enterprises that cut down production because of a lack of imported
  inputs; and
- enterprises in agro-industrial complexes and building materials.

In such cases foreign investors were permitted to acquire stock and
controlling stakes in companies due to be privatized.[30]

The state privatization programme introduced in 1992 liberalized the
conditions of foreign participation in the privatization process. Foreign
companies were granted the right to take part not only in investment
tenders but also in auctions and public price competition, including
cases where an FIE was the only participant. Decision-making on the
participation of foreign investors in the privatization of small and medium-sized firms (with the number of employees not exceeding 200 or
the book value of assets up to 1 million roubles on 1 January 1992) has
also been decentralized.

More importantly, the governments of the republics within the Russian Federation have been granted the right to take part in decision-
making on foreign participation in the privatization of the energy and
mining sectors: these include enterprises in the extraction of petrochemicals, ores, precious and semi-precious stones, and radioactive elements. The programme stipulates explicitly that any other restrictions

on foreign participation in privatization should not be imposed, and affirms the right of foreign investors to use their rouble assets for the purpose of privatization.[31]

In this way, the privatization programme for 1992 seems to have given more adequate legal background for foreign participation than the Law of 1991. While statistics of foreign participation in privatization are lacking, sketchy data provide several examples of foreign companies acquiring relatively big stakes in former state enterprises.

At the end of 1991, the German company Madrina AG acquired a 30 per cent equity stake in Elektrosila, a large producer of power-generating equipment: the total investment of the Western partner stands at 300 million dollars.[32] Acquisitions of local factories are also actively used by international tobacco concerns keen to tap one of the largest cigarette markets in the world. More recently, Philip Morris and R.J. Reynolds Tobacco International purchased a controlling interest in Russian tobacco-processing plants in St Petersburg and Krasnodar.[33]

Anecdotal evidence suggests further that foreign investors are particularly interested in the privatization of mining enterprises. One of the deals already agreed upon was the acquisition in April 1992 of a 31 per cent equity stake in the Lenzoloto joint stock company, 69 per cent state-owned, by the Australian company Star Technology Systems Ltd. This company has committed itself to invest 250 million dollars to increase the output of the Sukhoi Log mine in Eastern Siberia with total reserves of extractable gold estimated at 500 tonnes.[34]

The prospects of foreign participation in privatization are difficult to predict given the poor economic situation at the beginning of 1993 and the reluctance by decision-makers to grant foreign investors national treatment in the privatization process. However, it is reasonable to expect that foreign investors will be interested in privatizing larger Russian companies that can be made competitive in a foreseeable time span. This may be the case of some machine-building enterprises, including those in the defence sector, which have an important indigenous technological potential (such as the aircraft industry). Under solid state guarantees, foreign companies will also be willing to buy into local mining companies, once the domestic and foreign markets for their output are secured.

Growth and Scale of Foreign Investment

Joint ventures were first permitted on Soviet soil in 1987: in that year, 17 joint enterprises were set up in Russia – out of a total of 23 for the Soviet

Union. During 1987–90, the number of registered joint ventures in Russia made up 73 to 74 per cent of the all-Union total. By the end of 1991 — which saw the collapse of the Soviet Union — joint ventures numbered 2002, or 48 per cent of the estimated total (see Table 10.1).

The decrease in Russia's share of the total number of joint venture registrations during 1990–1 reflected the increasing interest by foreign investors in the other republics, along with the devolution of decision-making from the centre to the periphery. At the same time, the reorientation of foreign investment was statistically overstated. In the Baltic republics, in particular, many of the former all-Union enterprises reporting to central ministries were re-accounted as having foreign participation or as joint ventures with local partners, thus inflating the total number of FIEs.[35] Comparable statistics for the CIS show that Russia's share of the total number of new FIEs at end 1991 was as high as 78 per cent.

Since independence – end 1991 — the total number of FIEs in Russia grew by 67 per cent, reaching 3373 at the end of 1992. This figure is roughly equivalent to 48 per cent of the CIS total of 7000.

The evaluation of foreign investment stock in economies in transition in general, and in Russia, in particular, is an independent statistical problem, the analysis of which goes beyond the objectives of the present chapter.[36] Briefly, with respect to Russia, several factors should be taken into account.

First, the official statistics from the state committee on statistics (Goskomstat) represent part of the statutory capital of newly established FIEs (joint ventures and wholly owned subsidiaries), which are commitments by their Western partners to contribute a certain amount of capital goods. Some joint ventures never reach the stage of an actual transfer of capital (cash, equipment or technology) by the Western partner. Second, many FIEs do not report to Goskomstat additional paid-in capital and the resulting increases in their statutory funds. According to this body, the reporting is worse for larger FIEs. Third, in many cases the partners to foreign investment agreements use their discretion to assess their respective contributions, implementing rouble/convertible currency exchange rates that do not necessarily coincide with those stipulated by law or offered by the currency exchange. The use of individual exchange rates depends on the partner's shares of non-cash contributions, which may account for 80 per cent of the total capital value.

The evaluation of the assets of Russian enterprises undergoing privatization gives an indication of the magnitude of possible deviations of

Table 10.1 Foreign investment projects in the Russian Federation 1988–93

	Registered statutory capital				Foreign share cumulative	Operational (with output) no.	Output (SURm.)	Export[a] (SUSm.)	Import[a] (SUSm.)	Domestic sales[a] (SURm.)	Domestic sales[a] (SUSm.)	Employment
	No.	Total (SURm.)	Foreign (SURm.)	Foreign (SUSm.)								
1.01.1988 (1987)	17	129.7	47.6	76.8	0.38							
1.01.1989 (1988)	140	647.3	248.4	407.7	0.403							
1.01.1990 (1989)[b]	933	2592.1	1072.2	1708.8	0.433							
1.01.1991 (1990)[b]	1535	3826.0	1588.9	2485.5	0.415	620	18400.0	284.0	943.0		581.0	
1.01.1992 (1991)	2022	4151.8	2183.8	2827.4	0.526	1168	448929.4	422.0	470.0	11300.0	329.0	137 000
1.01.1993 (1992)	3373	19752.5	8257.5	2858.7	0.45	2519		1862.9	2036.9	169946.5	1364.6	195 037

[a]Before 1 January 1992, exports, imports and domestic sales for convertible currency figures are given in millions of valuta roubles.
[b]Number of registered FIEs refers to those for which information on capitalization is available; total number of registered FIEs was 947 on 1 January 1990 and 1971 on 1 January 1991.

Note: For the period ending 1 January 1991, foreign capital figures are converted in dollars at average monthly official/commercial exchange rates; for 1991, foreign capital increment figures are converted at 1.74 roubles per dollar yearly average commercial exchange rate; for 1992, foreign capital increment figures are converted as 193 roubles per dollar yearly average market exchange rate.

Source: United Nations Economic Commission for Europe.

these *ad hoc* exchange rates vis-à-vis their market counterparts.[37] Whereas the first accounting convention overstates the value of foreign investment stocks, the last tends to decrease it. In particular, against the backdrop of accelerating inflation and the fall in the value of the rouble, the market rouble–dollar exchange rate has deviated progressively from purchasing power parities in foreign investment transactions in favour of the dollar. In this way, the reverse conversion of foreign capital stocks denominated in roubles into convertible currencies (dollars) at market exchange rates - and those are the only rates available – minimizes the growth of that aggregate.

This being said, during 1991–2, in rouble terms the foreign part of the statutory capital of FIEs grew from 1.6 billion in January 1991 to 2.2 billion a year later, and to 8.3 billion at the start of 1993: that is, over five-fold. During 1992, the value of foreign investment almost quadrupled.[38] On a yearly basis, in 1992 the implicit GDP price deflator increased almost 18 times, while on a December to December basis, prices in investment construction increased 16-fold and wholesale industry prices by 34 times.[39] This suggests that the real growth in foreign investment was minimal.

The latest reliable dollar estimates of the cumulative foreign component of joint ventures' statutory capital from the UN/ECE database refer to the beginning of 1991, when it amounted to 2485.5 million dollars (1588.9 billion roubles). The rouble equivalent of this figure is an aggregate of the Ministry of Finance's registration data pertaining to new FIEs, while the former estimate is obtained by converting the rouble stock value at monthly average official/commercial exchange rates. Subsequently, the regular keeping of registration records was discontinued.

To arrive at our dollar estimates, the 1991 increment in foreign investment was converted at the year's average commercial exchange rate (1.74 roubles to the dollar). During 1992, the Russian state bank published only the official market exchange rate from the inter-bank currency exchange. Following the Goskomstat methodology, for that year the rouble–dollar yearly average market rate (193 roubles per dollar) was used to convert the rouble-denominated foreign investment stock increment into dollars. In this way, the cumulative value of foreign investment (cumulative value of foreign components of FIEs' statutory capital) increased from 2485.5 million dollars at the end of 1990 to 2827.4 million dollars a year later. During 1992, according to the official methodology, this indicator hardly grew (it increased by about 31 million dollars) and stood at 2858.7 million dollars at year end.

It is interesting to compare the estimated foreign investment stock figures with the balance of payments data on flows of foreign investment computed by the Goskomstat and the central bank for the first nine months of 1992. During that period, the gross foreign investment inflows in Russia amounted to 1.1 billion dollars. However, the outflow was 0.5 billion dollars for joint ventures and 0.825 billion for the banks. Hence, the resultant inflow was negative, amounting to 225 million dollars.[40] Since the methodology of the balance of payments compilation has not yet been documented, these figures do not tell us whether the foreign investment of banks was effected by banks with foreign participation, their purely Russian counterparts or both.[41] If the outflows of capital represent a divestment of FIEs, this would be in line with the Goskomstat data on stocks, which show a drop in the value of the foreign component of FIEs' statutory capital in the third quarter and a marginal growth for the year as a whole.

An alternative estimate made by PlanEcon in a study prepared for the World Bank puts the cumulative volume of foreign investment in Russia in June 1992 at 1218.4 million dollars, while the IMF has estimated the net inflow of FDI in Russia in convertible currencies for 1991 at 100 million dollars.[42]

The World Bank study (PlanEcon) stock estimate has one important advantage over its official, respectively the UN/ECE, counterpart. It refers to the foreign investment stocks of operational FIEs, and this brings it closer to the IMF and OECD FDI stock definitions.[43] However, the authors could not avoid the reverse conversion of data from roubles into dollars at yearly average exchange rates. As was already indicated, particularly for 1992, this may undervalue the foreign investment stocks.

In sum, at the end of 1992, foreign investment stocks in Russia were worth some 2.0 to 2.5 billion dollars, and at the time of writing (1993) a more accurate evaluation was hardly possible. In principle, the estimate of the end-1992 foreign investment stocks based on the commitments of Western partners (Goskomstat -UN/ECE methodology) is a more credible one. One should not forget, however, that during 1992 at least, the unrealistically low rouble exchange rate tended to minimize the growth of this value in dollar terms. A lower estimate by the World Bank (PlanEcon) may be more practical, although the value of foreign investment stocks can be underestimated because of the incomplete coverage of operational FIEs. In view of the growing interest of decision-makers in attracting foreign capital, the compilation of comprehensive and up-to-date foreign investment statistics remains a challenging but rewarding task for Russian statisticians.

Major Investors

According to available data from the UN/ECE Secretariat, the bulk of foreign investment in Russia originates from Western Europe. At the end of 1992, this region accounted for over 53 per cent of the total foreign component of the statutory capital of FIEs. It should be noted, however, that during 1991–2 its importance as a source of entrepreneurial capital declined, mostly in favour of the USA (almost 18 per cent) and Japan (6 per cent). Companies from the developing countries and Eastern Europe committed over 5 per cent of total foreign investment in each case, and their shares also declined recently.

Table 10.2 assembles information on 10 major investor countries in the Russian Federation on 1 January 1993. The top 5 investor-countries accounted for over 46 per cent of total volume (48 per cent at the start of 1991), while the top 10 made up 69 per cent (67 per cent). US companies invested by far the largest share of foreign capital, followed by German, Austrian, Finnish and Chinese investors. In terms of numbers of projects registered, German firms outpaced US enterprises, accounting for over 14 per cent of the total. However, in terms of capitalization, projects with US participation on average tend to be over twice as large as those with German participation. It should also be noted that, by the end of 1992, Japan joined the list of major investors in Russia, while this had not been the case two years earlier.

Overall, the aforementioned pattern broadly corresponds to the available estimates of the geographical distribution of FDI stocks worldwide at the beginning of 1990.[44] At the same time, though the share of Western Europe is very close to the worldwide average (52 per cent in 1990), both US and Japanese involvement in inward investment in Russia is lower than their respective shares in world FDI stocks (26 per cent and 12 per cent respectively). To a certain extent, the lack of investment from the US and Japan has been compensated by that from developing and transition economies. However, over the last few years, the geographical structure of capital inflows to Russia has tended to get closer to that of FDI stocks worldwide.

Industrial Distribution

Up-to-date data on the industrial distribution of FIEs are practically inaccessible (the official data on industrial breakdown of foreign investment-related output available are presented in Table 10.3). It is known, however, that at the end of the third quarter of 1991, 509 of the 1102

Table 10.2 Major source countries of foreign investment in the Russian Federation

| Country | 1.1.1991 (1987–90) | | 1.1.1993 | |
	No.	Foreign capital (SUR m.)	No.	Foreign capital (SUR m.)
USA	198	190.6	451	1466.7
Germany	224	179.1	482	735.5
Austria	84	64.5	170	602.0
Finland	115	193.2	245	520.9
China	23	13.5	96	514.0
Japan	32	28.6	119	484.2
Italy	104	115.1	177	406.9
UK	93	65.4	175	331.8
Sweden	48	48.8	93	321.9
Canada	40	46.1	67	302.2
Top 5	644	640.8	1444	3839.1
Top 10	961	944.9	2075	5686.1
Total	1535	1588.9	3373	8257.5
Per cent of total				
USA	12.9	12.0	13.4	17.8
Germany	14.6	11.3	14.3	8.9
Austria	5.5	4.1	5.0	7.3
Finland	7.5	12.2	7.3	6.3
China	1.5	0.8	2.8	6.2
Japan	2.1	1.8	3.5	5.9
Italy	6.8	7.2	5.2	4.9
UK	6.1	4.1	5.2	4.0
Sweden	3.1	3.1	2.8	3.9
Canada	2.6	2.9	2.0	3.7
Top 5	42.0	40.3	42.8	46.5
Top 10	62.6	59.5	61.5	68.9
Total	100.0	100.0	100.0	100.0

Source: United Nations Economic Commission for Europe.

ventures in operation (46 per cent) were engaged in industrial production, and 56 (5 per cent) in construction. About 9 per cent were in Research and Development, 8 per cent in trade and public catering and 31 per cent in other industries.[45] Because of the implicit statistical conventions, these data give only a rough idea of the actual lines of FIEs' activities.[46] However, they indicate that over half were engaged in the production of goods (industry and construction).

This trend is confirmed by independent data sources. Of the 2100 Russia-based joint ventures operating in June 1992, according to the

Table 10.3   Operational foreign investment projects in the Russian
Federation, by industry

Industry	Output (SUR m.)	%
Agriculture	715.0	1.1
Forestry	179.1	0.3
Industry	49799.6	73.8
Construction	3100.7	4.6
Transport	1841.3	2.7
Communications	80.3	0.1
Trade and public catering	3892.3	5.8
Material supply	315.8	0.5
Information and computer services	341.2	0.5
Other material production	2167.0	3.2
Real estate and communal services	105.3	0.2
Healthcare	3302.3	4.9
Education	44.5	0.1
Culture	574.1	0.9
Science, R&D	857.3	1.3
Financial services	21.4	0.0
Management services	21.4	0.0
Social organizations	13.3	0.0
Other	123.2	0.2
Total	67495.1	100.0

Note: 1.7.1992 (1Q-2Q 1992).

Source: UN/ECE Doc. Trade/R.588.

PlanEcon data bank, 1240 or 59 per cent were in manufacturing. Of
these, 56 per cent produced consumer goods, and the remainder were
split between the extractive sector (energy and mining), and the production of machinery and transport equipment.[47] The industrial concentration of FIEs in the above-mentioned sectors is dictated largely by
structural imbalances in the Russian economy, the wearing out of technological equipment and the reliance on imports. As an example,
according to Russian experts, the 'rational consumption norm' of
cloth should be 50 square metres per person per year, while in 1985
average consumption amounted to only 36 square metres. To reach the
desired level of consumption, 6 billion square metres of cloth should be
produced yearly. Meanwhile, in 1992 the production of cloth in Russia
plummeted to 3 billion square metres and has continued to fall. In 1991,
Russia produced 313 million pairs of shoes and imported another 23
million.[48] In the early 1990s, the annual sales of passenger motor vehicles did not exceed 700 000 while the average age of a car increased from

7.5 years in 1980 to over 12 years in 1993. Experts have estimated the yearly deficit of car sales at 1.5 to 3 million.[49]

According to Russian estimates, the share of imported equipment has made up almost 48 per cent in the oil and oil-refining industries, and 42 to 43 per cent in the manufacture of wearing apparel. A considerable part of this equipment needs to be replaced.[50]

The demand-led import-replacing foreign investment in the consumer goods and technological equipment sectors can help saturate the domestic market without additional strain on depleted convertible currency resources.

Foreign Investment Operations

During 1991, the number of operational FIEs nearly doubled, from 620 to 1168. Simultaneously, their share in the total number of registrations grew from 31 to 58 per cent. The following year, in terms of numbers, their growth accelerated further: by the end of 1992 there were 2519 enterprises with foreign capital participation in Russia producing goods or services (over 75 per cent of those registered).

In 1992, the total employment of FIEs went up from 137000 to 195000 (a 42 per cent increase). By the end of the year, foreign-investment-related employment was equivalent to 0.3 per cent of total employment and 1.2 per cent of total employment in the non-state sector of the Russian economy.[51]

At current prices, the total value of output of operational FIEs rose from 18.4 billion roubles in 1991 to 448.9 billion roubles a year later, that is a 24-fold increase. At constant prices, if an implicit GDP deflator is used, this nominal growth represents a rise in output of about 37 per cent, while Russia's GDP volume dropped by 19 per cent as compared with 1991. As a ratio of GDP at current prices, the foreign investment output also increased, from 1.8 per cent in 1991 to 3.0 per cent in 1992.[52] Although both proportions are marginal, one can note that the foreign investment output–GDP ratio is higher than the share of enterprises with foreign participation in total employment.

The data available on the sectoral distribution of foreign-investment output refer to the first half of 1992 only. Table 10.3 shows that, in terms of value, almost 74 per cent of FIEs' production was concentrated in industry, 6 per cent in trade and public catering, 5 per cent in construction and less than 3 per cent in transport services. Together these five sectors accounted for 92 per cent of the value of total production.[53] Thus, output data show an even higher concentration in the production of goods than the data on the number of operational FIEs.

During 1991–2, the domestic sales of FIEs in roubles increased more than 15-fold (from 11.3 to 169.9 billion roubles), while the retail sales turnover (also at current prices) grew 7.6 times. As a result, the ratio of foreign investment sales to the total value of retail turnover grew from 2.4 to 4.7 per cent.[54] During 1992 the domestic sales of foreign investments for convertible currency amounted to 1364.6 million dollars, that is 73 per cent of foreign-investment-related exports.

The above-mentioned figures suggest that, during 1992, the production of FIEs was growing despite a critical slump in the Russian economy. Simultaneously, their role in satisfying consumer demand (with the retail trade turnover as a proxy) increased more than in production.

The dynamics of FI-related exports and imports are difficult to follow because after 1991 Goskomstat switched to accounting foreign trade in dollars instead of roubles. At the end of 1992, the total exports of FIEs amounted to 1862.9 million dollars, and imports to 2036.9 million dollars. These figures were equivalent to 4.9 per cent of total Russian exports and 5.8 per cent of Russian imports, and were considerably higher than in 1991, when the respective shares did not exceed 0.7 and 1.1 per cent.[55] Thus, the participation of FIEs in foreign trade has been more significant than that in production, and has been close to their share in domestic trade.

While in 1991, foreign investment exports and imports were almost balanced (the deficit amounted to 48 million roubles), and during the first half of 1992 exports exceeded imports by 261 million dollars, for that year as a whole the foreign trade deficit of FIEs made up 338 million dollars. The latter figure compares unfavourably with Russia's overall foreign trade surplus in 1992, estimated at 3.1 billion dollars.

Data on the product structure of FI-related exports and imports are not available. However, there are indications that, recently, FIEs have become active in oil exports. Although the origin of these is not clear (own extraction or resale), in 1991 four oil joint ventures sold abroad just under 1 million tonnes (1.8 per cent of the total).[56] In 1992, excluding deliveries to the ex-Soviet republics, FI-related exports grew to 4.4 million tonnes of oil (6.7 per cent of the total),[57] and in 1993 FIEs were set to export up to 7.5 million tonnes[58] to markets outside the CIS. At the same time, FIEs seemed to strengthen their positions on the domestic market, not only through an increase in production but also through an enhanced sale of imported goods and services.[59]

At the beginning of the 1990s, by all yardsticks, the role of foreign capital in the Russian economy was modest but growing. Operational FIEs increased their output in real terms against the backdrop of overall stagflation. The impact of foreign investment operations became noticeable in the supply of consumer goods and in foreign trade, in particular oil exports. At the same time, the Russian economy failed to attract foreign investment in amounts commensurate with both its investment potential and its needs for external financing and new technology.

Geographical Distribution

At the time of writing (1993) data on the geographical distribution of foreign investment were available only for the period ending in 1991. Table 10.4 refers to operational FIEs and some of their output indicators by economic region (which do not coincide with administrative divisions).

The data show that, during 1989–91, foreign investment activities were shifting from the central region (including Moscow) to the outlying regions of Russia. While their number was growing in absolute terms, the share of operational FIEs domiciled in the Central region fell from 84 to 55 per cent of the total. The major beneficiaries of that shift were the Northern and North-Western regions situated in European Russia, as well as the Far-Eastern economic region. At the end of the period under review, these three areas accounted for 7, 9 and 8 per cent respectively of the total number of operational FIEs.

In terms of domestic sales and imports by FIEs, the above-mentioned shift is less significant. However, with respect to foreign-investment-related exports, the gain in the weighting of the outlying regions is particularly pronounced: while the share of the Central region plummeted from over 75 to only 29 per cent, that of the Far East and Western Siberia soared from 11 to 25 per cent, and from 1 to 12 per cent respectively.

The redistribution of FI-related exports is apparently linked to the growing penetration of foreign enterprises in the development of mineral deposits, concentrated mainly on the outskirts of Russia. If this is the case then more up-to-date information is likely to show an even more intensive concentration of foreign investment activities in the east and north of the country.

Foreign Investment in Mineral Resources

The scope of foreign involvement in the development of Russia's natural and mineral resources increased recently. Several large-scale projects

224

Table 10.4 Foreign investment projects in the Russian Federation, by region of operation

Economic region	Operational (no.)			Domestic sales (SUR m.)			Domestic sales (valuta SUR m.)			Exports (valuta SUR m.)			Imports (valuta SUR m.)		
	1989	1990	1991	1989	1990	1991	1989	1990	1991	1989	1990	1991	1989	1990	1991
Northern	5	30	86	5.7	45.1	399.0	0.1	1.7	1.9	0.8	5.3	26.9	0.5	7.2	14.0
North-Western	23	26	109	79.0	269.0	1223.9	4.7	49.2	16.0	2.5	6.8	26.5	8.1	12.1	33.6
Central	271	308	676	399.1	1526.3	7161.2	171.5	437.6	288.1	84.0	108.9	122.6	229.5	489.3	277.7
Volga-Vyatka	1	2	26	0.0	1.8	155.0	0.0	0.0	0.3	0.0	0.0	9.9	59.0	69.0	11.3
Central-Black Earth	0	2	18	0.0	49.2	326.0	0.0	0.0	0.0	0.0	1.2	5.1	0.0	29.4	7.4
Povolzh'e	7	26	52	23.8	147.6	574.3	1.1	16.7	5.6	1.1	5.7	39.9	9.7	37.1	7.1
North-Caucasian	2	19	52	4.9	76.2	387.6	1.2	4.8	7.8	0.0	3.9	16.0	0.0	3.7	7.0
Ural	2	7	41	18.9	75.1	323.7	0.2	0.0	0.6	0.0	0.2	5.3	1.2	7.9	9.7
Western-Siberian	3	9	42	26.1	15.8	223.3	0.0	0.3	3.7	1.3	37.7	51.4	7.1	12.8	29.3
Eastern-Siberian	1	3	17	8.9	13.1	40.3	0.0	0.1	0.2	8.9	8.3	10.3	0.0	0.6	0.6
Far-Eastern	7	33	93	33.0	51.5	412.6	0.2	1.8	3.7	12.8	31.3	107.6	2.2	8.2	72.0
Kaliningrad	0	0	12	0.0	0.0	22.0	0.0	0.0	0.7	0.0	0.0	0.5	0.0	0.0	0.3
Total: Russian Federation	322	465	1224	599.4	2270.7	11248.9	179.0	512.2	328.6	111.4	209.3	422.0	317.3	677.3	470.0

Per cent of total

Northern	1.6	6.5	7.0	1.0	2.0	3.5	0.1	0.3	0.6	0.7	2.5	6.4	0.2	1.1	3.0
North-Western	7.1	5.6	8.9	13.2	11.8	10.9	2.6	9.6	4.9	2.2	3.2	6.3	2.6	1.8	7.1
Central region	84.2	66.2	55.2	66.6	67.2	63.7	95.8	85.4	87.7	75.4	52.0	29.1	72.3	72.2	59.1
Volga-Vyatka	0.3	0.4	2.1	0.0	0.1	1.4	0.0	0.0	0.1	0.0	0.0	2.3	18.6	10.2	2.4
Central-Black Earth	0.0	0.4	1.5	0.0	2.2	2.9	0.0	0.0	0.0	0.0	0.6	1.2	0.0	4.3	1.6
Povolzh'e	2.2	5.6	4.2	4.0	6.5	5.1	0.6	3.3	1.7	1.0	2.7	9.5	3.1	5.5	1.5
North-Caucasian	0.6	4.1	4.2	0.8	3.4	3.4	0.7	0.9	2.4	0.0	1.9	3.8	0.0	0.5	1.5
Ural	0.6	1.5	3.3	3.2	3.3	2.9	0.1	0.0	0.2	0.0	0.1	1.3	0.4	1.2	2.1
Western-Siberian	0.9	1.9	3.4	4.4	0.7	2.0	0.0	0.1	1.1	1.2	18.0	12.2	2.2	1.9	6.2
Eastern-Siberian	0.3	0.6	1.4	1.5	0.6	0.4	0.0	0.0	0.1	8.0	4.0	2.4	0.0	0.1	0.1
Far-Eastern	2.2	7.1	7.6	5.5	2.3	3.7	0.1	0.4	1.1	11.5	15.0	25.5	0.7	1.2	15.3
Kaliningrad	0.0	0.0	1.0	0.0	0.0	0.2	0.0	0.0	0.2	0.0	0.0	0.1	0.0	0.0	0.1
Total: Russian Federation	100.0	100.0	100.0	100.0	100.0	100.0	100.0	100.0	100.0	100.0	100.0	100.0	100.0	100.0	100.0

Source: UN/ECE DOC. TRADE/R.588.

were negotiated in the prospecting and extraction of petrochemicals, copper, precious metals (gold) and coal (see the appendix to this chapter for details).

In the early 1990s, the oil-extracting sector became of particular interest to foreign investors. The output of oil in Russia reached its peak in 1987 when it amounted to 569 million tonnes. It has since declined: in 1991 production was some 100 million tonnes lower than in the peak year of 1987. In 1992, Russia extracted 393 million tonnes, that is 66.6 million tonnes less than in 1991 and 176 million tonnes below 1987 levels.[60]

The causes of the steep drop in oil production are linked to the depletion of major deposits, inefficient extracting, distributing and processing equipment, and chronic under-investment. In the early 1990s– compared with a decade earlier–the capital intensity of oil extraction increased threefold. By 1991, the twenty largest oil deposits in operation, representing some 60 per cent of all extractable stocks, had been depleted by 70 per cent.[61] As much as a third of total output was lost through leaking pipes, wasteful refineries and inefficient factories.[62] In 1990, in Western Siberia, the lack of pipes connecting drilled pits and oil collectors resulted in a 12 million tonnes drop in output at an exportable value of 2 billion dollars.[63]

Sources from the Ministry of Fuels and Power Engineering reveal that at the beginning of 1992, 22 500 oil wells were stopped for overhaul. The government intended to attract foreign investors to rehabilitate 8000 wells.[64] The overhaul of 6000 to 7000 oil pits at an estimated cost of $500 m would increase oil output by 25 million tonnes, which, if exported, would net in over 3 billion dollars in additional revenues.[65]

Until recently, both foreign investors and the government took a cautious approach to petrochemicals. Selected companies with government backing have been given access to marginal deposits inaccessible to domestic producers. Foreign investments in the oil sector in 1992 did not exceed 200 million dollars; only sixteen joint ventures were operational.[66]

The operations of the few investors were aimed essentially at raising the output of depleted oil wells with the use of modern technology unavailable to local producers. Such projects often included replacing pipes and reopening wells that were closed for lack of spare parts. The first 'trial' joint undertakings in the oil extraction industry had been agreed upon even before the law on subsoil (mineral deposits) was enacted. Despite their marginal impact on the overall level of production, they proved advantageous to Western partners because of the relatively small capital expenses, which paid back within months.[67]

In this way, a joint venture formed with the participation of Canadian Fracmaster and Royal Dutch Shell has increased output of idle oil wells in Siberia by 10 000 barrels per day through the use of hydraulic fracturing. The joint venture has already recouped 23 million dollars' worth of initial investment by the Western partners through export sales of oil to Italy and Spain.[68] The French Total Oil concern has set up a small joint venture with Tatneft (capitalized at 2 million dollars), which intends to increase output by 30 to 50 per cent by pumping polymers into oil-beds at the Romashkino oil field. The total investment in the next few years should total 300 million dollars, and output is expected to rise to 1 million tonnes a year. Total will be paid 25 per cent of the increase in output in kind.[69] Along the same lines, at the beginning of 1992, Mobil Oil announced that it was investing 300 million dollars in the Tyumen oil fields.[70]

During 1992 and 1993, the foreign participation in oil production and exports increased in importance. By the end of 1992, FIEs in the oil sector had rehabilitated 300 oil wells in the Tyumen region. By the same date, Siberian enterprises had concluded 5000 contracts with foreign companies for the overhaul of oil wells worth 1 billion dollars. Joint ventures are estimated to have extracted 7.5 million tonnes of oil in 1992.

Along with implementing small-scale trial petrochemical projects, larger oil companies have started exploring the opportunities of prospected deposits. Here again, foreign investors rely on their superior technology to extract oil in unfavourable geological conditions and geographically remote areas.

In 1991, the German company Deminex set up the joint venture Volgodeminoil with Nizhnevolzhskneft to exploit oil and gas deposits in the Volgograd region. This enterprise plans to capitalize on the technology and know-how of the German partner required to drill and extract oil from the depth of 4 to 5 km. Within five years, it plans to increase the output of oil to 1.2 million tonnes (the total oil resources of the fields to be developed are estimated at 110 million tonnes). In the longer term, the total investment may be as high as 3 billion dollars.[71]

In 1991, Conoco, the subsidiary of DuPont de Nemours, founded a joint venture – Polyarnoye Siyaniye (Polar Lights) – aimed at developing three oil fields: Dosyushevskoye, Ardalinskoye and Kolvinskoye in the Komi autonomous region. The resources of Ardalinskoye alone are estimated at 16 million tonnes, and the joint venture intends to invest up to 3 billion dollars in the development of the three fields over a period of ten years. At the time of writing (1993), other Western energy concerns were concluding or negotiating similar agreements.[72]

A number of large energy companies have also finalized lengthy negotiations on their right to prospect for petrochemicals and develop deposits in areas so far neglected by geologists.

One of the largest research projects is the exploration of two oil and gas fields on the shelf of Sakhalin Island in the Russian Far East (the Lunskoye and Piltun-Astokhskoye fields). According to Japanese estimates, the Sakhalin deposit could produce some 3 billion barrels of crude oil and at least a trillion cubic metres of natural gas. The Russian Ministry of Ecology and Natural resources has conservatively estimated the reserves of the two major Sakhalin shelf deposits at 100 million tonnes of oil (the equivalent of yearly oil exports by the former USSR) and over 400 billion cubic metres of natural gas.

For several years, four international groups of companies have been contesting the right to explore and extract oil and gas from the two Sakhalin fields.[73] The international tender was finally won by the MMM consortium consisting of the Japanese trading company Mitsui Bussan, Marathon Oil Co. (US) and McDermott International Inc. (US). The consortium was awarded a contract to conduct a feasibility study of the two oil fields. At a later stage, Royal Dutch/ Shell and Mitsubishi joined the consortium and shared the costs of the feasibility study. It is expected that the enlargement of the consortium will significantly increase its chances of winning the development rights.[74]

The estimates from the feasibility study of the tender's winners suggest that the total cost of the project will amount to 12 to 14 billion dollars, much of which to be spent on subcontracting Russian enterprises and on employee remuneration.[75] The production of crude oil and gas is scheduled to start at the end of 1995, and the production of liquified natural gas in 1999. The total profit from the operation of the two deposits spread over a period of twenty-five years is estimated at 27 to 32 billion dollars, of which the foreign partners will receive between 9 and 16 billion dollars.[76]

The appendix to this chapter lists some of the large-scale foreign investment projects in mineral resource development in February 1993. The value of the initial foreign investment (that is, for the first one to four years of operation) in ten projects, for which data are available, amounts to over 1.5 billion dollars. This value is equivalent to over half of the estimated volume of foreign investment commitments accumulated by the Russian Federation by the end of 1992 (2.9 billion dollars).

The value of total foreign investment planned for twelve projects for which data are available is as high as 42.2 billion dollars. It should be noted, however, that this capital commitment will be spread over a period of 25 to 40 years. The bulk of contracts negotiated or agreed upon (19 out of 22) deal with the prospecting and extracting of oil and gas. The data on nine projects suggest that, in 5 to 15 years' time, oil output in Russia may increase by 59 million tonnes.

The recent foreign penetration in mineral resources has aroused concern among Russia's oil- and gas-producing enterprises, which see a competitive threat from transnational concerns in the formerly closed energy sector. The major complaint of local entrepreneurs is that foreign companies in the energy sector have acquired concessions to develop the best deposits, while their local competitors have been 'elbowed' to a second-best position.[77] In order to face this challenge, Russian petrochemical producers have started regrouping their forces. At the end of 1991 a new Russian oil corporation, Sinco, was formed. It incorporates nine regional oil-producing conglomerates from Siberia as well as an international company, Euro-Sov Petroleum Ltd, with British, Australian and US interests. With a modest statutory capital (11 million roubles), the corporation plans to lease and develop idle oil fields. In this way, it intends to increase its equity capital, privatize the company and further enlarge the scope of its operations.[78] Three other recently established oil companies – Lukoil, Surgutneftegaz and Yukos – control almost one-third of oil output in Russia. In the course of their privatization, some 40 per cent of the stock will be sold off to the public, and as much as 15 per cent will be made available to foreign investors.[79]

The lobbying by petrochemical companies both in the press and among policy-makers has clearly borne fruit. Signs of an emerging protectionist stance *vis-à-vis* foreign investment in mineral resources have started to appear. Recently, President Yeltsin granted the exploitation rights of the giant Chtokmanskoye gas deposit and the Prirazlomnoye oil field to the Russian consortium Rosshelf.[80] This decision was taken after a preliminary agreement had been reached with a group of Western companies including Conoco, Finnish Metra and Norsk Hydro. This pro-Russian presidential decision was a clear sign of the authorities' sensitivity to the newly emerging protectionist sentiment among local industrialists, particularly the powerful mining and military-industrial lobbies.

The protectionist approach has also become prevalent in the development of the largest untapped copper deposit at Udokan in South-East

Siberia. The contract was awarded to a Russian – Cypriot joint venture – Udokan Mining Company – (45 per cent owned by the Cypriot firm Chita Minerals, itself an affiliate of the US and German firms Somerset Holdings and SFV). The unsuccessful bidder was the Australian company BHP, one of the most experienced developers of this type of deposit.[81] The Russian–Cypriot venture received the backing of a number of Russian machine-building enterprises expecting to subcontract the production of equipment and associated construction work worth 700 million dollars and 3500 new jobs.[82]

The Financing and Operations of Foreign banks

The financing of foreign investors' activities in transition economies, particularly in the former Soviet Union, has generally encountered difficulties. Domestically, the state-controlled banks were loath to extend loans to joint ventures, unless a government agency (normally a branch ministry) served as guarantor. On the other hand, commercial banks only started to emerge in the 1990s and, because of their lack of resources, could not provide sufficient funding to the FIEs. In this way, these companies often had to rely on external financing, with foreign partners arranging and guaranteeing loans.

In Russia, the problems of foreign investment financing have been similar to those encountered by FIEs in former Soviet times. As regards rouble financing, the funding of FIEs through securities issues has so far been limited because of the underdeveloped securities market. At the same time, domestic sources of investment financing have started to emerge owing to the developing network of commercial banks.

By the beginning of 1993, the number of commercial banks in Russia had approached 2000 (4000 if branches are included).[83] The crediting facilities of commercial banks are relatively small, while the technical equipment and the level of staff competence are often insufficient. On 1 January 1993, the combined statutory capital of the 100 largest commercial banks did not exceed 148.9 billion roubles, or less than 360 million dollars at exchange rates applicable to date.[84] The recently established affiliate of Crédit Lyonnais, with a statutory capital of 20 million ecus, became one of the top five banking institutions in the Russian Federation.

Although the rouble financing of FIEs is feasible, owing to the developing network of commercial banks, foreign currency funding is more problematic. Russian experts estimated that, at the end of 1992, only 10 out of 1550 operating banks in Russia had sufficient resources and expertise to conduct operations in foreign currencies.[85] In these conditions, the operation of foreign banks on the Russian market, as well as the activities of joint and foreign investment funds, represent potentially important sources of finance for the FIEs.

As a rule, foreign and joint investment funds are organized to finance foreign (joint) investment projects in individual industrial sectors and/ or regions. Thus, the Austrian company Newa-Arge and the Russian firm Arctis founded an investment fund to finance joint military conversion projects in St Petersburg. The fund sponsored by UNIDO has an initial capitalization of 1.5 million dollars.[86] The Staritsky Development Corporation registered in the USA, with a statutory capital of 100 million dollars, aims to develop agricultural and food production in the Tver region; the projected investment over the next three years is estimated at 1 billion dollars.[87] One more joint investment fund targeted at conversion projects with foreign capital participation was set up in the USA in late 1990.[88]

The financial basis of foreign investment activities would be enhanced by facilitating foreign bankers' access to the domestic market. The penetration of foreign banks in Russia started after the law on banks and banking activities was enacted in December 1990. Since then, a number of joint banks have been established, such as the International Moscow Bank, with a relatively important foreign share (60 per cent). A joint Russian–American Investment Bank with an initial capitalization of 10 million dollars and 50 million roubles was founded by a number of US and Russian bankers. Its role is to offer financial advice and project finance, mostly to oil enterprises of Siberia.[89]

International financial organizations contribute, to a certain extent, to setting up joint ventures in the banking sector. Recently, the EBRD took a 35 per cent stake in the newly founded Russian Project Finance Bank. This bank, with the participation of ten local banks and an initial capitalization of 6 million dollars, will extend medium-term and long-term loans to foreign investors and FIEs, as well as act as an investment bank. The bank plans to raise its capitalization to 100 million dollars within two years, and the European Union has agreed to provide staff training worth around 7 million ecus.[90]

Two leading Western banking institutions have set up affiliates in the Russian Federation: as mentioned above, in 1991 the French bank Crédit Lyonnais obtained a general licence to set up its first affiliate. The Austrian Z-Zanderbank was also granted the right to act as an offshore bank. These pioneering measures were followed by some other Western banks, which applied for general licences allowing them to extend their full range of services to foreign and local investors, and the general public.

The penetration of foreign banks in Russia has aroused opposition on the part of the local banks. Russian commercial banks view their foreign counterparts as a threat to their positions, using the 'infant industry' argument in their defence, namely their inability to compete with foreign banks in terms of available resources, technical infrastructure and financial know-how.

For this reason, in the autumn of 1992, the Association of Russian Banks submitted to Parliament draft amendments to the law on banks and banking activities. These, in particular, recommended that the licensing of subsidiaries of foreign banks in Russia be frozen so that they could not conduct rouble operations for a period of at least two or three years.[91] If adopted, these amendments would have cut off foreign banking subsidiaries from the bulk of domestic financial operations, limiting their role to off-shore operations.[92]

Reportedly, at least in the short run, the uncertainty associated with the offensive of Russian bankers against the penetration of competitors from abroad has influenced the investment decisions of foreign financiers. Apart from the above-mentioned affiliates of the French and Austrian banks, which had already acquired licences for operations in Russia, by the end of 1992 not more than four or five foreign banks had applied for opening subsidiaries in that country.

At the same time, the proposal of the Association of Russian Banks to freeze the licensing of foreign banks' subsidiaries was rejected by Parliament at the end of 1992, under considerable pressure from the reform-minded government. As a compromise, the latter decided to work out rules of access and operation for foreign banks, which would create certain privileges for banking institutions with purely Russian capital.[93]

It should be noted that the reasoning of local bankers is not entirely groundless, and, perhaps, before local and foreign banks obtain equal treatment, the former should be given the opportunity to stand on their own two feet. At the same time, the policy-makers have to decide to what extent the users of financial services should bear the cost of fortifying the indigenous banking industry in terms of reduced financial opportunities and diversity of services. Temporary barriers to entry should give local banks room for growth and experience, but not discourage competition in the financial sector.

The governmental economic policy paper for 1993 called for restricted access by foreign banks to the domestic market as one of the means to raise the efficiency of foreign economic relations. To this end, the government may raise the cost of operational licences, as well as introduce high minimal capitalization and reinvestment requirements.[94] To a certain extent, these instruments will raise sectoral barriers to foreign penetration. However, they are likely to deter relatively small investment projects. Larger projects initiated by major banks, which have already incorporated the Russian market in their long-term strategies, will probably not be discouraged.

Home Country Incentives

At the end of the 1980s, the governments of the leading Western economies did not show particular interest in the activities of national private companies in the former Soviet Union. A more practical approach emerged with the dismantling of the USSR after the failed coup of August 1991. The deteriorating economic situation in Russia withered away hopes that the intergovernmental assistance to the former USSR could by itself radically change the negative economic trends. In turn, this contributed to a better understanding of the potential role of private capital inflows in stabilizing the economy and implementing market reforms. Since then, to varying degrees, Western governments have started incorporating foreign investment in Russia in the existing framework of foreign investment support.

In September 1991, the US president waived a provision of the Foreign Assistance Act barring the Overseas Private Investment Corporation (OPIC) from assisting communist countries.[95] In that month, OPIC was ready to offer 1 billion dollars worth of insurance to American firms willing to invest in the former USSR.[96] In late 1991, companies registered with OPIC were willing to invest in the ex-Soviet republics as much as 1.5 billion dollars, particularly in the oil and gas sectors.[97] In November 1991, OPIC made a first conditional agreement to insure up to 100 million dollars of the 250 millions of investment by Batterymarch Financial Management, which targeted several investment projects under the auspices of the Russian defence conversion programme. At the end of 1991, OPIC had in its portfolio 100 investment proposals by US firms representing a potential investment of over 3 billion dollars aimed at improving the communications and transportation infrastructure, energy, food production and the hotel industry.[98]

The interest of US companies in foreign investment insurance has been growing. By March 1992, as many as 300 firms had asked OPIC to consider their investment projects in the ex-USSR for insurance purposes. Of these, 37 worth about 1 billion dollars, were agreed upon by

OPIC. In June 1992, OPIC's president noted that he was considering the coverage of 15 billion dollars in risk insurance for investment projects in Russia.[99] The agency has also made a available direct soft loans, not exceeding 5-6 million dollars, to small ex-Soviet–American joint ventures.[100]

Additional financial support to US investors is available from the US Export-Import Bank, which recently signed an agreement with the Russian authorities to open a credit line of 2 billion dollars to finance projects in Russia including those in the oil and gas sectors.[101] The first venture partly financed by the aforementioned bank is for the development of oil wells in West Siberia, and involves the US-based Anderson/Smith Operating Corporation. The Ex-Im Bank provided a loan of 44 million dollars (an equivalent sum was also provided by the EBRD), while the total investment cost of the project was estimated at 250 million dollars.

Similar steps, albeit on a more modest scale, have been undertaken by the governments of some other developed market economies. The French agency SOFARIS (Société Française pour l'assurance du capital-risque) set up a guarantee fund of 100 million French francs to cover the risk of capital losses in Eastern Europe, including the former USSR.[102] In 1992, the Canadian government agreed to provide 200 million dollars (Canadian) in insurance for investment in Russia through the state Export Development Corporation.[103] Reportedly, the Japanese Ministry for International Trade and Industry earmarked 1.8 billion dollars in state insurance for the business operations of Japanese companies in Russia. By October 1992, investment worth 16.8 million dollars in fifteen joint ventures had been covered.[104] A credit line recently extended by the Italian government involved 438.5 million dollars available for loan financing in joint investment projects up to 85 per cent of their cost. The FIEs eligible for loans include those producing refrigerators and other consumer durables, medical equipment, steel, food, synthetic rubber, electrical goods and diesel engines.[105]

Western governments' guarantees for investment in Russia often require reciprocal guarantees from the host country. Thus, the British company John Brown was unable to proceed with its 1.6 billion dollars joint project to produce polyethylene in Russia because the British Export Credit Guarantee Department (ECGD) insisted on sovereign guarantees on the Russian side, as well as on IMF approval of the economic reform programme, before providing its own guarantees.[106] Reportedly, in some East European countries, the ECGD now guarantees foreign investment in the non-state sector of the economy without reciprocal sovereign guarantees. At the same time, the stance of some other Western government agencies has not changed. For example, Hermes, a private insurance firm working on behalf of the German government, extends guarantees to private investors only if conditions of counter guarantees from the host country state bank are met.[107]

Some international institutions have shown a willingness to finance foreign investment in Russia although, so far, their role has been limited. The EBRD extended a 6.5 million dollar loan to the joint venture IBN-Sovintel to set up a modern international telecommunication system in Moscow. It is noteworthy that it did not require credit guarantees from either the Russian government or the joint venture's American partner.[108] The World Bank agreed to invest 870 million dollars in the West Siberian oil and gas complex. However, it expressed several reservations before its commitment could be implemented (the prices of hydrocarbons must be raised to world levels within two years, taxation in the sector must be reduced and restructured and legislation for the oil industry must be adopted).[109]

At present, it is premature to appraise the efficiency and effects of Western governments' support for private foreign investment in Russia. It is clear, however, that politically their willingness to cooperate may be used in the debate between Russia's reformists and conservatives.

Foreign Investment Prospects

In the period following the failed August putsch of 1991 the investment climate in Russia deteriorated. The economic situation was characterized by stagflation: according to Goskomstat, in 1992 the decline in production continued for a third consecutive year. On a year-by-year basis, GDP in 1992 declined by 19 per cent on top of a 17 per cent fall in 1991; national income and industrial production fell by 20 per cent (on top of 11 and 8 per cent respectively in 1991).[110]

Simultaneously, the price liberalization undertaken at the beginning of 1992, the government's hesitant stance in pursuing a stabilization policy and the uncontrollable flow of roubles from the other ex-Soviet republics all contributed to accelerating inflation. During 1992 (as compared with December 1991) consumer prices grew 26-fold, while industrial wholesale prices increased 34-fold. Inflation, coupled with high taxation and commercial interest rates, undermined the investment potential of enterprises. As compared with the end of 1991, 1992 saw investment levels fall by 45 per cent. Simultaneously, real incomes plummeted: in 1992 they stood at 60 per cent of 1991 levels.[111]

On the political front, the situation was characterized by a growing power struggle between the reform-minded presidency and the conservative parliament, increasing separatist trends in the autonomous republics and other regional entities, and intensifying ethnic clashes in some areas of the country.

At the beginning of 1993, there were eighteen constitutions and constitutional drafts in the autonomous republics of the Russian Federation, either operational or about to be ratified by their Parliaments. The constitutions of some of the autonomous republics declared an 'independent state' in Chechnya and 'a state associated with Russia' in Tatarstan. The draft constitutions of other autonomous republics (Tuva, Karelia and Yakutia-Sakha, Kalmykia, Buryatia and Bashkortostan) stipulated the supremacy of their laws over federal ones. Accordingly, the republics that signed the Federation Treaty tended to overrule decisions by both the federal parliament and the Russian president. For example, Yakutia-Sakha increased the local budget allocations from mining and the processing of diamonds from 27 per cent (as agreed in the Federation Treaty) to between 35 and 40 per cent.[112] In 1992, the central government allowed the regions to keep 19 per cent of their revenues; however, through effective lobbying in Moscow some managed to keep as much as 50 per cent.[113]

The growing separatism of the autonomous republics and regions had direct implications on negotiations involving large investment projects with foreign capital participation. A vivid example was the dragging out of negotiations on the Sakhalin petrochemical deposits development rights caused by the bargaining of central and local authorities over revenue-sharing and other conditions. Recently, a growing number of agreements with foreign investors have been signed by republics and regional administrations.

Moreover, protectionist tendencies in Russia are likely to grow in sectors where emerging Russian entrepreneurs can reap immediate gains (such as banking and insurance). At the same time, their impact will be weaker in areas where the technological superiority of Western investors is incontestable (for instance, in oil extraction), and where large investments are required for modernization purposes (such as in textiles and oil refining).

The deteriorating foreign investment climate in Russia has been reflected in international risk ratings. At the beginning of 1993, the US financial newspaper *Institutional Investor* gave Russia a score of 23.6 out of a maximum of 100 for reliable host countries. In this way, Russia was classified at approximately the same level as Poland, Romania, Ukraine and Belarus, but significantly lower than Hungary (42.3) and the Czech Republic (46.1).[114] An American Express survey covering 126 leading executives of companies with interests in Eastern Europe found that 62 per cent of businessmen rated the business environment in Russia as poor, while 48 per cent and 43 per cent said that it was good or excellent in Hungary and the Czech Republic. While the rating of Poland improved as a result of the economic stabilization programme, most business executives found that economic stability in Russia had deteriorated.[115]

At the time of writing (1993), when infighting between the proponents of reform and the conservatives reached a peak, the political component of the investment climate came once again to the forefront. Although the return to totalitarian rule seems improbable, the future of the political system in Russia remains uncertain. The outcome of the current political struggle may have an important impact on the West's support of the market reforms and encouragement of foreign investment in Russia. Western governments will cooperate more readily in financing foreign investment activities in Russia if the reform momentum is sustained.

On the domestic side, there seems to be a high degree of understanding among policy-makers that the economy can not be revitalized without external financing and the inflow of entrepreneurial capital. Therefore, the odds are high that efforts to attract foreign capital will continue. In the short run, these are likely to bear fruit primarily in the primary sector, and in particular in hydrocarbons (oil). The basis for an agreement between the host country and international energy concerns is relatively straightforward: potential Western investors are interested in securing a share of prospected oil deposits, while the Russian authorities face declining production levels which risk bringing the economy to a standstill. Moreover in the next few years an upsurge in the production of petrochemicals and in mining is the only means of raising export earnings and replenishing convertible currency reserves. Therefore, it seems probable that, under a stable government, foreign penetration in the primary sector will go on, and its scale may reach billions of dollars a year.

In manufacturing and services, the bulk of foreign investment has been effected by small and medium-sized companies, which are very sensitive to political and economic conditions. These smaller firms also tend to rely on their home governments' support for guaranteeing and financing investments. In the short to medium term, therefore, a massive inflow of foreign capital in manufacturing and services is less certain.

Appendix Russian Federation – selected major foreign investment projects in natural resources' development (agreed upon or negotiated during 1990–February 1993)

Investing company name	Country of origin	Initial foreign investment^a ($USm)	Total foreign investment ($USm)	Type of foreign investment	Local partner	Product line	Stage	Additional information
1. Marathon Oil McDermott International, Mitsui Bussan Mitsubishi Royal Dutch/ Shell	USA Japan Netherlands UK	...	13 000.0	Concession, production-sharing	Sakhalin Morneftegaz	Development of Sakhalin sea shelf oil and gas deposits (Piltun-Astokhskoye and Lunskoye)	Negotiated, feasibility study agreed upon in January 1992	Reserves of two fields are estimated at 100 m tons of oil and 400 bn cubic metres of gas; production may start at end 1995; total foreign investment may reach $US12–14 bn and profit spread over 25 years $US27–32 bn; foreign partners will obtain $US16 bn
2. Tokyo Boeki Development Ltd/Far East Energy Inc	Japan USA	30.0	12 000.0	Concession	Russian and Saha (Yakut) governments	Development of oil and gas deposits in Saha (Yakut) Republic	Negotiated, feasibility study agreed upon	Field contains 1 tn cubic metres of natural gas and 2.25 bn barrels (357.1 mn tons) of oil; project can cost $US10–14 bn and can yield 300 000 barrels a day of oil and 1.2 bn cubic metres of gas a day in 10 years; two 4000 km and 5000 km pipelines to Japan and Korea are projected

	Company	Country			Type	Partner	Object	Status	Details
3.	Elf-Aquitaine	France	450.0	5 500.0	Production-sharing agreement	...	Exploration of Saratov-Volgograd oil field	Agreed on 6.02.1992	Exploration costs of $US400–500 m over 8 years are expected; subsequently $US5–6 bn will be invested in production if oil is found; annual output is estimated at 20 m tons; ELF will be exclusive operator for 20 years
4.	Deminex	Germany	...	3 000.0	Joint venture	Nizhnevolzhskneft'	Exploration and extraction of oil and gas in Volgograd region	Negotiated	Oil resources of fields to be developed are estimated at 130 mn tons; it is planned to start production in 1994, increase output to 1.2 mn tons yearly in 5 years, and to 10 mn tons subsequently; part of the output will be exported to Germany
5.	Conoco (Subsidiary of Du Pont de Nemours)	USA	...	3 000.0	Joint venture	Archangelsk-Geologiya	Joint venture to develop Dosyuchevskoye, Ardalinskoye and Kolvinskoye oil fields to the North-East of Urals (Nenets Autonomous District)	Agreed, exploitation licence issued in January 1993	Combined resources of deposits are estimated at 16.6–17.49 m tons of oil; all output will be exported; after-tax profits will be distributed 50–50% between partners, while Russian side will obtain 70% of profits (including taxes)

Appendix 10 (Continued)

Investing company name	Country of origin	Initial foreign investment[a] ($USm)	Total foreign investment ($USm)	Type of foreign investment	Local partner	Product line	Stage	Additional information
6. Total	France	...	1 700.0	Concession, production-sharing	Ukhtaneftgaz Geologiya	Oil extraction in Republic of Komi	Agreed, awaiting government approval	Four oil fields to be developed are located at TIMAN-PECHORA Basin and have estimated reserves of 300 mn barrels (48 mn tons); annual oil output is to be increased at an annual rate of 2.3 mn tons
7. Total	France	400.0	1 000.0	Concession, production-sharing	Komineft'	Technical re-equipment and operation of Hariaga oil fields	Agreed, awaiting government approval	Total will invest $US400 mn in the first 3 years and a total of $US1 bn in the development of Hariaga oil fields in northern Russia; annual output will be raised at an annual rate of 1.5 mn tons; French side will get 25% of output

No.	Company	Country		Value	Type	Partner	Description	Status	Notes
8.	Chita Minerals Company (Joint Venture by Somerset Holdings and SFV)	Cyprus (USA and Germany)	...	1 000.0	Joint venture	...	Extraction of copper at UDOKAN deposit in East Siberia	Agreed in January 1993	Copper resources are estimated at 18 mn tons, total cost of the project at $US1 bn and state budget revenues at $US4.5–5.5 bn over project life; half of yearly output (300 000 tons in 7 years) will be exported to China and half sold domestically
9.	Occidental Petroleum	USA	...	800.0	Joint venture	Chernogorneft'	50–50% joint venture to modernise two oil fields	Agreed	Joint venture will increase output from 40 000 barrels (6300 tons) to 65 000 barrels (10 300 tons) a day; $US800 mn foreign investment is projected for the next 25 years
10.	Panoco Holding (Pan Ocean Oil Group)	Switzerland	...	600.0	Joint venture	Tatneft'	Development of seven oil fields in Tatarstan.	Agreed in September 1991	Joint venture will develop seven oil fields with proven reserves of 268 mn tons (1.69 bn barrels); output should grow from 2000 barrels a day (317 tons a day) to 125 000 barrels a day (19 800 tons a day); new oil refinery with production capacity of 50 000 barrels a day (7900 tons a day) will be built

Appendix 10 (Continued)

Investing company name	Country of origin	Initial foreign investment[a] ($USm)	Total foreign investment ($USm)	Type of foreign investment	Local partner	Product line	Stage	Additional information
11. Mobil Oil	USA	...	300.0	Unknown	...	Oil and gas production	Agreed	Investment in oil and gas industry of West Siberia
12. Star Technology System	Australia	...	250.0	Equity stake	Lenzoloto	Development of Sukhoi Log gold mine	Agreed in April 1992	Western partner obtained a 31% equity stake in Lenzoloto; total reserves of Sukhoi Log are estimated at 500 tons worth $US5 bn; Russian partner will invest 640 mn SUR (at November 1992 prices); gold will be sold exclusively to the state
13. Total	France	300.0	...	Concession, production-sharing	...	Development of Romashkino deposit in Tatarstan	Agreed	Investment is stretched for the 'next several years'; Total will get 25% of the output in kind
14. Gulf Canada Corporation	Canada	154.0	...	Joint venture	Komineft'	Development of Vozey oil deposit in Komi Republic	Agreed in 1991	Venture relies on modern technology of western partner; total investment of $US200 mn will be required; within three years up to 2000 barrels a day will be extracted

	Company	Country	Value (mn)		Type	Partner	Project	Status	Date	Notes
15.	Anglo-Suisse/Phibro Energy	USA	116.0	...	Joint venture	Varyeganeftegaz	Exploration and production of oil in Tyumen' region	Agreed		...
16.	West Siberian Services	Switzerland (Croatia, UK)	25.0	...	Unknown	...	Overhaul of oil wells in western Siberia	Agreed in 1991		Company was founded by Ina-Naftaplin (Croatia) and Marc Rich (UK); company will overhaul 150 existing and drill 31 new wells
17.	Fracmaster Royal Dutch/Shell	Canada UK Netherlands	23.0	...	Joint venture	...	Rehabilitation of oil wells	Agreed in 1990		Joint venture has increased output of wells by 10 000 barrels a day; western partners get 25% of production gains each; initial investment has been recouped through oil exports to Spain and Italy
18.	Anderman/Smith Operation Co	USA	12.0	...	Joint venture	Chernogorneft'	Development of western Siberian oil field	Initial agreement reached; negotiated		US Export–Import Bank and the EBRD will supply $US44 mn project loans each (without Russian government guarantees); each partner will initially invest $US12 mn
19.	Morris Cartright & Company	UK	9.0	...	Joint venture	Polosukhinskaya Mine	Extraction of coal at Polosukhinskaya in Kemerovo region	Agreed in February 1991		Increase of yearly coal output from 2.3 mn tons to 5 mn tons by 1995; part of coal will be exported; western partner will get 60% of profit

Appendix 10 (Continued)

Investing company name	Country of origin	Initial foreign investment[a] ($USm)	Total foreign investment ($USm)	Type of foreign investment	Local partner	Product line	Stage	Additional information
20. GHK Corporation	USA	...	...	Joint venture	Kuibyshevneft', Logovaz	Restoration of idle oil wells in Samara region	Agreed on 9.05.1992	Joint venture will rehabilitate 111 idle oil wells in SAMARA region; total investment by foreign and local partners will amount to $US15–20 mn
21. TEIKOKU SEKIYU MITSUI SEKIYU KATHATSU TOYO ENGINEERING SANTEK	Japan	...	...	Joint venture	...	Rehabilitation of idle oil wells at deposits between Volga river and Ural mountains	Negotiated	Joint venture will increase output of 20-30 oil wells with the use of modern technology (pumping of chemical agents); project will be financed by an association of Japanese oil companies; Japanese partners will be paid in oil
22. SAGA Petroleum/ Royal Dutch/Shell	Norway UK ... Netherlands	...	...	Joint venture	Severgazprom; Arkhangel'sk Geologiya; Ukhtaneftegaz Geologiya	Development of Negotiated discovered oil and gas fields at Timan-Pechora Basin in Arkhangel'sk region	Negotiated	Joint venture seeks to obtain an exploitation licence to develop Sredne- and Severokhariaga oil fields, and five gas and gas condensate fields

[a] Foreign capital to be invested during the first one to four years of the project.
Source: East-West Investment News (Incorporating East-West Joint Ventures News), no. 1 (Spring 1993).

Notes

1 *Osnovnye Pokazateli Balansa Narodnogo Khozyaistva SSSR i Soyuznykh Respublik. Statisticheskii Sbornik [Major Indicators of National Economy Balance of the USSR and Union Republics]* (1990) pp. 22, 34; *Narodnoye Khozyaistvo SSSR v 1990* [Statistical Yearbook of the USSR] (1990) pp. 68, 358, 360.

2 *Narodnoye Khozyaistvo SSSR v 1990*, p. 668.

3 *BIKI* (24 Oct. 1991).

4 *Narodnoye Khozyaistvo SSSR v 1990*, p. 210.

5 *BBC Summary of World Broadcasts*, Weekly Economic Report, SU/WO209 (13 Dec. 1991) p. A/17.

6 *Journal of Commerce* (16 Nov. 1990).

7 Law of the Russian Federation, *Ekonomika i Zhizn'* (Aug. 1991) no. 34, supplement.

8 *Commersant* (Russian edn) no. 8, 4 Mar. 1997.

9 MIGA's guarantees cover 90 per cent of the value of initial investments for a fifteen year period. In addition, expected earnings can also be covered up to 180 per cent of the original investment. The premium rates range from 0.3 to 2 per cent of the amount of guarantee (*Business Eastern Europe* [24 Sep. 1990]).

10 *Interflo*, 7/92, p. 26.

11 *Business Moscow News* (Russian edn), no. 5 (31 Jan. 1993) p. 13.

12 *Ekonomika i Zhizn'*, no. 20 (May 1992). One should note that a day after the law on subsoil was adopted, the Russian president signed a decree forbidding the free sale and purchase (including export and import operations) of certain goods and services, including precious metals and stones, and uranium (*East–West Investment and Joint Ventures News*, no. 12 [Jun. 1992]).

13 *Vedomosti Rossiiskoi Federatsii*, no. 11 (1992) p. 699.

14 State Tax Service, *On Taxation of Bank Incomes*, no. 10 (7 Apr. 1992); *Ekonomika i Zhizn'*, no. 20 (May 1992).

15 *Business Eastern Europe* (15 Feb. 1993).

16 *Vedomosti Rossiiskoi Federatsii* (1992) no. 11, pp. 699–701.

17 Ekonomika i Zhizn', no. 1 (1 Jan. 1992).

18 *Business Moscow News* (Russian edn) no. 1, Jan. 1993.

19 In March 1993 the first positive operational results could be observed in the free economic zones of Kaliningrad and Nakhodka, in which 130 and 300 FIEs were registered respectively (*Izvestiya*, 18 Mar. 1993).

20 When spelling out guarantees for foreign investment, for example, the law does not define what 'national interest' considerations, which may cause the nationalisation of foreign investors' property, are. Equally, while according to the law, the FIEs 'own produce' can be exported without licences, the notion of 'own produce' has yet to be defined one and a half years after the law was enacted (see *Ekonomika i Zhizn'*, no. 43 [Dec. 1992]).

21 See *The Journal of Commerce* (30 Apr. 1992).

22 BBC *Summary of World Broadcasts*, Weekly Economic Report, SU/W0240 (24 Jul. 1992) p. A/1.

23 *Financial Times* (13 May 1992); *International Herald Tribune* (21 May 1992); *Journal of Commerce* (25 Feb. 1992).

24 *East–West Investment and Joint Ventures News*, no. 13 (Sep. 1992).

25   At the same time, these enterprises found themselves in a slightly more favourable position than other companies with foreign participation: while joint ventures with a foreign share of less than 30 per cent had to sell 30 per cent of export receipts to the State Bank at exchange rates lower than the market rate and only 20 per cent at free market rates, wholly foreign-owned subsidiaries and joint ventures in which the foreign share exceeded 30 per cent could sell all the required amounts at free market exchange rates. (*Ekonomika i Zhizn'*, no. 27 [July 1992]).

26   *Izvestiya* (23 Mar. 1993).

27   *Business Eastern Europe* (20 Apr. 1992).

28   *The Economist* (2 May 1992) p. 87. Later in 1992, the government decided to exempt from export tax FIEs with a foreign share in stock exceeding 30 per cent and those registered before 1 January 1992. However, this applied, reportedly, only to exports of 'over and above plan production'. (*BBC Summary of World Broadcasts, Weekly Economic Report*, SU/W0242 [7 Aug. 1992] p. A/7).

29   Foreigners could freely take part in investment tenders as regards transport, trade and public catering (dining) enterprises, as well as small companies in industry and construction (less than 200 employees or 1 million roubles worth of assets). At the same time, their participation in auctions and price bidding needed authorization by the State Committee on State Property Management.

30   In particular, they were given the right to: (i) buy controlling stakes and stock left over after the shares had been distributed to the workers of the enterprise to be privatized; (ii) acquire an additional package of shares at market prices, after 10 per cent of stock had been sold at an auction (in case the stock had appreciated); (iii) obtain rights to manage the stock packages belonging to property funds.

31   *Ekonomika i Zhizn'*, no. 29 (Jul. 1992).

32   *East-West Investment and Joint Ventures News*, no. 14 (Dec. 1992).

33   UN/ECE Secretariat.

34   *Izvestiya* (17 Nov. 1992).

35   In Estonia, for example, in mid-1992, 1633 enterprises were considered in joint ownership with foreign capital. At the same time, there were only 321 newly established joint ventures with foreign participation (*Statistika Aasta-Raamat*, 1992 [Statistical Yearbook] p. 54). Among 1300 FIEs in Latvia at the end of 1992, 647 were formed with Russian partners. On the same date, the respective figures for Lithuania were 1963 and 683 (*BBC Summary of World Broadcasts*, Weekly Economic Report, SU/W0267 [5 Feb. 1993] p. C1/1-2).

36   This problem is discussed in *East-West Joint Ventures and Investment News*, no. 10 (December 1991).

37   When independent auditors evaluated the assets of Lenzoloto, the state gold-mining company, in dollars, the implied exchange rate amounted to 2.5 roubles per dollar (while the free market exchange rate at the end of 1992 exceeded 400 roubles/1 dollar). As was already mentioned, the Australian company Star Technology Systems Ltd. bought a 31 per cent stake in Lenzo-loto worth 625 million roubles for 250 million dollars, which suggests that a rouble invested in the gold-mining enterprise weighed about 160 'normal' roubles (*Izvestiya* [17 Nov. 1992]).

38 The Goskomstat data show a fall in the foreign component of cumulative statutory capital in the third quarter of 1992, which is difficult to interpret. The most trivial explanation of a mere under-reporting of FIEs to statistical bodies put aside, this drop may indicate an actual divestment by these enterprises.

39 *O Razvitii Ekonomicheskikh Reform v Rossiiskoi Federatsii v 1992 Godu*, pp. 18, 21.

40 *Ekomomika i Zhizn'*, no. 10 (Mar. 1993).

41 It is equally unclear, whether official estimates cover the capital flow exclusively in the form or cash, or in kind as well.

42 The flow estimate covers investments in cash only and excludes those in kind (*Foreign Direct Investment in the States of the former USSR* [World Bank, 1992] pp. 8 and 9).

43 The criterion used to define operational enterprises is, however, arbitrary. The authors consider FIEs to be operational if they have opened bank accounts. It is known that the opening of a bank account is a first step towards registration but does not necessarily imply the start of operations. Official Russian (as well as the former-Soviet) statistics regard as operational those FIEs which produce goods or services, or have employees on their payrolls. Despite a certain vagueness, this definition seems more reliable than that of the World Bank (*PlanEcon*).

44 J. Rutter, *Recent Trends in International Direct Investment* (US Department of Commerce, Aug. 1992) Appendix table 4.

45 *Vneshneekonomicheskiye Svyazi SSSR. Ezhekvartal'nyi Statisticheskii Byulleten'*, no. 9, p. 116.

46 The former-Soviet (respectively Russian) classification of foreign investment activities was based on the industrial allocation of local partners, and not on the nature of FIEs' operations themselves. (See UN/ECE Documents Trade/R.575, p. 34.)

47 *Foreign Direct Investment in the States of the former USSR*, p. 104.

48 *Business Eastern Europe* (25 Jan. 1993).

49 *Finansovye Izvestiya*, no. 19 (6–12 Mar. 1993).

50 *Business Moscow News* (Russian edn) no. 4, (Feb. 1992).

51 Calculated from *Table 10.1* and *O Razvitii Ekonomicheskikh Reform v Rossiiskoi Federatsii*, pp. 46, 47.

52 Calculated from *Table 10.1* and *Ekonomika i Zhizn'*, no. 4 (Jan. 1993) p. 13.

53 UN/ECE Document *Trade/R.588*, p. 23.

54 Calculated from *Table 10.1* and *O Razvitii Ekonomicheskikh Reform v Rossiiskoi Federatsii* pp. 7, 8, 24. It is clear that FIE sales for roubles include deliveries not only of consumer products but investment goods as well. The sales of the latter, in contrast, are not included in the overall retail turnover figures.

55 Calculated from *Table 10.1* and *Ekonomika i Zhizn'*, no. 13 (Mar. 1992) p. 14 and no. 4 (Jan. 1993) p. 15.

56 *Business Eastern Europe* (6 Apr. 1992) calculated from *Ekonomika i Zhizn'*, no. 13 (Mar. 1992) p. 15.

57 Calculated from *Ekonomika i Zhizn'*, no. 4 (Jan. 1993) p. 15.

58 *BBC Summary of World Broadcasts*, Weekly Economic Report, SU/WO265 (22 Jan. 1993) p. A/11.

59   If the foreign trade deficit of FIEs in 1992 is converted in roubles at average yearly exchange rates (193 rouble/1 dollar), it amounts to 33.6 billion roubles, which is roughly equivalent to 20 per cent of foreign investment sales for domestic currency in 1992.

60   *O Razvitii Ekonomicheskikh Reform v Rossiiskoi Federatsii v 1992 godu*, p. 59.

61   *Business Moscow News* (Russian edn) no. 5, (Feb. 1992).

62   *Financial Times* (6 Mar. 1992).

63   *Ekonomika i Zhizn'*, no. 12, (Mar. 1991).

64   *BBC Summary of World Broadcasts*, Weekly Economic Report, SU/WO214, (24 Jan. 1992) p. A/11.

65   *Ekonomika i Zhizn'*, no. 28 (Jul. 1992).

66   *Financial Times* (6 Mar. 1992).

67   According to the Minister of Fuels and Energy, in 1992, joint ventures invested 150 million dollars in the energy complex and exported oil and petroleum products worth $600 m: *Business Moscow News* (Russian edn) no. 11 (March 1993).

68   *Interflo*, 4/91, p. 30; *Moscow City Guide* (Jun.–Jul. 1991) p. 72.

69   *BBC Summary of World Broadcasts*, Weekly Economic Report, SU/W0218 (21 Feb. 1992) p. A/6–A/7; *Business Eastern Europe* (6 April 1992); *Ecotass*, no. 28 (22 Jun. 1992) p. 5.

70   *BBC Summary of World Broadcasts*, Weekly Economic Report, SU/WO214 (24 Jan. 1992) p. A/10.

71   Izvestiya (13 Dec. 1991); *Business Moscow News* (Russian edn), no. 4 (Jan. 1993).

72   Saga Petroleum, the leading non-state Norwegian oil company, and Royal Dutch-Shell have set up a joint venture with a number of Russian enterprises to develop oil and gas deposits in the Timan-Pechora basin (*Business Moscow News* [Russian edn] no. 4 [Jan. 1993]. Total is working on two projects in the Komi Republic (Hariaga deposits). The initial investment in each of those is expected to amount to $600–700m. in the first three years of operations and over $1 bn during the next ten years. Total intends to raise total output to 35 million tonnes at an annual rate of 1.5 million tonnes. Total is also planning to invest $1.7 bn in rehabilitating four more oil deposits (Sandivey, Veyakoshor, Makarekhin and Iverobagan) in the Timan-Pechora basin and to increase their output to 40 million tonnes – *BBC Summary of World Broadcasts*, Weekly Economic Report, SU/WO218 (21 Feb. 1992) p. A/6–A/7; *Business Eastern Europe* (6 Apr. 1992); *Ecotass*, no. 28 (22 Jun. 1992) p. 5. *Summary of World Broadcasts*, Weekly Economic Report, SU/WO227 (24 Apr. 1992) p. A/8.

73   *Journal of Commerce* (30 Sep. 1991); *Izvestiya* (12 Feb. 1992).

74   *BBC Summary of World Broadcasts*, Weekly Economic Report, SU/WO251 (9 Oct. 1992) p. A/10.

75   *Business Moscow News*, (Russian edn) no. 5 (Jan. 1993).

76   Izvestiya (12 Feb. 1992).

77   See, for example, the article by the president of the Germes concern, V. Neverov, in Izvestiya (24 Jan. 1992).

78   *Commersant*, Russian edn (25 Nov.–2 Dec. 1991).

79   *Petroleum Economist* (Dec. 1992) p. 10.

80 The Chtokmanovskoye deposit with total reserves in excess of 3000 billion cubic metres of gas, is seen by specialists as a potential source of gas exports to Western Europe (up to 18 billion cubic metres yearly) and of liquified gas to the United States (15–16 billion cubic metres). The extraction of 40 billion cubic metres of gas at the Chtokmanovskoye deposit will require imports of equipment for deep sea operations worth $ 1.72bn. About $ 2.65bn. will be needed to build a turnkey plant to produce the liquified gas, while the network of pipelines connecting the new deposits with Western Europe will require investment of 360 million dollars: *Business Moscow*, News, Russian edition, no. 5 (Feb. 1992).

81 The deposits, copper resources, are estimated at 18 million tonnes, and the total cost of the project at $1 bn. Half the output of the new mine is planned to be sold domestically at world prices, and the budgetary revenues at all levels of Government will reach $4.5–5.5bn over the project's life. Udokan Mining also has plans to market copper to China at the yearly rate of 200000 tonnes over a period of twenty-five years from 1997. These exports should guarantee half of the financial needs of the company (*Finansovye Izvestiya*, no. 6 [3 Dec. 1992]; *Financial Times* [15 Jan. 1993]; *Izvestiya* [18 Jan. 1993]).

82 *Finansovye Izvestiya*, no. 6 (3 Dec. 1992); *Financial Times* (15 Jan. 1993); *Izvestiya* (18 Jan. 1993).

83 *Ekonomika i Zhizn'*, no. 5 (Feb. 1993) p. 7.

84 Calculated from *Finansovye Izvestiya*, no. 14 (4–10 Feb. 1993).

85 *Finansovye Izvestiya*, no. 9 (24–9 Dec. 1992).

86 *Commersant*, Russian edn (25 Nov.–2 Dec. 1991).

87 *Commersant*, Russian edn (3–10 Feb. 1992).

88 See *East–West Investment and Joint Ventures News*, no. 14 (Dec. 1992).

89 *Interflo* (11/92) p. 19.

90 *Financial Times* (12/13 Sep. 1992).

91 *Izvestiya* (26 Oct. 1992). As V. Yakunin, the chairman of Tokobank put it: 'A young banking system in Russia cannot compete with the banks from Europe, the United States and Japan. Russian banks need protectionism, and not conditions equal to those granted to foreign banks' (*Finansovye Izvestiya*, no. 4 [19 Nov. 1992]).

92 In the same way, the Statute implementing the Law on Insurance limits the share of foreigners in joint stock and limited liability companies to 49 per cent in order 'to defend the insurance market under formation in Russia'. This stipulation excludes foreign insurers from directly operating in the Russian market through their branches (*Business Moscow News*, Russian edn, no. 5 [31 Jan. 1993]).

93 *Finansovye Izvestiya*, no. 5 (26 Nov. 1992).

94 *Izvestiya* (26 Jan. 1993).

95 This government agency issues investment guarantees and insures foreign investment projects mostly in developing countries. It also participates in the financing of FIEs, focusing on those set up by small and medium-sized companies.

96 *Interflo* (10/1991) p. 15.

97 *BIKI* (19 Oct. 1991).

98 *United States Mission Daily Bulletin* (Geneva, 13 Nov. 1991); *Business Eastern Europe* (2 Dec. 1991).

99   *United States Mission Daily Bulletin* (Geneva, 18 Jun. 1992).

100 *Izvestiya* (9 Mar. 1992).

101 *Interflo* (5/92) p. 21.

102 N. Simon, French Firms and the Joint Venture Challenge in the USSR, *Moct–Most*, no. 2 (1991) p. 104.

103 *Interflo* (7/92) p. 12.

104 *Ecotass*, no. 39 (28 Sep. 1992) p. 6.

105 *Eastern Europe Reporter* (13 Apr. 1992) p. 314.

106 *Interflo* (3/92) p. 25.

107 *Business Eastern Europe* (16 Nov. 1992).

108 *BBC Summary of World Broadcasts*, Weekly Economic Report, SU/WO253 (23 Oct. 1992) p. A/2; SU/WO261 (18 Dec. 1992) p. A/12.

109 *BBC Summary of World Broadcasts*, Weekly Economic Report, SU/WO242 (7 Aug. 1992) p. A/8.

110 *Ekonomika i Zhizn'*, no. 5 (Jan. 1991); *O Razvitii Ekonomicheskikh Reform v Rossiiskoi Federatsii v 1992 Godu*, p. 6; *Naradnoye Khozyaistvo Rossiiskoi Federatsii, 1992* [Statistical Yearbook of the Russian Federation, 1992] p. 14.

111 *O Razvitii Ekonomicheskikh Reform v Rossiiskoi Federatsii v 1992 Godu*, pp. 6, 7, 15.

112 *Moskovskiye Novosti*, no. 6 (7 Feb. 1993).

113 *Financial Times* (17 Mar. 1993).

114 *Finansovye Izvestiya*, no. 11 (14–20 Jan. 1993).

115 *Financial Times* (11 Mar. 1993).

11
The Russian Far East: The Role of Japan

Terutomo Ozawa

I imagined that by means of signs I might make myself understood by the Japanese. For this purpose I caused a cask to be
sawed in two, and set both parts afloat in water in front of the
town. In the inside of one half of the cask were placed a glass
containing fresh water, a piece of wood, and a handful of rice,
to denote that we were in want of these articles; the other half
contained a few piastres, a piece of yellow cloth, and some
crystal beads and pearls, meaning thereby to intimate that we
would give them either money or other articles in exchange for
provisions.

Captain Golownin (who in 1811 was sent on a mission to
survey the Kurile Islands), *A Narrative of My Captivity in Japan*,
1818.[1]

Introduction

Japan had been under self-imposed seclusion for over two hundred years
until 1854 when Commodore Perry's squadron ('black ships' as they
were called by the Japanese) forced Japan to open its doors for trade
with the West. The purpose of seclusion was to ward off any Christian
proselytization. During two centuries of practical isolation, only Dutch
and Chinese merchants were allowed to trade with Japan, but even such
limited commercial exchanges were permitted to take place solely at
Dejima (which literally means 'a jetted islet'), a small port enclave
created for that specific purpose in Nagasaki on Kyushu, the southern
major island of Japan. The volume of trade was minimal, and Japan was
practically an autarkic economy. As might well have been expected, the
Japanese standard of living then remained low and backward, compared

251

with that in the Western world, which actively exploited and gained from trade, although local crafts including porcelain, lacquerware, and sword-making metallurgy flourished in Japan.

It was still in the extended period of seclusion that Captain Golownin of Russia landed on Kunashiri, the island next to Hokkaido and the most southerly of the Kuriles, in his futile efforts to open commerce with Japan. He was arrested and detained for the next two years. When he was released, a letter given to him had the following to say:

> Among us there exists this law: if any European residing in Japan shall attempt to teach our people the Christian faith, he shall undergo a severe punishment, and shall not be restored to his native country. As you however have not attempted to do so, you will accordingly be permitted to return home. Think well on this.[2]

Ever since then, Russia and Japan have been rather isolated from each other in commercial relationships despite their geographical proximity. Russia became increasingly westward-orientated (that is, Europe-focused) after the sale of Alaska to the USA in 1867; the Russo-Japanese war (1904–5) and the subsequent communist revolution (1917) further increased a political cleavage between the two countries.

It was only when Mikhail Gorbachev's *perestroika* began to be reflected in a more open economy policy that the volume of trade between the two countries began to expand in the latter half of the 1980s. His speech delivered at Vladivostok on 28 July 1986, in particular, created momentum towards closer economic ties among the USSR, Japan, China, and South Korea. The Vladivostok Initiative, however, faltered as *perestroika* led to separatism and social fragmentation in the former Soviet Union. Gorbachev's historic visit to Japan and South Korea in 1991 could not invigorate the Pacific rim move.[3] The collapse of Soviet Communism and its aftermath unfortunately reversed the momentum.

The relationship between Japan and Russia is further strained by the Northern Territories issue involving the four islands of Etorofu, Kunashiri, Shikotan, and Hobomai occupied by Soviet forces at the end of the Second World War in 1945.

The two countries are close neighbours with vastly different — hence complementary — factor endowments and small transportation costs for trade. An enormous potential for trade thus has long existed between Russia — especially Far Eastern Russia — and Japan, but has remained largely unexplored; ideological, geopolitical, and institutional factors have so far converged into a persistently insurmountable barrier to any large-scale commercial exchange commensurate with the two countries' national incomes and geographical contiguity.

Nonetheless, if Russia's present political effort towards a market economy proves successful, there will be a long-awaited opportunity for expanded trade and investment relations between Russia — and the Commonwealth of Independent States (CIS) at large — and Japan. Political stability in the CIS is the prerequisite for any normal growth in commercial exchanges. As will be detailed below, however, new Russo-Japanese relations are not likely to be built so much at the national (central) level involving the entire Russia, but rather in a more or less *ad hoc*, semi-market-orientated manner at the regional level — and especially centred on the Russian Far East.

'Taking-Off Class III' – and a Subsequent Divergence in Economic Performance

Russia and Japan had many common characteristics as late starters for industrialization. Both began to industrialise at about the same time — and under the imperial tutelage of their respective rulers, the tsar in the former and the Meiji emperor in the latter. W.W. Rostow (1960) categorized countries into four different classes with respect to their take-off periods. Great Britain as Take-off Class I (1783-1802); the USA, France and Germany as Take-off Class II (1830–50); Sweden, Japan, Russia-USSR, Italy, Canada, and Australia as Take-off Class III (1870–1901); and Argentina, Turkey, Brazil, Mexico, Iran, India, China, Taiwan, Thailand and South Korea as Take-off Class IV (1933 to the present).

Russia and Japan thus began as classmates, so to speak, for the take-off stage of economic development. To be more exact, Rostow identified the Russian take-off approximately from 1890 to 1914, and Japan's from 1878 to 99.[4] In the next stage of 'the drive to maturity' (in which 'a society has effectively applied the range of [then] modern technology to the bulk of its resources'), 1950 was a 'rough symbolic date for technological maturity' for Russia, and 1940 for Japan.[5]

Consequently, Japan was slightly ahead of Russia through the drive-to-maturity stage. But Japan's lead accelerated especially after 1950 when it regained political autonomy upon the signing of the San Francisco Peace Treaty, and its economic miracle was soon to be made – with an ever-widening gap. For the next stage (after the 'drive-to-maturity' phase) is the age of high mass-consumption in which Russia was victimized by its own political system, totalitarian communism, since such a system proved incompatible with democratic consumerism that would make mass-consumption capitalism flourish. The collapse of communism was the telling testimony to the intrinsic incompatibility between the age of consumerism and the centrally planned and military-dominated totalitarian society.

Rostow's (1960) prognosis concerning the self-contradictory course of Soviet communism back in the late 1950s shows great foresight:

> We come now to the age of high mass-consumption, where, in time, the leading sectors shift towards durable consumers' goods and services: a phase from which Americans are beginning to emerge [in the late 1950s]; whose not unequivocal joys Western Europe and Japan are beginning energetically to probe; and with which Soviet society is engaged *in an uneasy flirtation*. (p. 10; emphases added)

> For the United States, the turning point was perhaps Henry Ford's moving assembly line of 1913–14; but it was in the 1920s, and again in the post-war decade, 1946–56, that this stage of growth was pressed to, virtually, its logical conclusion. In the 1950s Western Europe and Japan appear to have fully entered this phase, accounting substantially for a momentum in their economies quite unexpected in the immediate postwar years. The Soviet Union is technically ready for this stage, and by every sign, its citizens hunger for it: but communist leaders face difficult political and social problems of adjustment if this stage is launched. (p. 11; emphasis added)

The basic incompatibility between totalitarian communism and the age of consumerism gave the communist leaders the only option: in order to retain power, they had to keep the Soviet economy in the pre-consumerism phase of industrial production, namely, heavy and chemical industries, as will be explained further below. In the meantime, the West, including Japan, quickly proceeded to the phase of high mass-consumption, as its political system, democracy, turned out to be structurally congruous with the new age of consumer capitalism.

Developmental Phases of Capitalist Production and Structural Upgrading

In order to understand the predicament Soviet communism faced, it is necessary to appreciate that the underlying currents that have been sweeping the modern economic system of production and consumption originated in the Industrial Revolution.

At some cost of simplification, capitalist production can be chronologically divided into five major phases, with each represented by the dominant growth (lead) industry. The primary form of capitalism originated in *mercantilism*, in which *wool* was the predominant commodity manufactured. The Industrial Revolution in England and the *laissez-faire* doctrine led to *liberalism*, which was represented by cotton textiles. The subsequent search for raw materials and markets overseas ushered in the age of *imperialism* symbolised by *iron and steel*, the age that culminated in two world wars as the imperial powers clashed with each other.[6]

After the Second World War, the capitalist economies rapidly shifted to the phase of *consumerism* best exemplified by the widespread private ownership of automobiles among consumers (as suggested by Rostow above). Presently, the advanced world is in the new age of *informationalism* characterized by the widespread use of computers and software. To put it differently, capitalist production was originally a *labour-dependent* system (textiles), which became a *resource-dependent* system (iron and steel, chemicals, and heavy machinery), which then turned into *an assembly-dependent system* (automobiles) and most recently, an *information-dependent* system (computers and software). At present, the advanced West – and Japan – is already firmly in this new 'technological paradigm' of capitalist development in which R&D-based knowledge and information have become key inputs for industrial activity (Ozawa, 1992b).

How swiftly Japan succeeded in upgrading itself in the postwar period – thereby widening its lead over Russia – can be analysed in terms of an 'industrial restructuring' paradigm developed to explain post-war Japanese economic development (Ozawa 1991). Needless to say, Japan's postwar economic miracle was achieved under the sponsorship of the West, especially the USA. America's industrial hegemony and leadership crystallised into the Pax Americana which served as a nursery, as it were, for Japan's quick recovery and economic growth.

Indeed, as illustrated in Figure 11.1, ever since the beginning of the 1950s, Japan's industrial structure has gone through continuous metamorphic changes, a process that so far can be chronologically divided into four sequential stages of industrialization:

I   Expansion and reliance of labour-intensive (that is, labour-dependent) manufacturing in textiles, sundries, and other light industry goods as the leading export sector (1950 to the mid-1960s). These industries (Tier 4) may be classified as 'Heckscher – Ohlin' industries because of the standardized manufacturing technologies used and the importance of factor abundance (low-cost labour) for export competitiveness.

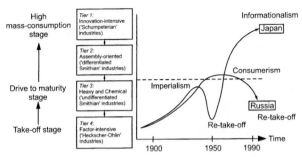

Figure 11.1   Sequential catching-up development: Japan vs. Russia

II Scale-economies-based modernization of heavy and chemical industries (which are highly resource-dependent) such as steel, aluminium, shipbuilding, petrochemicals, and synthetic fibres as the leading growth sector (the late 1950s to the early 1970s). They (Tier 3) may be called 'undifferentiated Smithian' industries because of their rather homogeneous nature and their dependence on Smithian economies of scale and learning effect.

III Subcontracting-dependent and assembly-dependent mass production of consumer durables, such as automobiles and electric/electronic goods as the dominant sector (the late 1960s to the present). They (Tier 2) may be identified as 'differentiated Smithian' industries, since their products are highly differentiated, yet their competitiveness derives basically from scale economies.

IV Mechatronics-based, computer-aided flexible (or 'lean') manufacturing of highly differentiated multi-variety goods, along with technological breakthroughs such as HDTVs, new materials, fine chemicals, and more advanced microchips (the early 1980s onwards). They (Tier 1) are called 'Schumpeterian' (that is, information-dependent) industries because of the key role of innovations in their growth and competitiveness.

The transition from one phase to another has surely not been clear-cut but has overlapped in chronological approximations. Nevertheless, each phase is characterized by the dominance of certain industries as the leading sectors, a pattern that duplicated the evolutionary sequence of capitalist production, as outlined earlier.

It was in the period before the Second World War that Russia and Japan were basically neck- and-neck in building up heavy and chemical (Tier 3) industries.[7] Both countries succeeded in promoting Tier 3 industries under state sponsorship: Russia under communism and Japan under militarist nationalism. But the Russian political system proved unsuitable for the development of consumer-orientated industries of Tier 2 and above. In other words, communism was a useful instrument only for Tier-3-based industrialization but no longer – and even became an obstacle – for the higher stages of economic development.

On the other hand, Japan's transition to Tier 2 was fortunately facilitated by the USA, thanks to the deepening cold war of the post-war period. The Allies initially wanted to penalize Japan for military aggression by dismantling its industrial manufacturing facilities, especially heavy and chemical industries, by way of transferring capital equipment and machinery as reparations to the Asian countries, such as the Philippines and Indo-China, to which Japan caused havoc during the war. In other words, Japan's industrial base was to be degraded down to Tier 4; that was their original intention.

Luckily for Japan, however, the communist revolution in China and the US – Soviet ideological confrontation forced the Allies, especially the USA, to reverse their occupation policy. Japan was now looked at as a potential ally, a bulwark against the spread of communism. America began to assist Japan in reconstructing its heavy and chemical industries (Tier 3), especially after the outbreak of the Korean War. War procurements by the USA-led forces were a shot in the arm. Indeed, the war triggered the first postwar economic boom in Japan, as ammunitions, jeeps and trucks, and other war-related goods and services (ship repairs, for example) were procured from Japan, the closest supply base for the Korean War.

This was an ironical twist of events. *Russia wanted to catch up with – and take over – the West by adopting communism. Yet its aggressive stance in the post-war period slowed down its own progress by hindering a transition to the age of high mass-consumption but created an ideal (godsent) opportunity for Japan to catch up with the advanced West. Japan thus enjoyed undreamed-of positive political externalities.*

More importantly, America helped Japan rebuild itself in the image of American democracy and consumerism. The transplantation of Western democracy and individual freedom and the 'forced' renouncement of armament (hence the absence of a defence burden) were the most critical factors in Japan's success with the subsequent development of Tier 2 and Tier 1 (that is, mass-consumption-orientated) industries.

Moreover, the USA initially not only supplied badly needed raw materials, such as cotton, coal, petroleum and the like, for Japanese industry but also opened its vast domestic markets for imports from Japan, especially steel, ships, and a variety of consumer goods, such as textiles and transistorized radios in the 1950s. The external political change thus enabled Japan to metamorphose itself from the Tier 4-based economy in the 1950s to the Tier-3-based one in the 1960s – and further, toward the subsequent development of Tier-2 industries. Its heavy and chemical industries, whose foundation had been pre-viously laid under Japan's militarism, were modernized and further built up. Their outputs expanded through exports, reaping economies of scale in the process, thereby turning themselves into the dominant industrial sector throughout the 1960s.

The Vietnam War (another flare-up in the cold war) was an additional stimulus to the Japanese economy throughout the latter half of the 1960s. By then, Japanese industry had already begun to move into the consumer-orientated Tier-2 industries, especially TV sets and automo-biles, which saw rapid growth throughout the 1970s despite the oil shocks of 1974 and 1979. In fact, Japan's fuel-efficient subcompact cars became an overnight hit product in the USA, thanks to the oil price hikes. As cars and electronics took over as the leading sector of the Japanese economy, Japan was *in the full Rostovian age of mass consumption – way ahead of the Soviet Union in per capita income and industrial (if not military) technology.*

Not only has Japan succeeded in building Tier-2 industries that became more cost-efficient through the medium of Japan-originated 'lean production' than their Western counterparts, but it has also marched on to develop Tier-1 industries of its own type in competition with its original tutors, the USA and Europe.

Japan's soaring export competitiveness against the backdrop of the arrival of high mass-consumption in export markets, as well as at home, is clearly revealed in Figure 11.2. The dominance of textiles and steel as Japan's major exports in the 1950s and the 1960s was replaced by that of high-income consumer durables in the subsequent decades – notably cars and colour TVs in the 1970s, and computers, VCRs, camcorders, fax machines and compact-disc players in the 1980s.

This structural metamorphosis is described in Japan as a shift away from the production of those goods characterized by '*ju-ko-cho-dai*' ('heavy-thick-long-big'), the major attributes of heavy and chemical industries (Tier 3), to the production of those goods symbolized by 'kei-haku-tan-sho' ('light-thin-short-small') in the resource-saving, high-value-added, knowledge-based industries (Tier 2 and Tier 1). Japan has emerged as an economic superpower, part and parcel of the tripolar global economy. When the cold war was over, as Chalmers Johnson wryly observed, Japan won.[8]

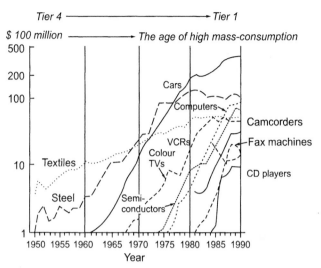

Figure 11.2 Trends in Japan's major exports of manufactures

Source: MITI (1991a, p. 145).

As Lester Thurow (1992) pointed out, the pattern of trade among the tripolar powers is now in 'head-to-head' rivalry, as each strives to develop and retain strategic high-tech industries such as microelectronics, biotechnology, advanced materials, telecommunications, and civilian aircraft. The head-to-head competition is more directly confrontational than what he calls 'niche' competition that prevailed in the early post-war era when, say, Japan was selling labour-intensive manufactures or inexpensive small cars, while 'the United States exported agricultural products they could not grow, raw materials they did not have, and high-tech products ... that they could not build'.[9] In other words, trade was initially based on a developmental-stage gap.

In the meantime, communist Russia was stuck with the pollution-prone heavy and chemical industries and began to experience the high social costs of environmental destruction (pollution of air, water and land) which the communist bureaucracy had no incentive to solve. Communism was indeed instrumental in enabling Russia to take off into Tier-3-phase industrialization, a phase of industrialization based on heavy and chemical industries that required large-scale investment and operation and could usually be supported by government procurement demand (especially military, as in the case of munitions, chemicals, shipbuilding, aircraft and utility vehicles).

As mentioned above, Japan's heavy and chemical industrialization in the period before the Second World War was also propelled and facilitated by nationalism and military buildup at home. This coincides with what Rostow (1960) noted:

> Communism is by no means the only form of effective state organization that can consolidate the preconditions in the transition of a traditional society, launch a take-off, and drive a society to technological maturity. But it may be one way in which this difficult job can be done... Communism takes its place, then, beside the regime of the Meiji Restoration in Japan, and Ataturk's Turkey, for example, as *one peculiarly inhumane form of political organization* capable of launching and sustaining the growth process in societies where the preconditions period did not yield a substantial and enterprising commercial middle class and an adequate political consensus among the leaders of the society. (pp. 163–4; emphasis added)

As Rostow observed, communism was indeed a 'disease of the transition' (p. 162). For that matter, then, militarism in Japan and Germany – and to a similar extent, imperialism in the West at large – was equally 'a disease of the transition'.

Russia's Pent-Up Demand for Consumer Goods: Developmental-Gap-Based Trade and Investment

The sudden collapse of communism in the former Soviet Union is currently weakening even its heavy and chemical industries long nurtured in the context of the arms race with the West, and regressing its economy back to the resource-dependent stage (Tier 4) of economic activities. Aside from the 'illegal' exports of surplus arms, the only commodities Russia can now sell to the outside world competitively are the natural resources it is richly endowed with, such as oil, gas, minerals, and forest and marine resources. Russia is confronted with a dire shortage of consumer goods which it cannot expect to produce sufficiently at the moment.[10]

In sharp contrast, Japan, well into the mature age of high mass-consumption, is suffering from its excess capacity for – and supplies of – consumer goods, especially at a time when its domestic economy is in a serious slump and its export markets in the West are constrained by recession and rising protectionism.

Reflecting the two countries' structural disparities, a fascinating pattern of border trade is quickly developing between the Russian Far East and Japan's northern island, Hokkaido:

> Although Japan's Foreign Ministry is holding back large-scale economic aid to Russia until the territorial issue is resolved, Nemuro [a fishing town in Eastern Hokkaido only 3.7 kilometres away from the nearest islet of the Habomai archipelago] has become the site of a bustling, though primitive, border trade ...
>
> Every Tuesday and Friday at 8 a.m., Russian fishing boats pull into Hanasaki Harbour hauling tons of crab. While some Russian crew members transact sales at the fish market, others wander down the wharf to strike bargains for used cars which they buy with yen proceeds from the crab exports. The cars are lowered, wooden beams running through window spaces, by cranes onto the boats bound for Sakhalin or Vladivostok later in the day.
>
> Under the [no visa] exchange programme launched in April [1992], relaxed border controls allow Russian fishermen, their families and friends who inhabit the disputed islands ... to visit Nemuro and certain other Hokkaido ports. They return home not only with used cars but also with appliances, electronics, clothes, cosmetics and groceries.
>
> With the rouble long in a tailspin ... crab has effectively become a stable unit of Russian currency in regional commerce ... The going rate for a used car is about Y50000 ($400), which is what five king crabs at Y10000 ($120) each, or 10 kegani crabs at Y5000 ($40) each fetch at the fish market.
>
> According to the Nemuro mayor's office, Russian ships unloaded Y845 million worth of seafood from January through July [in 1992] — almost four times the Y218 million worth imported in all of 1991.[11]

This 'crab-for-cars' border trade symbolizes the fundamental pattern of commercial exchange that is likely to persist for the foreseeable future between Russia – and notably, its resource-based Far East – and Japan; the former exports natural resources, the latter consumer goods and related capital goods. Such trade is based on the absolute availability of goods – that is, the principle of complementarity in trade.

Japan and other key Pacific Asian economies (the newly industrializing economies, or NIEs), such as South Korea, Taiwan, and Singapore, are all resource-scarce, but are already in the phase of high mass-consumption. This characteristic leaves the 'resources-for-manufactures' type of trade relatively unencumbered by the politics of domestic interest groups; in fact, perfect harmony exists between private and public interests in promoting such trade on the part of the Asian economies.

Simultaneously, the newly semi-autonomous republics and provinces of the erstwhile Soviet Union are now increasingly gaining control on their own natural resources, although there are uncertainties in the current process of decentralisation of power from Moscow.[12] Yet, as the republics and regional provinces secure administrative autonomy, they become eager to base their regional economies on the overseas sales of natural resources in exchange for consumer goods; and this absolute complementarity in trade is creating a good basis for barter trade, at least for the time being, for cash-strapped Russia and especially for the resource-rich Russian Far East.

In this connection, South Korea, which established diplomatic ties with Russia in September 1990, is particularly active in exploring the opportunities for 'consumer-goods-for-resources' barter trade. Lucky-Goldstar, Korea's major trading company, completed the exchange of 500 000 dollars in personal computers for 20 000 tons of aluminium with a Siberian mining firm. Samsung is similarly arranging several barter deals with local firms in Ukraine, Kazakhstan and Uzbekistan.[13]

This type of 'consumer-goods-for-resources' trade is certainly serving as an opener of commercial exchange with the Pacific Rim economies. Nevertheless, Russia will eventually move up the ladder of capitalist production, if it is to catch up with the West, by building Tier-2 and Tier-1 industries. For a start, Russia has already begun to convert its hitherto military-based heavy and chemical industries into consumer-orientated ones; that is, to transform some Tier-3 sectors into Tier-2 industries: and there are reportedly some success cases.

The primary example is Metalkhim, still a government-owned company which once produced the SS-20 medium-range missiles, tanks, howitzers, and nuclear, chemical and biological weapons. It is now producing refrigerators, red-plastic boomboxes, bicycles, washing machines, watches, plastic squeeze toys, and 25 million tampons a year. But it is reported that the quality of most of these consumer goods is poor; 'the radios are perhaps five years behind Japanese quality and technology and the plastic squeeze toys are crude'.[14] Another high-tech Russian firm, Khrunichev Enterprise, has also formed a venture with Lockheed Corporation to market the Russian-built Proton rocket for commercial satellite launches.[15]

Given the high concentration of top-quality manpower and industrial experiences in Russia's defence industry, such industry may be able to develop international competitiveness fairly quickly if it is properly restructured. In fact, the Japanese government is concentrating its assistance on Russia's conversion of military-related production into civilian manufacturing. Specifically, the Japanese Ministry of International Trade and Industry (MITI) has suggested to Russia that the latter's naval shipyards in Vladivostok could possibly subcontract work for Japanese shipbuilders and its tank and plane engine factories manufacture small tractors — although no specific arrangement has been made as yet.[16] The South Korean government too is showing interest in assisting Russia to reorientate its defence industry for commercial applications; Korea specifically selected 21 sectors – out of the 56 originally submitted by Russia – which include airplanes, production technologies, underwater electronic equipment, missiles, computer software and telecommunications.[17]

The 'Japan Sea Rim' Economic Zone: Full Economic Integration as a Political Solution of the Territorial Issue – Pragmatism over Nationalism

Valentin Fedorov, governor of the Sakhalin region of Russia, expressed what may be called a 'beyond the territorial issue' approach to Russo-Japanese economic cooperation. He is quoted as saying:

> We inherited this matter from the past. You cannot review boundaries. You have to do away with boundaries. I have suggested that to Japan. I have also suggested that we have visa-free travel, free trade and cross-investment between Sakhalin and Hokkaido. But the Japanese side refused. We should develop economic cooperation and relationships that integrate Japan and the Russian Far East. That would be the basic foundation for a good and healthy relationship.[18]

This proposed approach has a lot of promise if the governors of Far Eastern Russia can play an active role in creating a conducive environment for industrial cooperation between the region and Japan, now that Russia's central administration has been disintegrating in the wake of the collapse of totalitarianism. In this respect, Japan is advocating the appropriate use of industrial policy at the regional level and dispatching missions to Russia's republics and regional governments. For instance, the MITI is preaching the Japanese brand of industrial restructuring as an alternative to the IMF formula that stresses the speedy implementation of financial and trade liberalization; it instead emphasizes the development of Russia's industrial and entrepreneurial base prior to such liberalization by arguing that Russia is not ready for immediate liberalization. The MITI missionaries are urging the adoption of policies to nurture infant industries and presenting Japan as a model, because Japan in 1945 had to 'democratize and demilitarize' its economy rapidly — and did so very successfully.[19]

In other words, the traditional IMF – and for that matter the World Bank – approach is built on Keynesian macroeconomic management (fiscal, monetary, exchange rate, and demand-stabilization policies), whereas the MITI is advocating the use of sector-focused industrial policy. It is actually what John Dunning (1992) conceptualized as 'macro-organizational strategy' – through which 'to retain or attract mobile assets and to advance the industrial competitiveness of these assets' at the national level. Japan's advice, however, is more likely to be targeted at the regional level – namely at the Russian republics and provinces on an individual basis, and especially in Far Eastern Russia, rather than at the central level, namely Moscow.

As far as Japan's official economic aid so far offered to Russia is concerned, it is limited in amount and rather small because of the unsettled territorial dispute. The Japanese government would certainly be much more 'willing' to offer aid if such a political obstacle did not exist. As explained below, however, Japan's political front (mostly for domestic grand-standing) is quite different from the economic pragmatism exhibited by its government agencies, notably the MITI, and the private business sector.

As shown in Table 11.1, the total 'pledged' amount of 2823 million dollars at the end of 1992 is bare-minimal – and relatively small when the enormity of political stakes involved in assuring a smooth transition of Russia to democracy is taken into full account. Besides, as much as 92.1 per cent (2600 million dollars out of the total of 2823 million dollars) of the aid is offered in loans and trade insurance. Trade insurance alone amounts to 1.8 billion dollars providing insurance to Japanese exporters. Japan's exports to Russia exceeded the 3 billion dollars level in 1986 but began to decline sharply after 1989, and dwindled to a little over 1 billion in 1992. On the other hand, Japanese imports from Russia continued to rise from 2 billion in 1986 to 3.3 billions in 1991, but dropped sharply to 2.4 billion in 1992.

It is said that Russian enterprises, especially those old ones of the former Soviet Union, owe the Japanese general trading companies about 1.5 billion dollars.[20] Hence, the trade insurance provided by the Japanese government will surely serve as a special aid as it encourages

Table 11.1   Japan's pledged economic aid to Russia at the end of 1992 (million US dollars)

	$USm.	Aid
1990	8	Food, medical goods (humanitarian aid)
	100	Loans from Japan's Export-Import Bank
1991	20	Medical equipment (humanitarian aid)
	1 800	Trade insurance ($700m. already applied)
	200	Suppliers' credit extension from Japan's Export-Import Bank
	500	Loans from Japan's Export-Import Bank
1992	50	Food, medical goods (humanitarian aid)
	20	International fund for scientists (not yet provided)
	25	International fund for nuclear facilities repair ($12m. provided)
	100	Food, medical goods (humanitarian aid)
Total	2 823	($890 provided)

Sources: Based on statistics from the Japanese Ministry of Foreign Affairs, as reported in *the Nikkei Weekly* (22 Mar. 1993) p. 1.

exports from Japan. In fact, under the expanded trade insurance pro-gramme for Russia, a 700 million dollar deal between Japanese steel-makers and Gazprom, a Russian gas company, has been most recently signed to supply large-diameter pipes, seamless pipes, and drilling equipment on a deferred payment basis.[21] The deal is expected to improve and strengthen Russia's vitally important energy industry, which can earn much-needed foreign exchange.

Despite the presently sagging trade relationship between the two countries, there has recently occurred some close cooperation between the Russian Far East and Japan's regions on the Japan Sea coast, notably the Niigata area and Hokkaido (Japan's main northern island). For example, in November 1992 a group of some 20 small and medium-size Japanese trading houses signed an agreement with the authorities of 10 regions in the Russian Far East and Siberia to establish a joint venture in Buryat aimed at expanding trade. The accord stipulates that the local authorities, including those of Buryat, Sakha, Irkutsk, Sakhalin and Krasnoyarsk, will each establish a fund of hard currency. And the new joint venture in Buryat will provide them with credit five times the fund and serve as a channel through which loans from the Export-Import Bank of Japan can be secured for Russo-Japanese business tie-ups.[22]

Separately from this joint venture, 3 diamond-cutting factories (there will be 12 more in the future), each employing 200 workers, have recently opened in the Sakha town of Suntar. The factories are run by Sakha-Japan Diamond, a joint venture between the Sakha government and a small Japanese trading company. The Sakha government secured the right to sell 20 per cent of its rough diamonds independently of Moscow in March 1992. The joint venture initially intends to ship out 20000 carats of polished diamonds to Japan, starting in 1993 – and eventually 30000 carats, which would equal 10 per cent of the Japanese market, the world's largest gem market. Furthermore, FR Corporation, a Tokyo-based jewellery retailer that has acquired exclusive rights to import polished diamonds from Sakha-Japan Diamond, will train Russian workers at its cutting centre in Japan.[23]

In addition to these individually – and rather sporadically – contrived ventures, the Japanese government has been actively exploring the possibility of setting up a large economic zone in a multi-border region involving the Russian Far East, north-eastern China, North and South Korea, and Japan, a plan tentatively called 'the Japan Sea Rim Joint Development Plan'. The Research Institute for International Trade and Industry, an official policy research arm of Japan's MITI, and its Russian counterpart are reportedly formulating a regional industrial development policy to make this plan materialize. Furthermore, this joint development zone is expected to be the focal point for Japan to plan its medium-term and long-term economic assistance programmes for Russia.[24] In other words, Japan's economic aid to Russia will be centred on Far Eastern Russia.

The potential industries in the region targeted are energy, agricultural and fisheries processing, and other natural resources, and tourism. The proposal is designed to bring the Russian Far East into the industrial dynamism of the Pacific Rim. The zone can 'mesh Russia's untapped natural resources with the abundant labour supply in China, technology in South Korea, and the capital and high-tech know-how of Japan'.[25] Thus, Japan and the Asian NIEs' investments will be initially targeted at exploration, development, extraction, primary processing, and exportation of natural resources from the Russian Far East.

In addition, Japanese industry is participating in the Tumen River Delta project initiated by the United Nations Development Programme, a plan for regional development on the Tumen River Delta dividing North Korea, China and Russia. The plan calls for the dredging of the river mouth, the improvement of ports, and the establishment of free-trade zones within the region – at an estimated cost of 30 billion dollars and a completion period in excess of twenty years. The Japan Federation of Economic Organizations (*keidanren*) has joined a Japanese investment consortium already consisting of about twenty large Japanese companies such as Nomura Securities, the Bank of Tokyo, Marubeni, Nissho

Iwai, and others.[26] There is no doubt that the Tumen River Delta project constitutes one of the key components of Japan's broader regional development plan for the Russian Far East.

On the eastern side of the Japan Sea, some Japanese localities are also gearing up for the coming age of Far Eastern Russia as a dynamic growth region. The Japanese Ministry of Transport is planning to build a major port and Japan's largest liquefied natural gas storage facilities in Niigata to accommodate the import of natural gas from Sakhalin and Siberia during the period 1996–2000 for construction with a budget exceeding 8 billion dollars.[27] In addition, the Japanese Ministry of Posts and Tele-communications is initiating a move to improve telecommunication links within the Japan Sea Rim zone, especially around Vladivostok, Khabarovsk and Nakhodka, since the need for better international and intra-regional communication services will increase among Japanese investors, traders, and tourists. As the first step of this effort, a joint venture will be set up in Vladivostok between KDD (Japan's largest international telecommunications carrier) and Nissho Iwai (a major trading company) on the Japanese side, and Interdaltelecom (a regional telecommunications organisation) on the Russian side.[28]

There are thus some promising movements initiated by the Japanese government and its private business sector, on one hand, and Russia's Far Eastern governments, on the other, toward laying down the founda-tions for economic exchanges. Economic relations are being formulated and organised in a quasi-governmental/semi-market-orientated fashion on both sides. If the Russian republics and provinces can secure greater and lasting autonomy from Moscow, the present trend is expected to be strengthened, since there is so much complementarity between them and Japan – and the East Asian economies. The growth of the Russian Far East will probably play a role similar to that of presently booming South China in 'importing' and transmitting inland the industrial dynamism of the Pacific Rim. The only difference is, however, that the initial phase of economic development in the Russian Far East will be resource-based, while that in South China is largely labour-based.

Conclusions

The Rostovian stage theory of economic growth provides an important framework within which to interpret the emergent economic relation-ships between Far Eastern Russia and Japan. The demise of Soviet communism was a reflection of its failure to catch up with the West – and Japan – in the age of high mass-consumption. For totalitarian communism has proved to be structurally incompatible with the stage of consumer-based capitalism in which democracy and individual freedom in choice of lifestyle, the basic principles of the Western political system, happen to be simultaneously the driving forces of the market system. And the leading industrial sector of modern capitalism is the consumer durables and services, notably automobiles, personal computers, other electronic high-income goods, tourism, leisure activities, and personal financial services.

At the moment, in the aftermath of the collapse of communism, Russia has slipped away even from scale-dependent heavy and chemical industries (Tier 3) and degenerated back to the elementary stage of capitalist production, namely, the resource-dependent (Tier 4) stage of economic growth. National efforts now must be made to move the Russian economy all over again up the ladder of industrialization toward more consumer-orientated stages (that is, to base its economy on Tier 1 and Tier 2 industries).

As the resource-abundant Russian republics and provinces, many of them located in the Russian Far East, attain autonomy, a strong basis for trade and investment built on a developmental-stage gap is opening up between the region and Japan – as well as other natural-resource-scarce Asian economies.

Despite the politically charged territorial dispute, the Japanese government and industry are focused squarely on the enormous potentiality of economic exchanges with the Russian Far East and planning to assist – and to capitalise on – regional development on Russia's Japan Sea coast by way of official economic aid, foreign direct investment, and trade. As is typically the case with the Japanese approach to overseas market development, all the available national means, both public and private, will be mobilized as an integrated holistic package of economic activities – once political stability is assured in Russia. Japan is presently in a rather confrontational phase of 'head-to-head' rivalry *vis-à-vis* the USA and Europe, now that its industrial structure has advanced and become similar – hence, competing in relationship – at the same mature stage of high mass-consumption or the Schumpeterian stage of high-tech manufacturing. In contrast, the trade and investment relationships between Far Eastern Russia and Japan are expected to be of the highly complementary 'niche' type for the time being, given the vast gap that exists in stages of growth and factor endowments between the two economies.

Regional economic integration on the Japan Sea Rim, if successfully promoted, will be an effective temporary substitute for – and a promising prelude to – the possible settlement (compromise) of the knotty territorial dispute that is anyhow unlikely to materialize in any immediately foreseeable future.

Notes

1 Quoted in Williams (1963 p. 25).
2 *Ibid.*, p. 30.
3 Borthwick (1992 p. 491).
4 Rostow (1960) states, however, that the timing of the Japanese take-off cannot be identified exactly because of the lack of adequate data. He asserts: 'By 1914 the Japanese economy had certainly taken off. The question is whether the period from about 1878 to the Sino-Japanese War in the mid-1890s, is to be regarded as the completion of the preconditions or as take-off. On present evidence we incline to the latter view' (p. 38, fn.).
5 In terms of industrial composition, Rostow describes this stage as follows: 'After the railway take-offs of the third quarter of the nineteenth century – with coal, iron, and heavy engineering at the centre of the growth process – it is steel, the new ships, chemicals, electricity, and the products of the modern machine-tool that come to dominate the economy and sustain the overall rate of growth' (p. 59).
6 The stage theory based on the sequence of 'mercantilism', 'liberalism', and 'imperialism' was originally conceived by a Japanese Marxian economist, Kozo Uno (1954). Albritton (1991) added a more recent stage, 'consumerism', for the post-Second World War period. I am further adding 'informational-ism' as the latest stage of capitalist development.
7 Rostow (1960) observed: 'It is clear that an enlargement and modernisation of armed forces could play the role of a leading sector in take-off. It was a factor in the Russian, Japanese and German take-offs; and it figures heavily in current Chinese Communist plans' (p. 56).
8 As quoted in a telecourse programme, *The Pacific Century*, produced by the Annenberg Foundation and the Public Broadcasting Corporation, 1992.
9 Thurow (1992 p. 29).
10 Adjubei (1993) observes: 'Of particular attraction to the foreign investors are the high levels of domestic demand for some raw materials and manufac-tured products (inter alia, personal computers, telecommunications, copying equipment, chemicals, drugs, high quality paper and consumer durables), as well as a wide range of business and personal services which are either unavailable in the local market or imported' (manuscript, p. 8).
11 *Nikkei Weekly*, 12 September. 1992, pp. 1 and 3.
12 The following observation sums up the current situation: 'Relations between the regions and the central government were defined in three agreements signed [in 1992]. The most important was the federation treaty, signed by the central government and 18 republics (regions of Russia with large non-Rus-sian populations and extensive powers of local government). It gave the republics new powers, extending their influence over foreign policy, foreign trade, land and natural resources and ownership rights. There are several problems with this treaty, not least of which is that it has not been imple-mented'. 'A country of countries', *The Economist*, 28 March. 1992, p. 22.

Nevertheless, as pointed out by Adjubei (1993), 'immediate export prospects exist for joint ventures which process and commercialize domestic natural resources — which have attracted 24 per cent of foreign capital. Given the increasing interest of both foreign investors and host Governments in this type of venture, their share is likely to grow in the future' (manuscript, p. 8). 'Recently, Russia and Kazakhstan, both well endowed in natural resources, have become more favourably disposed towards foreign investors wishing to develop their oil, gas, and timber reserves. Press reports confirm this trend in some other former Soviet republics. The pressing need for convertible currency, which can be earned through the export of natural resources, opens better prospects for multinationals, which have some experience of large-scale concessions, joint ventures and production-sharing agreements in the primary sector' (manuscript, p. 23).

13   *Japan Times*, 3 August 1992, p. 7.
14   As reported in Wall Street Journal, 25 February 1993 p. A6. It also observes: 'Western experts say at least the defence plants are functioning, unlike most of the rest of Russia's economy. To a large extent, these plants are the Russian economy. Alexander P. Vladislavlev, chairman of the Industrialists and Entrepreneurs Union of Russia, estimates that defence plants produce more than 20 per cent of the Russian gross domestic product, employ the best 7.5 million workers in the country and consume more than 75 per cent of all government outlays on science.'
15   *Wall Street Journal*, 29 December 1992, p. A3.
16   *Japan Times*, 7 August 1992, p. 14.
17   *Wall Street Journal*, 15 October 1992, p. A16.
18   *International Herald Tribune*, 31 August 1992, p. 2.
19   Wall Street Journal, 21 July 1992, p. A9; *Nikkei Weekly*, 22 August 1992, p. 3.
20   Based on statistics prepared by the Japanese Ministry of International Trade and Industry as reported in *Nikkei Weekly*, 25 January 1993, p. 3.
21   *Nikkei Weekly*, 1 February 1993 p. 8.
22   *Nikkei Weekly*, 14 December 1992, p. 10.
23   *Ibid.*, p. 10.
24   *Daily Yomiuri*, 16 March 1993, p. 6.
25   *Nikkei Weekly*, 18 July 1992, p. 3.
26   *Nikkei Weekly*, 8 February 1993, p. 10.
27   *Nikkei Weekly*, 26 September 1992, p. 3.
28   *Nikkei Weekly*, 20 June 1992, p. 9.

12
Ukraine

Faye Sinclair

In terms of population, Ukraine is the second largest of the successor states (approximately 25 million inhabitants). It has a developed industry based on deposits of coal and iron ore, and its geographical position is conducive to highly efficient agriculture. Since the dissolution of the USSR, and its declaration of independence, Ukraine has embarked on the road of market reform, which entails the opening of the economy, allowing for a free flow of goods, labour and entrepreneurial capital. The inflow of the latter, in particular, is increasingly perceived as a catalyst in transforming Ukraine from Kornai's 'shortage' economy to a Western-type 'pressure' economy, which operates under hard rather than soft budget constraints.

So far, however, the inflow of foreign capital in Ukraine has been rather modest. The estimated stock of foreign investment (FI) accumulated by the end of 1992 (480 million dollars) was comparable to that of Romania (540 million dollars), but was significantly lower than in the neighbouring transition economies (Hungary, Poland), which have gone further along the road of market transformation.

The purpose of this chapter is to assess the scope of foreign investment in Ukraine's economy after one and a half years of independent development. The issues addressed include the magnitude of FI, its origin and industrial distribution, as well as the scale of operations of FIEs (foreign investment enterprises). The chapter also discusses the legal environment of FI, the comparative advantages of the economy from the point of view of prospective investors, and the implications of the current economic crisis on future investment trends.

Magnitude of Foreign Investment (1987–93)

(a) Growth and Capitalization

During 1987–90, when the Soviet Union was still in place, Ukraine outpaced the other constituent republics in terms of growth in the number of joint venture registrations. On 1 January 1991, the total number of joint ventures registered on Ukraine's territory amounted to 209, or 7.2 per cent of the former-Soviet total (as compared with less than 5 per cent during 1987–8). On the same date, the total capitalization of Ukraine-based joint ventures stood at 330.5 million roubles or 6.7 per cent of the USSR total, while its foreign component amounted to 133.3 million roubles or 206.5 million dollars at current official/commercial exchange rates.

FI projects registered during 1987–90 had a smaller than average (all-Union) statutory capital. The average statutory capital allocated to a joint venture amounted to 2.2. million roubles (8.3 per cent lower than the former Soviet average). The same holds true of the foreign part of the ventures' capitalization) with average foreign capital committed not exceeding 1.4 million dollars.[1] During that period, individuals or small-company owners of Ukrainian descent with limited resources represented the predominant type of investors in Ukraine, while medium-sized enterprises or multinationals were largely reluctant to invest in what appeared a relatively risky environment. This factor helps explain the small average size of FI in Ukraine.[2]

The majority (over 57 per cent) of joint ventures registered in Ukraine by 1 January 1991 were engaged in industry, primarily in manufacturing. Agriculture (with 2 per cent of the total number of registrations) was much less attractive to foreign investors than business services, which accounted for 13.5 per cent of the total number of registered joint ventures. Overall, the sectoral distribution of Ukraine-based joint ventures in 1990–1 largely adhered to the all-Union pattern.[3]

Since independence on 16 July 1990 the number of FIEs in Ukraine has grown at a relatively high speed. According to the Ministry of Statistics, the number of joint ventures increased from 209 in early 1991 to 1203 at the beginning of 1993 – that is, almost sixfold. Simultaneously, the foreign component of their capitalization rose from 206.5 million dollars to an estimated 480 million dollars (total capitalization stood at 6.5 billion roubles).[4]

During the first half of 1992, gross fixed investment in Ukraine declined by 41 per cent, compared with the first half of 1991.[5] This suggests that during this period of economic decline, although small in magnitude, FI to a certain extent tended to counteract the slump in production.

No less important is the fact that recently Ukraine's business environment seems to have become increasingly attractive to 'large-scale' foreign investors. Several multinationals have successfully negotiated joint ventures in the telecommunications, oil refining and consumer goods sector. These have a higher capitalization than investments previously undertaken by small-scale entrepreneurs. For example, one of the largest joint venture deals within the CIS in terms of capitalization was concluded in October 1992 by Pepsico with Ukraine's shipbuilding enterprise and largest beverage producer. The venture's objective is to export up to a billion dollars worth of Ukrainian ships over the next eight years. The convertible currency proceeds will be used as the working capital to finance the expansion of Ukraine's bottling and ship-building capacities.[6]

(b) Foreign Partners

The USA and Germany represent Ukraine's most important aggregated FI partners. Out of a total of 600 FI projects registered by mid-1992, as many as 80, or 13 per cent, had partners from the USA, while those with German partners accounted for 10.5 per cent (see Table 12.1).[7]

More generally, enterprises from both Western and Eastern Europe are the sources of the largest number of FIEs: 247 (41 per cent) and 189 (32 per cent), respectively. In the latter case the role of investors from the Czech and Slovak republics (7 per cent), Hungary and Poland (9 per cent each) predominates. The relatively high FI activities of companies from these three countries may be explained by Ukraine's geographical proximity and its sizeable internal market.

(c) Operational FIEs

The number of operational FIEs represents a better indicator of both foreign investors' interest in the host economy and their role therein. By the beginning of 1991, there were 113 operational joint ventures in Ukraine. Their number more than doubled during that year (267) to reach 416 by July 1992 (see Table 12.2). The continuing growth in the number of operational joint ventures, despite the deepening economic crisis and sustained political tension between Ukraine and Russia, testifies to the growing confidence of foreign investors, partly attributable to a more stable legal environment created by the March 1992 foreign investment law.

Table 12.1 Foreign investment projects in Ukraine, by origin of foreign partner, on 1 July 1992

Country/region	No.	%
Western Europe	247	41.2
EU	153	25.5
Belgium	12	2.0
France	16	2.7
Germany	63	10.5
Greece	4	0.7
Ireland	2	0.3
Italy	25	4.2
Luxembourg	2	0.3
Netherlands	6	1.0
Spain	6	1.0
UK	17	2.8
EFTA	70	11.7
Austria	32	5.3
Finland	8	1.3
Iceland	1	0.2
Sweden	4	0.7
Switzerland	24	4.0
Liechtenstein	1	0.2
Other Europe	24	4.0
Cyprus	9	1.5
Turkey	6	1.0
Yugoslav successor states	9	1.5
Canada	17	2.8
Japan	2	0.3
Israel	5	0.8
USA	80	13.3
Developing countries	40	6.7
Economies in transition	189	31.5
Bulgaria	27	4.5
CIS	12	2.0
Belarus	1	0.2
Moldova	3	0.5
Russian Federation	8	1.3
Czech and Slovak F.R.	42	7.0
Estonia	1	0.2
Hungary	51	8.5
Latvia	1	0.2
Poland	53	8.8
Romania	2	0.3
Non-European planned economies	9	1.5
China	6	1.0
Vietnam	3	0.5
Other countries	11	1.8
Australia	11	1.8
Total	600	100.0

Source: UN/ECE DOC. TRADE/R.588.

Table 12.2 Foreign investment projects in Ukraine: major indicators, 1991–2

Date/year	No.			Output (mn SUR)	Exports (mn valuta SUR)	Imports (mn valuta SUR)	Domestic sales		Employment
	Registered	Operational	Operational with output				(mn SUR)	(mn valuta SUR)	
1.01.1991 (1991)	209	113	102	374.0	33.0	88.0	310.0	32.0	13900
1.01.1992 (1991)	n.a.	267	250	1730.7	88.6	155.7	1614.6	78.3	21900
1.07.1992 (1Q-2Q 1992)	600	416	349	11652.9	3097.7	3259.1	9416.7	245.4	29389
Percentage, as at 1 January 1991 (1990 = 100):									
1.01.1991 (1991)	100.0	100.0	100.0	100.0	100.0	100.0	100.0	100.0	100.0
1.01.1992 (1991)		236.3	245.1	462.8	268.5	176.9	520.8	244.7	157.6
1.07.1992 (1Q-2Q 1992)	287.1	368.1	342.2	3115.7	9387.0	3703.5	3037.7	766.9	211.4

n.a. = not available.

Source: UN/ECE DOC. TRADE/R.588.

During 1991, operational joint ventures increased their output to 1731 million roubles, as compared with 379 million roubles in 1990, representing a growth of 457 per cent at current prices. If one further compares the value of joint venture output to gross social product, the ratio increased from 0.1 per cent during 1990 to 0.3 per cent in 1991, whereas the respective ratio to national income rose from 0.3 per cent to 0.8 per cent. During the first six months of 1992, FIEs' output grew further to 11 653 million roubles.

Employment in enterprises with foreign capital participation increased from 13 900 in 1990 to 25 400 by mid-1992.[8] If one compares the number of employees at FI enterprises with that in the emerging non-state sector of the economy, the employment-creation effect appears to be relatively small. For example, during 1991, the increment in FI-related employment amounted to only 8000, while some 1.5 million workers, or 6 per cent of Ukraine's labour force, moved out of the state sector. The released labour was absorbed by emerging domestic non-state enterprises.[9]

The growth in FI operations is further illustrated by the increasing domestic trade turnover of FIEs, which rose from 310 billion roubles in 1990 to 1615 million roubles a year later, reaching 9417 million roubles during the first half of 1992. One should note, however, that the partial price liberalization of January 1992 accelerated inflation in Ukraine and generated a somewhat distorted image of the growth in local currency (rouble) sales by FIEs during the first half of 1992. A more reliable indicator is that of convertible currency sales, the value of which increased from 32 million dollars during 1990 to 78 million dollars in 1991, and exceeded 245 million dollars during the first two quarters of 1992. On a yearly basis, this represented a fifteenfold increase in value terms over a two-year period.

(d) Foreign-Investment-Related External Trade

Joint venture exports practically tripled in value terms during 1991: from 33 million (valuta) roubles to 88.6 million (valuta) roubles. In that year, joint venture exports represented 1.4 per cent of total Ukrainian merchandise exports. Similarly, the value of joint venture imports grew by 77 per cent increasing from 88 million (valuta) roubles to 155.7 million (valuta) roubles.

During the first six months of 1992, both FI-related exports and imports rose steeply to 3098 million (valuta) roubles and 3259 million (valuta) roubles respectively. The figure for exports accounts for about 5 per cent of total Ukrainian exports.

During 1991, some 80 per cent of joint venture exports were to Western Europe, with the EU accounting for 75 per cent of the total. Germany, which is Ukraine's main Western European trading partner, absorbed 49 per cent of these exports. Joint venture imports largely reflect the pattern of the foreign investors' countries of origin. During 1991, 66 per cent of joint venture imports came from Western Europe (52 per cent from the EU). Germany alone accounted for 43 per cent of joint venture imports that year. The transition economies delivered 27.5 per cent of FI-related imports, with Poland the major source of imports.

During the first half of 1992, the proportion of FI-related exports to Western Europe fell to 39 per cent of the total, with Germany accounting for only 19 per cent. This decline was largely offset by growth in the share of exports to transition economies and developing countries. Their shares increased from 6 and 4 per cent of total joint venture exports during 1991 to 22 and 16 per cent in the first two quarters of 1992, respectively. Western Europe's contribution to total joint venture imports also declined during the first half of 1991 to 21 per cent of the total, with Germany reducing its import share to 14 per cent. While the transition economies also decreased the volume of their imports, with their weighting declining from 27 per cent in 1991 to 7 per cent during the first six months of 1992, Cuba turned out to be the major source of joint venture imports, accounting for almost half of their value.

The volatility of FI-related foreign trade largely reflects the absence of established commercial links by the newly set-up FIEs, coupled with the reduced export-absorbing capacity of the major markets of Western Europe moving deeper into recession.

(e) Regional Distribution of Foreign Investment

By mid-1992, FI activities were concentrated in Western, Southern and Central Ukraine.[10] On that date, as many as 115 out of 416 (28 per cent) operational FIEs were located in Kiev city, attracted essentially by the business infrastructure and proximity to decision-making bodies. The Odessa region, which enjoys relatively well-developed seaport facilities, was the second most attractive location (13 per cent). During the first half of 1992, joint ventures operating from these areas accounted for a significant proportion of FI domestic sales (14 per cent and 9 per cent respectively); in addition, Odessa-based FIEs were geared towards export markets. During the same period, 54 operational joint ventures in Odessa jointly accounted for over a third of total FI-related exports, and for about 60 per cent of imports (see Table 12.3).

Table 12.3   Foreign investment projects in Ukraine by region of operation, on 1 July 1992 (1Q–2Q 1992)

Region	No.			Domestic sales		Exports Imports
	Registrations	Operational	Operational with output	(SUR m.)	(valuta SUR m.)	(valuta SUR m.)
Krim Republic	10	8	107.3	24.2	5.1	40.2
Cherkasy	9	8	39.6	n.a.	0.5	0.3
Chernigiv	4	4	100	n.a.	321	5
Chernivtsi	12	11	314.9	n.a.	7.6	3.5
Dnipvopetrovsk	24	21	675.8	22.3	126.6	40.0
Donetsk	36	32	1413.9	53.5	803.1	668.8
Ivano-Frankivs'k	12	11	111.6	4.4	45.9	77.4
Khar'kiv	20	17	717.0	1.3	5.6	25.2
Kherson	n.a.	n.a.	n.a.	n.a.	n.a.	n.a.
Khmel'nyts'k	n.a.	n.a.	n.a.	n.a.	n.a.	n.a.
Kiev City	115	93	1352.0	40.0	31.7	281.1
Kiev Region	7	6	86.4	0.4	3.0	8.9
Kirovograd	n.a.	n.a.	n.a.	n.a.	n.a.	n.a.
Lugans'k	8	8	2511.4	0.1	605.2	58.0
Lviv	38	35	147.8	10.6	71.4	16.6
Mikolaev	5	5	5.4	n.a.	0.6	n.a.
Odessa	54	43	826.2	87.9	967.8	1937.0
Poltava	n.a.	n.a.	n.a.	n.a.	n.a.	n.a.
Rivno	8	8	270.9	n.a.	25.1	0.3
Sumy	1	1	286.8	n.a.	0.3	0.2
Ternopil	6	6	108.4	n.a.	n.a.	4.0
Vinnitsa	4	2	11.4	0.1	n.a.	72.1
Volyn'	5	4	4.1	n.a.	0.4	n.a.
Zakarpati'ya	28	17	86.9	0.6	77.1	20.8
Zaporizh'ya	7	6	227.9	n.a.	n.a.	n.a.
Zhitomyr	3	3	11.0	n.a.	n.a.	n.a.
Total	416	349	9416.7	245.4	3097.7	3259.1

n.a. = not available.

Source: UN/ECE, TRADE/R.588.

The Lviv and Donetsk regions ranked third and fourth in terms of numbers of operational joint ventures, with 38 and 36 FI projects (about 9 per cent each). Although the share of Lviv-based FIEs in operational indicators was minimal, joint ventures from the Donetsk region, where Ukraine's largest coal basin is situated, were actively involved both in domestic and foreign trade, their share generally exceeding 20 per cent of the respective total values of FI-related domestic trade turnover, and exports and imports. According to the Statistical Committee of the CIS, by mid-1992, the total number of operational FIEs in the CIS had risen to 2604. On that date, Ukraine accounted for 16 per cent of the total, as compared with 66 per cent for the Russian Federation, 6 per cent for Belarus and 4 per cent for Kazakhstan. The Ukraine's share matches its weighting in the CIS population and national income produced (19 and 17 per cent respectively in 1991).

Foreign Investment and Privatization Legislation

Prior to Ukraine's secession from the former Soviet Union on 24 August 1991, inward foreign investment was regulated by the 1987 Soviet decree on joint ventures. This law emphasized the importance of joint ventures as a means of 'attracting into the Soviet economy modern technological and managerial skills'; of raising production and supply for the domestic market; and of decreasing 'irrational' imports while promoting exports.

Initially, the foreign share in the statutory capital was limited to 49 per cent. The subsequent presidential decree of 20 October 1990 allowed foreign investors to set up wholly foreign-owned subsidiaries. Joint ventures were subject both to profit and income repatriation taxes, at the basic rates of 30 per cent and 20 per cent respectively.[11]

Since independence, several laws pertaining to FI activities have been enacted. The adoption of the Law on Investment Activity on 18 September 1991 was followed by a decree from the Council of Ministers on the protection of foreign investment. The latter guaranteed foreign investors the right to repatriate profits in roubles and convertible currency, and provided several concessions, namely a two-year tax exemption period and a subsequent 35 per cent reduction in profit tax. Joint ventures were exempted from customs duties for an initial period of two years, and FIEs, in which foreign partners controlled over 30 per cent of the capital, were in addition exempted from customs duties, even after the initial two-year concession period had elapsed.[12]

On 23 March 1992, the Ukrainian parliament endorsed the law on foreign investment, which entered into force on 31 March 1992. Its major provisions are summarized below.[13]

(a) Definition and Types of Foreign Investment

The law defines FIEs as those in which foreign partners control a minimum of 20 per cent of the declared authorized (statutory) capital, or where FI amounts to at least 100 000 dollars (article 2). An FIE may establish subsidiaries that enjoy the rights of legal entities. Provided that 51 per cent of its statutory fund is financed by the FIE, a subsidiary is entitled to preferences and guarantees equal to those of its parent.

Foreign investment can be effected in various forms, including the ownership of land, enterprises' securities and intellectual property rights. The types of FI are not restricted: foreign companies may establish joint ventures, wholly foreign-owned subsidiaries, acquire the stock of and take over existing enterprises, as well as obtain the right to use land or concessions to exploit natural resources on Ukrainian territory.

(b) Access to the Economy

In order to acquire legal status, partners to the FI agreement should apply for registration with the Ministry of Finance (MF), which registers a new FIE within three working days.[14] The registration may be denied if an applicant fails to meet registration requirements, for example, if the activity of an enterprise is deemed to be dangerous to the environment.

In conformity with its charter, an enterprise with foreign capital participation may engage in any type of activity that is not prohibited by law. However, in order to engage in insurance or brokerage activities, an FIE must obtain a licence from the MF. Banking operations need to be licensed by the National Bank of Ukraine (NBU). Certain activities by foreign investors are restricted for reasons of national security.

(c) Legal Status and Guarantees

As stipulated by the laws of most other successor states, the Ukrainian FI law introduces a 'national regime' for FIEs. In addition, additional privileges may be granted to foreign investors operating in 'key' economic and social sectors.

The law also extends important guarantees to foreign investors. Article 10 explicitly states that foreign investments in Ukraine may not be subjected to nationalization. Expropriation is only permitted in the event of an emergency such as a natural disaster, accident or epidemic. Expropriation can be contested (see article 49).

Foreign investors are entitled to 'prompt, adequate and effective' compensation for tangible or intangible losses arising from government actions or omissions, which contradict the legislation, as well as those resulting from negligence by government bodies or officials. Compensation, including the accrued interest, is paid either at current market rates or at rates established by independent auditors. In the event of termination, the foreign investor is entitled, within six months of termination, to a return on investment based on market value.

Equally, foreign investors are entitled to remit abroad income and other assets obtained legally in the course of their investment activities. To this end, they have the right to purchase foreign currency in accordance with Ukrainian currency legislation or, alternatively, to export domestically purchased goods without a licence (article 14).

Unlike its Russian counterpart, the Ukrainian law protects foreign investors against legislative changes detrimental to their interests. At the foreign investor's request, the legislation in effect at the time of registration will be applicable for a ten-year period.

(d) Taxation and Tax Incentives to FIEs

The FI Law generally stipulates that FIEs are subject to the national taxation regime. Simultaneously, foreign investors are offered considerable tax incentives.

Enterprises with foreign investments are exempt from income tax for a period of five years from the declaration of their first income, and subsequently enjoy a 50 per cent tax reduction. Enterprises engaged in wholesale and retail trade, and brokerage operations have shorter income tax holidays (three years and two years respectively), and a smaller tax reduction (30 per cent in each case).

Generally, reinvested profits are exempt from taxation. In addition, the taxable income of wholly foreign-owned subsidiaries is reduced by the sum of the actual investment. Equally, if the value of the investment exceeds the FIE's income in any fiscal year, it can be subtracted from the taxable income of future years.

For a five-year period after official registration, the FIEs' output is exempt from value added tax. Additional tax privileges may be granted to enterprises operating within designated priority sectors, or in particular regions of the country (free economic zones, article 49). This also holds if the foreign investment involves the transfer of new technologies to Ukraine. FIEs are subject to a 15 per cent income repatriation tax.

(e) Non-Tax Incentives

Property imported as a contribution to statutory funds and purchases abroad of current production inputs are exempt from customs duties and import taxes. This also applies to property imported for the personal use of FIEs' employees.

FIEs are allowed to export their own produce without a licence, and the convertible currency proceeds from exports remain entirely at their disposal.

(f) Labour Regulations

All matters relating to labour relations are to be settled on an individual contractual basis between the enterprise with foreign capital and its employees. The contractual terms should be at least as favourable as those stipulated by Ukrainian labour law.

Social insurance and security matters in FIEs are regulated by the relevant legislation. As indigenous enterprises, companies with foreign capital participation contribute to the Social Insurance Fund (SIF) for both foreign and national employees. Contributions to Ukraine's Pensions Fund (PF) are restricted to Ukrainian citizens (article 37).

The employer contributes 37 per cent of the wage bill as a payroll tax to the state, with 26 per cent of this sum being allocated to the SIF and PF, and the remaining 11 per cent to the Economic Stabilization Fund; 1 per cent of Ukrainian employees' wages is allocated to the PF.[15]

(g) Convertible Currency Regulations

On 5 February 1992 the Ukrainian Supreme Soviet adopted a resolution on the formation of foreign exchange reserves in Ukraine in 1992, which introduced a tax on convertible currency export earnings (surrender requirement), whose rate (quota) varies in respect of different goods or services. The rate rises from 15 per cent of earnings from exports of animal products, to 65 per cent for those derived from construction services overseas, insurance and other services related to foreign trade. Joint ventures in which the foreign share is equal to, or exceeds 30 per cent, as well as wholly foreign-owned subsidiaries, are exempt from this tax.[16]

The taxing of the export earnings of FIEs with a foreign share of 20 to 30 per cent implicitly contradicts the relevant provisions of the FI law.

Government regulations have also restricted the FIEs' right to purchase convertible currency. In November 1992, with the opening of the official (convertible) currency exchange, the rights of authorized banks to buy and sell foreign currency were curtailed.[17] Simultaneously, legal entities (including FIEs), were instructed to exchange currency solely at authorized banks. For profit repatriation purposes, foreign investors must buy and sell foreign exchange from one of these banks at the exchange rate established for this purpose. Before this regulation was enacted, foreign investors had been able to obtain convertible currency from authorized banks at free market exchange rates. As a result, this regulation may restrict the freedom of profit repatriation contained in the FI law.

(h) Privatization and Foreign Investment

The FI law stipulates the right of foreigners to participate in the privatization of state and municipal enterprises (article 41). The conditions of foreign investors' participation in this process are spelled out in the relevant laws and government regulations.

Ukraine's privatization programme was initiated by the adoption of laws on the privatization of small and large enterprises, enacted in March 1992. Under the March 1992 law on small privatization, enterprises are to be transferred to private ownership by means of buy outs by employees, auctions and public bidding, in which foreign investors have the right to participate.

Large enterprises are to be privatized in two phases (law on large-scale privatization). During the initial phase, Ukrainian citizens will obtain the right to buy certificates (vouchers) to a limit of 30 000 roubles; during the second phase, a mechanism of exchange of vouchers for shares is to be established.[19]

During 1992, some 60 large enterprises were identified for privatization. These included the ZAZ car plant, Avtokraz, a tractor plant, and Vulkan, a chemical factory.[20] Overall, it is expected that some 5000 to 7000 industrial enterprises and 150 000 trading enterprises will be denationalized.[21]

In July 1992, the Council of Ministers unveiled Ukraine's privatization programme: one explicit objective is to encourage foreign investment activities. The programme defines sectoral priorities for privatization: wholesale and retail trade, catering services, the construction industry, wood processing and 'light' (consumer goods) industry.[22] The privatization timetable is ambitious: in May 1992, the proportion of state-owned assets (excluding kolkhoz and sovkhoz farms, as well as housing) was 96 per cent. This is to be reduced to 85 per cent by the end of 1993, 66 per cent in 1994, and 56 per cent by the end of 1995.[23]

Although Ukraine's privatization programme foresees an increased role for FI, its stance *vis-à-vis* foreign participation remains contradictory. Contrary to the FI Law, which enabled foreign investors to purchase state enterprises with the currency in circulation at the time, foreign investors have since been restricted to using convertible currency for privatization purposes. The valuation of assets to be privatized and sold to foreign investors is to be effected at a special privatization exchange rate established by the NBU. In addition, to prevent the 'underselling' of Ukrainian assets to foreigners, the programme recommends a 'reconstruction cost' for asset valuation. This values an enterprises at current prices – that is, the cost of its construction from scratch at the moment of privatization.

Recently, Ukrainian decision-makers have displayed a more liberal stance *vis-à-vis* foreign participation in privatisation. In October 1992, the Ministry of External Economic Relations and Trade put forward a mechanism for holding auctions, with the intent of increasing the participation of foreign capital in various sectors of the economy, including housing. Significantly, this new procedure enables foreign investors to use both domestic and convertible currency for privatization purposes. Direct contractual agreements between prospective investors and targeted Ukrainian enterprises have also been eased.[24]

(i) Assessment of the Legal Environment for Foreign Investment

Since independence, Ukraine has endorsed an important package of laws pertaining to foreign investment activities. The law on foreign investment has established a relatively favourable legislative environment for FI activities, partially compensating foreign investors for domestic economic instability. The following privileges and incentives to foreign investors can be singled out:

- short registration periods;
- guarantees of a stable legal and tax environment;
- long (five-year) income tax holidays;
- eligibility for tax incentives, starting from the 20 per cent foreign share in the statutory capital (in most other successor states the threshold is 30 per cent).

The acceleration in FIE registration in late 1992 may be a first sign that prospective investors are reacting optimistically to a more stable and predictable legal environment.[25]

At the time of writing (May 1993), because of persisting political and economic instability, the future prospects of FI participation in privatization remained unclear. Its magnitude and pace will be determined largely by the interplay of economic efficiency considerations emphasized by the reformers, and the reluctance of the conservative faction to loosen its hold on state-controlled assets.

Foreign Investment Opportunities

Motives and Potential Benefits

Traditionally, the motives for FI have been determined by the investor's perception of the host country's actual or potential (dynamic) comparative advantage. When making investment decisions, entrepreneurs attempt to combine firm-specific advantages (superior technology, managerial expertise, knowledge of a particular market, reputable brand names) with those of the host economy. Among Ukraine's country-specific advantages one should mention its geographical position, the abundance of certain natural resources, developed industrial and agricultural sectors, as well as a relatively skilled and inexpensive labour force.[26] It is acknowledged that inward foreign investment can be an important mechanism in replenishing the host country's savings, foreign exchange reserves and the stock of technological and managerial expertise. Under certain conditions, this can provide the impetus for accelerated economic growth.[27]

These arguments are valid for Ukraine, which suffers from a paucity of domestic savings, a shortage of foreign exchange, and a quasi-complete ignorance of Western managerial practices. Moreover, FI can accelerate the removal of former Soviet command structures, which generated resource misallocation and wastage. Joint ventures and other forms of FI penetration facilitate the adoption of 'pressure economy' techniques of operations, which should enable the emergence of the 'Schumpeterian drive' among local entrepreneurs, and replace soft-budget with hard-budget constraints, thereby enabling the transition to intensive (resource-efficient) economic growth.

In practice, the potential benefits of FI depend on a variety of external and internal factors, which often act in a contradictory manner.

In this way, the legal environment for FI in the successor states has been created during a period of relatively unfavourable global economic conditions. Whereas deeply indebted developing countries are competing for inflows of external resources, the developed economies are overwhelmed by domestic economic problems. In Europe, in particular, Germany, potentially one of the most important FI source countries, has faced the economic cost of reintegration. Global recession has further diminished the FI potential, forcing host countries to compete more fiercely for limited capital inflows. On the domestic front, the successor states have been faced with a structural economic crisis. In Ukraine, this is reflected in the steep decline of economic indicators since 1990. A slump in production emphasizes the need for FI, but at the same time discourages potential investors.

The next section discusses some features of the Ukrainian economy, focusing both on the host country demand for external resources and the existing opportunities to foreign investors.

Labour

As mentioned above, Ukraine possesses a skilled and relatively inexpensive labour force of 24.2 million people. In comparison with the Soviet average, Ukraine has a high proportion of workers with secondary or higher education. In 1989, it had 1319 specialists with secondary or higher education per 10 000 inhabitants, compared with 1272 for the former USSR, while 569 persons per 10 000 inhabitants had higher education, compared with the ex-Soviet average of 553.[28]

The experience of operational joint ventures shows that the Ukrainian workers can adapt to Western production techniques and augment their labour productivity, provided the appropriate training and incentives are in place. In this way, the plant director of the British-US-Ukrainian joint venture Femtech, producing tampons in the Kiev region, declared: 'I am very surprised that there are not more companies producing here. The skills of the local people are excellent'.[29]

Although Ukraine's labour productivity on average is lower than that of the ex-USSR as a whole, it is accompanied by lower wages.[30] For example, in 1987 the average monthly wage in the construction industry was 257 roubles per month in the Soviet Union as a whole, 235 roubles in Belarus, but only 224 roubles in Ukraine.[31]

Since the January 1992 price liberalization, in nominal terms Ukrainian wages have increased and even outstripped those of Russia. At the same time, the continuing depreciation of Ukraine's 'interim' currency, the karbovanets, kept the average unit labour costs at considerably lower levels than in the developed market economies: for example, in February 1993, the minimum monthly wage of 4500 karbovantsi was equivalent to approximately 3 dollars at market exchange rates. The combination of low remuneration and high levels of labour education offer good FI opportunities in labour-intensive industries.

Mineral Resources

Ukraine has an abundance of natural resources, including coal, iron and manganese ores, but relatively little oil or natural gas.[32] This makes Ukraine dependent on energy imports from Russia and the other CIS states, and deprives it of an important motive for FI penetration, as transnational energy concerns have shown an interest in the development of mineral resources (hydrocarbons) worldwide.

Mineral deposits, especially coal, encountered acute resource depletion during the 1970s and 1980s. This phenomenon was particularly apparent in the Donbass coal region, once a pillar of the economy, where all 150 mines are loss-making and heavily subsidized. Resources depletion led to investment diversion to more cost-effective sources of energy, such as oil and natural gas. This policy change was reflected in gross fixed investment per capita in Ukraine during the 1980s being some 60 per cent below that of Russia.[33]

Largely because of resource depletion, Ukraine's minerals have been of only limited interest to foreign investors. The application of Western cost-accounting methods has demonstrated the lack of potential for coal and iron ore extraction. To date, foreign investment in mineral resources has focused on manganese ore mining.[34] In July 1992 Portman Mining from Australia set up a joint venture with the Ukrainian government to expand the output of manganese in the Nikopol basin. The foreign share in this joint venture's statutory capital is 55 per cent. Portman has agreed to build a plant with a capacity of 1 million tonnes per year, compared with the present yearly output of 250 000 tonnes, to provide the working capital, as well as implement Western managerial and marketing techniques. The output of the mine will be purchased by manganese alloy producers in Europe, China and Russia.[35]

Industry

Ukraine has a developed industry largely moulded by its mineral resource base – that is by coal and iron ore extraction. Although the country has attempted to diversify its industrial sector, coal mining and ferrous metallurgy continue to play a major role as producers of primary inputs, accounting for 20 per cent of total industrial output during 1990. To a lesser extent, this also holds for machine-building, whose share of industrial indicators is also marginally higher than the former all-Union average.

In 1989, Ukraine's steel production accounted for over 34 per cent of the former Soviet total, and machine-building for a quarter. The country, largely due to Khrushchev's initiative, also possesses a developed chemical sector.[36] In general terms, in 1990 'heavy industry' (investment goods production known as 'Sector A') accounted for almost 80 per cent of total industrial assets (at 1982 prices), while light industrial and food processing made up less than 11 per cent and 10 per cent respectively.[37] Ukraine's industry bias towards 'Sector A' was inherited from Stalin's policies of accelerated industrialization, when the emphasis was on heavy industry and defence-related production.

The industrial sector suffers from the obsolescence of a significant proportion of the capital stock due to chronic under-investment.[38] It is estimated that some 11 per cent of installed machinery and equipment in industry is over twenty years old.[39] Ukraine's industrial production is inefficient and energy-intensive, while the quality of final output is well below Western standards. This, in particular, holds for the machine-building industry, which in 1990 accounted for 43 per cent of industrial assets and output (at 1982 prices).[40]

Because considerable resources are required to restructure major industrial sectors, these have been largely overlooked by foreign investors. Future inflows of entrepreneurial capital from abroad, however, could raise the efficiency of heavy industry and remove distortions in Ukraine's industrial structure by channelling resources into consumer goods production.

As stated above, decision-makers are trying to encourage foreign entrepreneurs to invest in food processing, consumer goods industries and the distributional infrastructure with the help of tax concessions.[41] Given the provision of adequate incentives, enhanced foreign participation in these sectors could help stabilize the consumer goods market and remove domestic inflationary pressures.

The attraction of foreign investors is also essential in terms of export prospects. At present, Ukraine's specialization in basic industrial products (steel) leaves little room for exports to European markets, which face structural crises in similar sectors. In the medium term, however, more efficient FIEs could act as a catalyst in diversifying industrial exports and entering new markets, primarily those of the EU.

Defence Conversion

Another potential opening for FI is the conversion of defence industries. This is fraught with particular difficulty in Ukraine because of the disproportionately high share of the defence-related sector. Some 14 per cent of the former Soviet defence-related industrial capacity is located on Ukrainian territory, employing 19 per cent of Ukraine's labour force.[42] According to O. Havrylyshyn, the Ukrainian deputy finance minister, about three-quarters of industrial capacity was related to military uses.

Guidelines for enterprises undergoing restructuring, promulgated in July 1992, focused on producing medical equipment, which is in short supply, as well as aircraft, cargo and passenger automobiles, agro-industrial machinery and domestic appliances. By September 1992, consumer goods accounted for 9 per cent of the Ukrainian defence complex's production.[43] It is assumed that an additional impetus to defence conversion will be provided by privatization: eventually, over half of Ukraine's 700 defence plants will be privatized.

Despite the efforts of policy-makers, defence conversion has encountered considerable obstacles, mostly because of a shortage of funds in convertible currency. In 1992 alone, 140 billion roubles were required to implement 216 targeted conversion projects, but only 30 billion roubles were allocated.[44] The lack of foreign assistance forces Ukraine to finance conversion through exports of military equipment.

The prospects for greater foreign involvement in the conversion sector are more promising in areas where Ukrainian enterprises and research centres can offer a pool of indigenous technological expertise. In August 1989, the Israeli company Elscint established a joint venture with the Ukrainian Ministry of Health for the production of medical diagnostic equipment in cooperation with a defence-related enterprise based in Kiev.[45] In July 1992, a consortium of US firms established a conversion fund, which allocated 30 million dollars to the development of a ceramic aviation engine in cooperation with local engineers.[46]

At the same time, the interest of foreign companies to date has been limited. Experts indicate that the absence of market mechanisms is the major obstacle to foreign capital participation in defence conversion.[47]

Agriculture

Thanks to its geographical position, climate and rich soil, Ukraine enjoyed some of the highest yields within the former Soviet Union, accounting for approximately 20 per cent of Soviet agricultural output.[48] According to several commentators, agriculture represents Ukraine's potentially most efficient export industry.[49]

As mentioned above, despite relatively favourable conditions for agricultural production, this sector has been less attractive to foreign investors than industry, wholesale and retail trade, or business services. However, several joint ventures and cooperative agreements have been signed with the objective of raising agricultural efficiency. For example, in July 1991 the Plodorodiye Association was established in the Sumy oblast in cooperation with the US firm Monsanto. This venture aims to transfer Western agricultural technologies and increase the use of pesticides. In addition, American experts in crop growing (sugar beet, potatoes, maize and soya) have cooperated with Ukrainian farmers to augment yields on a contractual basis.[50] A similar agreement was reached in December 1991 between the French company Nodet and several sugar beet sovkhozes in Ukraine. The Western partner will introduce French technology and managerial techniques in sugar beet production. The agreement also foresees the setting up of a communication system, including telephone and satellite links.[51]

Communications

As in the other former Soviet republics, the inadequate communication network in Ukraine has considerably impeded the development of private business. At the beginning of the 1990s, Ukraine had only 7 million telephone lines, of which a mere 1 million were in rural areas. Although 37 per cent of Kiev's inhabitants possessed a telephone, this was well below Western standards. Moreover, Ukraine's international communications network was tied to Moscow's facilities, which hampered links abroad, vital for business operators.

Recently, foreign investors have been actively engaged in eliminating this bottleneck. In January 1992 the Ukrainian State Committee for Communications, AT&T and Dutch PTT established a telecommunications joint venture, contributing 51 per cent, 39 per cent and 10 per cent of the statutory capital respectively. This venture has the dual objective of establishing an international telephone link between Ukraine and the rest of the world, and of increasing the number of domestic connections, covering thirteen of Ukraine's 25 telephone regions. The three parties intend to invest 150 million dollars during the next 15 years, and have committed themselves to a threefold increase in the number of telephone lines during the next 8 years, with the target of 22 million lines by the year 2000.[52]

A second joint venture pertaining to the expansion of Ukraine's telecommunications network, capitalized at 100 million dollars, was agreed upon in May 1992. The foreign partners are represented by companies from Denmark, the Netherlands and Germany. The project's aim is to invest 1 billion dollars over a 15-year period in the establishment of a mobile telephone network. A satellite launched by Dutch Telecom will link Ukraine with Western Europe.[53] Along the same lines, in 1991 Siemens declared its intent to invest 95 million dollars in a new enterprise, which was due to start producing digital communication switches with a planned initial capacity of 1 million digital lines a year, to be raised to 3 million lines by the end of the century.[54]

The Banking System

Despite the growing number of commercial banks emerging as a second layer in the financial system, limited local and convertible currency resources have caused considerable obstacles to FI activity.

As in the other successor states, the participation of foreign banks in domestic finance could significantly contribute to alleviating this hurdle. Information on the activities of FIEs in financial services is sketchy. It is known, however, that by the end of 1992, over fifty joint ventures between Western and Ukrainian banks had been established. One of the larger enterprises of this kind – the First Ukrainian Bank (FUB) – was founded in May 1992. This bank's activities are targeted at financing foreign trade transactions, and it already has affiliate offices in Donetsk, Amsterdam and New York. The FUB has been described as 'filling the gap' in financial services that stems from the inadequate local banking system.

The Current Political and Economic Situation

A survey of obstacles to FI in Eastern Europe and the former Soviet Union, conducted by the World Bank research team in 1991, revealed that political and economic instability represented the strongest deterrent to foreign capital penetration.[55] Political and macroeconomic components of the investment climate, which in the Ukrainian context are closely interrelated, appear to be a determining factor in the foreign investors' perception.

Since the early 1990s, the economic situation in Ukraine has been continuously deteriorating. In 1992, national income fell by 15 per cent on top of the 4 per cent and 11 per cent falls in 1990 and 1991. In the same year, industrial production fell by 9 per cent compared with 0.1 per cent and 5 per cent decreases in the previous two years. Steeper still was the drop in gross fixed investment in the state sector, which plummeted by 40 per cent in 1992. Simultaneously, inflation accelerated after the January 1992 partial price liberalization. On a year-by-year basis, during January to September 1992 the consumer price index increased more than eightfold and in December prices grew by 30 per cent on a monthly basis. Finally, according to official sources, by the end of 1993 unemployment was expected to rise to 6 per cent of the labour force, as compared with 0.3 per cent in December 1992.[56]

Ukraine's economy is characterized by a considerable dependence on inter-republican trade. In 1990, the value of the latter amounted to a third of net material product.[57] The import dependence is particularly high in fuels: the country only produces 5 million tonnes of crude oil annually, whereas 60 million tonnes need to be imported. Equally, Ukraine has to import 79 per cent of its natural gas requirements.[58] Russia supplies 80 per cent of Ukraine's consumption.[59] In addition, Ukraine imports 100 per cent of its rubber consumption, 60 to 80 per cent of non-ferrous metals, motor cars, chemical fibres and cosmetic products; and 40 to 50 per cent of medical supplies, timber products and textiles.[60]

During 1991 and 1992, as a result of disruptions in supply linkages, Ukraine's machine-building sector was increasingly unable to fulfil its contractual obligations *vis-à-vis* producers in the other successor states.

The non-fulfilment of inter-republican agreements had a detrimental impact on the functioning of some 1350 enterprises.[61] It also further undermined the supply of consumer goods: their production declined by 5 per cent in 1991 and continued to fall during 1992.[62] In the first half of that year the output of the food-processing industry plummeted by 23 per cent.[63] The re-establishment of disrupted links with long-established suppliers remains crucial for Ukraine's domestic stabilization, as well as that of its CIS trading partners, which depend on Ukraine's machinery, spare parts and other deliveries.

Against the backdrop of economic crisis and the disruption of production links, the dependence on inter-republican trade (especially fuel imports) makes the country particularly vulnerable. Whereas the Russian government, facing an uncontrollable slump in oil production, aims at setting up oil prices at world levels, it is vital for Ukraine's economy to secure fuel deliveries in required quantities and at minimal prices. The oil dispute constitutes one of the major sources of political tensions with the Russian Federation.

On the political side, since Ukraine's Declaration of Independence in August 1991, domestic instability, exacerbated by tensions with Russia, has been closely linked with the conflicting perceptions by reformers and conservatives of the scope, sequencing and pace of economic transformation.

Ukraine's strategy of transition has so far been 'gradualist'; observers have remarked that even this gradualist approach has been pursued too cautiously and half-heartedly.[64] Recently, the worsening situation has forced policy-makers to realise that the 'foot-dragging' of reforms has contributed to the deepening economic crisis. In this way, the gradualist strategy has been adjusted to include some practical market-orientated measures.

In November 1992, Prime Minister Kuchma declared that Ukraine could no longer afford to operate as a 'soft' budget economy; he proposed to remove subsidies to state enterprises, and to offer the future unemployed work at new construction projects at the minimal wage.[65] In December 1992 state subsidies on almost all food products were removed, with price hikes in state shops of between 300 and 550 per cent. A package of agricultural reforms drawn up by the government would allow 'free market' prices to replace their administered counterparts.[66]

In the same way, the finance minister's November 1992 'anti-crisis' programme intended to reduce the budget deficit to between 4 and 6 per cent of GDP by the end of 1993, while inflation (which at the beginning of 1993 ran at 50 per cent per month) was to be brought down to 3 or 4 per cent a month.[67]

Ukrainian policy-makers started to realize the important role that FI could play in overcoming the present crisis and in transforming the economy along market lines. In a somewhat polemical way, V. Simonenko, the finance minister declared: 'I am completely against the idea of aid from the West, but fully support mutually beneficial foreign investment and cooperation.'[68]

The Ukrainian government started elaborating policy guidelines pertaining to FI in more detail. Several priority areas for foreign financial and technological assistance were identified, including agriculture, energy, transportation, and computerisation.[69]

Some Conclusions

So far, Ukraine has had only limited success in attracting foreign entrepreneurial capital. The magnitude of FIEs' operations does not exceed percentage points in any of the macroeconomic indicators, and with few exceptions (exports, telecommunications) their impact on the domestic economy has been negligible.

Foreign investment is concentrated in manufacturing and business services, and, to a lesser extent, in wholesale and retail trade, while in terms of capitalization the bulk of FIEs has been small. It remains to be seen whether the government will succeed in attracting larger FI projects in the newly defined priority areas.

A major achievement has been the enactment of relatively liberal legislation regarding FI operations. Foreign investors have received important guarantees against expropriation, changes in legislation and taxation, as well as tax incentives.

However, the economic crisis, compounded by political instability, has hindered foreign investor interest. Given the uncertainty of future economic reforms, the pace of FI penetration is difficult to forecast. The optimistic scenario predicts deeper foreign involvement in sectors where the combination of factor endowments can be most efficiently synthesized with FI company-specific advantages.

In these terms, as in the other successor states, companies from abroad will seek to participate in the development of Ukraine's mineral resources by focusing on new deposits. Some food-processing and consumer-goods-producing industries could also be of interest to foreign investors. Though the domestic market for these products is enormous, foreign companies could cost-effectively combine modern Western technology with educated Ukrainian labour. Another possible area of cooperation is the conversion of defence-related industries to civilian uses. Here, foreign companies could capitalize on the results of indigenous R&D and the expertise of local engineers and workers.

Notes

1 UN/ECE *East-West Joint Ventures News*, no. 10 (December 1991) p. 6.
2 World Bank (1992, p. 6).
3 UN/ECE *East-West Joint Ventures News*, no. 10 (December 1991) pp. 10-13.
4 UN/ECE Secretariat. An alternative estimate puts the total value of foreign investment in Ukraine at $900m. at the beginning of 1993. It is not clear, however, to which date this figure refers and how it was calculated: see *Business Moscow News* (Russian edn), no. 18 [May 1993].
5 'Ukrainian Economic Performance During the First Half of 1992: Not Even Pretending to Reform', *PlanEcon Report*, vol. VII, nos 35-6 (15 September 1992) p. 2.
6 'Pepsico to finance Ukraine's Expansion with Ship Exports', *Financial Times* (23 October 1992).
7 If not otherwise indicated, figures in the subsections which follow are taken or calculated from the UN/ECE doc. Trade/R. 588.
8 *BBC Summary of World Broadcasts*, Weekly Economic Report, SU/WO247 (11 September 1992) p. A/9.
9 Arenda enterprises and cooperatives absorbed half of this released labour, while small enterprises and individual farms absorbed a quarter of it, each (*Ukraine in Figures*, 1992, p. 17).
10 UN/ECE, Trade/R. 588, p. 27.
11 Dyker (1991, p. 8).
12 D. Robinson, 'Ukrainian Exporters have high hopes', *Journal of Commerce* (21 October 1991).
13 The summary is based on the English translation of the foreign investment law made available to the UN/ECE Secretariat by the Ukrainian permanent mission in Geneva, as well as on that reproduced in Interflo (8/92).
14 Registration takes twenty-one working days if a foreign investor requests 'additional privileges'.
15 International Monetary Fund (1992, pp. 32–3).
16 Exemption from this tax is also extended to enterprises' export proceeds used to repay convertible currency loans which financed the imports of equipment and technology ('Hard-Currency Tax in Ukraine', *Business Eastern Europe* (25 May 1992) p. 254).
17 The exchange rate for the coupon (karbovanets) is henceforth established by the NBU on the basis of the latest trading results at Ukraine's currency exchange. The individual exchange rates established by authorised banks must not exceed the NBU's exchange rate by more than 2.5 percentage points ('Currency exchange mechanisms more restrictive in Ukraine', *Business Eastern Europe* (23 November 1992).
18 Small enterprises are defined as those with a book value of assets equal to or below 1.5 million roubles.

19 'Move sought for Jvs to direct foreign participation', *Finance Eastern Europe* (22 May 1992) p. 14.

20 'Foreign Investment Law passed', *Finance Eastern Europe* (18 March 1992) p. 13.

21 *BBC Summary of World Broadcasts*, Weekly Economic Report, SU/WO153 (9 November 1990) p. A/8.

22 'Ukraine legt Privatisierungsprogramm vor', Neuer Zürcher Zeitung (27 August 1992).

23 Ibid.

24 'Ukraine encourages auctions to attract foreign capital', *BBC Summary of World Broadcasts*, Weekly Economic Report, SU/WO252, (16 October 1992) p. A/1.

25 Recently, however, two governmental decrees have led to a deterioration in the operational environment of FIEs. Contrary to the FI law, the decree of 26 December 1992 revoked the five-year VAT exemption period for these enterprises. A second Decree in 12 January 1993 terminated the licence-free export of goods purchased on the domestic market (*Kiev Times*, 25 May 1993). Both decrees, however, were revoked in May 1993 and did not have tangible implications for FI operations.

26 Marples (1991 p. 14).

27 Todaro, (1989, p. 475).

28 International Monetary Fund (1992, p. 25).

29 'A rash of difficulties', *Financial Times* (27 January 1993) p. 12.

30 In 1990, Ukraine's industrial labour productivity was 20 per cent below the Soviet average and 30 per cent lower than that of Russia. However, in agriculture, labour productivity was 8 per cent higher than the Soviet average and equivalent to that of Russia (UN/ECE 1997, p. 146).

31 International Labour Office (1990, p. 841).

32 In April 1992, a new deposit of natural gas with estimated reserves of 15 billion cubic metres was discovered in the Khar'kiv region. In the medium term, the exploitation of this deposit may alleviate Ukraine's dependence on natural gas imports—*BBC Summary of World Broadcasts*, Weekly Economic Report, SU/WO252 (17 April 1992) p. A/4.

33 UN/ECE Economic Survey of Europe, 1991–1992, p. 146.

34 It is estimated that the total manganese ore reserves of the Ukrainian Bolshoi-Tokmak deposit exceed 1 billion tonnes, which makes it one of the largest in the world.

35 *Business Eastern Europe* (27 July 1992) p. 369; and 'Ukrainian Manganese Deal', *East-West*, no. 541 (28 July 1992) p. 7.

36 'L'Ukraine face à la désunion', *Le Courier des pays de l'Est*, no. 358 (March 1991) p. 13.

37 Ukraine: an Economic Profile through the first Nine Months of 1991, PlanEcon Report, vol. VII, no. 42 (27 November 1991) p. 9.

38 The share of totally depreciated equipment in industry exceeds 47 per cent, and in some sectors is as high as 50 per cent, while the respective average for the ex-USSR was about 46 per cent. In 1989 Ukraine's share of gross fixed investment in the former USSR was less than 13 per cent, far lower than its contribution to output indicators. ('L'Ukraine face à la désunion', *Le Courier des pays de l'Est*, no. 358 [March 1991] pp. 11, 13).

39 Marples (1991, p. 15).
40 Ukraine: an Economic Profile through the first Nine Months of 1991, *PlanEcon Report*, loc. cit., p. 9.
41 Recently, the US firm Cargo has signed a contract to retool the Donetsk food processing enterprises, the equipment at which has completely depreciated (*BBC Summary of World Broadcasts*, Weekly Economic Report, SU/WO153 [9 November 1990] p. A/7).
42 Cooper (1991, p. 13).
43 *Business Eastern Europe* (28 September 1992).
44 *Finance Eastern Europe* (16 July 1992) p. 17.
45 *East European Markets* (25 August 1989).
46 *Finance Eastern Europe* (16 July 1992) p. 17.
47 *BBC Summary of World Broadcasts*, Weekly Economic Report, SU/WO182 (7 June 1991) p. A/1.
48 In 1989, Ukraine produced some 21 per cent of total Soviet agricultural output. This percentage was even higher in the output of meat, cereals and dairy products, while its shares in the production of sugar beet and sugar were predominant (54 per cent and 83 per cent respectively) ('L'Ukraine face à la désunion', *Le Courier des pays de l'Est*, no. 358 [March 1991] p. 13).
49 Marples, (1991, p. 15); and 'Reforms Aim to Free Farmers', *Financial Times* (27 January 1993) p. 12.
50 *BBC Summary of World Broadcasts*, Weekly Economic Report, SU/WO191 (9 August 1991) pp. A/6e, A/7.
51 'Des Français vont aider L'Ukraine à améliorer sa production de betteraves à sucre', *La Tribune Ukrainienne*, no. 2 (April 1992) p. 3.
52 'Téléphonie: AT&T;', *La Tribune Ukrainienne*, no. 2 (April 1992) p. 4.
53 'Ukraine's Second Contract with Western Telecommunications Companies', *East-West* (29 May 1992) p. 11.
54 *Financial Times* (22 June 1990).
55 Other perceived obstacles were the absence of legislation relating to property rights; the lack of wholesale and retail trade networks to replace the former administrative supply system; the inability to repatriate earnings and capital gains; and poor economic prospects. (*Foreign Direct Investment in the States of the Former USSR*, pp. 49–50.)
56 UN/ECE, (1993).
57 *Ibid.*, pp. 3–163.
58 Tedstrom (1992).
59 'Freiheit ist freiheit', *Der Spiegel* (9 March 1992) p. 154.
60 Ibid.
61 *BBC Summary of World Broadcasts*, Weekly Economic Report, SU/W1153 (17 August 1991).
62 UN/ECE (1977 p. 147).
63 'Ukrainian Economic Performance During the First Half of 1992', pp. 12–13.
64 The fight between proponents and adversaries of the reforms resulted in changes in the high echelons of government. In July 1992, V. Lanovoy, the reform-minded Finance Minister closely collaborating with the IMF, was replaced by former Communist Party First Secretary V. Simonenko, who appeared to be more cautious with respect to Ukraine's transition strategy

(A. Robinson, 'Ukraine Opposition Seeks Referendum on New Poll', *Financial Times* [17 July 1992].

65 C. Freeland, 'Deepening Crisis pushes Ukraine into urgent reform', *Financial Times* (19 November 1992).

66 *Ibid.*

67 C. Freeland, 'A Very Ukrainian Reformist', *Financial Times*, (27 November 1992); C. Freeland, 'Deepening Crisis Pushes Ukraine into Urgent Reform', *Financial Times* (19 Nov. 1992); and E. Balls and C. Freeland, 'Reform club's new member', *Financial Times*, (23 February 1993).

68 A. Robinson, 'Ukraine's opposition seeks referendum on new poll', *Financial Times* (17 July 1992).

69 *United States Mission Daily Bulletin* (Geneva: 8 September 1992) p. 6.

13
Kazakhstan

Yuri Adjubei and Alexandra Swetzer *

Of the constituent republics of the former Soviet Union, Kazakhstan was one of the last to proclaim its independence (mid-December 1991), when it became clear that the USSR *de facto* no longer existed. Kazakhstan has been one of the most active member states of the Commonwealth of Independent States (CIS), advocating closer economic cooperation and political coordination.

In territory (2 717 000 square kilometres), Kazakhstan is the second largest state in the CIS, about the size of Western Europe. However, this vast territory in Central Asia is land-locked, with only an outlet to the Caspian Sea (a lake).

In terms of population, it ranks fourth after the Russian Federation, Ukraine and Uzbekistan, with 17 million inhabitants (6.1 per cent of the CIS).[1] The population is sparse and multi-ethnic, with the Kazakhs making up less than 40 per cent of the total.[2]

Economically, Kazakhstan lags behind the Slav members of the Commonwealth. Its shares of fixed assets (5.8 per cent of the CIS in 1991), national income (5.4 per cent) and industrial production (4.7 per cent) are lower than its share of population, but 7.3 per cent higher in terms of agricultural output. In the early 1990s national income per head was some 30 per cent below the CIS average.[3] At the same time, Kazakhstan is one of the richest successor states in terms of mineral resources, although its deposits have been underexploited so far. In 1991 Kazakhstan produced 26.5 million tonnes of oil and 7.9 billion cubic metres of natural gas (5.2 per cent and 1.0 per cent of the CIS total). Coal

---

* The authors work for the secretariat of the United Nations Economic Commission for Europe. The views expressed here are their own, and do not necessarily reflect those of the secretariat.

extraction, at 130 million tonnes, made up 20.7 per cent of the CIS coal output.[4]

This chapter reviews foreign investment (FI) trends in Kazakhstan, by considering in turn the legal basis for FI, its participation in the privatization process, the available statistics and some of the problems encountered by foreign firms in the field of mineral resources.

Legal Framework and Privatization

The legal basis for foreign investment stems from a number of laws and regulations enacted between 1990 and 1992. The Kazakh law on foreign investment was adopted in December 1990 (effective from January 1991), a year before the republic became independent and earlier than that of Russia. Subsequently, it was complemented by Council of Ministers regulations on procedures for the establishment and operation of enterprises with foreign capital (October 1991). Other relevant provisions include the law on concessions of December 1991, and the code on subsoil resources and processing of mineral resources of May 1992.

According to the FI law, the establishment of a foreign investment enterprise (FIE) does not require prior authorization; it needs only to be registered with the local administration, the Ministry of Finance or the Ministry of Foreign Economic Relations.

All types of foreign investment are allowed: foreign companies are permitted to buy into existing enterprises and to acquire rights to exploit natural resources.[5] Nor does the FI law impose any equity limitation on foreign investors' ownership: wholly foreign-owned subsidiaries are allowed.[6] As far as the sectoral limitations are concerned, the law excludes FIEs from the armaments production and forbids other activities 'prohibited by law'.

The December 1995 presidential decree allowed the private ownership of land, including that purchased by foreign investors. The decree authorized the sale and transfer of state land to private domestic and foreign owners for temporary or permanent use, although not for agricultural purposes (agricultural land may only be owned by Kazakh citizens).[7]

The FI law extends other legal guarantees to foreign investors: the nationalization of FIEs is not allowed, while foreign property can be requisitioned only in 'exceptional circumstances' with appropriate compensation. Commentators have noted, however, that guarantees to foreign investors should have been spelled out in more detail, referring to 'prompt, adequate and effective' compensation in case of expropriation.

National treatment applies in respect of the taxation of FIEs: these pay the same taxes as national enterprises (a basic 30 per cent income tax for FIEs with over 30 per cent in foreign participation). At the same time, the law authorizes a five-year tax holiday (since the first declaration of profit) and a 50 per cent tax reduction in the subsequent five years, if foreign investors hold over 30 per cent of the FIE equity and operate in an industry designated as a 'priority sector'.[8] A similar provision can only be found in Ukraine's FI law, while in most other successor states the regulations are not particularly favourable to foreign investors.[9] Moreover, FIEs benefit from the accelerated depreciation of assets, while those operating in free economic zones are entitled to additional concessions. Finally, as in the other successor states, imported inputs used for production by companies with foreign participation are customs-free. Furthermore, the law stipulates the free repatriation of after-tax profits and proceeds from liquidation or sale of the stock.

Major legal provisions relevant to large-scale FI projects have been introduced by the concession law dealing with mineral resource development. This legal act spells out the rights of foreign investors to utilize natural resources and stipulates that the concessions must not be shorter than 5 years or longer than 40 years. It also guarantees the foreign investors' rights to full compensation in case of early discontinuation of a concession, or of loss caused by breach of contract by government authorities.[10]

Arguably, the most important provision relates to the rules governing foreign capital in the mining sector. Investors from abroad should be granted development rights 'on a competitive basis'. It is implied, however that these may result not only from tenders but also from direct negotiations with individual companies.[11] In this way, government agencies can speed up the implementation of large-scale deals with chosen partners. The centralized decision-making with respect to ventures in mineral resource development, which does not require lengthy coordination with the regions (as in the case in Russia), contributes to the same result.

Thus, Elf-Aquitaine, for example, has started work on the Temir project after less than a year of negotiations – a unique case in the CIS. The Oman Oil Company has concluded an agreement on the development of the Danga oil field (to the North of Tenghiz) with estimated reserves of 70 million tonnes in an even shorter period.[12]

Anecdotal evidence shows that, in the absence of a fixed payment scale, the financial conditions of mineral-resource-related investment projects (royalties, bonuses and taxes) can be settled on an *ad hoc* basis for each project.[13] In this way, the Elf-Aquitaine venture, for example, has been exempted from all income taxes.[14] Thus, at the beginning of the 1990s, in spite of remaining lacunae (such as the absence of a law itemizing the rights of foreign investors in petrochemicals development), a rather liberal legal framework was created for the activities of foreign capital in Kazakhstan. These regulations are 'competitive' with those enacted in the other successor states, and in some respects are even more beneficial to foreign investors. Backed by the consistent presidential policy favouring the inflow of entrepreneurial capital (see below), and coupled with the flexible approach by the authorities to individual deals, the legal regime has become a constructive component of the FI climate.

Kazakhstan is also creating legal conditions for FI participation in privatization. The privatization law of 1 August 1991 was enacted several months earlier than its counterpart in Russia. According to this, the methods or privatization include, *inter alia*, the sale of state property to the workers of state-owned enterprises (SOEs), to private persons by competitive bidding or auction, the conversion of SOEs into joint-stock and other companies, and the establishment of concessions. Foreign investors can participate in the asset sales of state enterprises (commercial privatization). However, certain restrictions have been introduced. The purchaser of state assets must demonstrate residence in Kazakhstan for at least five years.[15] The contract of sale, in addition, may include special terms such as the retention of a certain number of employees and continuation of the enterprise's activities.[16] According to the Presidential decree of May 1992, calling for the acceleration of privatization, in the course of mass (voucher) privatization, foreign investors are entitled to buy 10 per cent of shares of SOEs to be transformed into joint-stock companies.[17]

The first stage of privatization in Kazakhstan (1991–3) focused mainly on small enterprises. By the end of 1992, 6000 out of 31 000 enterprises had been privatized. In March 1993, a new National Privatization Programme was started: it envisages the transfer of state property into private hands through auctions (small-scale privatization), as well as the transformation of medium-sized and large companies into joint-stock companies, and the public offering of their shares. Very large enterprises (about 1500 companies with a workforce of more than 5000 employees each) will be temporarily controlled by the government through holding companies, to be privatized at a later date on a case-by-case basis.[18]

In addition to small SOEs privatized in 1991–2, under the new stage of small-scale privatization there are plans to privatize a further 8067 enterprises. By the end of 1995, 27 500 enterprises, with a workforce of less than 200, had been privatized.[19]

As far as medium and large enterprises are concerned, the major ambition of the current mass privatization programme is to transfer their assets directly to citizens through vouchers, whereas previous programmes favoured the employees of SOEs to be privatized. Originally the workers of SOEs were entitled to 25 per cent of ordinary stock free of charge, but this has been reduced to 10 per cent of the stock in the form of privileged (non-voting) shares. As much as 51 per cent of SOEs' shares were divided among 40 investment funds to be exchanged for vouchers distributed to the population.[20]

Apart from Philip Morris and RJR Nabisco, which bought respectively into the Almaty tobacco factory and the Chimkent Confectionery makers, anecdotal evidence of foreign investors' participation in privatization is lacking. Potential foreign investors are most likely to be attracted by the largest SOEs, particularly in the energy and mineral sectors but also in manufacturing.

With regard to agriculture, the decree on privatization of March 1993 stipulates that a maximum of 10 per cent of agro-industrial enterprises' shares enjoying a 'monopoly position' may be sold to foreign investors.[21]

Magnitude of Foreign Investment

(a) Growth of foreign capital

Under Soviet rule, the number of FIEs in Kazakhstan was growing slowly. By the end of 1990 – that is, almost four years after the all-Union regulations authorizing the establishment of joint ventures were adopted – the total number of FI registrations totalled only 14, while the foreign part of their capitalization at current official monthly average exchange rates was 19.6 million dollars. The Kazakhstan-based FIEs represented only a tiny fraction of those registered in the former USSR, in terms both of numbers and of foreign capital committed.

According to the CIS Statistical Committee, at the start of 1992 the total number of registrations stood at 164. By the beginning of 1993 (that is, after the first year of independence) the number of FIEs registered more than tripled (540) and further increased to 669 six months later. An alternative source estimates the total number of FI registrations on 1 January 1993 at 674 and six months later at 1140.[22]

The process of FI registrations in Kazakhstan seemed to evolve at the same speed as in the other CIS member states; as a year before, at the start of 1993 Kazakhstan accounted for some 6.5 per cent of the total number of FIEs registered in the CIS.[23]

While registration data are not available for recent periods, according to the Kazakh State Committee on Statistics and Analysis, during the period of independent development (from 1991) the total number of operational FIEs grew from 14 in January 1992 to 736 four years later. At the end of June 1996 their number stood at 817 (see Table 13.1).

The FI stock data from the Kazakh National Bank refer mainly to large enterprises and therefore underestimate foreign investment in medium and small companies. Keeping this in mind, by the beginning of 1994, FI stock in Kazakhstan had reached 1271.4 million dollars. Over the next two years, its growth rates tended to increase, and its value more than doubled. Growth continued in the first half of 1996 when the FI increment made up 450.4 million dollars, bringing the total stock value to 3243.9 million dollars at the end of June 1996. It should be noted that the increase in FI stock resulted partly from a broader coverage and better reporting by enterprises in recent periods.

It is worth mentioning that the bulk of foreign investment in Kazakhstan is made up of loans extended by foreign parents to their subsidiaries. At the end of 1995, the proportion of intra-company loans in the FI cumulative total was as high as 88 per cent, the equity of affiliated enterprises making the balance. As compared with equity, intra-company loans are easier to recover in the event of a sudden deterioration in the host's economic situation. Therefore, the exceptionally high share of intra-company loans reflects the uncertainty inherent in foreign investors' perceptions of current Kazakh conditions.

In terms of major source countries, the structure of FI in Kazakhstan is dominated by US investors. At the beginning of 1996, they accounted

Table 13.1 Foreign investment in Kazakhstan, 1994–6

Date/Year	FDI Stock		Number of FIEs	
	Increments	*Cumulative*	*Increments*	*Cumulative*
		($ m.)		
1.01.1994 (cum.)	1271.4	1271.4	260	260
1.01.1995 (1994)	638.7	1910.1	231	491
1.01.1996 (1995)	883.4	2793.5	245	736
1.07.1996 (1Q–2Q)	450.4	3243.9	81	817
Total	3243.9	3243.9	817	817

Source: East-West Investment News, no. 4, Winter 1996.

for two-thirds of FI stock (1.8 billion). As a leading consolidated investor, United States companies were followed by their counterparts from
South Korea (9 per cent), the UK (6 per cent), Turkey and France (about 4
per cent each). These top five investor countries together accounted for
88 per cent of cumulative FI.

It is worth noting that, on the same date, the share of US firms in the
total number of FIEs (8 per cent) was substantially lower than in terms of
FI volume. This confirmed the relatively important capitalization of a
few US – controlled enterprises, while the opposite was true of investors
from several countries with the largest numbers of affiliates. In terms of
enterprise numbers, companies from Turkey, China and the Russian
Federation were the most active investors, with between them over a
third (36 per cent) of the total number of operational FIEs.

In terms of industrial distribution, at the beginning of 1996 foreign
investment in Kazakhstan was focused strongly on mining, oil and gas
extraction in particular. This sector accounted for three-quarters of FI
stock. Manufacturing investment (24 per cent) was represented primarily by foreign participation in basic metals and tobacco manufacturing.
This suggests that, so far, foreign investment in Kazakhstan has been
almost exclusively attracted by mining and primary processing in natural resources.

(b) Foreign Investment Operations

The importance of foreign investment for the host economy is
illustrated by the magnitude of FIEs' operations and their weight in
macroeconomic indicators.

Employment in FIEs increased from less than 1000 at the beginning of
1991 to 6476 two years later. During 1993 and 1994, the rapid growth in
FI-related employment continued: each year its volume almost doubled.
In 1995, the number of salaried workers in FIEs grew more slowly: at year
end, it was 25 132 (see Table 13.2).

During the same period, overall employment was contracting. In
1995, as compared with 1992, it dropped by almost 14 per cent. The
simultaneous growth of FI-related employment and decrease of its overall level resulted in the rising share of the 'foreign sector'. The proportion of FIEs in total employment increased from less than 0.2 per cent in
1992 to 0.4 per cent in 1995.

During 1990–2, the current price growth in FIEs' output (in Soviet
roubles) outpaced that of inflation. While in 1991 and 1992 GDP
decreased by 13 per cent in real terms, the ratio of FI-related output to
GDP rose from 0.2 per cent to 1.3 per cent in one year. As from 1993, the

Table 13.2 Foreign investment enterprises in Kazakhstan, major indicators

Date (Year)	Operational FIEs						
	Number	Output	Exports	Imports	Domestic Sales		Employment
		(KZTm.)	($ m.)	($ m.)	(KZTm.)	($ m.)	
1.01.1991(1990)	6	14.4	9.7	2.2	7.9	n.a.	n.a.
1.01.1992(1991)	14	195.0	20.7	49.7	167.3	n.a.	n.a.
1.01.1993(1992)	139	28095.3	52.9	96.5	5883.6	0.2	6476
1.01.1994(1993)	260	352.3	164.2	82.6	55.6	3.7	12633
1.01.1995(1994)	491	4182.1	229.2	148.5	5535.4	19.5	22149
1.01.1996(1995)	736	28823.2	371.0	218.5	21629.9	13.1	25132
1.07.1996(1Q–2Q)	817	25379.4	222.6	168.1	18811.6	13.1	27603

n.a. = not available.
^a Data for 1990–2 are given in million SUR; (2) Data for 1990–1991 are given in million (valuta) roubles.
Note: Exports and imports data for years preceding 1994 refer to extra-CIS exports and imports.

Source: *East-West Investment News*, no. 4, Winter 1996.

Kazakh statistical aggregates were valued in Kazakh tenge (KZT), which impeded the compilation of time series. This being said, in 1994 the growth of FIEs' output (12-fold) was slower than price rises (industrial producer price index). In contrast, in 1995 the output of FIEs outpaced the measure of inflation (6-fold and 2.4-fold growth, respectively). During the same period, at current prices the Kazakh GDP grew 16-fold in 1994 and 2.2-fold in 1995 (implying a contraction of 25.4 and 9 per cent on a yearly basis in real terms). As in 1994 nominal GDP growth was steeper than that of FIEs' output, the ratio of the latter to the former decreased from 1.3 per cent in 1993 to 0.9 per cent twelve months later. In 1995, in contrast, FI-related output grew faster than nominal GDP; as a result the FIEs' output-GDP ratio increased that year to 2.9 per cent.

The domestic sales of FIEs increased 35-fold in 1992 as compared with 1991, and reached 22.4 billion roubles in the first half of 1993. In 1992, their volume was equivalent to 2.6 per cent of Kazakhstan's retail trade turnover (0.5 per cent in 1991).

Subsequently, the domestic sales of FIEs valued in KZT continued to grow in real terms, outpacing the rate of inflation. The ratio of domestic sales by FIEs to the overall retail trade turnover (which dropped dramatically in 1994) grew from 0.1 per cent in 1993 to 10.7 per cent in 1994 and 14.3 per cent in 1995.

At the beginning of the 1990s, the foreign trade involvement of FIEs was growing, but its magnitude remained relatively small. During 1992, excluding intra-CIS trade, these companies exported 52.9 million dollars' worth of goods and services, and imported 96.5 million dollars' worth. These figures compare unfavourably with those of Russia-based FIEs (1.9 billion and 2.0 billion dollars respectively). However, these negligible export and import volumes accounted for a large component in total extra-CIS foreign trade: in the same year, operational FIEs accounted for 3.8 per cent of total exports and almost 21 per cent of total imports of Kazakhstan (respectively 4.3 per cent and 17.0 per cent in Russia).[24]

As opposed to previous years, the reported value of FIEs' exports and imports in 1994 and 1995 included both intra- and extra CIS transactions. In 1995, at current prices, FIEs' exports increased by 62 per cent as compared with 1994, while the growth of imports made up 47 per cent. In the same year, also at current prices, total exports and imports of Kazakhstan grew by 54 per cent and 7 per cent respectively. Since both rates were lower than those of FI-related exports and imports, the share of the latter in the respective totals increased from 7.1 per cent in 1994 to 7.5 per cent in 1995 (exports), and from 4.3 per cent to 5.8 per cent (imports).

In contrast to the early 1990s, the trade balance of FIEs was positive in both 1994 and 1995. Each year, exports exceeded imports by about 80 million dollars. This development supported the general trend in Kazakh foreign trade, which after a deficit of around 250 million dollars in 1994 reached a positive balance of about 1.2 billion dollars in 1995.

In sum, so far the role of foreign investment in the Kazakh economy has been limited: by either yardstick (output or employment) the share of FIEs does not exceed 3 per cent; their role, however, is generally more important in the foreign trade sector. The steady rise in the number of workers employed by FIEs compares favourably with the overall employment contraction. At the same time, the recent FIEs' output growth seems to have been relatively unstable.

In the medium term, the implementation of a number of large-scale investment projects may increase the scope of FI-related activities in terms of both production and exports.

Foreign Investment Potential

The economy of Kazakhstan is characterized by a heavy reliance on the extraction of mineral resources and agriculture.

In 1988, the last year in which the Kazakh economy was growing, the share of industry (including mining) in net material product (NMP or national income produced in material production) amounted to 25.1

per cent; agriculture accounted for 34.2 per cent. For the sake of comparison, in Russia the respective percentages stood at 44.5 per cent and 18.7 per cent.[25] In the late 1980s and early 1990s, Kazakhstan produced 7 per cent of Soviet agricultural output and 3.5 per cent of industrial production.[26]

As mentioned above, the production of coal is the most important sector of Kazakhstan's industry. Some branches of machine-building are also developed. For example, Kazakhstan produced 6.2 per cent of Soviet agricultural machinery. The consumer goods sector in manufacturing (light industry) in 1988 accounted for 15 per cent of total industrial production.[27] However, in per capita terms, consumer goods production lags behind that of the other CIS member states; at the beginning of the 1990s, this indicator in Kazakhstan was only 55 to 60 per cent of the CIS average.[28] Within agriculture, grain production, as well as meat and wool (about 23 per cent of the former Soviet total during 1986–9) are the most developed.[29] In 1992, Kazakhstan exported 10 million tonnes of wheat, mostly to Russia.[30]

Another distinctive feature of Kazakhstan's economy is its dependence on intra-republican deliveries of foods and services among the former Soviet republics. In 1988, the value of goods and services obtained from the other Soviet republics at domestic prices was equivalent to 20 per cent of its gross social product (GSP, total value of material production), while its deliveries to those republics amounted to 12 per cent of GSP. The deficit in intra-republican trade was thus equivalent to 8 per cent of GSP. For the sake of comparison, in Russia this quasi-foreign trade had a positive balance, while 'exports' and 'imports' did not exceed 8 per cent of GSP in each case.[31]

Its dependence on the other CIS states (both in terms of export markets and supplies) and primarily Russia is even more important for individual goods. While at the beginning of the 1990s Kazakhstan accounted for about 20 per cent of the CIS production of coal, it delivered 69 per cent of intra-CIS exports of this commodity. On a smaller scale, this discrepancy also holds for oil (respectively 5 per cent and 16 per cent), iron and steel (5 per cent and 17 per cent) and some other industrial and agricultural goods (grain, wool).[32] On the other hand, in 1992 imports from Russia made up 67 per cent of its domestic consumption of wood, 96 per cent of paper, 63 per cent of oil, 80 per cent of trucks, 37 per cent of rolled steel and 41 per cent of metal-cutting lathes.[33]

This dependence makes the Kazakh economy particularly vulnerable to conjunctural moves in other CIS member states, and provides the basis for Kazakhstan's interest in maintaining good political relations within the Commonwealth. At the same time, it gives Kazakh policy-makers an impetus to reduce the country's dependence and diversify both in its export markets and sources of supply.

Finally, the Kazakh economy suffered badly from the devastating environmental effects of centralized planning under the old system. Decision-makers are more sensitive than their Russian counterparts to environmental issues such as the aftermath of radioactive leakages at the Semipalatinsk nuclear testing site, the drying-up of the Aral Sea, acute water shortages, soil erosion and atmospheric pollution from its coal-fired power plants.

The investment potential of Kazakhstan resides first and foremost in the stock of its mineral riches. The proven reserves of oil are conservatively estimated at over 2 billion tonnes and those of gas at 1.8 trillion cubic metres.[34] The Caspian shelf deposits may contain 2 billion tonnes of oil (according to official estimates) and about 8 billion according to Western experts.[35] This makes Kazakhstan's reserves comparable to those of the main producers of petrochemicals.

Kazakhstan produced 7 per cent of Soviet gold output and 50 per cent of silver. It also has the largest uranium mines in the world. Kazakhstan's reserves of chrome amount to 90 per cent of the former Soviet Union, while the respective shares for lead, tungsten, copper and zinc are as much as 50 per cent. The country is also rich in other non-ferrous metals, cadmium, iron ore and beryllium.[36]

Though the development of mineral resources by foreign investors may be oriented primarily towards supplying the home country and the world market, the medium-sized domestic market for manufactures creates reasonable opportunities for those foreign companies aiming to set up local (import-substituting) production on the basis of low domestic labour costs. This strategy, which may in future involve exports to the neighbouring central Asian countries, is valid, primarily, for the manufacture of consumer goods – first of all, consumer durables – and medicines.[37]

Though the information available is sketchy, several examples suggest consumer market scarcities, which provide important investment opportunities for foreign companies.

Thus, since the dissolution of the CMEA and the disruption of links with the other former Soviet economies, Kazakhstan has experienced a critical shortage of medicines. It produces only 26 per cent of medical drug requirements and depends for the rest on imports.[38]

In 1992, according to expert estimates, 40 per cent of lorries and 50 per cent of buses and taxis in Kazakhstan were worn out and needed to be replaced. Russia and Ukraine could not maintain deliveries, but opportunities from Hungary, as well as Fiat, General Motors and Volkswagen were investigated.[39]

So far, foreign investment commitments in manufacturing have been less spectacular than those in the mineral resource development (see the next section). However, a number of manufacturing joint ventures have been agreed upon, while several FIEs already produce consumer goods on a growing scale.

In 1992, Fiat negotiated with the government a venture to produce small cars and utility vans for farmers. The total cost of the project was estimated at 4 billion dollars, while the projected output of the plant was put at 300 000 Fiat Pandas and 20 000 vans per year.[40] In the course of privatization, Philip Morris has won the right to buy into the Almaty tobacco factory. Total foreign investment in the modernization of the factory, which eventually will be 90 per cent owned by this investor, will reach 400 million dollars. As a result, the output will grow from 12 billion to 20 billion cigarettes a year.[41]

At the beginning of 1993, several operational Chinese–Kazakh joint ventures manufactured consumer durables – assembled calculators, audio and video tape recorders – from Chinese components.[42]

Foreign Investment in Mineral Resources

Recognizing the development of petrochemical resources as a cornerstone of the future wealth of the country, policy-makers have decided to triple the production of oil by the year 2010 (a target of 1.6 million barrels per day, or 92.7 million tonnes a year), while gas output is anticipated to rise four-fold.[43] This will allow for a substantial rise in Kazakhstan's oil exports, from 4.8 million tonnes in 1992 (crude and refined petroleum) to 40 million tonnes.[44]

At the same time, the paucity of technology and capital required for the large-scale exploration and development of oil and gas deposits has prompted a favourable attitude towards foreign capital, which is expected to play a leading role in the supply of petrochemicals. Projects agreed upon or negotiated at the time of writing (1997) tended to be large-scale. As a rule, projects are negotiated on an individual basis, and frequently foreign partners obtain important concessions.

In Soviet times a number of large-scale petrochemical projects involving foreign capital were considered. The Tenghiz oil deposit project[45] became a trial venture negotiated as far back as 1989; on 30 June 1990 a letter of intent was signed between Chevron and a Soviet Ministry.[46]

Subsequently, negotiations dragged on mostly because of bureaucratic hurdles.[47]

The final agreement on the creation of the Tenghizshevroil joint venture was endorsed by Kazakhstan president Nazarbayev and the chairman of the Chevron board, K.T. Derr, some three years later, in April 1993. In the first three to five years of the agreement, foreign investment in the deposit development will amount to 1.5 billion dollars and to an estimated 30 billion dollars over the entire period of exploitation (40 years). By 2010, output is projected to rise to 38.8 million tonnes a year (as compared with the current 3.8 million tonnes per annum). Most of the oil extracted will be exported. Total revenue from the development of the Tenghiz oil field will amount to 210 billion dollars. As much as 80 per cent (80 billion dollars, including royalties and taxes) of the net income will go to the Kazakh partners, and 20 per cent to the Chevron Corporation.[48]

Major impediments to an increase in oil output at the Tenghiz deposit include the cost of reducing the amount of highly corrosive sulphur components, and the limited capacity of pipelines connecting the deposit to export markets. In order to provide a new outlet, a Caspian pipeline consortium was founded with the participation of Russia, Kazakhstan, Oman and Azerbaijan. The objective is to build a pipeline connecting Tenghiz with the Russian port of Novorossiisk on the Black Sea coast. The pipeline's capacity, which is to be commissioned in three years, will be 15 million tonnes per year, to be raised subsequently to 75 million tonnes a year.[49]

At the beginning of 1992, Elf-Neftegaz (a subsidiary of Elf-Aquitaine) signed a production-sharing agreement to prospect and develop the Temir deposit (with an area of 19300 square kilometres) in the Aktyubinsk region (north-west). The Temir area is believed to contain about 120 million tonnes of oil (extractable reserves), while the whole of the Aktyubinsk region currently extracts only 2.7 million tonnes of oil a year. Prospecting, which started at the beginning of 1993, will last ten years and is expected to cost up to 480 million dollars.[50] Overall, the development cost is estimated at several billion dollars and the output forecast is 30 million tonnes a year. The Kazakh share of net income will depend on the volume of output, and may reach between 75 and 90 per cent of the incremental output value, once the foreign partner has recovered its costs.[51]

One more sizeable project negotiated in 1992–3 is the development of the Karachaganak oil and gas fields in North-Western Kazakhstan, one of the largest in the world. According to the Ministry of Energy, the

Karachaganak deposit holds 222.2 million tonnes of oil, 714.3 million tonnes of condensates and 1300 billion cubic metres of gas,[52] while different sources give even higher estimates of proven reserves.[53] The development rights for this deposit have been won by British Gas and Agip, the Italian state company, and the final agreement was expected to be signed late in 1993.[54] The Western partners' investment share may amount to 6 billion dollars in the first 10 years, and up to 20 billion dollars over the 40-year lifetime of the project. Karachaganak is expected to produce 150 000 barrels of condensates a day (8.7 million tonnes a year).[55]

At the time of writing, several other major petrochemical projects were at various stages of negotiations. In mid-1993, a preliminary agreement on the exploration of new oil fields in the Caspian Sea with a total surface of over 100 000 square kilometres was reached. Seven oil companies (Royal Dutch/Shell, British Petroleum, British Gas, Total, Agip, Statoil and Mobil) signed this agreement. The reserves of the Caspian Sea deposits may prove to be larger than those of Tenghiz. According to various estimates, exploration will cost between 130 million and 150 million dollars, and production is expected to start by the year 2000.[56] Negotiations with Western companies also concern the Baiganinskii deposit – with 2.8 billion barrels (444 million tonnes) of oil and condensates, and 375 billion cubic metres of gas,[57] Kumkol,[58] Kamenskii and Chinarovskii[59] and several other oil and gas fields. Prospective foreign investment in these projects may reach tens of billions of dollars in the next 10 to 30 years.[60]

The Kazakhstan Ministry of Energy has called for the development of more than forty petrochemical deposits in partnership with foreign companies. Kazakh decision-makers have tried to loosen the country's dependence on oil-processing facilities, most of which are situated outside Kazakhstan. Oil refineries at Atyrau, Pavlodar, Chimkent, Aktau and other sites are earmarked for modernization and expansion.[61]

For the time-being, the development of mineral resources (other than petrochemical) is a lower priority. However, press reports suggest an increasing interest on the part of foreign investors in that area. In August 1992, for example, a joint venture to develop the Bakyrchik gold deposits was set up between the Australian–US company BK Gold and the Kazakh government. Bakyrchik is one of the largest deposits in the world and the production promises to be highly profitable. The western partner, which owns 40 per cent of the joint venture capital (27 million dollars), has pledged to invest 113 million dollars in the enterprise to increase its capacity to 1 million tonnes of ore (230 000 ounces of gold) a year. In return, it will appropriate 75 per cent of net income during the payoff period, and 40 per cent subsequently. During the first 5 years of the joint venture agreement, it will be relieved of taxes, and over the next 5 years will only pay half of profit taxes.[62] Along the same lines, the Australian company Moonstone Mines has expressed interest in participating in the development of the diamond deposits in southern Kazakhstan (Kokchetav region).[63]

Recent Economic Situation and Host Country Policy

At the beginning of the 1990s, the economic situation in Kazakhstan was deteriorating. In 1992, as compared with 1988, NMP plummeted by 24 per cent. On a year-to-year basis, in 1992 NMP dropped by 14 per cent and GDP by 13 per cent. As already indicated, the slide in real GDP continued into the mid-1990s.

One of the major causes of the deepening economic slump was the disruption of economic ties with the other successor states at enterprise level.

Stagflation features started to emerge. Throughout the first half of the 1990s, high inflation accompanied decreasing employment. The crisis in the first half of the 1990s further highlighted the dangerously high dependence of the Kazakh economy on unstable supplies, and put to the forefront the task of both diversifying those sources and developing indigenous production for a number of goods critical to the economic health of the country.

The aforementioned state of the economy will clearly determine the country's strategy *vis-à-vis* foreign investment. According to Kazakhstan's policy-makers, the inflow of entrepreneurial capital from abroad may assist in:

- Structurally transforming the economy by overcoming its raw-material orientation and creating a modern manufacturing and service sector;
- Reducing its economic dependence on the other successor states to economically and politically acceptable levels; and
- Diversifying external economic links both in terms of partner countries and types of cooperation.

In May 1992, the president of Kazakhstan outlined his country's economic strategy: first, to replenish the consumer market (3 years); second, to develop the infrastructure and overcome the raw-materials orientation of the economy (7 to 10 years). The latter is earmarked as a priority in foreign economic policy.[64]

Along these lines, foreign investment is expected to raise the export supply of petrochemicals and other minerals, and augment convertible currency revenues from exports, royalties and taxes. In turn, this would increase the resources available for modernization and underpin the market reforms. As indicated above, FI is also called upon to promote import-substituting industries, particularly in the consumer goods sector. The setting up of a local input-based consumer goods industry, the processing of agricultural products, and the development of technology-intensive industries have all been quoted as priority areas for FI in Kazakhstan.[65]

Thus, Kazakhstan's policy-makers seem to have a clear-cut view of the potential role of foreign capital in the country's development. This would explain why this country has not known abrupt policy changes *vis-à-vis* FI, which have been a common feature in the other successor states (see the chapters on Russia and Ukraine). Furthermore, Kazakhstan does not hesitate to put foreign investors in a privileged position *vis-à-vis* local enterprises.[66] The establishment of a National Foreign Investment Agency has become a focal point of FI-related negotiations, as well as of contacts between foreign businessmen and government bodies.

Western experts, who have examined the investment climate and business opportunities in Kazakhstan, note the stable political situation as the most valuable asset.[67] Despite the deteriorating economic situation, the relatively liberal legislation coupled with a consistent government policy has created a favourable basis for foreign investment in the development of mineral resources. Given the scale of current negotiations, one can expect the volume of FI to run into billions of dollars in the short to medium term, and into tens of billions in commitments from foreign companies over the next 10 to 40 years. However, the large-scale ventures in the mining sector are likely to become relatively closed, self-contained units, with few spill-over effects on the national economy, unless they are accompanied by systemic changes that unleash private entrepreneurship. The creation of a market infrastructure is even more important for foreign investment in sectors other than mineral sources, which aim to benefit from the relatively inexpensive labour and are geared to the domestic (Central Asian) markets. The irreversible course of market reform, as a guarantor of future economic liberalization, is paramount for attracting foreign investors of this type.

Notes

1 CIS Statistical Committee, *Statisticheskii Byulleten* [Statistical Bulletin] no. 16 (November 1992) p. 67.
2 According to the 1989 population census, Kazakhs made up 39.7 per cent of the population, while Russians accounted for 37.8 per cent, Germans for 5.8 per cent and Ukranians for 5.4 per cent. While most Kazakhs live in the south and the south-west of the republic, the Russian population is concentrated in the north-east, Almaty and in several industrial cities. The birth rate in Kazakhstan is the lowest among the central Asian CIS member states (1.1 per cent in the period 1985–90); however, among the Kazakh population between 1979–89, this exceeded 20 per cent. If this trend continues, Kazakhs may become a majority ethnic group in the country within the next twenty years; see Economist Intelligence Unit. (1992, p. 57).
3 Calculated from the CIS Statistical Committee, *Ekonomika Sodruzhestva Nezavisimych Gosudarstv (Kratkii spravochnik)* [CIS Concise Statistical Yearbook] (1992) pp. 18, 63.
4 CIS Statistical Committee, *Statisticheskii Byulleten* no. 16 (November 1992) pp. 67–70.
5 *Zakon* (Aug. 1992) p. 55; BIKI (2 June 1992).
6 According to the National Foreign Investment Agency, of the 540 FIEs registered by the beginning of 1993, as many as 64 (12 per cent) were wholly foreign-owned subsidiaries.
7 Andrusz (1996).
8 Priority sectors include the production of consumer goods, the processing of agricultural products, the production of electronics, bio-technological goods and those based on domestic technology, medicines, the processing of industrial waste and production of construction materials.
9 *East-West Investment and Joint Ventures News*, no. 13 (September 1992) pp. 20–1.
10 *Business Moscow News* (Russian edn) no. 3 (January 1992).
11 *Recht der Internationalen Wirtschaft* (November 1992) p. 900.
12 *Ekonomika i Zhizn'*, no. 33 (August 1993).
13 Generally, in addition to the regular income tax, enterprises in the mineral resource sector have to make additional payments to the budget. One of these, the geological tax, amounts to 8 per cent of receipts from the sale of oil, gas and gas condensates. These enterprises also have to pay fixed rental payments (3.8–5.7 dollars per tonne) when operating in particularly beneficial natural conditions allowing for profits to double the national average (*Central European*, July/August 1993, p. 62).
14 *Petroleum Economist* (January 1993) p. 7.
15 UN/ECE document, TRADE/WP.5/R.9/Rev. 1, pp. 29–43.
16 *East-West Investment News*, no. 2 (Summer 1993) p. 19.
17 *East-West Investment and Joint Ventures News*, no. 12 (June 1992) p. 5.
18 *East-West Investment News*, no. 2 (Summer 1993) p. 8.
19 *Business Moscow News* (Russian edn) no. 27 (4 July 1993).
20 *Central European* (September 1993) p. 14.
21 *BBC Summary of World Broadcasts*, Weekly Economic Report, SU/W0273 (19 March 1993) p. C2/2.

22 *Business Moscow News* (Russian edn; 19 September 1993).
23 Calculated from Table 13.1 and CIS Statistical Committee, *Statisticheskii Byulleten*, no. 10 (May 1993) p. 117.
24 For the time-being, the Kazakh economy is even more autarchic than its Russian counterpart. The overall foreign trade turnover in 1992 did not exceed 2 billion dollars, that is less than the foreign trade turnover of Russia-based FIEs.
25 Calculated from *Osnovnye Pokazateli Balansa Narodnogo Khoziaistva SSSR i Soyuznykh Respublik* [Major Indicators of the National Economy Balance] (1990) pp. 34, 36.
26 *Business Eastern Europe* (4 November 1991).
27 Economist Intelligence Unit 1992, pp. 62–5).
28 Estimated from the CIS Statistical Committee, *Ekonomika Sodruzhestva Nezavisimych Gosudarstv (Kratii Spravochnik)* [CIS Concise Statistical Yearbook] (1992) pp. 19, 64.
29 Economist Intelligence Unit (1992, p. 62).
30 *Financial Times* (8 April 1993).
31 Calculated from *Osnovnye Pokazateli Balansa Narodnogo Khoziaistva SSSR i Soyuznykh Respublik* [Major Indicators of the National Economy Balance] (1990) pp. 34, 36, 43–4.
32 Calculated from the CIS Statistical Committee, *Ekonomika Sodruzhestva Nezavisimych Gosudarstv (Kratkii Spravochnik)* (1992) pp. 27–9; CIS Statistical Committee, Statisticheskii Byulleten no. 16 (August 1993) p. 78.
33 Calculated from the CIS Statistical Committee, *Statisticheskii Byulleten* no. 16 (August 1993) p. 78.
34 *Ekonomika i Zhizn'* no. 33 (August 1993) and *Financial Times* (13 April 1993).
35 Higher Western oil reserves for Kazakhstan go up to 6.2 billion tonnes and even 15.9 billion tonnes (100 billion barrels). See *International Herald Tribune* (13 April 1993); *Far Eastern Economic Review* (4 February 1993) p. 48.
36 Economist Intelligence Unit (1992, p. 63); Far Eastern Economic Review (4 February 1993).
37 According to some estimates, the profitability of investment in Kazakhstan-based FIEs is on average 32 per cent (profit to capital ratio), while in Russia it does not exceed 10 per cent (*Business Moscow News*, Russian edition; 15 August 1993).
38 *Business Eastern Europe* (29 March 1993).
39 *BBC Summary of World Broadcasts*, Weekly Economic Report, SU/W0214 (14 January 1992) p. A/15.
40 *Izvestiya* (23 May 1992; 2 September 1992).
41 *Finansovye Izvestiya* (1–7 October 1993); *Business Eastern Europe* (18 October 1993).
42 *Interflo* (1/93).
43 *Petroleum Economist* (January 1993) p. 7.
44 CIS Statistical Committee, *Statisticheskii Byulleten* no. 8 (April 1993) p. 73; *Ekonomika i Zhizn'* no. 33 (August 1993).
45 Geologically proven resources in the Tenghiz and adjacent Korolev oil fields on the north-eastern shore of the Caspian Sea in western Kazakhstan are

estimated at 4 billion tonnes; the extractable reserves are estimated at 1 to 1.4 billion tonnes (*Business Moscow News*, Russian edn, no. 16 [April 1993]).

46 *Izvestiya* (8 May 1992).

47 *Argumenty i Fakty* (July 1991).

48 *Business Moscow News* (Russian edn; 18 April 1993).

49 *Business Moscow News* (Russian edn; 22 August 1993).

50 The development of this deposit is complicated by the fact that the oil lies beneath a thick layer of salt and needs to be extracted from a depth of 5 to 6 km.

51 *Commersant* (English edn; 5 May 1993); Izvestiya (30 April 1993); BBC *Summary of World Broadcasts*, Weekly Economic Report, SU/W0229 (8 May 1992) p. A/2.

52 *Petroleum Economist* (January 1993) p. 8.

53 These go up to 317 million tonnes (2 billion barrels) of oil and to 8000 billion cubic metres (20000 billion cubic ft) of natural gas (Independent, 2 July 1992).

54 *Financial Times* (20 August 1992).

55 *Petroleum Economist* (January 1993) p. 8.

56 *International Herald Tribune* (10 June 1993); *Moscow News* (Russian ed; 27 June 1993).

57 *Petroleum Economist* (January 1993) p. 7.

58 Situated in the Kzyl-Orda region (southern Kazakhstan), this deposit contains 300 million tonnes of oil: *BBC Summary of World Broadcasts*, Weekly Economic Report, SU/W0297 (3 September 1993) p. WD/2.

59 Both are situated near Karachaganak and contain 1.5 billion barrels of oil and condensates (238 million tonnes), and 695 cubic metres of gas: *Petroleum Economist* (January 1993) pp. 7–8.

60 See Interflo (3/93) p. 31; *BBC Summary of World Broadcasts*, Weekly Economic Report, SU/W0274 (26 March 1993) p. A/13; SU/W0297 (3 September 1993) p. WD/2.

61 *Interflo* (1/93).

62 *Finansovye Izvestiya* (6–12 August 1993).

63 *Business Moscow News* (Russian edn; 5 September 1993).

64 *BBC Summary of World Broadcasts*, Weekly Economic Report, SU/1386 (21 May 1992) p. ii.

65 *Izvestiya* (25 September 1992).

66 The special attitude toward potential foreign investors has been spelled out by the president himself in a number of interviews and public appearances. On meeting a French business delegation in September 1992, he declared 'Without foreign investment, we will not be able to solve our economic problems' (Izvestiya, 25 September 1992).

67 *International Herald Tribune* (11 March 1993).

14
The Transcaucasus Republics

Patrick Artisien-Maksimenko

Azerbaijan

Introduction

The Republic of Azerbaijan (formerly the Azerbaijan Soviet Socialist Republic) declared its independence on 18 October 1991; that same year, it adopted a new constitution that established a presidential republic.

Azerbaijan borders the Caspian Sea to the east, Iran to the south, Armenia to the west, Georgia to the north-west and the autonomous republic of Dagestan to the north. In territory (86 600 square kilometres) and population (7.2 million), it is the largest of the three Transcaucasus republics, although some 20 per cent of its territory is currently occupied by Armenian troops. The population is multi-ethnic, with the Azeris making up 78 per cent of the total, the Armenians and Russians 8 per cent each, and other smaller ethnic groups 6 per cent.

Economically, Azerbaijan still lags far behind some of its neighbours: the private sector accounts for only around 25 per cent of GDP. In 1996 agriculture still made the second largest contribution to GDP (26.7 per cent) after services (49.1 per cent) and ahead of industry (21.7 per cent).

Oil has in the past been a cornerstone of economic development and remains a determining factor in the country's economic prospects. Azerbaijan is with Russia and Kazakhstan one of the richest successor states in terms of mineral resources, although its deposits have so far been underexploited. The Baku Institute of Geology estimates that 60 per cent of the territory is oil-bearing. One offshore field – Guneshli – currently accounts for over half of the country's oil production. Proven resources include approximately 1 billion tonnes of oil, with estimated reserves of 4 to 5 billion tonnes. Natural gas resources amount to 800 billion cubic metres. Other minerals include alumina, alumite, gold and iron ore.

The government is committed to a three-pronged economic strategy for transition: first, to create a democratic market economy; second, to transform the economy into a modern industrial and technological base to enhance competitiveness on world markets; and third, to create a diversified economic structure.[1]

Recent Economic Trends[2]

After five consecutive years of negative economic growth caused by the disruption of trade with the former Soviet Union and catastrophic industrial recession, the collapse of large segments of the state manufacturing sector and the conflict with Armenia, 1997 registered the beginnings of an upturn with GDP growth reaching 5.8 per cent, as the agreements signed by the Azerbaijan International Operating Company (AIOC) for oil exports from the Caspian via Russian and Georgian pipelines become operational and early oil starts to flow.

By 1997, however, GDP was still only 40 per cent of its 1989 level, as previously guaranteed outlets for state enterprise production had dwindled away. Medium-term economic prospects depend increasingly on oil exports and the development of the hydrocarbons sector. At the time of writing (mid-1998) and after months of protracted negotiations between Russia and Chechnya over transit tariffs and repair costs, the state oil company, SOCAR, has started to send its crude through the northern pipeline route to the Black Sea port of Novorossiisk.

The agricultural sector, which accounts for about 30 per cent of GDP and employs over a third of the workforce, has suffered from a deterioration in its domestic terms of trade – as input prices have risen faster than those of outputs, a lack of up-to-date technology and deficiencies in farm equipment and the irrigation network. There are nascent signs that the fast-track privatization of farming is having a modest positive impact on production levels. Most foodstuffs, however, that were previously produced domestically are now imported.

Since 1995, after years of near-hyperinflation, the government has pursued a vigorous anti-inflationary policy under the aegis of an IMF-sponsored structural transformation facility. The Central Bank tightened the credit facilities of state-owned banks and halted large consumer subsidies on petrol and bread. As a result, year-on-year inflation declined from a high of 1660 per cent in 1994 to 20 per cent in 1996 and 4 per cent in 1997, in line with the objectives of the IMF-backed programme.

Privatization has progressed slowly, with the private sector accounting for some 30 per cent of GDP and 25 per cent of employment (excluding enterprises with less than 50 per cent private ownership). In July 1996 calls by the IMF for an acceleration of the process prompted President Heydar Aliyev to instruct the State Property Committee to break up and sell the assets held by the former ministries of public services and small enterprises. Under the terms of the IMF programme, 70 per cent of large and medium enterprises are due to be sold off by end 1999:extensive delays to date, however, make this deadline unrealistic. According to official estimates, 60 per cent of privatized enterprises are in the consumer goods sector, 25 per cent in services and 15 per cent in trade.[3] Partial privatization of the national airline and oil and gas industries is being considered, but defence equipment manufacturing, public television and radio and the railway network are to remain in state control.

The following section reviews the legal basis for foreign direct investment (FDI) in Azerbaijan, the available statistics and some of the problems encountered by foreign firms.

Legal framework and privatization

The legal basis for FDI stems from a number of laws and regulations enacted since 1992. The law on the protection of foreign investment was introduced on 15 July 1992 and guarantees equal treatment to both domestic and foreign investors, while providing full legal protection to foreign investors.

Most types of foreign investment are allowed, including joint ventures, wholly owned subsidiaries, branches and representative offices. The law also permits foreign investors to repatriate after-tax profits in foreign currency, set prices and choose suppliers, export without a licence goods and services originating from wholly foreign-owned subsidiaries and joint ventures with at least 30 per cent foreign participation, and import customs-free components of production.

A new law on investment activities approved by Parliament in November 1995 extended other legal guarantees to foreign investors: the nationalization and expropriation of property are prohibited, except where national or security interests are at stake, and only upon full compensation. Disputes involving foreign investors may be ruled upon by Azerbaijani courts or third-party arbitration. Thus, the AIOC's production-sharing agreement with SOCAR refers arbitration to the United Nations Commission on International Trade Law. Some Western investors doubt, however, whether national courts would recognize and enforce their legal rights against the state.

Azerbaijan is also creating legal conditions for foreign investment participation in privatization. Under the privatization programme of 21 July 1995, most state-owned enterprises are to be sold at auctions for cash or vouchers to be distributed to the entire adult population. Small and medium firms are to be sold to workers and management. Enterprises with more than 300 employees are to be converted into joint-stock companies and their shares sold to the public for cash and vouchers.[4]

An area of concern to foreign investors is the lack of transparency in the privatization of fuel and energy enterprises, namely oil and gas production and the petrochemical industries, where inconsistencies have arisen. On the one hand, the constitution specifies that natural resources are the property of the state, and the privatization programme envisages a 'golden share' device, through which the state can exercise effective control and the right of veto over shareholder decision-making in joint-stock companies.[5] However, with presidential consent, the privatization of energy sector projects can be authorized.

Furthermore, although foreign investors can acquire property in Azerbaijan, under the land code of 9 November 1991, land may not be passed on to or inherited by foreign legal and physical persons.[6] Under the same code, however, foreign firms can invest in real estate through the vehicle of joint ventures, but are advised to address their contractual rights in the event of dissolution or winding up. There are no restrictions on foreign participation in joint ventures. Under the land reformation law of 16 July 1996, foreign firms may also acquire leasehold rights in real estate.

Magnitude of foreign investment

FDI inflows to Azerbaijan have been below expectations. The combination of an inadequate legal system, an uncertain political situation and bureaucratic hurdles have made investing precarious. According to the United Nations, FDI increased from a mere 15 million dollars in 1993 to 601 million dollars in 1996 and to 1200 million dollars in 1997 (see Table 14.1). Projections from the Ministry of the Economy put cumulative FDI inflows at 1500 million dollars at end 1998. International oil contracts contributed as much as 80 per cent of cumulative FDI at end 1996.

The surge in FDI since 1995 is attributable to the signing of the first oil contract in 1994 to develop the Azeri-Chirag-Guneshli oil fields. Investment in this project amounted to 126 million dollars in 1995 and 416 million dollars in 1996. In 1997 three international oil

Table 14.1   Azerbaijan: cumulative FDI Inflows, 1993–8 (millions of dollars)

1993	1994	1995	1996	1997	1998^a
15.0	30.0	275.0	601.0	1200.0	1500.0

^{a}Projection.

Sources: *UN World Investment Report*, Geneva, 1997; Azerbaijan Ministry of the Economy, Baku, 1997; EBRD, Azerbaijan 1998 Country Report, 1998.

consortia developing offshore Caspian fields contributed some 604 million dollars of investment: namely, 569 million dollars from the AIOC to the Azeri-Chirag-Guneshli project; 20 million dollars to the Karabakh field through the Pennzoil-led CIPCO consortium and 15 million dollars from the BP-led Shah Deniz project. US companies have invested 42 per cent and 30 per cent stakes in the first and second projects respectively. There are two other major production-sharing agreements: the North Apsheron Operating Company (NAOC), with Amoco holding the largest stake (30 per cent), and the Lenkoran Deniz–Talysh Deniz Consortium, where Elf is the major investor with a 40 per cent stake.

Other sources of FDI in 1997 included the World Bank (11 million dollars for the reconstruction of Baku's water supply system), the EBRD (23 million dollars for the building of the Yenikand hydro-power station and upgrading of the gas supply network) and Turkey's Eximbank (11 million dollars for renovating Baku's airport).

According to the EBRD, Azerbaijan's oil deposits could become as significant to the international industry at the turn of the century as the North Sea was in the 1970s and the North Slope of Alaska in the early 1980s.

Although most of the FDI to date has been directed at the oil industry, the share of investment channelled to other sectors and supporting industries has increased from 20 per cent of total FDI in 1996 to 29 per cent in 1997, with the main recipients including construction, services, manufacturing, transport and telecommunications. Turkey and Iran are the leading investors outside the oil and gas sectors. FDI accounts for as much as two-thirds of total investment: at the end of 1997, Azerbaijan's Ministry of Justice had registered 242 fully owned subsidiaries of foreign companies, 161 joint ventures and 148 representative offices.

Recent investments outside the gas and oil sector include a contract signed in August 1997 by the US consortium RV Investment Group

Services, with the state-owned gold company, Azergyzyl, to mine metal ores; a contract with Mitsubishi and Sumitomo to supply 350 million yens' worth of agricultural equipment; and an undertaking by Daewoo in February 1998 to upgrade the telecommunications network in Nakhcivan.

Host Country Incentives and Drawbacks

A recent survey by MAI Consultants (UK) estimates that oil production in Azerbaijan could rise to more than 3 million barrels a day by 2007, that is more than is currently produced in the UK offshore sector. In the medium term, the oil sector is likely to play a major role in Azerbaijan's economic recovery, but the task of rebuilding a competitive oil industry is daunting.

First, few multinationals had anticipated the magnitude of infrastructural bottlenecks both in the oil industry and supporting sectors: at the time of writing (mid-1998) only one modern offshore drilling rig was operating in Azeri waters. Transport development, in particular, is essential: until new pipelines come into use and existing ones are fully upgraded, oil shipments by rail will remain significant.

Second, the much-publicized incentives of a large, cheap and well-educated workforce are frequently undermined by the time-consuming and bureaucratic local management practices entrenched in decades of Soviet centralization.

Third, the foreign business community has raised question marks about the absence of a long-term economic policy, which would minimize the potential distortions of the oil boom. The government's eagerness to sign new contracts with oil majors is adding unsustainable pressure to an already weakened infrastructure.

Finally, to the above difficulties are added the political complexities of choosing a main export pipeline capable of carrying a minimum of half a million barrels a day, which could rise to a peak of 800 000 barrels by the year 2002. The pipeline would also be likely to handle some oil from other Caspian Littoral states, namely Turkmenistan and Kazakhstan. An oil transit terminal at Dyubendi for handling Kazakh oil on its way to the Black Sea was officially opened in January 1998. A government decision on the main export route is due in October 1998. Georgia, Russia and Turkey are the main contenders, but each route is flawed. The Northern Route to the Russian Black Sea port of Novorossiysk is commercially attractive, but lacks long-term security as it needs to traverse Chechnyia. The Western Route would rely on a partially finished pipeline from Baku to Tbilisi and the Black Sea port of Supsa. This, the shortest and cheapest route, would, however, cross an area of previous or potential conflict. The third alternative through Turkey to the southern port of Ceyhan would be the longest and costliest, but with a potentially large market for oil in the Mediterranean.

One of the government's priorities is to attract non-oil foreign investment: the target is for 30 per cent of foreign investment to originate outside the oil sector: with this in mind, some tax incentives have been introduced which reduce corporate taxes on the foreign share of profits. The government further acknowledges that the long-term economic recovery cannot rely solely on oil production, but must include capital formation in manufacturing, services, transport and communications. Press reports do suggest, however, that bureaucratic hurdles and an inadequate legal system have to date kept foreign investors away from these sectors.

In May 1997 Sumgait, a town some 35 kilometres north of Baku, was declared a special economic zone and given two grants worth just over 1 million dollars by UNDP. The objective is to provide a favourable environment for private investment which could serve as a blueprint for industrial development throughout Azerbaijan.

Armenia

Introduction

Armenia is a landlocked country neighbouring Georgia, Azerbaijan, Iran and Turkey. With a territory of 29 800 square kilometres and a population of 3.7 million, it is the second most densely populated of the former Soviet republics. The ethnic makeup is overwhelmingly Armenian (93.3 per cent), with Azerbaijanis accounting for 2.6 per cent and others 4.1 per cent.

The Nagorno-Karabakh dispute with Azerbaijan, which escalated into full-scale war after the withdrawal of Russian troops in 1991, has remained unresolved since the 1994 ceasefire and cost Armenian economic development dearly. Trade embargoes from Azerbaijan and Turkey, the collapse of former markets in the Soviet Union, an inadequate legal environment for fostering private enterprise and the lingering effects of a devastating earthquake in 1988 have hampered economic recovery. As a result, incoming foreign investment has remained low. There is consensus among the foreign business community that the economy cannot achieve its potential in terms of foreign trade and investment until the Nagorno-Karabakh dispute is resolved and economic isolation is lessened.

Recent Economic Trends

The economy has made significant progress in recent years, although growth is showing signs of decelerating. Real GDP grew by 5.8 per cent in 1996 but slowed to 3.1 per cent in 1997, which compares unfavourably with a government growth target in excess of 5 per cent. There are also concerns over inflationary pressures: inflation rose from 5.7 per cent in 1996 to 22 per cent at end 1997, suggesting that growth was fuelled largely by a loosening of monetary and fiscal policy.

The IMF has been providing balance of payments and budgetary support in the shape of a three-year Enhanced Structural Adjustment Facility (ESAF) worth 150 million dollars awarded in 1996. The IMF's decision reflected the government's progress in improving tax collection. The government has relied heavily on external budgetary support: the 1997 and 1998 budget deficits were covered almost entirely by net foreign loans from multilateral and bilateral sources. However, the IMF wishes to see further improvement in revenue collection, combined with continued structural reform, notably in terms of privatization and banking sector reform.

Growth is being driven almost entirely by a booming service sector. Industry, particularly light industry and the food-processing sector, continues to suffer from a lack of export routes. Exports contracted by an estimated 19.6 per cent year-on-year in 1997, while imports rose by 2.7 per cent, resulting in a trade deficit estimated at 559 million dollars. Some 50 per cent of imports come from the CIS, with Russia, Georgia and Turkmenistan the major sources. Exports to the EU, which go mainly to Belgium and Germany, were facilitated somewhat by the conclusion in June 1997 of an EU–Armenia Interim Agreement. The agreement liberalizes trade in goods other than steel, textiles and coal, and offers most-favoured-nation status as regards tariffs and customs duties.

Structural reform has been patchy. The privatization of small enterprises is almost complete: according to the EBRD[7] 6021 small units out of a total of 7 720 had been privatized by January 1998. The privatization of housing is virtually complete; in the agricultural sector, almost all of the state and collective farms have been broken up and over 300 000 private farms created.

However, the sale of medium and large firms has been more sluggish, with lower-than-expected privatization revenues contributing to fiscal fragility. In order to increase privatization receipts, in June 1997 the government announced its intention to sell 18 major enterprises to foreign investors, including chemical works, three major hotel complexes, the Armentel telephone company and the Yerevan cognac distillery. The government also decided to privatize the state airline by putting it out to international tender with the support of the World Bank.

However, the environment for foreign investors remains poor. This results not only from post-Soviet legislative weaknesses, but also from energy shortages and the difficulties of importing component goods. Although some of the state firms offered for sale have attracted foreign interest, major Western investment in exporting or import-dependent industries is likely to remain limited while key overland routes are closed.

Legal Framework

The legal basis for FDI stems from several laws enacted since 1990. The law on Ownership (October 1990) granted both Armenian citizens and foreign investors the rights to own enterprises, equipment, intellectual property and securities. The right of land ownership, however, was restricted to Armenians. This law was seen as laying the foundation for private entrepreneurship. In March 1992, the law on enterprises and entrepreneurial activities established the forms of enterprises that foreign investors could enter as joint venture partners or fully owned subsidiaries. These include small, family-run, unlimited-liability enterprises, production cooperatives, joint-stock companies and limited-liability companies.

In July 1994 the new foreign investment law defined and extended the rights, guarantees and incentives for foreign firms operating in Armenia. Under the law, foreign investors can repatriate profits and other legally earned assets; they are entitled to a five-year grace period if the legislation at the time of the investment is subsequently amended; investments are exempt from customs duties on property imported for use in the production process; tax holidays are available; and a prompt compensation scheme at current market prices or prices determined by independent auditors is available if damages result from illegal government actions.

An area of concern to foreign investors – as in Azerbaijan – is the lack of transparency. Some critical legislation is still missing – such as an anti-monopoly law; some sectors are still state-controlled near-monopolies (for example aviation and telecoms). The absence of adequate laws to regulate the shadow economy, particularly in the trade sector where small companies are prevalent, is also thought to undermine competition. Furthermore, bureaucratic procedures have been reported to be burdensome and time-consuming: foreign investors negotiating contracts with the Armenian government must be prepared for protracted negotiations, as approval may be required from several ministries. Flaws in newly adopted laws and the absence of an effective law-enforcing mechanism have resulted in widespread corruption. Bribery is reported to be common in sectors involving government procurement, company registration, licensing and land allocation.

Foreign investment agencies designed to encourage incoming FDI include the State Council of Investment Stimulation and Protection, whose brief is to develop policies for attracting FDI.[8] The Armenian Development Agency was also set up to stimulate export and investment programmes: 700 million drams were allocated to the agency from the 1998 budget for the creation of a private investment fund with a total authorised capital of some 20 million dollars.

Magnitude of Foreign Investment

Until private capital flows increase substantially, Armenian public finances will remain heavily dependent on aid and credits from foreign governments and multilateral agencies, of which the country is one of the largest recipients in the CIS. Most recent inflows of foreign capital have been in the form of loans, including a three-year ESAF worth 150 million dollars awarded by the IMF in 1996; a 60 million dollars, 35-year loan from the World Bank in 1997 for structural reforms; and a 15 million dollars, interest-free World Bank loan for the modernization of the transport network. At the end of 1997, total World Bank credits issued to Armenia stood at 280 million dollars.

As in neighbouring Azerbaijan, foreign capital inflows to Armenia have been disappointing. The lack of incentives targeted at foreign investors combined with the reluctance of foreign lending institutions to take risks have hindered business opportunities. According to a US source,[9] in 1996 the number of fully foreign-owned companies in Armenia rose from 191 to 305, while that of joint ventures with foreign partners grew from 206 to 380, bringing the total number of companies with foreign capital to 685. Almost half of these enterprises are in trading activities (47 per cent); industry accounts for 15 per cent of firms and services for 11 per cent. Russia, Iran and the USA are the three main sources of foreign investment.

According to the Armenian Ministry of Economy, FDI inflows in 1996 and 1997 amounted to 34 million dollars and 50 million dollars respectively, although the real figures – taking account of the shadow economy – may be nearer twice those amounts. Economic improvements in

1995–6 and the last ceasefire with Azerbaijan have resulted in noticeable increases in FDI inflows, particularly from the USA. After a long period of hesitation in the first half of the 1990s, when a mere 2 to 4 US investments were registered annually, in excess of 30 new foreign investments were set up in 1995–6, and over 20 in the first half of 1997.

Armenia's outdated telecommunications network and equipment have been the targets of foreign interests: in 1995 the Ministry of Communications and AT&T signed a joint venture agreement to lay fibre-optic cables throughout Yerevan. Armtel, an Armenian–US joint venture, has also started to install facilities for mobile cellular phones, with Siemens providing 100 million dollars in credits towards equipment purchases.

In the energy sector, in August 1997 Armrosgazprom was set up as an Armenian – US joint venture to generate electric power from gas supplied from Russia. The Ministry of Energy and Gazprom each hold a 45 per cent stake.

Other recent investments include the Armenian Gold Recovery Company, a joint venture between Armzoloto and First Dynasty Mines of Canada, which plans to invest 86 million dollars in the exploration of the Meghradzor and Zod mines.

In the tobacco industry, an Armenian–Canadian joint venture, Grand Tobacco, was set up in 1998 to revive tobacco production in Armenia. The Canadian partner – Grand Tabak – invested 3.2 million dollars in 1997, with a further capital injection of 5 million dollars planned for 1998.

In February 1997 the US-based American–Armenian Exploration Company entered into a production-sharing agreement with the Ministry of Energy for the drilling of oil and gas deposits. The initial investment was 10 million dollars.

In sum, although the Armenian government has emphasized its continued commitment to economic reform, the economy is unlikely to achieve its potential in terms of foreign trade and incoming investment until the Nagorno-Karabakh dispute is settled. Foreign investors have to date given preference to Azerbaijan's oil potential and Georgia's strategic location.

Georgia

Introduction

Georgia, with a territory of 69 000 square kilometres and a population of 5.4 million, straddles Europe and Asia on the eastern shores of the Black

Sea. The collapse of the Soviet Union and central planning dealt a severe blow to most industrial sectors: the economy went through one of the worst recessions in the CIS and did not show signs of positive growth until 1995.

Since then, Georgia has become a focal point for the transit of goods, gas and oil from its Eastern neighbours to Europe. Georgian ports are likely to take on added significance as the Central Asian oil starts to flow. Foreign investment remains low to date; foreign firms have shown an interest in light manufacturing, energy and agriculture. The general consensus among the foreign business community is that trade and investment cannot be fully exploited until the infrastructure is upgraded.

Recent Economic Trends

As in neighbouring Armenia, the economy has made significant progress since the mid-1990s. Three key macroeconomic indicators are showing encouraging signs, although some of the factors behind these trends suggest underlying problems.

First, GDP growth has been relatively strong since 1996 and looks set to continue. GDP grew by 10.5 per cent in 1996 and 10 per cent in 1997, and growth rates of 8 to 10 per cent to the turn of the century appear sustainable. However, this impressive recovery started from an extremely low base, following the Soviet collapse and several years of civil strife. Agriculture, trade and services were among the fastest-growing sectors in 1996–7, while the leading growth sectors in industry included fuel, chemicals, pulp and paper.

Second, inflationary pressures have eased, with annual inflation falling from 13 per cent in 1996 to 10 per cent in 1997 and further annual contractions to single figures expected in 1998–2000. However, low inflation has only been partly the result of the central bank's tight monetary policy: prices are also held down by low levels of disposable income, with state sector wages as low as 60 dollars a month.

Third, according to the EU-sponsored Tacis team, the budget deficit was sharply reduced from 5.6 per cent of GDP in 1996 to around 2.2 per cent of projected GDP in 1998. This relatively small budget deficit (135 million dollars) stems largely from reduced state spending through downsizing government and eliminating gas and bread subsidies. However, there are wage arrears in the state sector, while the social welfare system is in a parlous condition. Persistent tax collection problems have also forced the government to borrow extensively from the IMF, the World Bank and the central bank.

Core industrial sectors need to be overhauled. In 1997, manufacturing, transport, communications and construction accounted for only 30 per cent of GDP. The energy sector, in particular, continues to inflict periodic reductions in power supply and stifle industrial growth.

Georgia's external balances are in a weak state. Imports in 1996 amounted to 638 million dollars but exports were a mere 213 million dollars making for a trade deficit of 425 million dollars, a trend reinforced in 1997 when the deficit widened to 485 million dollars. The problem of the growing trade deficit has been compounded by a steady increase in foreign debt, which reached 1.6 million dollars in late 1996 (around 60 per cent of GDP). Georgia's limited debt-servicing capacity has also limited the amount of new debts which can be contracted or guaranteed on non-commercial terms.[10] No debt-servicing payments were made in 1995 and 1996.

Russia remains Georgia's main trading partner, despite road and rail shipment problems over the Caucasus mountains through Abkhazia. Georgia's other major trading partners are Turkey, Azerbaijan and Armenia.

Debts owed to Turkmenistan for gas supplies temporarily soured relations between the two countries in 1995–96, but under a restructuring deal agreed in 1997 Georgia agreed to resume payment of capital and interest from 1998. Besides a number of free-trade agreements with CIS member states, in April 1996 Georgia signed a partnership and cooperation agreement with the EU.

The ongoing construction of a 920-kilometre pipeline from Azeri oil fields in the Caspian across Azerbaijan and Georgia to a new oil terminal at Supsa with an ultimate capacity of 15 to 18 million tonnes a year should, when operational in 1999, boost foreign exchange earnings. This project is matched by a smaller transit pipeline from Baku to the Black Sea port of Novorossiysk.

Privatization

Georgia's voucher-based mass privatization programme ended in 1996, when half a million citizens were reported to have become shareholders; one-fifth of the equity was purchased by foreigners.[11] Some 1000 medium and large-scale enterprises (out of a privatization target of 1189) were turned into joint-stock companies by the end of 1996. Of these, 524 were privatized by early 1997.

By the end of 1996, over 90 per cent of small firms were in private hands; much of the privatization of small, state-owned enterprises took place through cash payments. At the time of writing (1998), the private sector accounts for at least 60 per cent of GDP, and over 65 000 small businesses have been registered.[12]

The 1996 law on the ownership of agricultural land gave farmers clearer property rights and enabled entities to buy, sell, lease and inherit land, including building land. The privatization of housing is virtually complete. In May 1997 a new privatization law introduced 'no-minimum-price' auctions aimed at completing the privatization of firms unsuccessfully offered in cash auctions. Foreign investors are entitled to take part in the privatization process.

Legal Framework

The 1996 law on promotion and guarantees of investment activity signalled an improvement in Georgia's investment climate. The new legislation eliminated the need for licensing foreign investments by introducing a less cumbersome registration procedure. Registration at the Ministry for Trade and Economic Relations is required if the proposed investment exceeds 100 000 dollars. The law permits unlimited foreign ownership in some sectors through acquisitions, mergers, takeovers and greenfield investments, but sharply limits foreign participation in infrastructural projects and bans foreign ownership of agricultural land. The government is also legally bound to retain a controlling interest in the gas and oil sectors, electric power transmission, communications, transport, roads, railways, ports and airports. These restrictions clearly reduce the potential for foreign capital participation in modernizing a fast decaying infrastructure.

Georgia's law on entrepreneurship is also pertinent to foreign investment. It allows six different commercial forms, including limited and unlimited liability companies, limited partnerships, joint-stock companies, cooperatives and sole ownership. It exempts investments of a minimum duration of 10 years from subsequent legislative changes to investment conditions.

In March 1997 a presidential decree established the Foreign Investment Advisory Council, whose brief is to speed up incoming FDI flows by improving the investment climate.

Magnitude of Foreign Investment

FDI inflows to Georgia remain low: the end-1996 stock was around 195 million dollars. Investments are mainly small: South Korea's Daewoo is one of the most prominent foreign investors, but has invested a mere 9 million dollars in switching equipment in the state telecommunications company.

Much of the FDI stock was received in 1996 and 1997, suggesting improving investor confidence in the economy's longer-term prospects as preparations for the export of Caspian Sea oil gather pace. In particular, agriculture and food-processing, especially the tea and wine sectors, are beginning to attract the attention of foreign firms.

Tables 14.2 and 14.3 show that, as of 1 October 1997, the Ministry of Trade and Foreign Economic Relations had issued 161 licences to foreign companies. German companies were the leaders with 24 joint ventures, followed by Russia (22) and the United States and Britain (19 each). In terms of capital invested, Israel topped the league table with 16.3 million dollars; Ireland (15.2 million), the United States (10.2 million) and South Korea (9.1 million) were among the other main investing nations.

Recent FDI inflows have included purchases of 11.7 million shares in 40 companies across a range of industrial sectors by the US firm GIA, the largest single investor in Georgia to date; two investments by Martin Bauer (Germany) in the banking sector and the Odishi and Kalkha tea

Table 14.2   Georgia: registered foreign investments by country of origin, 1 October 1997

Country of origin	Licences issued	Value ($ m.)	Percentage of total
Israel	7	16.3	15.4
Ireland	6	15.2	14.4
US	19	10.2	9.7
Korea	2	9.1	8.7
Germany	24	8.0	7.6
Britain	19	7.7	7.3
Russia	22	6.8	6.5
Netherlands	9	6.5	6.2
Bermuda	2	4.1	3.9
Turkey	12	3.9	3.7
France	2	3.6	3.4
Austria	1	2.7	2.6
Italy	6	2.2	2.1
Switzerland	10	2.2	2.1
Cyprus	3	1.6	1.6
Greece	3	0.85	0.8
Austria	3	0.54	0.5
Bulgaria	3	0.54	0.5
Others	20	3.34	3.0
Total	153	105.32	100.0

Source: Georgia Ministry of Trade and Foreign Economic Relations, *Georgian Economic Trends*, 1997.

Table 14.3   Georgia: registered foreign investments by sector, 1 October 1997

Industrial sector	Licenses issued	Value ($ m.)	Percentage of total
Manufacturing	34	39.476	37.4
Communications	10	22.447	21.3
Food Industry	45	17.015	16.1
Banking	14	8.470	8.0
Agriculture	4	5.895	5.6
Trade	30	5.234	5.0
Construction	8	2.692	2.6
Transport	4	2.479	2.4
Service	11	1.559	1.5
Health	1	0.107	0.1
Total	161	105.374	

Source: Georgia Ministry of Trade and Foreign Economic Relations, *Georgian Economic Trends*, 1997.

factories; a 5 million dollar investment by British Petroleum; capital injections by the Commercial Bank of Greece and the EBRD into Georgia's first international bank, the Black Sea International Bank; production-sharing agreements and joint ventures in the Kura Basin and the Black Sea region by Atlantic Richfield (US), Frontera (US), Ramco Energy and JKX Oil and Gas (both UK) and Canadian Canargo Energy; and investments in the telecommunications sector by Deutsche Telekom, Siemens, Alcatel, Ericsson, Telrad (Israel) and Daewoo.

Among the factors deterring foreign investors to date have been:

1. Political uncertainty: although large-scale fighting in the breakaway regions of Abkhazia and South Ossetia has ceased, no final settlement has been reached in either case.
2. Lack of financial incentives: the 1996 investment law cancelled tax breaks for foreign investors. In part, this seems to have reflected higher investment inflows, which were making the tax breaks too expensive for state finances to bear.
3. Restricted privatization: there are strict limits (see above) on foreign participation in infrastructure investment. The depressed state of the power, telecommunications and transport sectors has exacerbated the poor business climate.
4. Poor infrastructure: this has contributed to the unreliability of distribution networks and deterred further investment in agriculture and food processing.

5. Legal environment: corruption is widespread and the business environment is still burdened with government influence and bureaucracy: personal contacts still play a significant role in winning a contract.

In sum, Georgia can benefit from its strategic location as the shortest and arguably safest oil and gas corridor between Central Asia and Europe. Its natural assets and the vast energy reserves of its Eastern neighbours enhance its position further as a host to FDI. Unlocking this potential, however, will require a transparent economic and legal framework in which foreign investors can put their trust.

Notes

1   Altai Efendiev, Azerbaijan: A Country of Enormous Potential and Challenging Economic Opportunities, *BSCC Bulletin*, September 1995.
2   A full review of economic trends is beyond the scope of this chapter. For an in-depth analysis, see Kaser (1998).
3   EBRD (1998 b).
4   Bureau of National Affairs, *Eastern Europe Reporter, Country Reports*, vol. 6, 1 July 1996.
5   Bureau of National Affairs, *Eastern Europe Reporter, Azerbaijan's Evolving Legal Environment*, 28 July 1997.
6   Ibid.
7   EBRD (1998a).
8   Ibid.
9   Business Information Service for the Newly Independent States, 9 April 1997.
10   See EBRD (1998c, p. 13).
11   See Kaser (1998).
12   EBRD (1998c, p. 13).

Part IV

East Asian Multinationals in Eastern Europe

The second half of the 1990s witnessed a marked acceleration in East Asia's outward investments to Eastern Europe. In this section, I asked Jim Slater to reflect on recent trends in East–East investment, and to consider the potential for closer economic cooperation with Japanese, Korean, Chinese and Malaysian multinationals.

15
Trends in East Asian Investment in the Transitional Economies

*Jim Slater**

Introduction

In the last decade or so the international economy has been characterized by a singular growth in foreign direct investment (FDI). While the developed countries have been largely both the leading drivers and recipients of FDI, the developing and newly industrialized countries of South East Asia have also shown a marked acceleration in their outward and inward FDI, along with rapid rises in the more familiar economic growth indicators. China, for example, as the largest developing economy is currently second to the US in terms of total inflow, but, – it is less well known – is also one of the largest outward investors among developing countries. Table 15.1 shows the recent rankings of countries according to annual *inflows*.

Table 15.2 compares annual *outflows* on a regional basis. Excluding Japan and Hong Kong, the magnitude of investment from South-East Asia is relatively small compared with global totals, but the increase in the 1990s compared with the previous decade is impressive. The figures imply considerable investment outflows from Hong Kong, but their interpretation is difficult. Hong Kong (and to a lesser extent, Singapore) acts as an entrepôt for capital as well as for goods. Large sums destined for China, particularly, (some, indeed, originating from China itself) are channelled through Hong Kong, and Hong Kong is not the original

* The author wishes to acknowledge and express gratitude for the assistance of Dr Anthony Bende-Nabende and Dr Isabel Tirado-Angel, former PhD students in the University of Birmingham Business School.

Table 15.1   Top five countries in FDI inflow, 1993–5 (billion US dollars)

Ranking	1993		1994		1995	
1	US	43.0	US	49.8	US	60.2
2	China	27.5	China	33.8	China	37.7
3	France	20.8	France	16.6	UK	32.2
4	UK	15.5	Mexico	11.0	France	23.7
5	Belgium	10.8	UK	10.3	Sweden	14.3

Notes: 1. Flow, based on balance of payments.
2. 1995 figures for China are local statistics

Source: Prepared by JETRO from international financial statistics, IMF and local Chinese statistics.

Table 15.2   Regional FDI outflows, 1984–96 (million US dollars)

	1984–9 annual average	1990	1991	1992	1993	1994	1995	1996
N. America	21511	31900	39111	42613	80662	58454	98690	92445
EU	62641	132959	106362	110521	96596	112836	149118	160372
Asia[a]	5147	12276	8151	17380	30280	34804	41627	45675
Asia[b]	3314	9828	5326	9126	12567	13367	16627	18675
Japan	20793	48024	31620	17390	13830	18090	22510	23440
Australia	3338	186	3022	854	1768	5243	4092	1343
S. America	383	1114	1313	685	2108	2919	2822	3022

[a] South, East and South-East Asia, excluding Japan.
[b] South, East and South-East Asia, excluding Hong Kong

Source: UNCTAD (1996, 1997).

source. There is 'real' FDI from Hong Kong destined for China and other South-East Asian countries, but there is little evidence from other sources of the type of activity in former Soviet Union (FSU) countries. Undoubtedly resources are moving from or via Hong Kong: for example, UNCTAD-DITED (1997) quote significant figures for the Russian Federation and Lithuania, but their origin and nature are not well publicized. Hong Kong's outward investment is, therefore, not discussed in the text that follows.

Table 15.3 shows outward investment from the remaining Asian home countries over the last seven years. Although most of this investment is intra-regional, if both the economic growth and outward investment rates prove sustainable then Asian transnational corporations (TNCs) are likely to increasingly search for suitable, more remote, destinations. Already significant investments are being made outside the

Table 15.3 Recent trends in FDI outflows from major Asian developing countries, 1990–6 (million US dollars)

	1990	1991	1992	1993	1994	1995	1996
Korea	1056	1500	1208	1361	2524	3529	4188
Taiwan	5243	1854	1869	2451	2460	2678	3096
Singapore	2034	526	1317	2021	3104	3906	4800
Thailand	140	167	147	233	493	886	1740
China	830	913	4000	4400	2000	2000	2200
Malaysia	532	389	514	1325	1817	2575	1906

Source: UNCTAD (1996, 1997).

South-East Asian region. Some of these are in Central and Eastern European (CEE) and FSU countries, and this chapter aims, first, to assess their size and nature and, second, to attempt to gauge trends in the likely future investment linkages between the two regions. It should be pointed out from the beginning that these 'regions' are terms of convenience and do not imply a homogeneity or unity of purpose. Therefore, from a short examination of the statistical aggregates, the chapter will spotlight cases on a country-by-country basis. The figures that follow are not collected according to consistent statistical definitions and are, therefore, not suitable for formal analysis.

Regional Investment Trends

Table 15.4 shows inward investment flows for the FSU for 1991–5 and stocks for end 1995. Not only have the dollar totals increased, but also the share of the total of world investment has risen from 1 per cent in 1991 to around 5 per cent in 1995. Evidently, most of the stock and recent inflows are concentrated in the Czech Republic, Hungary, Poland, Russia and Slovakia. The origins of these investments are discussed elsewhere in this book, and clearly Western Europe and the US are the principal sources. Interestingly, whereas Japan accounts for a considerable proportion of total world FDI, there seems to have been relatively little interest there in the FSU.

Table 15.5 summarizes outflow totals for East and South-East Asia. Although there are considerable year-to-year fluctuations, characteristic of the lumpiness of major investments and, often, sensitivity to political influence, Table 15.5 confirms the upward trend consonant with the growth in global investment and trade. Among the Asian economies

Table 15.4   FDI inflows into Central and Eastern Europe, 1991–5, million US dollars

Country	Inflows					Stock	
	1991	*1992*	*1993*	*1994*	*1995*	*1994*	*1995*
Albania	n.a.	20	58	53	70	130	200
Armenia	n.a.	–	–	8	10	8	18
Azerbaijan	n.a.	–	–	–	110	–	10
Belarus	n.a.	7	10	15	20	32	52
Bulgaria	56	42	55	106	135	263	398
Croatia	n.a.	–	–	–	–	–	–
Czech Republic	n.a.	–	654	878	2500	2508	5008
Estonia	–	82	162	214	188	458	646
Georgia	–	–	–	–	–	–	–
Hungary	1462	1479	2349	1144	3500	6434	9934
Kazakhstan	–	100	150	185	284	435	719
Kyrgyzstan	–	–	–	10	15	10	25
Latvia	–	29	45	215	250	289	539
Lithuania	–	10	12	31	50	53	103
Moldova	–	17	14	23	32	54	86
Poland	291	678	1715	1875	2510	4879	7389
Romania	40	77	94	340	373	551	924
Russian Federation	–	700	700	1000	2000	2400	4400
Slovakia	–	–	199	203	250	890	1140
Slovenia	–	111	113	84	130	308	438
Tajikistan	–	–	–	10	15	10	25
Ukraine	–	200	200	159	200	559	759
Uzbekistan	–	40	45	50	115	135	250
Yugoslavia	118	64	23	–	–	400	400
Total	1966	3657	6600	6603	12757	20808	33565

n.a. = not available.

Source: UNCTAD (1996).

Japan's stock of outward FDI is by far the largest, followed at some distance by (in order of magnitude) Hong Kong, Taiwan, China, Singapore, Korea and Malaysia. Most Asian investment, as mentioned earlier, is confined to the Asia Pacific Region, particularly within Greater China. Nevertheless, there seems a prima facie case to examine the leading investors first for evidence of investment links with the FSU countries. Table 15.6 summarizes available information concerning certain significant Asian investments in Central and Eastern Europe.

The following section examines Asian investment in CEE and the FSU countries on the basis of the *home* economies.

Table 15.5 Outward FDI of Asian economies, 1980–95 (million US dollars)

Region / economy	Outflows (annual average)			Outward stocks		
	1980–85	1986–90	1991–95	1980	1985	1995
Asia	5 749	39 893	49 637	21 504	49 952	469 919
Japan	4 641	32 073	23 963	18 833	44 296	305 545
NIEs						
Hong Kong	455	2 252	14 797	148	2 345	85 156
Korea, Republic of	66	361	1 919	142	526	11 079
Singapore	128	684	1 820	652	1 320	13 842
Taiwan	51	3 417	2 291	97	204	24 344
	700	6,714	20 827	1 039	4 395	134 421
ASEAN(4)						
Indonesia	9	3	16	−1	49	113
Malaysia	239	296	1 482	414	749	9 693
Philippines	8	2	2	171	171	167
Thailand	2	77	386	13	14	2 330
	257	378	1 887	597	983	12 302
China	150	711	2 956	–	131	17 268

Source: UNCTAD–DITED (1997).

The Asian Investing Nations

A feature of Table 15.6 is the absence of Japan as a significant investor in the FSU. In fact, recent figures confirm that only 0.2 per cent of Japan's overseas investments stock is located in the region. The ranking of Asian investors based on Table 15.6 thus suggests the Republic of Korea as the leading investor followed by Singapore, China, Hong Kong (possibly) and Taiwan.

Japan

Clearly Japanese companies do have a presence in the FSU, but have been reluctant to undertake large-scale investments. Such as they are, investments have been made primarily through joint ventures or via European-based Japanese affiliates. Examples include ventures by Fujitsu in Poland, and Kyocera and Alps Electric in the Czech Republic channelled through their UK and Irish affiliates. JETRO (1997) reports signs of stirring, however, with Matsushita Electric and Sony Manufacturing projects in the Czech Republic and Slovakia, respectively. JETRO also reports current manufacturing investments of total Japanese cumulative investment in the four main CEE host countries. The figures

Table 15.6   FDI of Asian developing economies in Central and Eastern Europe, latest available year (million US dollars and percentage); accumulated FDI From Asia

Host country	Year	Total	Economies	Share	Main investing economy
Estonia	1993	188	2.9	1.5	China ($2m.)
Hungary	1993	5802	29.0	0.5	Republic of Korea($23m.) China ($6m.)
Latvia	1994	315	0.5	0.2	China ($0.5m.)
Lithuania	1994	174	4.0	0.6	Hong Kong Republic of Korea China
Poland	1994	4321	43.0	1.0	China ($25m.) Singapore ($13m.) Republic of Korea ($5m.)
Romania	1995	1595	159.1	10.0	Republic of Korea($159m.)
Slovakia	1995	923	10.7	1.2	Republic of Korea ($11m.)
Russian Federation	1994	2919	403.6	13.8	Singapore ($195m.) China ($164m.) Hong Kong ($12m.) Republic of Korea ($11m.) Democratic People's Republic of Korea ($10m.) Taiwan Province of China ($5m.)

Source: UNCTAD–DITED (1997).

show dollar totals and Japan's share of the total inward investment into each of the host countries (see Table 15.7).

Approximately two-thirds of the Russian projects are located in the Russian Far East and include participation in some very large projects such as Sakhalin (offshore oil and gas). It would appear, therefore, that while Japanese investment has been characterized historically by its relative absence (to some extent paralleling trade relations), there are signs of increasing activity. The low investment levels have received some scrutiny: the recent UNCTAD report already cited (UNCTAD-DITED 1997), produced as an input to the Bangkok Asia–Europe Meeting (ASEM) in July 1996, questioned the exceptionally small Japanese FDI in CEE countries. The specific contributory factors can be summarized as:

- *Limited Japanese support services.* Japanese investment overseas has been preceded by the establishment of intelligence-gathering by trade and investment-support agencies spearheaded by the *sogo-sosha*, the conglomerate trading-houses. Neither they, nor the

Table 15.7 Direct investment in three Central European countries and Russia (million US dollars)

	Hungary	Poland	Czech Republic	Russia
Cumulative total of direct investment from other countries	11919 (end 1995)	10155 (end July 1996)	6704 (end Sept. 1996)	4724 (end of June 1996)
Cumulative total and share of direct investment from Japan	370 (3.1%) (end 1995)	83 (0.8%) (end July 1996)	160 (2.4%) (end Sept. 1996)	154 (3.3%) (end June 1996)

Notes: Figures for direct investments from Japan are based on local statistics. However, the figure for direct investment by Japan in Hungary is based on investments notified to the Japanese Ministry of Finance. Figures for Japanese investment in Poland are JETRO estimates.

Source: JETRO, based upon Central banks and foreign investment agencies of individual countries and State Statistical Committee (Russia).

banking sector that is often a part of them, nor even JETRO are represented to levels comparable with those in other parts of the world.

- *Japan's official aid policies.* Unlike policy with respect to some developing countries, Japan's aid to CEE is not closely linked to investment or trade generation.
- *Trade relations: low levels of trade* (0.7 per cent of Japanese exports are sold in CEE countries). There has been little incentive, therefore, for trade-supporting investment or to consider investment as an alternative supply strategy.
- *Alternative resource availability.* South-East Asia has provided low-cost land and labour, and relatively good skills with the additional advantage of low transportation costs to the major Asian markets (including Japan).
- *Psychological/cultural distance.* This is the perceived difficulty of operating in unfamiliar national and organizational cultural environments, possibly compounded by anticipated difficulties within the politico-legal framework. However, the UNCTAD-DITED report suggests that the learning/experience curve travelled by European affiliates is likely to partially offset these fears and lead to further investment initiatives of the type described above.

Also, the report suggests that Japanese small and medium enterprises (SMEs), faced with rising costs elsewhere, may look to the region in future. In fact, the Japanese government plans to target SME's for participation in particular projects associated with part of its development assistance programme. In particular one scheme is to generate SME investment through the Far East-Eastern Siberian Investment Fund jointly sponsored with the European Bank for Reconstruction and Development (JETRO 1997). In addition to the factors analysed in the UNCTAD-DITED document there is, however, another political dimension. Relationships between Japan and the Russian Federation have been cool as a result of longstanding territorial disputes (Kuril Islands) in the Far East. Recent developments (Boris Yeltsin's visit to Tokyo in November 1997) suggest that these differences are likely to be put aside in order to facilitate mutual gains from trade and investment. Government policies apart, it is likely that Japanese companies will begin to awaken to the benefits and opportunities already perceived by other Asian countries, particularly because of rivalry with Korea. This is not to say the awareness is not already there. Rather, the caution exercised by Japanese companies will attenuate as the perceived 'negatives' or threats diminish (and government gives the green light). As the legal framework becomes more apparent, the aftermath of privatization (not generally of great interest as a vehicle for Japanese FDI) begins to settle, cultural distance declines and FSU incomes rise, more positive decisions are likely to be taken. Japanese penetration of new export markets and outward investment activities typically progress on a follow-the-leader basis. Since some of Japan's leading companies are beginning to locate in CEE, more are likely to follow. Table 15.8 indicates the commencement of a new – albeit small at present – round of Japanese investment. The shift in governmental relationships and the activities of Korean companies, closely observed by their Japanese competitors, probably presage a snowballing of Japanese interest in the region.

The Republic of Korea

In contrast to Japan, Korea has become a relatively prolific investor in CEE, leading, in fact, the Asian nations. Korea's economic development has been rapid even by South-East Asian standards. To a large extent Korea has adopted and adapted the Japanese model of development: a close cooperative relationship between business (particularly the *chaebols*, which bear certain similarities to Japan's *sogo shosha*) and a government with outward-looking objectives. However, compared with Japan, there seems to have been more direct involvement by government. Like Japan, Korea is heavily dependent upon imports for food and raw materials. Initial industrial policies focused on exports have been followed largely since the mid-1980s by rapid growth in outward FDI. (see Table 15.9). Clearly, 'push' factors have been major motivators in

Table 15.8 Some recent investments by Japanese companies in the Transitional Economies
Where available, figures in parenthesis are in million US dollars and are reported intentions not necessarily yet realised.

	Czech Rep.	Hungary	Kazakhstan	Poland	Russia	Slovakia	Turkmenistan
Denon	Electronics						
Isuzu				Autos (645)			
Japan Chrome Corp.			Coal (140) Chrome				
Matsushita	TV (66.5)						
Mitsubishi					Oil[a]		Gas pipeline
Nissho Iwai	Metals (2.5)						
Nomura	Banking	Banking		Banking	Banking		
Panasonic							
Sony		Electronics				Electronics	
Suzuki		Autos (330)					
Toray	Textiles (150)						
Toyota				Autos			
Yakazi						Autos (23)	

[a] With Mitsui.

Table 15.9   Korea's total outward FDI, 1985–95 (million US dollars); approval basis

1985	1986	1987	1988	1989	1990	1991	1992	1993	1994	1995[a]
116	184	411	224	570	959	1115	1218	1260	2305	1246
(39)	(52)	(92)	(176)	(269)	(338)	(443)	(497)	(682)	(1475)	(570)

[a] January to May.
( ) = no. of projects.

Source: Bank of Korea: *Economic Statistics Yearbook*, 1996.

stimulating outward investment in general, while 'pull' factors have influenced the specific location of individual investments (Nam and Slater 1997).

By 1994 Korea's outward FDI was about 2.1 per cent of GDP compared with 6.2 per cent for Japan and 9.1 per cent for the USA. The likely Korean reaction to this benchmarking suggests that there will be active steps to continue to increase outward FDI.

Most of Korea's investment has been concentrated in South-East Asia and North America (46.9 and 24.9 per cent respectively in 1994), primarily in the manufacturing sector (Table 15.10). Commoditized products using labour-intensive production technologies, such as textiles, clothing and metal products have accounted for a high proportion of FDI, especially in Asia and Latin America. Investment in Europe, virtually zero in 1985, grew to a flow of around 500 million dollars in 1996 with the accumulated stock at about 2 billion dollars. Much of this has arisen from a surge in the 1990s. Like Japanese companies, the Korean *chaebols* tend to operate follow-the-leader strategies. Recent rapid investment in the UK, for example, followed a first move by Samsung. Korea's FDI in the CEE countries has also grown rapidly only very recently. Total stock was reported at about 71 million dollars in 1991 but rose ten-fold by 1996. In Europe generally, much of this investment has been focused upon the automobile and electronics industries, with some trade-supporting activity. In addition, in Eastern Europe some Korean companies are flirting with the banking sector. Unlike their Japanese counterparts, the Korean *chaebols* are not allowed under Korean domestic law to own banks. Some companies are circumventing this through their overseas operations (for example, Daewoo is opening or buying banks in Hungary, Uzbekistan and Romania, negotiating in Poland and apparently eyeing opportunities in Croatia, Ukraine and Azerbaijan.)

Table 15.10 Distribution of Korea's total outward FDI stock, 1980–92 (million US dollars)

Total (US$m.)		Of which (%)										
		Asian developing countries		Japan		Australia & NZ		N. America		EU		Rest of world
1980	1992	1980	1992	1980	1992	1980	1992	1980	1992	1980	1992	1980 1992
200	5600	22	32	1	2	2	4	17	38	30	7	28 18

Source: UNCTAD-DITED (1997) from Chia (1995).

Until the late 1980s Korea had no trade relations with the communist bloc. The end of the cold war and the political success of the Seoul Olympics was followed by a strengthening of diplomatic linkage through the government's 'northward' policy, and trade and investment have since grown rapidly.

The main 'pull' factors to CEE countries seem to be low labour costs and proximity to Western European markets in addition to anticipation of growth in the CEE domestic economies. Korean companies seem well aware of the existing EU/CEE preferential trade agreements and to have positive views on the extension of the EU (Nam and Slater 1997). Indeed, Daewoo's adept deal with the Polish government to avoid customs duty on disassembled vehicles, then classified as components, might be said to have anticipated a fuller union. The list of investors is unsurprisingly made up mainly of the major *chaebols*. Daewoo is the leading Korean investor in the FSU countries, with Hyundai, LG (formerly Lucky Gold Star), Samsung and the troubled Kia also well represented. Table 15.11 is a summary of recent reports of investments made by these companies, by sector and country. Where possible, orders of magnitude are also shown: these may be actual expenditures to date or simply reports of current and or planned future expenditures. The figures should, therefore, be interpreted as indicators of strength of interest only. Figures are quoted in millions of US dollars.

The 'push' factors in Korea seem unusually strong. Exporting success has led to high wages, labour shortages and domestic market saturation. Social unrest, high-level corruption and tense relations with North Korea make for an unsettled domestic investment climate. There are signs that the recent huge increase in outward investment may have overstretched the capital resources of some of the major companies, and

Table 15.11   Korean cumulative investment in former Eastern Bloc countries, 1991–6 (million US dollars); approval basis

(a) Country	1991	1992	1993
Russia	20.526 (15)	25.504 (20)	29.349 (39)
Poland	0.679 (2)	0.559 (2)	6.359 (4)
Hungary	49.363 (4)	12.044 (5)	15.238 (7)
Czech Republic	n.a.	10.780 (1)	11.780 (2)
Romania	0.500 (1)	0.500 (1)	0.500 (1)
Kazakhstan	n.a.	2.179 (7)	5.941 (7)
Uzbekistan	n.a.	n.a.	130.490 (4)
(b) Country	1994	1995	1996
Russia	n.a.	n.a.	n.a.
Romania	51.490 (2)	157.760 (3)	157.760 (3)
Bulgaria	n.a.	n.a.	n.a.
Slovakia	10.780 (1)	10.920 (2)	10.920 (2)
Slovenia	n.a.	0.100 (1)	0.100 (1)
Ukraine	n.a.	n.a.	4083 (2)
Uzbekistan	81.300 (2)	109.849 (7)	179.936 (13)
Georgia (U.K.)	31.204 (1)	n.a.	n.a.
Czech Republic	4.040 (3)	4.344 (4)	9.944 (4)
Kazakhstan	6.180 (6)	6.781 (10)	7.812 (15)
Tajikistan	n.a.	29.000 (1)	29.000 (1)
Poland	6.609 (4)	44.152 (7)	163.661 (11)
Hungary	19.788 (8)	39.960 (8)	40.902 (8)
C.I.S. *Total*	123.034 (53)	66.196 (68)	107.598 (79)

( ) = no. of approvals
n.a. = not available
Source: Korea Export–
Import Bank.

some observers suspect that Kia's insolvency may be a forerunner for similar problems. However, the drive is there and the success of some companies is likely to continue to reinforce the outward-looking trend.

China

Contrary to popular perception, China's links with international investment are not only one-way. Although in recent years China has been outranked only by the USA as a host economy for inward investment, the open-door and opening-up policies have resulted in a significant increase in outward investment, to the extent that China has become

Table 15.12 Korean investment interests in the FSU – a summary of recent reports (million US dollars)

	Azerbaijan	Bulgaria	Czech. Rep.	Hungary	Kazakhstan	Poland	Romania	Russia	Slovakia	Ukraine	Uzbekistan
Daewoo			√200	√30	?	√1100	√850	√			√658
Autos											
Electronics	?	?	?		√	√165					√
Financial				√		?	√			?	√[b]
Other							√213[a]				
Hyundai						√Autos		√Autos		√?Autos	
Kia											
LG						√Eng[c] √Bank48		?			
						?		?			
Samsung			?	?	√Copper 925 Gold 10.8				√Elec		? √

√ = firm commitment.
? = speculative.
[a] Shipbuilding/repair, oil and tractors.
[b] Includes cotton and telecommunications.
[c] In 1996 LG announced plans for 1200 million dollars' worth of investments in Central Europe, of which 746 million dollars is to be in Poland

one of the largest outward investors among developing home economies. During the period 1990–6 China ranked third in this category to Hong Kong and Taiwan. The perception of China purely as a centre of attraction for inward investment has arisen partly because the Chinese official outward investment figures have consistently severely underestimated the outflow. For example, the 1993 official MOFTEC (Ministry of Foreign Trade and Economic Cooperation) outward flow figure was 120 million US dollars. IMF figures, collected on a different basis, estimated the flow over the same year at 4.4 *billion* US dollars. Even so, the IMF figures still offer considerable scope for misinterpretation, given both the status of Hong Kong and Macau (accounting for around 60 per cent of Chinese outward FDI) and the phenomenon of 'round trip' and 'reverse-investment'. These issues are explained in Zhan (1995) and Slater (1997). While the aggregate figures are confusing, other sources do point to the transnationalization of Chinese companies.

First, China's own policies, dating from the mid-1980s, encourage specific outward FDI, which, *inter alia*:

- offers security of supply of raw materials scarce in China;
- generates foreign exchange;
- facilitates technology transfer to China;
- supports China's foreign policies.

More recently, outward investment has become subject to more liberal criteria and firms have responded accordingly. A problem has been that the outward rush has been largely unpoliced, and not all of the consequences appear to have supported the national interest. At present the Chinese government appears to wish to encourage transnationalization while curbing abuse through more effective regulation.

Second, some Chinese companies have become significant TNCs in their own right. Financial services apart (the Bank of China alone has overseas assets of over 150 billion dollars), in 1994, 8 Chinese companies appeared in the list of the top 50 TNCs based in developing countries (UNCTAD 1996) ranked by foreign assets, and six ranked in the top 25.

However, for the purpose of this chapter we aim to assess China's investment in the FSU countries. Clearly, some of the stock of FDI will relate to projects undertaken during periods of political proximity of the PRC to the USSR. According to Zhan (1995), about 3 per cent of China's outward investment stock (1979–94) is located in the CEE countries, the majority in the Russian Federation with some manufacturing investment in Poland. MOFTEC figures suggest 3.6 per cent for the period 1979–91 (CIS and Eastern Europe). If these two sets of figures are comparable in origin, they suggest a relative slowdown in China and the FSU, although the absolute flows will have increased. Table 15.6 has shown some of the more significant destinations: Estonia, Hungary, Latvia, Lithuania, Poland and the Russian Federation, with the total investment in these countries standing at about 200 million US dollars. As already quoted, Zhan (1995) estimated that some 3 per cent of China's outward investment stock by 1994 was located in Eastern Europe. Adding the global flow figures for individual years suggests a total outward stock of around 16 billion US dollars by end 1994, so that a total of some 450 million is implied for CEE countries. (This compares with around 300 million US dollars for the European Union calculated on the same basis.) MOFTEC stock figures treated similarly would suggest only about 150 million.

For the reasons given above, the MOFTEC figures are severe underestimates and can largely be discounted. Even the higher figures, however, are also likely to be underestimates. Methods of data collection, laxity, the desire to avoid attracting official attention and a general penchant for secrecy all point in the same direction. Working from host country statistics is also difficult. Chinese firms frequently set up complex networks of holding companies and subsidiaries in order to obscure ultimate ownership. This attitude extends from private companies through to state institutions including the People's Liberation Army and its extensive business operations. Therefore, unless none of the unreported investment has been hosted by the FSU, the figure above should define a lower bound.

Disaggregating these figures is difficult. Table 15.6 has shown the main destinations. The Russian Federation is the largest CEE host for Asian investment, and China's share is about 40 per cent (second to Singapore's 50 per cent). Sectoral details are not easily available: China's investments are geographically diverse and, reportedly (UNCTAD-DITED 1997) large in number and, relatively small in size. A priori, one would expect that low wages and other resource costs, technology acquisition and market proximity would be of little importance in drawing Chinese investment to the FSU countries, leaving security of supply of strategic raw materials and foreign policy support as the likely principal reasons. Certainly, there is evidence of the former. A sizeable number of China's Russian investments are located in the Far East, including the Sakhalin offshore oil and gas exploitation. In Turkmenistan, the National Petroleum Corporation is involved in a joint venture with Mitsubishi and Exxon. This project is huge: with investment estimated at 22 billion US dollars, it will pipe gas 8000 kilometres to Japan via China. Regarding policy support, it is probable that Chinese state-owned enterprises (SOEs) were encouraged into the Soviet Union and that these have become designated foreign affiliates. Additionally, the common border between the Russian Far East and China allows diffusion of economic activity. Anecdotal evidence indicates sizeable numbers of small Chinese enterprises and traders setting up shop in the area.[1]

Malaysia

Malaysia has been investing abroad for some years, but the figures began to look serious from 1993. Early outward FDI was led by the well-established Malaysian combines, such as Sime Darby, and much was related to Malaysia's natural resource expertise such as plantations and forestry (or, perhaps more accurately, logging). However, the last four years have seen not only rapid expansion, but also greater diversification in companies and sectors. Typical, and, apart from the notorious loggers, the most widely reported, was Proton's purchase of Lotus in the UK. Of particular importance in Malaysia has been the role of government, led by Prime Minister Datuk Seri Dr Mahathir Mohamad. His '2020 vision' of the economic development of Malaysia has included policies to stimulate the internationalization of Malaysian firms, in addition to encouraging outward investment for the economic benefits alone. Mahathir's foreign policy embodies Malaysian companies as key players in extending influence. The explicit policy of South – South cooperation, to reduce dependence upon and the influence of Western developed countries, has the Malaysian government leading politically, with Malaysian firms bringing expertise and technology to other developing countries while enjoying first-mover benefits in emerging markets. Priority targets among developing countries include the 'Moslem Market', i.e. the Islamic states of Central Asia together with Iran and Pakistan, which together contain about 300 million people. Mahathir's personal commitment has been considerable. He travels frequently, followed by a retinue of business leaders poised to take advantage of the doors opened by the diplomatic activity. While still a net inward investor, therefore, Malaysia has become an outward investor of some considerable magnitude in the last five years. Most Malaysian investment is within the South-East Asian region as companies have outgrown their domestic market. The forestry and other natural resource activities span North and South America, Oceania and Australasia as well as Asia. There are technology-seeking investments in Europe, and infrastructure projects underpin the South–South bridges.

Typical, but for different reasons, of companies that have outgrown their domestic markets are Proton and Petronas. The former, producer of Malaysia's first national car, was a joint venture with Mitsubishi using the Japanese company's technology. Proton's takeover of Lotus, possibly a reaction to the Japanese propensity to keep their most recent techno- logical advances to themselves, has already been mentioned. The origi- nal Proton, an independent version and a second domestic car, the Kancil, grew to account for about 70 per cent of Malaysian car sales. Proton now exports successfully in almost twenty countries. One would suspect that a serious strategic option for the company would be production operations in CEE. Petronas is Malaysia's state-owned oil and gas company. It has become wealthy on Malaysia's own reserves (the tallest office building in the world, the 88-storey twin Petronas Towers in Kuala Lumpur, is the company's own development and new home). However, Malaysian reserves are predicted to deplete well within the next 20 years, leaving the company little option other than to develop overseas operations. It currently operates across Africa and Asia, including upstream facilities in Turkmenistan, deriving about 10 per cent of its income from these operations, targeted to reach 30 per cent within 10 years.

Sceptics doubt the sustainability and depth of Malaysian outward FDI: some is politically motivated and requires subsidy; much is reported that is no more than memoranda of understanding and likely to come to nothing; some of the projects are conducted by Malaysian conglom- erates with financial and other expertise that does not appear relevant; the Malaysian economy, with persistent current account deficits and capital shortages, may simply not be strong enough. The 1997 collapse of the ringgit would reinforce this view. However, Mahathir's policies are unlikely to be buffeted off track by short-term setbacks. Outward investment is seen as a long-term solution for the payments problem counteracting the cash sucked from Malaysia by inward in- vestors. Substantial tax-breaks, enacted in 1995, and credit assistance are likely to combine to encourage outward investment. Table 15.3 shows the totals.

Within the transition economies, Albania, Tatarstan, Kazakhstan and Uzbekistan have been the main recipients. Malaysian official figures record separately only Kazakhstan with a 1996 figure of 10.6 million ringgits (4 million US dollars). However, other sources record the follow- ing major investments shown here. These are best interpreted as 'deals' rather than necessarily representing the realized value of the invest- ments:

Albania	Housing	Business Focus Sdn. Bhd	US$40m.
Kazakhstan	Power generation (B O T) Power generation (hydro and wind)	Usaha Sama Timur Barat Sdn Bhd Tenga PSC Sdn Bhd (Penang SCI Sdn. Bhd)	US$400m.
Uzbekistan	Education (Tashkent State Technical University)	Renong Bhd	n. a.
Tatarstan	Stock exchange, utilities, privatization, property	STI Corp. Sdn Bhd and Petra Group	US$2 to 3.5 bn.
Turkmenistan	Oil exploration and production	Petronas	n. a.

Informal sources also suggest Malaysian interests in gold, horticulture and tourism in Kazakhstan and Uzbekistan. Malaysia has also made aid contributions in Bosnia under the Dayton agreements which might help smooth the way for business if that country develops.

Singapore

Table 15.6 showed Singapore as a major, but focused, investor in the region, accounting for 50 per cent of Asian stock in the Russian Federation (195 million US dollars by 1994) and with other investments in Poland. According to Singaporean statistics, actual direct equity investment stock in CEE countries grew from under half a million Singapore dollars in 1990 to about 13 million (approximately 10 million US dollars) at year end 1995. Most of this recorded activity (95 per cent) was in manufacturing, with small investments in commerce and transport.

Table 15.13   Top Chinese TNCs' ranking among TNCs from developing countries, 1994

Rank	Corporation	Industry	Foreign assets (US$m.)
5	China State Construction Engineering Cooperation	Construction	2189
6	China Chemicals Imports and Exports	Trading	1915
17	China Metals and Minerals	Trading	710
22	China Harbours Engineering	Construction	554
25	China Shoujang Group	Metals	446

Source: UNCTAD (1996).

Table 15.14 Malaysia's outward FDI flows, 1990–6 (million ringgits)

	1990	1991	1992	1993	1994	1995	1996
Total[a]	1441.5	1071.0	1310.2	3412.4	5516.6	6643.7	6604.2
Total[b]	532	389	514	1325	1817	2525	
Kazakhstan							10.37
Uzbekistan		0.1			6.5	1.4	
Albania							12.1

[a] Million ringgits. *Source*: Bank Negara figures.
[b] Million US dollars. *Source*: IMF figures.

Other sources (UN/ECE) indicate that by January 1995 Singapore's investment stock in the Russian Federation alone had reached RUR 90134 million (about 220 million US dollars). Details of the nature of the investments seem difficult to obtain, but, compared with other Asian investors in Russia, the average size of investment is large, about 2 million US dollars. The largest seems to involve an initial investment of about 13 million US dollars with a total commitment of 73 million. Other, small-scale, probably trade-supporting investments included, at January 1995, stocks of 1.5 million US dollars (37 projects) in Romania, 0.2 million korunas (3 projects) in Slovakia and 8 projects of unspecified size planned in Kazakhstan.

Singapore is a heavily outward-oriented economy, and the Singaporean government is proactive in encouraging private outward investment through legislation and diplomatic initiatives. The Malaysian fiscal policies summarized above mirror those developed earlier in Singapore. The overall plan envisages Singapore as a strategic centre for finance, operations and R&D, with manufacturing activities located wherever there is competitive advantage. Much of Singapore's investment is in the ASEAN region, with, since 1990, rapidly increasing flows into Hong Kong and China. Both Europe and the USA are significant recipients, with the latter becoming increasingly favoured in recent years. Some of Singapore's investments in China have been massive. The Suzhou project, for example, involves building a whole city based upon the Singapore model. However, in both this type of government-led project and in private ventures, some Singaporean contractors have had their fingers burned. By Asian standards Singapore businesses operate in a regulated environment under a comprehensive framework of business law. Experience in China may slow down expansion in the FSU.

Other Asian Investors

While a number of the South-East Asian countries have become significant outward investors, they have paid little attention to FSU countries. Taiwan's outward investment total is the greatest among the Asian developing economies and is second in Asia only to Japan. However, Table 15.6 indicates that the only stock of significance was 5 million US dollars at January 1995 in the Russian Federation. Some 20 projects were reputedly involved. By end 1995, Taiwan's total global outward investment stock had reached 24.3 billion US dollars, about half having been invested between 1990 and 1995. Despite the presence of some very large global players, such as Evergreen and ACER, the Taiwanese economy is characterized by a large number of SMEs. While most Taiwanese FDI is distributed around ASEAN and the USA, Europe, particularly, the UK, has become increasingly targetted. China's opening up from the late 1980s may well have syphoned off a greater commitment of funds as Taiwanese entrepeneurs moved in to China in large numbers, mainly via Hong Kong. However, the interest in Europe continues to grow and is likely to prove a starting point for deeper forays into CEE. Interestingly, large numbers of Taiwanese now study in Europe, particularly in the UK. Ten years ago there were virtually none and the USA was the primary destination. Today the figures are almost even, and students are spread across Europe. Clearly a more sophisticated awareness of European culture is part of Taiwan's business strategy, reinforced by the political problem with China. Contingencies for flight of both capital and human resources undoubtedly influence some future plans. However, given that most Taiwanese FDI is in manufacturing and that the search for lower costs has been a major motivation, it will be surprising if more Taiwanese companies do not take an interest in CEE. In fact, the most recent reports (*Free China Review* 1997) indicate the Czech Republic as a target, with students studying in Prague. There are also small investments in trade support and in computing. Textania, a textile company, has invested 40 million US dollars in Hronov through a Malaysian subsidiary. Natural resource development is another possibility. One state-owned Taiwanese company, Chinese Petroleum, is reported to have signed a joint venture agreement to develop one of the oil fields in the Caspian Sea area. An initial investment of 4 million US dollars is confirmed, with a further $40 million to follow. In Romania, figures show a total stock of about 200 000 US dollars spread over 11 ventures. Taiwan is having to fight hard: the 'One China' policy, while possibly providing a contingency motivation for outward investment from

Taiwan, may simultaneously provide disincentives for potential host countries under pressure from Beijing.

Even though most countries within the expanded ASEAN area, excluding Malaysia and Singapore, are increasingly investing outwards, evidence of commitment to FSU countries is sparse. Thailand's official figures show flows of 20.7 and 1.0 million baht to Hungary in 1994 and 1995 respectively (less than 1 million US dollars), 1.7 million baht to Poland in 1992 (less than 100000 US dollars) and 10.1 million baht to the Russian Federation in 1994 (less than 5 million US dollars). Hong Kong/China attracts about a third of Thailand's total outflow (in 1996 about a billion US dollars). Indonesia's total outward investment stock at end 1995 was some 110 million US dollars (UNCTAD). However, these figures relate only to stock in the US. Another source (Chia 1995, quoted in UNCTAD-DITED, 1997) shows a much higher figure. The little information that derives from CEE countries suggests that Indonesian activity is small but non-zero. In the Russian Federation, 8 projects were reported at the beginning of 1995 involving a total of about half a million US dollars. Four projects are quoted in Romania, but with no recorded investment figure, and one in Slovakia.

Conclusion

During the years 1984–9 annual FDI flows from South-East Asian countries averaged 4.2 per cent of world outflows. In 1996 this percentage had risen to 13.2 per cent, a fall from the peak of 13.9 per cent in 1994. Annual global outflows increased 285 per cent during the same period. While most of the Asian stock is concentrated within the Pacific region, aggregate data also show significant interests in the European Union and North America. Investment in FSU countries as a percentage of the South-East Asian outward total was very small. However, closer inspection on a country-by-country and case-by-case basis shows wide diversity, with significant tranches lodged in certain areas. Table 15.6 summarized the important features of Asian FDI to CEE host economies. Korea's bullish surge accounted for 10 per cent of Romania's stock of inward investment in 1995, concentrated mainly in manufacturing. The Russian Far East and the Central Asian Republics account for large absolute sums, from a number of Asian countries principally devoted to natural resource exploitation.

From the Asian perspective there is capital available and a willingness to move it internationally to wherever there is perceived advantage. Eastern Europe's relative political risklessness and market proximity

Table 15.15   Singapore's investment stock in
Central and Eastern Europe, 1990–5 (million
Singapore dollars); direct equity investment

1990	1991	1992	1993	1994	1995
0.483	8.086	5.466	8.531	13.958	13.356

Source: Singapore: Ministry of Trade and Industry,
Department of Statistics.

seem favoured for export substitution. Geographical and cultural proximity, combined with natural resource abundance provide strategic
import substitution opportunities (that is, for alternative supplies of
strategically important raw materials) in the Far East. However, there
seems to be a problem in the heartlands of the Russian Federation.
Official estimates put the ethnic Chinese population in Moscow at
around 40 000. Unofficial estimates suggest a figure closer to 100 000.
These are mainly small traders. One Chinese entrepreneur, according to
press reports, plans to invest 100 million US dollars to provide accom-
modation in a Chinatown development – a second such project. However, large, productive investments appear to be absent. Even the strong
stomachs of Asian risk-takers seem to revolt at the indigestibility of
doing business in the Russian cities. ACER (Taiwan), having opened a
representative office in Moscow in 1994, finally decided to construct its
assembly plant in Finland. (Also from Taiwan, as a counter-example,
Pacific Technique Development Co. has, apparently, invested considerable sums in Nizhny Novgorod in an attempt to commercialize military
technology. The outputs are, it seems, expected to have applications in
the leisure industry.) Difficulties in the Federation seem to centre upon:
labyrinthine tax regulations; corruption; cross-border customs docu-
mentation and other such formalities; protection rackets; poor labour
motivation; and untrustworthy joint venture partners. Despite the
variability of effective business legislation in South-East Asian countries,
the absence of a coherent, transparent legislative framework and of
effective enforceability in the Russian Federation will continue to in-
hibit larger-scale productive inward investment. Other developing
countries have learned or are learning the benefits of inward investment
in contributing towards growth. A framework of laws, even in the business context, and means of recourse, seem to be lacking. Able and willing capital does not appear to be in short supply, whether from the
developed global sector or from the almost equally cash-rich Asian

economies, and FDI into the FSU is likely to increase only as business conditions become more congenial and bilateral political restraints loosen.

Note

1. The author is grateful to Professor P. Hanson for comments to this effect.

Bibliography

Adjubei, Y. (1993) 'Foreign Investment in the Commonwealth of Independent States', in Artisien-Maksimenko, P., Rojec, M. and Svetličič, M. (eds) *Foreign Investment in Central and Eastern Europe* (London: Macmillan)..

Albritton, R. (1991) *A Japanese Approach to Stages of Capitalist Development* (New York: St Martin's Press).

Andrusz, G. (1996) 'Kazakhstan', in M. McCauley (ed.) *Investing in the Caspian Sea Region: Opportunity and Risk* (London: Cartermill).

Artisien-Maksimenko, P. (1990) 'The Making of the East European Market', *Issues*, no. 10.

Artisien-Maksimenko, P., McMillan, C. H. and Rojec, M. (1992) *Yugoslav Multinationals Abroad* (London: Macmillan).

Artisien-Maksimenko, P., M. Rojec and M. Svetličič (1993) *Foreign Investment in Central and Eastern Europe* (London: Macmillan).

Artisien-Maksimenko, P. and Adjubei, Y. (1996) *Foreign Investment in Russia and Other Soviet Successor States* (London: Macmillan).

Artisien-Maksimenko, P. 'Armenia: an Isolated Economy', *Oxford Analytica*, 4 November 1996.

Artisien-Maksimenko, P. 'Azerbaijan: Economic Outlook', *Oxford Analytica*, 11 November 1996.

Artisien-Maksimenko, P. 'Kazakhstan: Recovery Signs', *Oxford Analytica*, 18 November 1996.

Artisien-Maksimenko, P. 'Kyrgyzstan: Economic Outlook', *Oxford Analytica*, 2 December 1996.

Artisien-Maksimenko, P. 'Turkmenistan: Economic Outlook', *Oxford Analytica*, 12 December 1996.

Artisien-Maksimenko, P. 'Uzbekistan: Foreign Investment', *Oxford Analytica*, 21 February 1997.

Artisien-Maksimenko, P. 'Foreign Investment in Eastern Europe' *Oxford Analytica*, 18 June 1997.

Artisien-Maksimenko, P. 'Foreign Investment in the CIS', *Oxford Analytica*, 19 June 1997.

Artisien-Maksimenko, P. 'Georgia: Economic Outlook', *Oxford Analytica*, 18 July 1997.

Artisien-Maksimenko, P. 'Armenia: Economic Outlook', *Oxford Analytica*, 10 September 1997.

Artisien-Maksimenko, P. 'Estonia: an Explosive Economy', *Oxford Analytica*, 5 November 1997.

Artisien-Maksimenko, P. 'Latvia: Economic Upturn', *Oxford Analytica*, 21 November 1997.

Artisien-Maksimenko, P. 'Eastern Europe: Intra-Regional Investment', *Oxford Analytica*, 24 June 1998.

Asia Business, July 1996.

Astapovich, A. and Grigor'ev, L. (eds) (1993) *Innostrannye Investitsii v Rossii: Problemy i Perspektivy* (Moscow: Informat).

BBC Summaries of World Broadcasts, Weekly Economic Reports: SU/WO153, 9 November 1990; SU/WO182, 7 June 1991; SU/WO191, 9 August 1991; SU/WO214, 24 January 1992; SU/WO218, 21 February 1992; SU/WO226, 17 April 1992; SU/WO227, 24 April 1992; SU/WO240, 24 July 1992; SU/WO242, 7 August 1992; SU/WO251, 9 October 1992; SU/WO253, 23 October 1992; SU/WO261, 18 December 1992; SU/WO265, 22 January 1993; SU/WO267, 5 February 1993; SU/WO273, 19 March 1993; SU/WO297, 3 September 1993).

Bank of Finland (1997) *Russian and Baltic Economies: The Week in Review*, 25 July.

Banerji, K. and Sambharya, R.B. (1994) *Vertical Keiretsu and International Market Entry: The Case of the Japanese Automobile Ancillary Industry* (West Virginia University and Rutgers University (Camden campus) (mimeo)).

Barclay, D. J. (1979) 'USSR: the Role of Compensation Agreements in Trade with the West', in Joint Economic Committee, US Congress, *Soviet Economy in a time of Change*, vol. 2 (Washington, DC: Government Printing Office).

Baykov, A. (1946) *Soviet Foreign Trade* (Princeton: Princeton University).

Best, M. (1990) *The New Competition* (Cambridge, MA: Harvard University Press).

BIKI: 19 October 1991; 24 October 1991; 2 June 1992.

Bobinsky, C. (1994) 'Survey on Poland', *Financial Times* 18 March.

Boguslavsky, M. M. and Smirnov, P. S. (1989) *The Reorganization of Soviet Foreign Trade* (Armonk, NY: Sharpe).

Borthwick, M. (1992) *Pacific Century: The Emergence of Modern Pacific Asia* (Boulder: Westview Press).

Brennan, G. and Buchanan, J.M. (1985) *The Power to Tax* (Cambridge University Press).

Brezhnev, L. I. (1976) *Otchet Tsentral'nogo Komiteta KPSS i ocherednye zadachi partii v oblasti vnutrennei i vneshnei politiki* (Moscow: Politizdat).

Buckley, P. J. and Casson, M. (1985) *The Economic Theory of Multinational Enterprise* (London: Macmillan).

Business Central Europe, 'Automotive Survey,' 8 February 1994.

Business Central Europe, May 1997.

Business Eastern Europe: 4 November 1991; 2 December 1991; 6 April 1992; 20 April 1992; 25 May 1992; 27 July 1992; 28 September 1992; 5 October 1992; 16 November 1992; 23 November 1992; 25 January 1993; 15 February 1993; 29 March 1993; 18 October 1993.

Business International (1992) 1992 East European Investment Survey (Vienna: Business International).

Business Moscow News, Russian edn: 3 January 1992; 4 February 1992; 5 February 1992; 1 January 1993; 4 January 1993; 5 January 1993; 11 March 1993; 16 April 1993; 18 April 1993; 27 July 1993; 15 August 1993; 22 August 1993; 5 September 1993.

Business Times, February 1997.

Cantwell, J.C. (1991) A Survey of Theories of International Production', in Pitelis, C. and Sugden, R. (eds) *The Nature of the Transnational Firm* (London and New York: Routledge).

Central Statistical Office (1995) *National Accounts, Hungary 1991–93* (Budapest).

Chia, S.Y. (1995) 'Foreign Direct Investment and Economic Integration in East Asia', paper presented at the 8th Workshop on Asian Economic Outlook, Asian Development Bank, Manila.

China Business Review, various Issues, 1996 and 1997.

Commersant, English edn, 5 May 1993.

Commersant, Russian edn: 25 November – 2 December 1991; 3–10 February 1992; 11–17 January 1993.

Cooper, J. (1991) 'The Soviet Defence Industry and Conversion: The Regional Dimension', *Radio Liberty Research Report on the USSR*, 23 August.

Courier des Pays de l'Est (1991) 'L'Ukraine face à la désunion', March, 358.

Czech Statistical Office (1996) *Reports and Analysis*, no. 27, January (Prague).

Daily Yomiuri 16 March 1993.

Davies, R. W. (1989) *The Soviet Economy in Turmoil, 1929–30* (London: Macmillan).

D'Cruz, J.R. and Rugman, A.M. (1993) 'Business Networks, Telecommunications and International Competitiveness', *Development and International Cooperation*, IX (December) 223–43.

Dongarov, A. G. (1990) *Innostrannyi Kapital v Rossii i SSSR* (Moscow: Mezhdunarodnye Otnosheniya).

Dunning, J. H. (1991) 'The Prospects for Foreign Direct Investment in Eastern Europe', *Development and International Cooperation*, 7 (12).

Dunning, J.H. (1991) 'Governments, Economic Organization and International Competitiveness', in Mattson, L.G. and Stymne, B. (eds) *Corporate and Industry Strategies for Europe* (Rotterdam: Elsevier Science) pp. 41–74.

Dunning, J.H. (ed) (1992) *The Theory of Transnational Corporations, United Nations Library on Transnational Corporations*, vol. 1 (London: Routledge).

Dunning, J. H. and Narula, R. (1993) '*Transpacific Foreign Direct Investment and the Investment Development Path: The Record Assessed*', Maastricht Economic Research Institute on Innovation and Technology, Maastricht.

Dunning J. H. (1993a) *Multinational Enterprises and the Global Economy* (Wokingham: Addison-Wesley).

Dunning, J.H. (1993b) *The Globalization of Business* (London and New York: Routledge).

Dunning, J. H. (1993c) 'The Prospects for Foreign Direct Investment in Eastern Europe', in P. Artisien-Maksimenko, Rojec, M. and Svetličič, M. (eds) *Foreign Investment in Central and Eastern Europe* (London: Macmillan).

Dunning, J.H. (1994) *Globalization: The Challenge for National Economic Regimes* (Dublin: Economic and Social Research Council).

Dunning, J.H. and Kundu, S. (1994) *The Internationalization of the Hotel Industry: Some New Findings From a Field Study*, Academy of International Business, Northeast Regional Meeting, 10 Best Papers Proceedings, June.

Dunning, J.H. and Narula, R. (1994) 'The R&D Activities of Foreign Firms in the US', *International Studies of Management and Organization*.

Dyker, D. (1991) *Restructuring the Soviet Economy* (London: Macmillan).

East European Markets, 25 Auguest 1989.

East-West: 29 May 1992; 28 July 1992.

Eastern Europe Reporter: 13 April 1992; 1 July 1996; 28 July 1996.

Economist Intelligence Unit (1992) *Georgia, Armenia, Azerbaijan, Central Asian Republics, Country Profile* (London).

Economist Intelligence Unit (1992–7) various bulletins (London).

Ecotass: 22, 28 June 1992.

Ekonomika i Zhizn' (1991, nos 5, 12, 34; 1992, nos 1, 13, 20, 27, 28, 29, 43; 1993, nos 5, 10, 33).

Eesti Pank (1997) *Annual Report 1996* (Tallinn).

Eesti Pank Bulletin (1997) no. 3.

Efendiev, A. (1995) 'Azerbaijan: A Country of Enormous Potential and Challenging Economic Opportunities', *BSCC Bulletin*, September.

Ellman, M. and V. Kontorovich (eds) (1992) *The Disintegration of the Soviet Economic System* (London: Routledge).

Enwright, M.J. (1994) 'Regional Clusters and Firm Strategy', paper presented at Prince Bertil Symposium on The Dynamic Firm: The Role of Regions, Technology, Strategy and Organization, Stockholm, June.

European Bank for Reconstruction and Development (1996) *Transition Report 1996* (London).

European Bank for Reconstruction and Development (1998a) 'Armenia 1998 Country Profile', Business Forum, Kiev, 9–12 May.

European Bank for Reconstruction and Development (1998b) 'Azerbaijan 1998 Country Profile', Business Forum, Kiev, 9–12 May.

European Bank for Reconstruction and Development (1998c) 'Georgia 1998 Country Profile', Business Forum, Kiev, 9–12 May.

Far Eastern Economic Review (1996, 1997) various issues.

Finance Eastern Europe: 18 March 1992; 22 May 1992; 16 July 1992.

Financial Times: 22 June 1990; 2 January 1992; 6 March 1992; 13 May 1992; 17 July 1992; 20 August 1992; 9 September 1992; 12–13 September 1992; 23 October 1992; 19 November 1992; 27 November 1992; 15 January 1993; 27 January 1993; 23 February 1993; 11 March 1993; 17 March 1993; 8 April 1993; 13 April 1993.

Finansovije Izvestiya: 19 November 1992; 3 December 1992; 10 December 1992; 24–29 December 1992; 14–20 January 1993; 6–12 March 1993; 6–12 August 1993; 1–7 October 1993.

Free China Journal (1997) various issues (Taipei: Government Information Office). *Free China Review* (1997) 47, no. 11, November (Los Angeles, CA: Kwang Ha).

Gerlach, M (1992) *Alliance Capitalism* (Oxford and New York: Oxford University Press).

Goldman, M.I. (1994) *Lost Opportunity: Why Economic Reforms in Russia Have Not Worked* (New York: Norton).

Gomes-Casseres, B. (1994) 'Group Versus Group: How Alliance Networks Compete,' *Harvard Business Review*, July.

Gugler, P. and Dunning, J.H. (1993) 'Technology Based Cross- Border Alliances', in Culpan, R. (ed) *Multinational Strategic Alliances* (Binghamton, NY: International Business Press).

Gutman, P. (1992) 'The Opening of the USSR to Foreign Capital: From Concessions during NEP to Joint Ventures under Perestroika', in Lavigne, M. (ed) *The Soviet Union and Eastern Europe in the Global Economy* (Cambridge University Press).

Gutman, P. and Arkwright, F. (1974) 'Multinationalisation et les pays de l'Est', *Politique Etrangère*, 4–5.

Hagedoorn, J. (1993) 'Understanding the Rationale of Strategic Technology Partnering: Inter-Organizational Modes of Cooperation and Sectoral Differences,' *Strategic Management Journal* 14, 371–85.

Hanson, P. (1990) *The Baltic States: The Economic and Political Implications of the Secession of Estonia, Latvia and Lithuania from the USSR*, Special Report no. 2033 (London: Economist Intelligence Unit).

Hanson, P. (1992a) *From Stagnation to Catastroika* (New York: Praeger/Washington Papers).

Hanson, P. (1992b) 'Centre and Periphery: the Baltic States in Search of Economic Independence', *Journal of Interdisciplinary Economics*, vol. 4.

Hanson, P. (1997) 'Russia's Baltic Outpost and Its Prospects', *Oxford Analytica*.

Harrison, B. (1994) *Lean and Mean: The Changing Landscape of Power in the Age of Flexibility* (New York: Basic Books).

Helper, S. (1993) 'An Exit-Voice Analysis of Supplier Relationships, in Grabher, G. (ed) *The Embedded Firm* (London and New York: Routledge).

Hewett, E. A. (1988) *Reforming the Soviet Economy* (Washington: Brookings).

Hewett, E. A. (1992) *Open for Business* (Washington: Brookings).

Hirschman, A. (1970) *Exit, Voice and Loyalty* (Cambridge, MA: Harvard University Press).

Holzman, F. D. (1991) 'Moving Toward Rouble Convertibility', *Comparative Economic Studies*, XXXIII (3) (Fall).

Hough, J. (1988) *Opening Up the Soviet Economy* (Washington: Brookings).

Independent, Supplement, 30 August 1997.

Institute of the State and Law, USSR Academy of Sciences (1989) *The Legal Status of Joint Ventures in the USSR* (Moscow: Nauka).

Interfax (1997) 26 August.

Interflo: 4/91; 10/91; 3/92; 5/92; 7/92; 8/92; 11/92; 1/93.

International Herald Tribune: 7 February 1992; 21 May 1992; 31 August 1992; 11 March 1993; 13 April 1993; 10 June 1993; 3 March 1994.

International Labour Office (1990) *ILO Year Book 1989* (Geneva).

International Monetary Fund *et al.* (1991) *A Study of the Soviet Economy*, 3 vols (Paris: OECD).

International Monetary Fund (1992) *Ukraine: Country Review* (April).

International Monetary Fund, *International Financial Statistics* (various issues) (Washington, DC).

International Monetary Fund, *Balance of Payments Statistics Yearbook* (various issues) (Washington, DC).

Ivanov, I. D. (1987) 'Restructuring the Mechanism of Foreign Economic Relations in the USSR', *Soviet Economy*, III (3) (Jul.–Sep.).

Izvestiya, 25 July 1991.

Japan Times: 3 August 1992; 7 August 1992.

Jentleson, B. (1986) *Pipeline Politics: The Complex Political Economy of East-West Energy Trade* (Ithaca: Cornell University Press).

Journal of Commerce: 16 November 1990; 30 September 1991; 21 October 1991.

Kaser, M. (1998) *The Three Caucasian Economies 1991–1997, Economic Survey of Europe, no. 1*, United Nations Economic Commission for Europe.

Khanin, G. (1992) 'Economic Growth in the 1980s' in Ellman, M. and Kontorovich, V. (eds) *The Disintegration of the Soviet Economic System* (London: Routledge) ch. 4.

Kiev Times, 25 May 1993.

Kobrin, S. (1993) *Beyond Geography: Inter-firm Networks and the Structural Integration of the Global Economy*, Wharton School Working Paper 93–10. (Philadelphia: William H. Wurston Center for International Management Studies).

Kogut, B. (1983) 'Foreign Direct Investment as a Sequential Process' in Kindleberger, C.P. and Audretsch, D. (eds) *The Multinational Corporation in the 1980s* (Cambridge, MA: MIT Press).

Kogut, B. and Kulatihala, N. (1988) *Multinational Flexibility and the Theory of Foreign Direct Investment* (Philadelphia: Reginald H. Jones Center for Management Policy, University of Pennsylvania (mimeo)).

Korhonen, I. (1996) 'Banking Sectors in Baltic Countries', Review of Economies in Transition, no. 3.

Kubielas, S. (1996) 'Technology Transfer through FDI and Structural Adjustment of the Polish Economy', Department of Economics, Warsaw University.

Kuboniwa, M. (1996) *Russian Output Drop in Early Transition and its Macro and Micro Economic Implications*, Working Paper D98–11, Hitotsubashi University Institute of Economic Research (November).

Lipsey, R. and Zimmy, Z. (1994) 'The Impact of Transnational Service Corporations on Developing Countries: Competition, Market Structure and the Provision of Unique Services', in Sauvant, K. and Mallampally, P. (eds) *Transnational Corporations in Services* (London: Routledge).

Marples, D. (1991) 'Ukraine's Economic Prospects', *Radio Liberty Research Report on the USSR*, 3 (40) 4 October.

Marshall, A. (1920) *Principles of Economics* (London: Macmillan).

Matejka, H. (1988) 'More Joint Ventures within the CMEA', in Hardt, J. and McMillan, C. H. (eds) *Planned Economies Confronting the Challenges of the 1980s* (Cambridge University Press).

Matyukhin, G. G. (1991) 'Instruktsiya no. 1: O poryadke regulirovanya deyatel'nosti kommercheskikh bankov', *Biznes i Banki*, no. 23 (June).

Maximova, M. (1977) 'Industrial Cooperation between Socialist and Capitalist Countries', in Saunders, C. (ed) *East-West Cooperation in Business* (Vienna: Springer).

McMillan, C. H. (1977) 'East-West Industrial Cooperation', in Joint Economic Committee, US Congress, *East European Economies Post-Helsinki* (Washington, DC: Government Printing Office).

McMillan, C. H. (1987) *Multinationals from the Second World* (London: Macmillan).

McMillan, C. H. (1991) *Canada–USSR Joint Ventures* (Toronto: Canada–USSR Business Council).

Ministry of Foreign Trade and Economic Cooperation (MOFTEC) *Almanac of China's Foreign Trade and Economic Cooperation*, various issues (Hong Kong: China Resources).

Naisbitt, J. (1994) *Global Paradox* (New York: Morrow).

Nam, S.K. and Slater, J.R. (1997) '*Korean Investment in Europe: Motives and Choices*', *in* Slater, J. and Strange, R. (eds) *Business Relationships with East Asia* (London: Routledge).

Neuer Zürcher Zeitung, 27 August 1992.

Nikkei Weekly: 20 Jun 1992; 18 Jul 1992; 12 September 1992; 22 August 1992; 26 September 1992; 14 December 1992; 25 January 1993; 1 February 1993; 8 February 1993.

Oman, C. (1994) *Globalization and Regionalization: The Challenge for Developing Countries* (Paris: OECD Development Centre).

Organisation for Economic Cooperation and Development (OECD) (1995) *International Direct Investment Statistics Yearbook* (Paris).

Ozawa, T. (1991) 'Japan in a New Phase of Multinationalism and Industrial Upgrading: Functional Integration of Trade, Growth and FDI', *Journal of World Trade*, vol. 25, no. 1, February.

Ozawa, T. (1992a) 'Foreign Direct Investment and Economic Development', *Transnational Corporations*, (1).

Ozawa, T. (1992b) *Japanese MNCs as Potential Partners in Eastern Europe's Economic Reconstruction*, 2 (Copenhagen: Institute of International Economics and Management).

Peng, M.K. (1993) 'Blurring Boundaries: The Growth of the Firm in Planned Economies in Transition', paper presented to the Academy of International Business Annual Meeting, Maui.

Perez, C. (1983) 'Structural Change and Assimilation of New Technologies in the Economic and Social Systems', *Futures*, 15 (October) 357–75

Perez, C. and Freeman, C. (1988) 'Structural Crises of Adjustment, Business Cycles and Investment Behavior', in Dosi, G., Freeman, C., Nelson, R., Silverberg, G. and Soete, L. (eds) *Technical Change and Economic Theory* (London: Pinter).

Peteraf, M. (1993) 'The Cornerstones of Competitive Advantage: A Resource Based View', *Strategic Management Journal*, 14, 174–91.

Petroleum Economist: December 1992; January 1993.

Piore, M.J. and Sabel, S.F. (1984) *The Second Industrial Divide* (New York: Basic Books).

Pitelis, C. and Sugden, R. (1991) (eds) *The Nature of the Transnational Firm*, (London and New York: Routledge).

PlanEcon (1991) VII (42) (27 Nov.).

PlanEcon (1992) VII (35–36) (15 Sep.).

Porter, M. (1990) *The Competitive Advantage of Nations* (New York: Free Press).

Powell, W. (1990) 'Neither Market nor Hierarchy,' in Staw, B.M. and Cummings, L.M. (eds) *Research in Organizational Behavior*, vol. 12 (Greenwich, CN: JAI Press) 295–316

Recht der Internationalen Wirtschaft, November 1992.

Robinson, A. (1994) 'Survey on Poland', *Financial Times*, 18 March.

Rojec, M. (1994) *Tuje Investicije v Slovenski Razvoj, Znanstveno in Publicisticno Sredisce* (Ljubljana).

Rojec, M. (1995) *Foreign Direct Investment and Privatisation in Central and Eastern Europe* (Ljubljana), ACE Project.

Rostow, W. W. (1960) *The Stages of Economic Growth: A Non-Communist Manifesto* (Cambridge University Press).

Rugman, A.M. (1979) *International Diversification and the Multinational Enterprise* (Lexington, MA: Lexington Books).

Rugman, A. and Verbeke, A. (1990) *Corporate Strategy After the Free Trade Agreement and Europe 1992* (Toronto: Ontario Centre for International Business) 27.

Russian Economic Trends (1993) II (z) (London: Whurr).

Rutter, J. (1992) 'Recent Trends in International Direct Investment', US Department of Commerce, August.

Scott, A.J. (1993) *Technopolis: High Technology Industry and Regional Development in Southern California*, (Berkeley and Los Angeles: University of California Press).

Sherr, A. B. *et al.* (eds) (1991) *International Joint Ventures: Soviet and Western Perspectives* (New York: Quorum).

Shmelev, N. (1978) 'Scope for Industrial, Scientific and Technical Cooperation between East and West', in Watts, N. (ed) *Economic Relations between East and West* (London: Macmillan).

Simon, N. (1991) 'French Firms and the Joint Venture Challenge in the USSR', *Moct-Most*, no. 2.

Statisticheskii Byulleten: 16 November 1992; 8 April 1993; 16 August 1993.

Stiglitz, J. (1989) *The Economic Role of the State* (Oxford: Blackwell).

Sutton, A. (1968) *Western Technology and Soviet Economic Development, 1917 to 1930* (Stanford: Hoover Institution).

Sydow, J. (1992) 'Enterprise Networks and Codetermination: the Case of the Federal Republic of Germany', in ILO (ed) *Is the Single Firm Vanishing? Inter-Enterprise Networks, Labor and Labor Institutions* (Geneva: ILO).

Taylor, F.W. (1967) *The Principles of Scientific Management* (New York: Norton; originally published in 1911).

Tedstrom, J. (1992) *USSR – Costs and Benefits for Ukrainian Independence* (Munich: RFE-RL Research Institute).

Teece, D.J. (1992) 'Foreign Investment and Technological Development in Silicon Valley,' *California Management Review*, Winter, 88–106.

Teece, D.J. (1994) 'Design Issues for Innovative Firms, Bureaucracy, Incentives and Industrial Structure', paper presented at Prince Bertil Symposium on The Dynamic Firm: The Role of Regions, Technology, Strategy and Organization, Stockholm, June.

The Economist (1996–7) various editions.

Thurow, L. (1992) *Head to Head: The Coming Economic Battle Among Japan, Europe and America* (New York: Murrow).

Todaro, M. P. (1989) *Economic Development in the Third World* (New York).

Tribune Ukrainienne (1992) no. 2 (April).

United Nations (1988) *Joint Ventures as a Form of International Economic Cooperation* (New York: Centre on Transnational Corporations).

United Nations (1992) *World Investment Directory, vol. II, Central and Eastern Europe* (New York).

United Nations Conference on Trade and Development (UNCTAD) (1993) *World Investment Report* (Geneva: UNCTAD Program on Transnational Corporations).

United Nations Conference on Trade and Development (UNCTAD) (1994) *World Investment Report: Transnational Corporations, Employment and the Workplace* (New York and Geneva).

United Nations Conference on Trade and Development (UNCTAD) (1995) *World Investment Report* (New York).

United Nations Conference on Trade and Development (UNCTAD) (1996) *World Investment Report* (Geneva).

United Nations Conference of Trade and Development (UNCTAD) (1997) *World Investment Report* (Geneva).

United Nations Economic Commission for Europe (1992) *Statistical Survey of Recent Trends in Foreign Investment in East European Countries*, Committee on the Development of Trade, Document TRADE/R. 588 (9 Nov.).

United Nations Conference on *Trade and Development*, Division on Investment Technology and Enterprise Development (UNCTAD-DITED.) (1997) *Sharing Asia's Dynamism*.

United Nations Economic Commission for Europe (1993) *Economic Survey of Europe in 1992–1993* (New York: United Nations).

United Nations Economic Commission for Europe. *East-West Investment News*, 1993: nos. 1 and 2; 1994–96: various issues (Geneva).

United Nations Economic Commission for Europe (1997) *Economic Survey of Europe in 1996–1997* (New York and Geneva).

United States Mission Daily Bulletin: 18 June 1992; 8 September 1992.

Uno, K. (1954) *Keizai Seisakuron* (Theories of Economic Policy), (Tokyo: Kobunsha).

Van Arkadie, B. and Karlsson, M. (1992) *Economic Survey of the Baltic States* (London: Pinter).

Van Tulder, R. and Junne, G. (1988) *European Multinationals in Core Technologies* (Chichester: John Wiley/IRM).

Wallis, J.J. and North, D.C. (1986) 'Measuring the Transaction Sector in the American Economy 1870–1970', in Engerman, S.L. and Gallman, R.E. (eds) *Long Term Factors in American Economic Growth* (Chicago: University of Chicago Press).

Wendt, H. (1993) *Global Embrace* (New York: Harper Business).

Wienert, H. and Slater, J. (1986) *East–West Technology Transfer, The Trade and Economic Aspects* (Paris: OECD).

Wilms, W.W. and Zell, D.M. (1994) *Reinventing Organizational Culture Across National Boundaries*, Carnegie Bosch Institute Working Paper 94–3, January (Pittsburgh, PA).

Williams, H. (1963) *Foreigners in Mikadoland* (Tokyo: Tuttle).

World Bank (1992) *Foreign Direct Investment in the States of the Former USSR*, Studies of Economies in Transition (Washington DC: World Bank).

Young, D. G. (1993) 'Foreign Direct Investment in Hungary', in Artisien–Maksimenko, P., Rojec, M. and Svetličič, M. (eds) *Foreign Investment in Central and Eastern Europe* (London: Macmillan, 1993).

Zemplinerova, A. and Benacek, V. (1995a) *Foreign Direct Investment: East and West: The Experience of the Czech Republic*, ACE Project Workshop, Prague, 6–8 April.

Zhan, J.X. (1995) 'Transnationalization and Outward Investment: The Case of Chinese Firms; *Transnational Corporations*, 4(3) 67–100.

Index